Bioterrorism

A Guide for Hospital Preparedness

Bioterrorism

A Guide for Hospital Preparedness

Joseph R. Masci, M.D. and Elizabeth Bass

CRC PRESS

Boca Raton London New York Washington, D.C.

Library of Congress Cataloging-in-Publication Data

Masci, Joseph R.
Bioterrorism : A Guide for Hospital Preparedness / Joseph R. Masci, Elizabeth Bass.
p. cm.
Includes bibliographical references and index.
ISBN 0-8493-1660-X
1. Bioterrorism. I. Bass, Elizabeth R. (Elizabeth Ruth), 1951- II. Title.

RC88.9.T47M37 2004
363.32—dc22

2004054244

Direct all inquiries to CRC Press, 2000 N.W. Corporate Blvd., Boca Raton, Florida 33431.

Visit the CRC Press Web site at www.crcpress.com

International Standard Book Number 0-8493-1660-X
Library of Congress Card Number 2004054244
Printed in the United States of America 1 2 3 4 5 6 7 8 9 0
Printed on acid-free paper

Preface

Biological agents have played a potent but often overlooked role in the annals of warfare. Smallpox, plague, syphilis, and other devastating infectious diseases — intentionally or unintentionally introduced into susceptible populations — have dramatically influenced the course of human history. Despite many examples over the centuries in which military advantage was gained more through infection than arms and strategy, the potential use of biological agents as instruments of terror in peacetime has only recently been recognized and exploited.

The most dramatic example of such bioterrorism occurred in the U.S. in the autumn of 2001, only weeks after the terrorist assaults on the World Trade Center and the Pentagon, when spores of the highly infectious and lethal disease anthrax were intentionally spread through the mail. Although only 22 people were infected, including 5 who died, thousands sought medical attention. More than 250,000 prescriptions were written for prophylactic antibiotics, numerous post offices and the Hart Senate Office Building were shut down, and mail delivery to Congress was stopped for 6 weeks. The broad impact of this very limited attack revealed a potential for much greater devastation if a wider and more sustained effort at bioterrorism were to occur.

It also revealed vulnerabilities in several key areas. The hospital systems in the cities that experienced the attacks, New York, Washington, D.C., and Boca Raton, FL, were called upon to respond to a fearful population and inquisitive media while evaluating their own systems of triage and care for potential victims of the attack. Even far from the epicenters of the attacks, hospitals and laboratories faced extraordinary demands. In Illinois, for example, laboratories processed more than 1500 samples for anthrax between October 8 and December 31, 2001; none was positive.

The national public health apparatus, which traditionally guides the medical profession and the hospital system in handling epidemics, was thrown into a confusing maelstrom: It was required simultaneously to monitor the extent of the attack, investigate individual cases, provide laboratory assistance, coordinate efforts with political and law enforcement agencies, and inform and reassure the public. The effort consumed the services of more than 90% of the CDC's epidemiological investigation officers and much of its laboratory capacity. Only the limited scope of that attack, which stopped as enigmatically as it began, prevented a crippling crisis for America's health care system.

In the aftermath of the anthrax and 9/11 attacks, concerns about the vulnerability of our health care and public health systems rose quickly. To the surprise of many, this vulnerability had been recognized in surveys and national exercises in the years leading up to the 2001 attacks, spurring attempts to improve preparedness at the national level.

Now that the hypothetical possibility of bioterrorism has become a sobering reality, efforts to prepare for future attacks have intensified greatly at the local, state, and national levels. A nationwide campaign to immunize a portion of emergency "first responders" and hospital workers against smallpox was one of the most conspicuous, direct results of these efforts. Participation in the first phase of that campaign fell far short of plans, however, as medical, labor, and liability issues arose — a sign of the complexities that lie ahead for medical institutions and workers.

In many ways, the challenge facing hospitals in preparing for bioterrorism remains daunting. At a time when hospitals in major cities frequently face problems of overcrowding, increasing use of emergency rooms, and increasingly stringent quality standards, planning for a biological attack often seems like a fanciful luxury.

Perhaps the greatest challenge facing us is in finding the border between complacency and overreaction to the risk of bioterrorism. Complacency makes it more likely that any future attack will bring confusion, delays in critical decision making, unnecessary spread of contagious agents and, as a result, medical and social catastrophe. Overreaction carries the risk that we will squander funds and resources on unrealistic scenarios while more immediate health needs go unmet, at high human cost.

The ideal balance — one that prepares us so well that it helps prevent bioterrorism from occurring in the first place while strengthening our ability to prevent and treat naturally occurring disease — is far from clear.

In this book, we have attempted to provide guidance to hospitals, health care workers, public health authorities, and others interested in effectively preparing for bioterrorism. We have included data from national and regional exercises in assessing preparedness and suggestions for implementing lessons learned from these exercises, as well as a brief overview of the current standards of the Joint Commission on Accreditation of Hospitals and Healthcare Organizations. We have examined the impact on the health care system from past bioterrorism as well as naturally occurring outbreaks such as SARS. We have tried to identify areas of concern in our current state of preparedness.

We have also provided a concise discussion of the likely agents of biological attack, including clinical information and management of specific attack scenarios both in text form and in the format of so-called tabletop exercises. Sections addressing seldom-discussed topics such as the unique needs of children, communication with the press, and management of the psychological impact of an attack have also been included. Throughout the book we assume a basic knowledge of the functioning of general hospitals. Our intent is to enhance knowledge regarding the challenges faced by hospitals, and we have, therefore, omitted selected basic information about hospital operations not specific to bioterrorism.

Employing a synthesis of these data, guidelines, and collective experience, we have attempted to provide concrete strategies that hospitals can use to establish and maintain an attainable level of preparation. We hope that our book aids in this important mission as the health community tries to develop sensible and effective ways to meet the unknown risk we face from bioterrorism.

Authors

Dr. Joseph R. Masci, M.D., is director of the Department of Medicine at Elmhurst Hospital Center and professor of medicine at the Mount Sinai School of Medicine. He graduated from New York University School of Medicine. After an internship and residency in internal medicine at Boston City Hospital, he completed a fellowship in infectious diseases at the Mount Sinai Medical Center in New York. Since that time he has been a full-time faculty member at Elmhurst Hospital, the municipal hospital teaching affiliate of Mount Sinai School of Medicine.

In the field of bioterrorism and emergency preparedness, Masci currently serves as chairman of the Emergency Preparedness Council of the New York City Health and Hospitals Corporation and as a member of the hospital subcommittee of the New York City Department of Health Weapons of Mass Destruction Committee. He formerly served on the Bioterrorism Advisory Committee of the Office of the Mayor of New York City. He is also chairman of the Emergency Preparedness Committee of the Queens Health Network in New York City. He has lectured extensively to lay and professional audiences on bioterrorism and emergency preparedness.

His other primary area of interest is HIV/AIDS. He is the medical director of AIDS services for the Queens Health Network, chaired the health workgroup of the New York City Health and Human Services HIV Planning Council from 1998 until 2003, and sits on the Medical Care Criteria Committee and Physicians Prevention Committee of the New York State Department of Health AIDS Institute. In 1992 he received the Dr. Linda Laubenstein Award for HIV Clinical Excellence from the New York State Health Department. He has conducted clinical research in AIDS and is the author of three textbooks, *Outpatient Management of HIV Infection,* first and second editions (Mosby-Yearbook) and third edition (CRC Press).

Elizabeth Bass is a journalist, specializing in medical writing and editing. As science and health editor of New York *Newsday* for 6 years, she supervised projects that won top awards in their fields, including the Pulitzer Prize. She has served as deputy national editor of *Newsday* and has taught reporting and editing at the Columbia University Graduate School of Journalism. Bass was an associate editor of *Human Diseases and Conditions* (Charles Scribner's Sons, 2001), a contributor to *Encyclopedia of Science and Technology,* edited by James Trefil (Routledge, 2001), and a coauthor of *KidsHealth Guide for Parents: Pregnancy to Age 5* (Contemporary Books, 2002), with Steven A. Dowshen, M.D., and Neil Izenberg, M.D. At the time of the September 11, 2001, terrorist attacks and the subsequent anthrax attacks, she was senior project editor at *Newsday* and worked extensively on coverage of the attacks and their aftermath.

Table of Contents

SECTION III Prevention, Diagnosis, and Treatment of Likely Biological Agents 167

SECTION V Appendices *313*

Dedication

To Jonathan Masci, our son

Section I

The Scope of the Problem

1 The Historical and Political Context of Bioterrorism Concerns

INTRODUCTION

On September 11, 2001, as the towers of the World Trade Center crumbled, doctors and nurses at several Manhattan hospitals paced outside their emergency departments next to lines of stretchers, waiting for the wounded who never came.

Public health authorities had other concerns. Minutes after jets hijacked by terrorists hit the skyscrapers, a 22-member National Guard unit from upstate Scotia, NY, was dispatched to New York City. By 8:30 P.M., it had set up its gear and was testing for biological agents and toxic chemicals.[1]

"The really difficult thing right now is not knowing if there is another shoe to drop," said Dr. Michael Osterholm, director of the Center for Infectious Disease Research and Policy at the University of Minnesota School of Public Health, to a reporter on September 11. "Has there been a biological agent released today?"[2]

The answer, all evidence indicates, was "no." But the attack on the World Trade Center and the Pentagon was so shocking in what it revealed — both about the vulnerability of U.S. society and about the deadliness of terrorists' intent — that it raised fears of another nightmare scenario: the use of biological agents to cause mass casualties. In the next two weeks, news outlets around the country ran stories quoting experts' opinions that the U.S. was vulnerable to a biological assault that could dwarf the 9/11 assaults.[3–9] Pharmacists reported heavy demand for ciprofloxacin by patients fearing an anthrax attack.[10]

In a column that ran September 12, 2001, former Defense Secretary William S. Cohen wrote:

> As horrific as yesterday's attacks were, we must be prepared for even worse. Americans must now think the unthinkable — that the next terrorist attack could well involve a contagious biological agent carried to our soil or airspace in a briefcase or bottle. We face opponents who are working diligently to become, in W. H. Auden's words, someone who "clutching a little case, walks briskly to infect a city whose terrible future may have just arrived."[11]

His words soon seemed prophetic. On October 2, three weeks after the World Trade Center and Pentagon attacks, a 63-year-old man, a newspaper photo editor, presented to a Florida emergency room with fever, vomiting, and confusion. Two days later, the diagnosis of inhalational anthrax was confirmed. He died the next day.[12] For the first time in the U.S., anthrax, one of the most potentially dangerous biological weapons, had been used in a lethal assault.

The 2001 anthrax attack did not, thankfully, mark the arrival of Auden's "terrible future." In the end, it involved only 11 cases, with 5 deaths. But the events of 2001 heightened concern about bioterrorism in several ways. The September 11 assaults on the World Trade Center and the Pentagon showed that terrorists could carry out a technically sophisticated, well-coordinated long-range plan on U.S. soil. It showed they could devise a novel and unexpected technique. And perhaps most ominous, it seemed to confirm that they were eager to cause mass civilian casualties, without limit, rather than targeting their attacks more narrowly.

The October anthrax incidents showed that this long-feared pathogen could be prepared as a weapon and distributed by low-tech means — in this case, as letters sent through the U.S. mail. It showed that responding to even limited use of a deadly biological agent could have heavy economic and emotional costs. Moreover, it revealed weaknesses in the nation's medical and crisis management responses, as well as its law enforcement capacity.

Despite the events of September 11 and the subsequent U.S. invasions of Afghanistan and Iraq, no new evidence has emerged publicly as of this writing to indicate that nations or terrorist groups possess biological weapons or are working to develop them. Indeed, it appears that contentions that Iraq's Saddam Hussein had usable biological weapons — contentions that helped lead to war — were unfounded.

However, public health and civil authorities remain concerned about the chances of biological attack, as they were long before 2001. For more than a decade earlier, studies, tests, and real-world events had been raising concerns that use of biological agents by terrorist groups or by nations — although still highly unlikely — was becoming a more realistic possibility, a risk that the nation's medical system was ill-prepared to meet.

Among the reasons for concern are:

- Biological weapons are much more accessible, cheaper, and easier to produce than nuclear weapons, yet potentially could have comparable destructive power.
- Unlike other terror tools, biological weapons could be used covertly. This could increase their destructive effect, but also make it harder to catch or even identify the perpetrators, another factor that might encourage their use.
- Research into making pathogens more virulent and resistant for use as weapons was reported to have been underway in recent decades, and advancing genetic knowledge could make such attempts likelier to succeed.
- Even small-scale use of biological weapons with low-teach means, as seen in the anthrax attacks, can cause large-scale social, psychic, and economic dislocation.
- Aside from nations that may have weapons or the capability to make them, nonstate extremist factions, both foreign and domestic, have expressed interest in biological weapons over the years.

- Terrorists' tactics have grown more lethal in recent years, with an apparent greater willingness to cause mass civilian casualties and a greater reliance on suicide attacks, both tendencies that could make use of biological weapons more likely.
- Key sectors of society — including hospitals, public health authorities, first responders, and the public — are not well prepared to respond to a biological attack, although improvements are being made, rapidly in some areas and less rapidly in others.

A standard feature of emergency-management planning for hospitals is analysis of hazard vulnerability. With that in mind, this chapter presents information about several factors that hospital planners may want to consider when they think about how much priority their institution should assign to bolstering preparedness for a biological attack. The issues of hospital and public health vulnerability to biological agents are discussed in Chapter 2.

For hospital planners, the key question is unanswerable: How likely is a biological attack that would affect my hospital? The political and military intelligence to answer this question is not available to us and may not, in fact, exist. The safest answer — such an attack is unlikely, or highly unlikely, but certainly possible — is not particularly helpful, but it may be the best we can do.

EASE OF USE OF BIOLOGICAL AGENTS

Many biological agents, including some that can be effectively weaponized, are relatively inexpensive and available, with sources in biological supply companies, hospital and commercial laboratories, and in nature.[13] In small amounts, some are relatively easy to culture and to deliver, as shown by several small-scale events:

- In 1984, members of a religious cult called the Rajneeshees added *Salmonella typhimurium* to restaurant salad bars in Oregon, sickening 751 people. The cult operated a health clinic and state-licensed laboratory; members cultured the salmonella from "bactrol discs" purchased from a medical supply house, ostensibly for laboratory quality assurance testing.[14]
- In 1990, nine people in an Edinburgh apartment block became ill with giardiasis, apparently after an infected person intentionally contaminated water tanks on the roof.[15]
- In 1996, a hospital laboratory technician in Dallas used *Shigella dysenteriae* type 2 taken from a hospital lab to contaminate pastries she placed in a breakroom, sickening a dozen coworkers.[16]

In a suicide scenario, little technical skill would be necessary to disseminate pathogens. During World War II, for instance, Japanese germ warriors infected Chinese prisoners of war with typhoid and freed them to spread the illness. Similar techniques could be used with a few volunteers, or even one.

However, preparing and delivering biological agents in a manner sufficient to cause large numbers of casualties would require a far higher degree of knowledge and skill, as well as financial and technical resources.[13,17]

Some have speculated that weaponizing and delivering microbial pathogens on a large scale would be beyond the scope of terrorist groups, requiring the resources of a nation.[18] Nonetheless, many have expressed concern that the required know-how and equipment are increasingly available around the world.[19–21] As just one measure of how widely disseminated the relevant knowledge is, more than 42,000 people around the world are members of the American Society for Microbiology, most with graduate degrees in microbiology.[22] Along with rising levels of scientific education have come greater freedom of travel, wider dissemination of information through the Internet, and advancing use of bioengineering techniques — all developments that can deliver great benefits but that also can enable bioterrorists to strike.

The Case of Aum Shinrikyo

The experience of Aum Shinrikyo, the Japanese cult that released sarin gas in the Tokyo subway with deadly results in 1995, shows that despite the nightmare scenarios that can be devised, deadly dissemination of biological agents may not be easy. The cult had scientific resources; officials estimated Aum Shinrikyo had 10,000 members in Japan and 30,000 in Russia, many of them well educated, with scientific or technical training. About 1,400 of the Japanese adherents and 5,500 of the Russians were hardcore followers, living in Aum facilities. The cult had financial resources as well. Its net worth was estimated at $1 billion or more, with money raised through a chain of restaurants, a computer company, expensive training courses, tithing, and other means.[23]

Its biological attacks began in April 1990, when the sect made several attempts to spread botulinum toxin from a vehicle driving around government buildings in central Tokyo and at the U.S. Navy base in Yokohama. In June 1993, it again tried to spread botulinum. In addition, over 4 days in June and July 1993, it tried to aerosolize anthrax spores from the roof of an eight-story building that the cult owned in Tokyo. Experts have said that the anthrax strain was not virulent enough to have the intended effect, although pet deaths and odd smells and stains were reported at the time.[24] In March 1995, just before the sarin subway attack, preparations were made to release botulinum toxin in the Tokyo subway using attaché cases equipped with vents and blowers, to be triggered by the vibrations of the subway. The attack fell through, reportedly because the appointed cult member chose not to fill the cases.[24] No casualties were reported from any of Aum's bioterrorist attempts.

The biowarfare effort was led by a graduate-level microbiologist. The cult had two laboratories and was building a more advanced lab when it was raided after the sarin attack.[25]

In terms of the risks of bioterrorism, the ineffectiveness of Aum's efforts can be seen as reassuring: A well-funded and well-educated group of fanatics, working over a period of years with two of the deadliest biological agents, apparently were unable to harm a single person.

However, a less reassuring morale can also be drawn from the fact that a well-funded and well-educated group had no scruples about repeatedly attempting such a project — trying to indiscriminately unleash mass destruction through disease.

Having failed at bioterrorism, Aum turned to chemical weapons, with greater effect. In late 1993, the cult members began using sarin and VX nerve gas, targeting specific enemies in seven attacks within a year. In the worst of these, 7 people died and more than 100 were injured when cult members sprayed vaporized sarin for 10 minutes in June 1994 in a parking lot in the city of Matsumoto. Even after the Tokyo subway attack and the raids on Aum facilities that followed, the cult still sought to cause mass casualties, making two unsuccessful attempts to release hydrogen cyanide gas in the Tokyo subways.

The group, it might be noted, has continued to exist under the name Aleph. In 2002, it had 1650 followers in Japan, including 650 adherents living in group facilities, and 300 in Russia, according to Japan's Public Safety Investigation Agency, which by law monitors the group. In 2003, the Japanese justice minister said a danger remained that it could launch "indiscriminate mass killings."[26]

DIFFICULTY IN CONTAINING INFECTIOUS DISEASE OUTBREAKS

Concerns about intentional dissemination in recent years coincided with a series of novel outbreaks of infectious agents. Although occurring naturally, these outbreaks raised awareness of how global interconnections — in food supply, immigration, business, and leisure travel — can help enable an infectious agent, once it is loose in the world, to spread and thrive.

The catastrophic example of this has been HIV/AIDS, an illness that has blanketed the globe since it first was reported in 1981 as a mysterious disease of gay men in the U.S. By the end of 2001, 20 years later, there had been more than 60 million cases of this sexually transmitted retroviral illness. An estimated 40 million people around the world were living with HIV, and an estimated 14 million children of 14 years or younger had lost at least one parent to the disease, with the heaviest impact in Africa. In the U.S., an estimated 500,000 people had died of AIDS through 2002.[27–29] HIV's social and economic impact challenges comprehension. As just one measure, it is notable that life expectancy in sub-Saharan Africa, which would have been 62 without HIV, fell to 47 in 2001.[30]

More limited examples include the following:

- Severe acute respiratory syndrome (SARS): A respiratory illness caused by a previously unknown coronavirus, SARS-associated coronavirus (SARS-CoV), it was first seen in Asia in late 2002 and was recognized in February 2003. Before the outbreak ended in July 2003, it had spread to more than two dozen countries in Asia, Europe, North America, and South America, with severe social consequences. To contain the SARS outbreak, thousands of people were quarantined, schools were closed, international travel was restricted and, in some countries, mandatory temperature-taking and surveillance were instituted. The disease spread largely in hospital settings, putting medical workers at risk, and in some cases stigmatizing them and their families. In East Asia, the World Bank estimated the direct economic impact to be between $20 billion and $25 billion.[31] As of July 31, 2003, a total of 8098 probable cases were reported to the World Health Organization, with 774 deaths, for a case fatality rate of 9.6%. Canada had 251 probable cases, including 43 deaths. The U.S. had 29 probable cases with no deaths. (For a discussion of the psychological impact of SARS on hospital staff, see Chapter 6.)

- West Nile virus: A flavivirus transmitted by mosquitoes that infects birds and horses, it had been seen in humans in Africa, Europe, the Mideast, Asia, and Oceana since it was first identified in Uganda in 1937. However, a human case had never been reported in North America until August, 1999, when a hospital-based physician in the New York City borough of Queens contacted the New York City Department of Health to report two patients with encephalitis.[32] Since then, outbreaks have grown each year in the U.S. In 2003, as of November 5, the Centers for Disease Control and Prevention (CDC) reported 8219 cases in 45 states with 182 deaths, a case fatality rate of 2.2%.
- Monkeypox: The first known cases of this disease outside Africa were reported in June 2003 in Wisconsin, Indiana, Illinois, and several other Midwestern states. They were linked to contact with prairie dogs that were believed to be infected by a giant Gambian rat, imported from West Africa where the disease is endemic, to be sold as a pet. Because the virus is related to smallpox virus, smallpox vaccine was used as prophylaxis. The CDC reported 72 suspect cases as of July 30, 2003, with 37 confirmed by laboratory results.

Unfortunate as these recent outbreaks have been, they can be seen as having strengthened the public health system's ability to respond to biological attacks, serving in effect as involuntary training exercises. The likelihood that other novel natural outbreaks will occur should be factored into hospital planners' considerations because the preparations made for bioterrorism could be expected to improve the hospital's ability to respond to natural outbreaks.

POTENTIAL DESTRUCTIVENESS OF BIOLOGICAL WEAPONS

Studies indicate that, if disseminated under optimal conditions, some biological agents have the potential to kill on a scale matched only by natural disasters or nuclear attack. This may be attractive to those seeking the maximum destructive capacity.

Conversely, it is believed that powerful psychosocial pressures militate against the use of biological weapons. It has been said that biological weapons, in their perversion of the age-old human quest to prevent and cure disease, are so morally objectionable as to be almost taboo, especially for use by a nation.[33] The Biological and Toxin Weapons Convention of 1972, which banned nations from developing or retaining biological weapons for hostile purposes, declared that their use "would be repugnant to the conscience of mankind."[34] A total of 150 nations signed the convention.

If a nation or terrorist group were identified as having used biological weapons, it could expect to experience universal opprobrium and severe retaliation, with political consequences that could last many years. In addition, if a contagious agent were used, the offender nation might be unable to ensure the safety of its own people and allies. Powerful as these constraints may be, the attempted biological attacks by Aum Shinrikyo, described previously, indicate that they are not universally persuasive.

Projections of Destructive Power

In a 1993 report, the U.S. Congress' Office of Technology Assessment quantified the risks of weapons of mass destruction. It estimated that if a single aircraft released 100 kg of anthrax spores in a line-source while flying over Washington, D.C., on a sunny day with a light breeze, the attack could kill 130,000 to 460,000 people. If the release were made at night or on an overcast day, with a moderate wind, it could kill 420,000 to 1.4 million people. If the night were clear, the death toll would rise to 1 million to 3 million people.

By comparison, the report estimated that a hydrogen bomb delivered by missile to Washington, D.C., would kill 570,000 to 1.9 million people (Figure 1.1). "In principle, biological weapons efficiently delivered under the right conditions against unprotected populations would, pound for pound of weapon, exceed the killing power of nuclear weapons," the report said. "On the other hand, if warning is provided, effective civil defense measures are considerably easier to take against chemical and biological weapons than against nuclear weapons."[13]

The Office of Technology Assessment (OTA) report was perhaps the most frightening tally, but it was hardly the only one. Many authors have projected levels of illness and death from biological attack that would overwhelm existing medical resources, as shown in the examples that follow.

In 1997, scientists from the CDC published two models looking at the impact from intentional release of pathogens.

One model compared the economic and health impacts of three possible bioterrorism agents — *Brucella melitensis, Franciscella tularensis,* and *Bacillus anthracis* — if each pathogen were sprayed separately under optimal conditions on a 100,000 population suburb of a major city.[35] If no postexposure prophylaxis were administered, the following was projected: 50,000 cases of inhalational anthrax with 32,875 deaths; 82,500 cases of pneumonic or typhoidal tularemia with 6,188 deaths; 82,500 cases of brucellosis with 413 deaths (Figure 1.2).

Prompt postexposure prophylaxis could reduce these totals. Most dramatically, if prophylaxis were begun on the day of the release or the day after, it would reduce the number of deaths by more than two thirds in each of the three cases, the study projected.

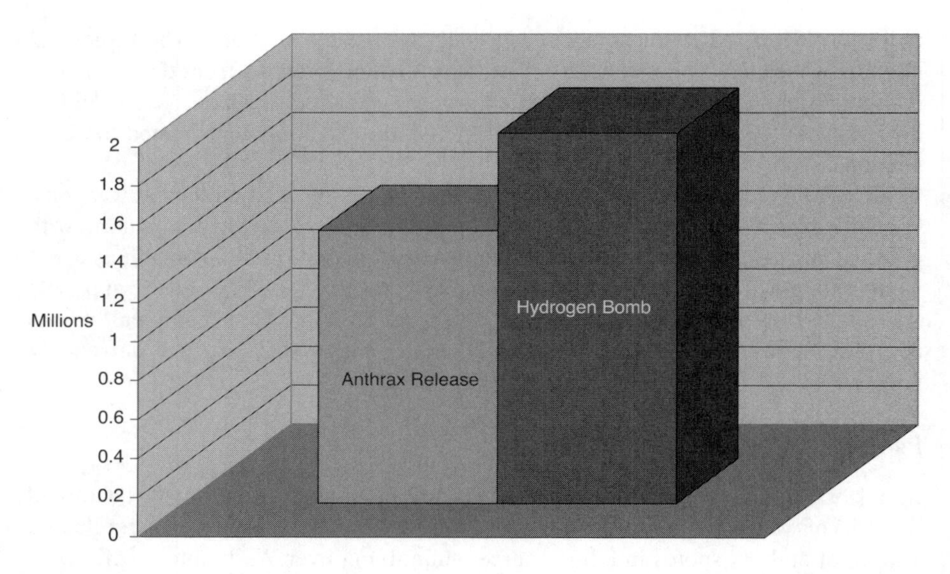

FIGURE 1.1 Projected deaths: anthrax atmospheric release vs. hydrogen bomb (Washington, D.C.). (From Jernigan, D.B. et al., OTA-ISC-559, U.S. Government Printing Office.)

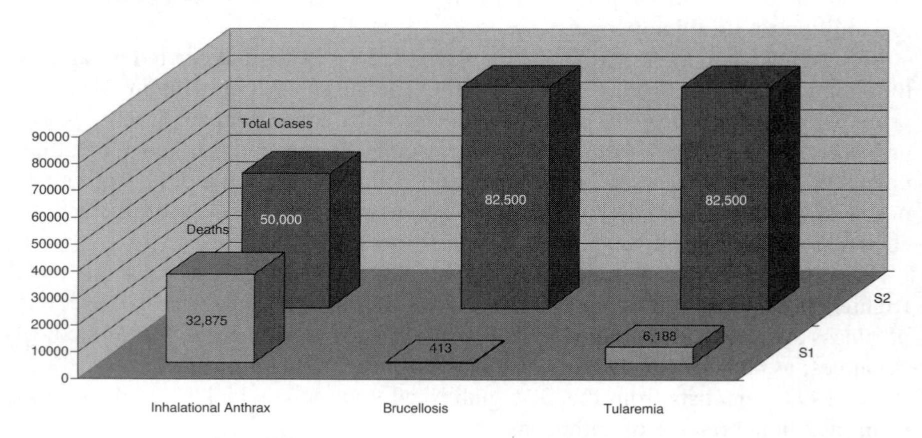

FIGURE 1.2 Effects of aerosol release over suburb of 100,000 population. (From Kaufmann, A.F., Meltzer, M.I., and Schmid, G.P., The economic impact of a bioterrorist attack: Are prevention and postattack intervention programs justifiable? *Emerg Infect Dis*, 3,

The other model projected the spread of smallpox, assuming an initial infection of 100 people.[36] The model assumed each person would infect three others, a higher rate than the historical average, but reasonable given the nearly total susceptibility of the U.S. population in the post-smallpox vaccination era. The model concluded that a combined vaccination and quarantine campaign would stop the outbreak in 365 days if the vaccination effort reduced transmission by a third and the daily quarantine rate reached 25%. In that scenario, 4200 cases of smallpox would occur.

Tests of Biological Agents or Simulants

Indications of the destructive power of biological weapons were also provided by hundreds of tests of biological weapons and dispersal systems that the U.S. military secretly conducted from 1943 to 1968. Although relatively few details of these tests have been made public, some results from the studies are known:

- In the so-called Shady Grove tests, conducted in 1964, Marine Corps bombers sprayed *Pasturella tularensis* and *Coxiella burnetti*, the etiologic agent of Q fever, into the air off Johnson Atoll in the Pacific, where boats bearing rhesus monkeys were arrayed in a line 100 miles long. In the biggest release, a plane sprayed a line of agent for 32 miles; it remained infectious more than 60 miles downwind.[37]
- In 1964, Air Force jets sprayed staphyloccal enterotoxin B over Eniwetok Atoll, earlier the site of nuclear bomb tests; monkeys were placed on the atoll and on boats. As reported in *The Biology of Doom: The History of America's Secret Germ Warfare Project,* an unclassified paragraph in the final report on the test stated, "The agent proved to be stable and did not deteriorate during storage, aerosolization, or downwind travel. A single weapon was calculated to have covered 2400 square kilometers, producing 30 percent casualties for a susceptible population under the test conditions. No insurmountable problems were encountered in production-to-target sequence."[37] The 2400 square kilometers covered by the weapon in that test is almost three times the area of New York City. If such a weapon were sprayed over a major city under optimal conditions, it theoretically could cause millions of casualties.
- Scientists from the Army's Special Operations Division, its germ-warfare unit, also explored simpler ways to spread pathogenic organisms. In 1966, Army testers went into the New York City subway system and dropped lightbulbs filled with powdered *Bacillus globigii*, an organism genetically related to the anthrax bacillus, on sidewalk ventilation grills and onto the tracks as trains sped along. The powder from the shattered bulbs aerosolized in clouds that were pulled along behind the trains. The Army's report on the exercise concluded: "A large portion of the working population in downtown New York City would be exposed to disease if one or more pathogenic agents were disseminated covertly in several subway lines at a period of peak traffic."[38]

The Sverdlovsk Accident

The models of biological attack and projected casualties listed above have provided an insight into the potential devastation that such attacks could cause. Real-life confirmation of the dangers of biological weapons was provided in 1979 when an outbreak of anthrax followed an accidental release of spores of *Bacillus anthracis* in the Soviet city of Sverdlovsk (now Ekaterinburg) and killed about 65 people over a 6-week period.

For years afterward, Soviet authorities claimed the illnesses represented cases of intestinal anthrax caused by consumption of contaminated meat. However, in 1992, just after the dissolution of the Soviet Union, Russian President Boris Yeltsin — who coincidentally had been the Communist Party chief for Sverdlovsk at the time of the outbreak — confirmed in general terms U.S. suspicions that the cases represented inhalational anthrax caused by an accident at a military facility.[39]

American scientists visited the area and reported in 1994 that most victims had worked or lived in a narrow zone extending from the facility to the southern city limit. Farther south along the zone, they found, livestock died of anthrax. "The zone paralleled the northerly wind that prevailed shortly before the outbreak," they reported.[40] Their findings were consistent with an airborne release from the military facility.

According to Ken Alibek, a high-ranking Soviet biological warfare official who defected to the U.S. in 1992, anthrax spores were accidentally released from the facility, a biological weapons factory, when workers failed to replace a clogged filter that had been removed from an exhaust pipe that vented anthrax-contaminated air.[41] Had the wind been blowing toward the city, casualties would have been much higher, Alibek maintained.[42]

The episode served as ominous confirmation both of the Soviets' long-hidden germ warfare activities and of the deadly power of aerosolized anthrax. Although by all accounts accidental, the Sverdlovsk incident was regarded as a model of how an intentional release might work.

SOCIAL AND ECONOMIC BURDENS OF BIOTERRORISM

Biological weapons may be attractive to terrorists because infectious-disease outbreaks can cause major economic and social disruption and psychic dislocation. This was amply demonstrated in the recent series of novel infectious disease outbreaks, especially SARS fever. Responding to a pathogen — or even to the false threat of a pathogen — can be costly for public security and health agencies even when little or no damage is done to the public health. That was the case with a series of anthrax hoax letters sent to abortion clinics in the 1990s, as discussed in the following subsection.

Potential biological agents need not even target humans to be economically and socially costly. In 2001, Britain experienced a natural outbreak of foot-and-mouth disease, a highly contagious viral disease of cattle and other hoofed animals. The outbreak led to the slaughter of more than 6.5 million farm animals, postponement of national elections, mobilization of troops, cancellation of many activities, banning of British meat imports, and widespread psychological trauma. It cost the British economy a total of more than £8 billion (the equivalent of more than $11.3 billion at the time).[43,44] The virus that causes foot-and-mouth, an apthovirus in the family Picornaviridae, is considered a potential agent of agricultural terrorism.

COSTS OF THE ANTHRAX INCIDENTS OF 2001

The anthrax attacks of 2001 provided a vivid example of the disproportionate social and economic costs that biological weapons can inflict.

In the October 2001 anthrax attacks, in which envelopes containing powdered anthrax spores were sent through the U.S. mail, 22 people became ill (half with inhalational anthrax and half with cutaneous anthrax) and 5 people died out of a U.S. population of 285 million.[45] By comparison, in the same month the CDC tallied 2790 deaths from pneumonia or influenza in 122 U.S. cities.[46]

Four anthrax-contaminated pieces of mail were found — letters to Senators Thomas Daschle of South Dakota and Patrick Leahy of Vermont, to NBC news anchor Tom Brokaw and to the *New York Post*. Other letters are believed to have contained or been cross-contaminated with anthrax spores but were not recovered. There was no use of multiple or contagious or antibiotic-resistant organisms, the features that figure in the most-feared scenarios.

At the time, of course, it was impossible to predict how widely the mail had been contaminated and how many anthrax cases would eventually emerge. In response to the handful of cases, health officials prescribed 60 days of antibiotic prophylaxis for about 10,000 people.[47] But prescriptions for ciprofloxacin and doxycycline rose by about 250,000 in October, reflecting far wider concern.[47a]

Essential mail delivery to Congress was suspended for 6 weeks, and the Hart Senate Office Building was evacuated. The Brentwood postal distribution center in Washington, D.C. remained closed for 2 years. In early 2004, the Hamilton Township (New Jersey) facility was still closed, and mail to Congress was still being irradiated, causing delays in delivery and some destruction of documents.[48]

Hundreds of millions of dollars were spent on responding to fearful individuals, testing white powders, examining mail, and testing and cleaning up postal facilities and other public and private buildings around the country. Cleanup of Capitol Hill cost the Environmental Protection Agency $27 million.[49] Shortly after the attacks, Congress appropriated $587 million to the U.S. Postal Service for protection of employees and screening and sanitizing of mail, as well as repair of facilities damaged on September 11.[50] The Postal Service planned to spend far more than that — a total of $1.366 billion by September 2005 — on emergency preparedness, almost all of it related to bioterrorism. That included $268.8 million to clean up and restore its Brentwood (Washington, D.C.) and Hamilton Township (New Jersey) distribution centers, as well as other facilities; $426.7 million for a biohazard detection system; $635.7 for ventilation and filtration upgrades; and $16 million for a mail irradiation facility for Washington, D.C.[51]

For the health system, a sampling of the response provides some sense of scale:

- Public health laboratories that are part of the CDC's Laboratory Response Network for Bioterrorism tested about 1 million environmental specimens and more than 125,000 clinical specimens.[52]
- The CDC's Emergency Operations Center responded to 11,063 bioterrorism-related telephone calls from October 8 to November 11, 2001. Of these, 882 calls were referred for follow-up investigation, including 226 that

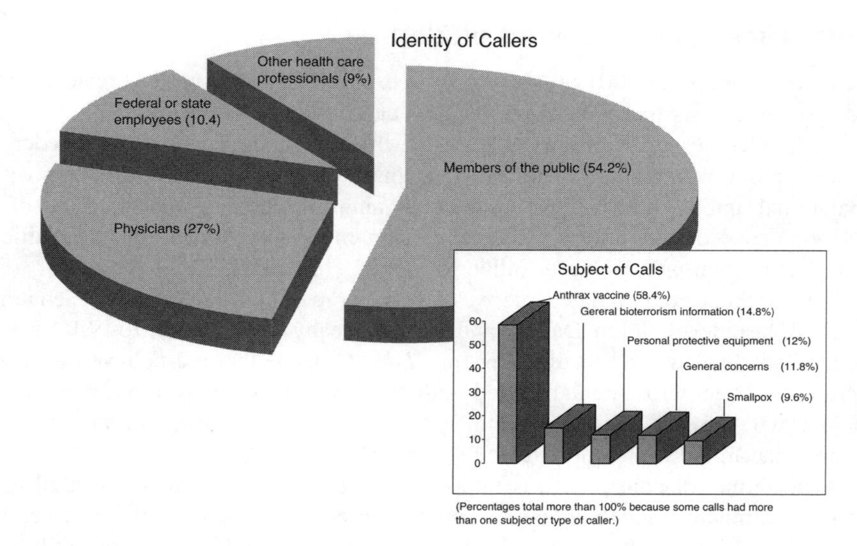

FIGURE 1.3 Anthrax calls to the CDC.

included reports of clinically confirmed illness compatible with anthrax or direct exposure to an anthrax-contaminated environment (Figure 1.3).[53]

- In New York City, where 8 of the 22 cases occurred, the city Bioterrorism Response Laboratory went from processing one specimen every 2 to 3 months, with two staffers on rotating call, to processing 2700 nasal swabs in 2 weeks and 3200 environmental specimens in 2 months. About 75 people, many borrowed from the CDC and the Department of Defense, worked round the clock in 10 laboratories (Box 1.1).[54]

Although the anthrax cases were confined to the East Coast — South Florida, the Washington, D.C., area, southern New Jersey, and the New York City metropolitan area — the attacks took a heavy toll in false alarms and precautionary testing around the country, including places far from the action.

- In Illinois, state public health laboratories processed 1496 environmental specimens from October 8 through December 31, 2001.[55]
- In Jefferson County, Alabama, where Birmingham is located, officials reported handling about 400 phone calls and responding to about 200 incidents during the anthrax period, at a cost of about $1 million. Most incidents involved packages or letters that recipients considered suspicious. About 100 specimens were sent to the state health laboratory.[56]
- In Idaho, the centralized State Emergency Medical Services Communications Center received 133 biohazard calls, all related to suspicious powders, from October 8 to December 31, 2001, as well as 53 routine hazmat calls. In a typical month, the system received no biohazard calls. Most of the biohazard calls were made by local law enforcement officials.[57]

BOX 1.1
The Anthrax Toll: One Lab's Experience

For the New York City Public Health Laboratory everything changed when a letter was found to be contaminated by anthrax. The lab's experience provides a glimpse into the costs of even a small-scale bioterrorist incident.

	Before October 12, 2001	After October 12, 2001
Specimens seen	1 every 2 to 3 months	2700 nasal swabs/2 weeks 3200 environmental specimens/2 months
Space	1 room	10 laboratories Secure new entryway for specimens Receiving area with decontamination site Office suite command center, open 24 hours/7 days
Staff	2, on rotating call	More than 75, some on loan from CDC, Department of Defense, or NYC Department of Health (DOH), working 12- to 20-hour shifts
Infection control	BSL-2 with routine infection control Quarterly environmental monitoring	BSL-2 and BSL-3 units External decontamination of all specimen packets Routine sampling of about 70 data points, including personnel's skin Continuous monitoring of all personnel movement by DOH police
Supplies	General lab supplies	6 tons flown in from CDC
Tracking	Each specimen handled uniquely	Database developed for tracking specimens and results
Technology	Basic microbiology	Two PCR units and an enzyme immunoassay (EIA) rapid screening unit. Average sample, even if negative, required at least 14 testing procedures

Source: Heller, M.B. et al., Laboratory response to anthrax bioterrorism, New York City, 2001, *Emerg Infect Dis*, 8, 1096, 2002.

POTENTIAL PERPETRATORS

Nations with Suspected Biological Weapons Programs

Biological weapons were last used on a large scale during World War II, when Japan killed thousands of Chinese civilians and Allied captives with plague, anthrax, typhoid, and more than a dozen other diseases. In the postwar period, many nations had active germ-warfare research programs.[58,59]

In 1969, President Richard M. Nixon ended the U.S. germ warfare program.[60] Three years later, the Biological and Toxin Weapons Convention of 1972 banned nations from developing or retaining biological weapons for hostile purposes. The 150 signers of the convention included the U.S. and the Soviet Union.

The convention, however, lacked a verification system. Talks to establish one began in 1994 and were broken off in July 2001 when a draft agreement being developed was rejected by the U.S, which argued that it would be ineffective and proposed alternate measures.[61]

Since the late 1990s, the U.S. repeatedly has charged that five nations — Iran, Iraq, North Korea, Libya, and Syria — were pursuing, or probably pursuing, biological weapons programs in violation of the convention. U.S. officials have said that 13 nations may have such programs; according to knowledgeable sources, they may include China, Israel, Egypt, Russia, Taiwan, and Cuba.[62,63] But, as described later in this chapter, U.S. claims proved wrong in Iraq, calling into question the reliability of U.S. intelligence in this matter.

Besides verification problems, the convention's vague wording made it unclear whether certain forms of ostensibly defensive research were allowed. Some of the U.S.' own research activities in the late 1990s were thought by some to have come close to the line of banned research or possibly to have crossed it.[64,65]

Potential Proliferation of National Research

As with nuclear weapons, the danger of biological weapons may reside largely in the possibility that they may be passed on to terrorist groups or outlaw nations who will not feel constrained by the taboos against their use or by the prospect of retaliation.

The Soviet Union

There long has been concern that biological warfare agents or information may have been disseminated to terrorist groups or terrorist states after the breakup of the Soviet Union, which had been running a massive germ warfare development program that included the genetic engineering of more resistant and virulent disease agents.[66]

Throughout the 1980s, the U.S. government maintained that the Soviet Union was conducting research that violated the Biological and Toxin Weapons Convention.[67]

These fears were seemingly confirmed in the early 1990s when defecting Soviet scientists reported that Soviet germ warfare development had been far more extensive than even the most alarmist U.S. officials had predicted. Vladimir Pasechnik, a biologist who had been the director of the Institute for Ultra-Pure Biological Preparations in Leningrad, defected to Britain in 1989. He told British authorities that hundreds of scientists at his institute were working on adapting cruise missiles to spray aerosolized biological weapons. He also reported that his institute had created a genetically modified plague that had increased resistance to antibiotics, as well as to heat and cold. This modified plague, he said, had been put into powdered form and packed into bombs and shells.[64]

The picture grew even more chilling after Kanatjan Alibekov, deputy director of Biopreparat, the Soviet germ warfare agency, defected to the U.S. in 1992. Alibekov, who changed his name to Ken Alibek, reported that the Soviets had employed more than 60,000 people in a massive bioweapons research and manufacturing enterprise that spanned more than 40 sites. These scientists and technicians had produced hundreds of tons of anthrax, smallpox, and plague germs for use as weapons, he said, and had used recombinant technology to engineer more dangerous agents.[66]

The breakup of the Soviet Union brought financial hardship, even destitution, for many of these thousands of workers, while security deteriorated at weapons facilities.[68] As a result, the possible dissemination of Soviet research and personnel to terrorist groups or unreliable nations, chiefly Iran, became a major concern. Since the early 1990s, the U.S. Congress has approved spending several hundred million dollars a year to safeguard and destroy Soviet weapons of mass destruction and to help fund employment for former Soviet weapons scientists, as part of the Cooperative Threat Reduction program established by the Nunn–Lugar Act of 1991. Although the vast majority of these funds were spent on trying to prevent nuclear proliferation, some went toward preventing spread of biological and chemical weapons.[69–71] Nor is the U.S. alone in this concern. The European Union and Japan help sponsor the International Science and Technology Center in Moscow, which the U.S. created in 1994 to provide peaceful employment for underpaid former Soviet weapons scientists. Besides, in 2002, the G8 nations* pledged to contribute $20 billion over the following decade to a global program to prevent terrorists from acquiring weapons of mass destruction from the former Soviet states.[69,72]

South Africa

Concerns about weapons proliferation also were raised after the fall of South Africa's apartheid regime, which had been researching biological and chemical means of assassination and population control on a smaller scale. Scientists told the South African Truth and Reconciliation Commission in 1998 that Project Coast, the chemical and biological weapons program, had produced botulism-laced chocolates and anthrax-laced cigarettes and had issued cholera bacteria and other pathogens to "operatives." Anthrax spores were said to have been placed in the food of three Russian advisors to the African National Congress, one of whom died.[73,74] Although South African officials had said the program's pathogens were destroyed in 1993,

* The G8 nations are the U.S., Canada, the U.K., France, Germany, Italy, Japan, and Russia.

many pathogens, including some genetically altered strains, were reported to be in private hands almost a decade later.[75–77]

Iraq

U.S. authorities have seen Iraq as a possible source for dissemination of state-sponsored biological weapons research or products.

At the close of the 1991 Persian Gulf War, a United Nations Security Council resolution required a defeated Iraq to declare all weapons of mass destruction so that they could be destroyed. In 1995, after 4 years of denying they had ever made biological weapons, Iraqi leaders made a series of admissions to UN inspectors. They said that their nation had made thousands of gallons of anthrax and botulinum between 1985 and April 1991 and had produced shells, bombs, and missile warheads to deliver those agents. With the Persian Gulf War looming, those agents were packed into 150 bombs and 25 warheads; several other bombs were filled with aflatoxin, a carcinogen.[78] According to UN officials, the Iraqis said they had decided not to use the biological weapons because they feared the U.S. would retaliate with nuclear weapons.[79] The Iraqi biological weapons program also studied *Clostridium perfringens* (which causes gas gangrene), enterovirus 17, human rotavirus, camelpox, tricothecene toxins, ricin, and wheat cover smut (which destroys wheat crops).[78]

Iraq maintained that it had destroyed all its biological (and chemical) weapons in 1991, but did not produce proof.[78,80] On March 20, 2003, the U.S. and its coalition partners invaded Iraq. The administration of President George W. Bush contended, in part, that Iraqi leader Saddam Hussein was pursuing chemical, biological, and nuclear weapons programs that threatened the world.[81,82]

But after an extensive investigation, including questioning of the captured Hussein, a U.S. inquiry concluded that Iraq had destroyed its weapons stockpiles in 1991, as it had claimed. The report, by special advisor Charles A. Duelfer, said that Iraq sought to covertly continue biological weapons research until 1996, when it destroyed its last plant.[83] "Indeed, from the mid-1990s, despite evidence of continuing interest in nuclear and chemical weapons, there appears to be a complete absence of discussion or even interest in BW [biological weapons] at the Presidential level," according to a summary of the 1000-page report, released by the CIA in October, 2004.[84]

Some experts expressed concern, however, that Iraqi weapons technology might have found its way to others.[19,85] David Kay, Duelfer's predecessor as chief U.S. investigator into Iraqi WMDs, told a Senate committee in May 2004 that, given "the number of willing buyers in the market," he considered such proliferation a bigger risk than the possibility that Hussein might have restarted his weapons programs.[85]

Terrorist Groups

Almost all terrorism to date, with the notable exception of September 11, 2001, has relied on bombs and other conventional weapons. In recent years, terrorists appear to have used biological agents in only a few cases: the anthrax attacks of 2001; the

Rajneeshee cult's use of salmonella to contaminate salad bars in 1984; and Aum Shinrikyo's failed attacks with anthrax and botulinum toxin during the early 1990s.

However, experts have identified trends among terrorists toward increasingly lethal assaults, greater reliance on suicide missions, and more religiously based rationales.[86,87] These trends, which appear to be interconnected, could make use of biological weapons by terrorists more attractive in that pathogens could produce mass casualties, and more feasible in that their risk to the perpetrators might not be considered a drawback. In addition, terrorists may feel freer than nations to use biological agents because they are less identifiable, have less to lose, and are less invested in the social web of nations.[33] Even if nations ultimately supplied the biological agents or expertise, some degree of deniability might be preserved in a terrorist attack.

"Additional non-state actors are becoming more interested in the potential of using biological warfare as a relatively inexpensive way to inflict serious damage," according to a CIA unclassified report to Congress on the acquisition of technology related to nuclear, chemical, biological, and advanced conventional weapons.[21]

Referring to weapons of mass destruction in general, the report stated: "Even in cases where states take action to stem such transfers [of weapons-related technology], there are growing numbers of knowledgeable individuals or non-state purveyors of WMD-related materials and technology who are able to act outside the constraints of governments. Such non-state actors are increasingly capable of providing technology and equipment that previously could only be supplied directly by countries with established capabilities."

International Terrorists

Osama bin Laden, the leader of al Qaeda, the terrorist organization responsible for the 9/11 attacks, reportedly has expressed interest in biological and chemical weapons.

The CIA unclassified report to Congress for January 1 to June 30, 2002, stated:

> One of our highest concerns is al Qaeda's stated readiness to attempt unconventional attacks against us. As early as 1998, Bin Ladin publicly declared that acquiring unconventional weapons was "a religious duty."
>
> Terrorist groups worldwide have ready access to information on chemical and biological, and to some extent, even nuclear weapons, via the Internet, publicly available scientific literature, and scientific conferences, and we know that al Qaeda was working to acquire some of the most dangerous chemical agents and toxins. A senior Bin Ladin associate on trial in Egypt in 1999 claimed his group had chemical and biological weapons. Documents and equipment recovered from al Qaeda facilities in Afghanistan show that Bin Ladin has a more sophisticated unconventional weapons research program than was previously known.[21]

Details of the documents and equipment recovered in Afghanistan were not disclosed. In light of the doubts that have been cast on U.S. intelligence estimates, in the wake of the failure to find weapons of mass destruction in Iraq, these statements are difficult to assess.

Since the September 11, 2001 attacks, the U.S. has attacked al Qaeda and captured or killed some of its leaders, although not, as of this writing, Osama bin Laden. The network, however, appears to remain active: In 2002 and 2003, it was linked to fatal bombings in Tunisia, Pakistan, Kenya, Saudi Arabia, Turkey, and to the group believed responsible for the Bali nightclub bombing that killed 190 people.[88–90]

In early 2003, more than a dozen persons were arrested in Britain and Germany, and three Algerian men were charged with terrorism after authorities found traces of ricin, a poison derived from castor beans, in a London apartment.[91,92] These episodes represented al Qaeda-related attacks that had been thwarted, according to a statement by the director of U.S. central intelligence.[93]

U.S. Domestic Extremists

U.S. domestic extremists have shown interest in biological weapons in recent years, writing approvingly of their lethal potential in online articles and providing instructions for their manufacture in books circulated at gun shows.[94]

Antiabortion extremists are thought to have perpetrated hundreds of anthrax hoax mailings to abortion clinics since 1989, sending letters or packages containing powdery substances and death threats mentioning anthrax. Two waves of anthrax hoaxes, with letters signed "Army of God," occurred in the fall of 2001 when authorities were desperately dealing with real anthrax sent through the mail. The 2001 hoaxes were believed to be unrelated to the lethal mailings. An antiabortion activist, Clayton Lee Waagner [sic], was charged in those hoaxes. In an earlier trial, he had said that he was preparing himself to carry out a mission from God to kill doctors who perform abortions.[95,96] In light of the killing of five abortion clinic doctors and two associates in the years 1993 to 1998, and the nonfatal shooting of five more doctors during the same period, such comments are not easily dismissed.

U.S. extremists have amply demonstrated their willingness to inflict mass casualties. The 1995 bombing of the Alfred P. Murrah Federal Building in Oklahoma City, which killed 168 people, was carried out by U.S. citizens who espoused precepts of the far-right militia and white supremacist movements. The bombing, at the time the most deadly terrorist attack on U.S. soil, led law enforcement agencies to increase their scrutiny of such groups in the late 1990s, and several Americans with ties to survivalist, right-wing militia or white supremacist groups were arrested in connection with possession of biological material. The agents involved included *Yersinia pestis* and anthrax, although the latter turned out to be a nonpathogenic veterinary vaccine.[33,94]

After the suicide in 2000 of a California gynecologist, authorities found ricin, with a blowgun and darts, in his family room, as well as more than 200 containers of pathogens, including salmonella, cholera, botulism, and typhoid, in refrigerators in his home and office. Machine guns and plastic explosives were found buried in his yard. The physician, Larry C. Ford, had served as a consultant to the South African apartheid regime's chemical and biological weapons program and had espoused radical racist views.[97]

TRENDS IN TERRORISM

Over the last 10 or 15 years, some experts have warned that terrorism was increasingly the province of groups whose world-views make mass murder morally acceptable to them.[87,98]

Some of these groups, like Aum Shinrikyo, are apocalyptic cults. Some — like the Christian Patriot movement that inspired Timothy McVeigh, the Oklahoma City bomber — are racist, antigovernment sects. Some — like al Qaeda, Islamic Jihad, and Hamas (Islamic Resistance Movement) — are ethnonationalist separatist movements, cloaked in Muslim religious fervor, that seek control of what they consider their homeland.

Whether or not religion is truly their driving force, groups that fight in God's name are seen by experts as more likely than "traditional" terrorists to seek mass casualties and therefore more likely to use biological weapons or other weapons of mass destruction.[76,77]

However, secular organizations such as the Tamil Tigers in Sri Lanka and some Palestinian groups have also conducted increasingly lethal attacks, often suicide bombings. The Tamil Tigers, a Marxist-Leninist group, have been responsible for 75 of the 188 suicide attacks that occurred worldwide from 1980 to 2001, according to political scientist Robert A. Pape.[99,100]

Suicide attacks tend to be particularly lethal. From 1980 to 2001, they accounted for 3% of terrorist incidents and almost half of the deaths caused by terrorism.[99,100]

In the 1960s and 1970s, terrorists typically used violence in a limited and targeted way, perhaps fearful of stimulating a backlash of outrage that would make it harder for them to achieve their goals.

In 1979, when Iranians seized American hostages at the U.S. embassy in Tehran, they demanded that the U.S. turn over to them the former shah of Iran. The "hostage crisis" galvanized attention to the anti-American views of the Iranian revolutionaries, reshaped the U.S. news media, and helped defeat President Jimmy Carter's reelection bid against challenger Ronald Reagan in the 1980 election. Although 52 Americans were held for 444 days, the only loss of life came when U.S. aircraft crashed during a failed rescue mission. The hostages were released — to worldwide attention — only minutes after the new American president was sworn in.

In such terrorist operations, victims were often singled out because they belonged to a particular group, such as British troops in Northern Ireland. Some of the most notorious of terrorist attacks — such as the 1985 hijacking of the Achille Lauro cruise ship, in which Leon Klinghoffer, a wheelchair-bound Jewish American, was killed and thrown overboard, or the 1985 hijacking of TWA Flight 847, in which U.S. Navy diver Robert Dean Stethem was beaten to death — seemed particularly horrific because the killing was so personal and discriminate. With mass deaths in more recent attacks, who can name the victims?

In the decades before September 11, 2001, terrorist incidents had been growing less common and more deadly.[78] Only 17% of international terrorist incidents in the 1970s and 19% in the 1980s caused at least one casualty.[33] In the early 2000s, however, 31% of international terrorist incidents caused at least one death.[101]

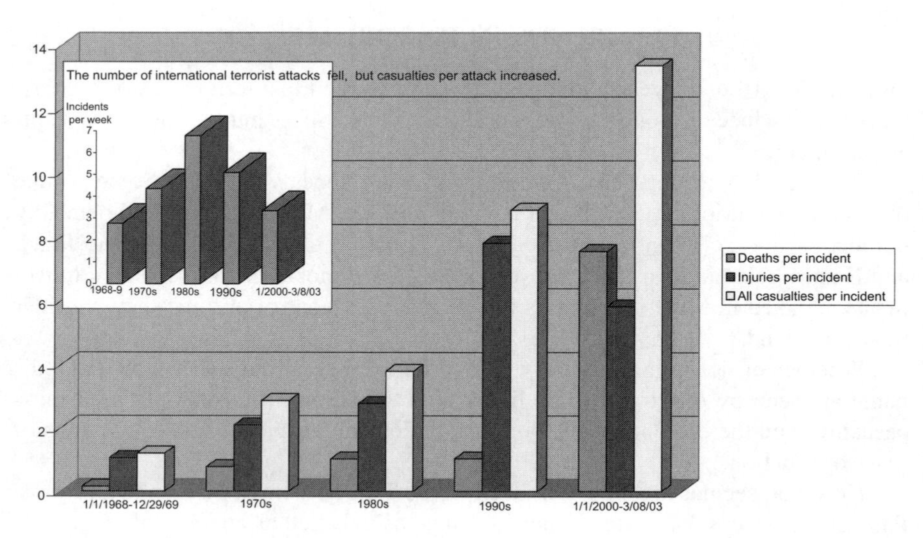

FIGURE 1.4 Trends in Terrorism: 1968–2003.[102]

The number of international terrorism incidents fell steadily from the 1980s, with an average of 29 attacks a month, through the early 2000s, with an average of 15 attacks a month. Meanwhile, the number of deaths and injuries per incident rose steadily from 1.2 in 1968–1970 to 13.3 in the early 2000s. Even if the death toll from the September 11, 2001, attacks could have been erased, the casualty rate in the early 2000s would have been 9.6 (Figure 1.4).[102]

Of course, September 11, 2001, cannot be erased. Whether it was an aberration or a step in a process of growing lethality, we cannot know. But certainly, it was preceded by a number of attacks on U.S. targets that caused deaths in the triple digits and by a string of what could be called phantom attacks — terrorist plans that allegedly aimed to kill thousands but were thwarted by chance or intelligence:

- The bombing of the World Trade Center underground parking garage in 1993, which killed six people and injured more than 1,000, was intended to topple the twin towers causing 250,000 deaths, the mastermind of the attack, Ramzi Yousef, allegedly told a Secret Service agent. The agent testified that Yousef said he wanted to cause destruction on the scale of the Hiroshima atom bomb attack in order to get the U.S. to end its support of Israel.[103]
- In June 1993, 10 Islamic radicals, linked to those responsible for the World Trade Center bombing, were charged with plotting to simultaneously blow up UN headquarters, a federal building, the George Washington Bridge, and the Lincoln and Holland tunnels. They were later convicted.[104]
- In January 1995, a plot to blow up 11 or 12 U.S. commercial airliners, carrying some 4,000 passengers, was uncovered after a fire broke out in a Manila apartment. Terrorists linked to the World Trade Center bombing, including Ramzi Yousef, were later convicted of plotting the attack that

was to take place on a single day. As part of their preparations, Yousef allegedly placed a bomb that exploded on a Philippines airliner in December 1994, killing a Japanese tourist.[105,106]

- In December 1999, an Algerian named Ahmed Ressam was arrested as he tried to drive into Washington state from a British Columbia ferry with a load of explosive materials in his trunk. His intent, he later said, was to blow up a passenger terminal at Los Angeles airport on New Year's Day, to mark the millennium. As a result of his arrest, Seattle cancelled its gala millennium celebration, which was to take place at the Space Needle, near a motel where Ressam had booked a room. Ressam, who said he was trained in Osama bin Laden's training camps in Afghanistan, was convicted in 2001.[107,108]

At the time, some of these plans may have seemed absurdly grandiose. But it is sobering to recall that none was more unlikely than the one that was carried out on September 11, 2001. It seems fair to regard September 11 as simply the one — perhaps the first one — that worked.

REFERENCES

1. Broad, W.J. and Petersen, M., Nation's Civil Defense Could Prove To Be Inadequate against a Germ or Toxic Attack, *New York Times*, 1B12, September 23, 2001.
2. Garrett, L., A Shocked City; Health Care Workers' Skills Are Put to Test, *Newsday*, W20, September 12, 2001.
3. Verrengia, J.B., Even Worse Threat: Bioterrorism, Associated Press in *South Bend Tribune* (Indiana), A3, September 17, 2001.
4. Perlman, D., Bacteria and Viruses Pose Grave Threat, Experts Say, *San Francisco Chronicle*, A10, September 18, 2001.
5. Lipman, L., U.S. Called Ill-Prepared for Germ Attack, *Palm Beach Post* (Florida), 11A, September 18, 2001.
6. Knickerbocker, B., Cities Gird for "Bio" Attacks, *Christian Science Monitor*, 1, September 20, 2001.
7. Seeman, B.T., Chemical and Biological Attacks Remain Threat; U.S. Ill-Prepared; Urgency Stressed, Newhouse News Service in *Times-Picayune* (New Orleans, LA), 1, September 23, 2001.
8. Weiss R. and Nakashima, E., Biological Attack Concerns Spur Warnings; Restoration of Broken Public Health System Is Best Preparation, Experts Say, *Washington Post*, A4, September 22, 2001.
9. Nelson, T., Biological Warfare Would Cause Many More Casualties, Expert Said, Knight Ridder/Tribune News Service in *Saint Paul Pioneer Press* (Minnesota), September 14, 2001.
10. Lewin T., Fear of Infections; Anthrax Scare Prompts Run on an Antibiotic, *New York Times*, B8, September 27, 2001.
11. Cohen, W.S., American Holy War, *Washington Post*, A29, September 12, 2001.
12. Jernigan, J.A. et al., Bioterrorism-related inhalational anthrax: the first 10 cases reported in the United States, *Emerg Infect Dis*, 7, 933, 2001.

13. U.S. Congress, Office of Technology Assessment, Proliferation of weapons of mass destruction: assessing the risks, OTA-ISC-559, U.S. Government Printing Office, 1993.
14. Carus, W.S., The Rajneeshees (1984), in *Toxic Terror: Assessing Terrorist Use of Chemical and Biological Weapons*, Tucker, J.B., Ed., MIT Press, Cambridge, MA, 2000, chap. 8.
15. Ramsay, C.N. and Marsh, J., Giardiasis due to deliberate contamination of water supply, *Lancet*, 336, 880, 1990.
16. Kolavic, S.A. et al., An outbreak of Shigella dysenteriae type 2 among laboratory workers due to intentional food contamination, *JAMA*, 278, 396, 1997.
17. Tucker, J.B., Introduction, in *Toxic Terror: Assessing Terrorist Use of Chemical and Biological Weapons*, Tucker, J.B., Ed., MIT Press, Cambridge, MA, 2000, chap. 1.
18. Leitenberg, M., Biological weapons and 'bioterrorism' in the first years of the 21st century, paper prepared for conference, April 16, 2002; updated April 3, 2003, accessed February 25, 2004, at Federation of American Scientists website, www.fas.org/bwc/recentpapers.htm.
19. Cronin, A.K., Terrorist Motivations for Chemical and Biological Weapons Use: Placing the Threat in Context, Congressional Research Service Report for Congress, 2003.
20. Public health response to biological and chemical weapons: WHO guidance, World Health Organization, May 2003.
21. Unclassified report to Congress on the acquisition of technology relating to weapons of mass destruction and advanced conventional munitions, 1 January through 30 June 2002, Central Intelligence Agency, accessed November 26, 2003, through cia.gov.
22. About ASM, American Society for Microbiology, accessed November 26, 2003, at www.asm.org/general.asp?bid=14777.
23. Kaplan, D.E., Aum Shinrikyo (1995), in *Toxic Terror: Assessing Terrorist Use of Chemical and Biological Weapons*, Tucker, J.B., Ed., MIT Press, Cambridge, MA, 2000, chap. 12.
24. Olson, K.B., Aum Shinrikyo: once and future threat?, *Emerg Infect Dis*, 5, 513, 1999.
25. Smithson, A.E. and Levy, L.-E., Ataxia: The Chemical and Biological Terrorism Threat and the US Response, Report No. 35, The Henry L. Stimson Center, Washington, D.C., 2000, chap. 3.
26. Yamaguchi, M., Justice Minister: Cult behind 1995 Tokyo Subway Nerve Gas Attack Still Dangerous, *AP*, April 11, 2003.
27. UNAIDS, Fact Sheet 2002: The Impact of HIV/AIDS, accessed November 26, 2003, at www.unaids.org/EN/media/fact±sheets.asp.
28. UNAIDS, Report on the global HIV/AIDS epidemic, 2002.
29. Centers for Disease Control and Prevention, Divisions of HIV/AIDS Prevention, Basic statistics, accessed November 26, 2003, at www.cdc.gov/hiv/stat-trends.htm#basic.
30. UNAIDS, Q&A II: Basic facts about the HIV/AIDS epidemic and its impact, accessed November 26, 2003, at www.unaids.org/EN/resources/questions_answers.asp.
31. World Bank Responds to SARS, press release, June 4, 2003, web.worldbank.org.
32. Asnis, D. et al., Outbreak of West Nile-like viral encephalitis — New York, 1999, *MMWR*, 48, 845, 1999.
33. Falkenrath, R.A., Newman, R.D., and Thayer, B.A., *America's Achilles' Heel: Nuclear, Biological, and Chemical Terrorism and Covert Attack*, MIT Press, Cambridge, MA, 1998, chap. 1.
34. Text of the Convention on the Prohibition of the Development, Production, and Stockpiling of Bacteriological (Biological) and Toxin Weapons and on Their Destruction, accessed at http://www.fas.org/nuke/control/bwc/text/bwc.htm.

35. Kaufmann, A.F., Meltzer, M.I., and Schmid, G.P., The economic impact of a bioterrorist attack: Are prevention and postattack intervention programs justifiable? *Emerg Infect Dis*, 3, 83, 1997.
36. Meltzer, M.I. et al., Modeling potential responses to smallpox as a bioterrorist weapon, *Emerg Infect Dis*, 7, 959, 2001.
37. Regis, E., *The Biology of Doom*, Henry Holt, New York, 1999, chap. 14.
38. A Study of the Vulnerability of Subway Passengers in New York City to Covert Action with Biological Agents, Miscellaneous Publication 24, Department of the Army, Fort Detrick, Frederick, MD, 1968, as cited in Cole, L.A., *The Eleventh Plague: The Politics of Biological and Chemical Warfare*, Henry Holt, New York, 1997, chap. 8.
39. Smith, R.J., Yeltsin Blames '79 Anthrax on Germ Warfare Efforts, *Washington Post*, A1, June 16, 1992.
40. Meselson, M. et al., The Sverdlovsk anthrax outbreak of 1979, *Science,* 266, 1202, 1994.
41. Alibek, K. with Handelman, S., *Biohazard*, Random House, New York, 1999, chap. 7.
42. Alibek, K., quoted in "Plague Wars," *PBS Frontline*, transcript accessed August 13, 2003, at http://www.pbs.org/wgbh/pages/frontline/shows/plague/sverdlovsk/alibekov .html.
43. Anderson, I., Foot and Mouth Disease 2001: Lessons To Be Learned, Inquiry Report (House of Commons paper), The Stationery Office Books, London, July 22, 2002.
44. The 2001 Outbreak of Foot and Mouth Disease, National Audit Office report (HC939 2001–2002), 2002, accessed October 24, 2003, www.nao.gov.uk.
45. Jernigan D.B. et al., Investigation of bioterrorism-related anthrax, United States, 2001: epidemiologic findings, *Emerg Infect Dis*, 8, 1019, 2002.
46. CDC 122 City Mortality Reporting System, accessed through cdc.gov.
47. Shepard, C.W. et al., Antimicrobial postexposure prophylaxis for anthrax: adverse events and adherence, *Emerg Infect Dis*, 8, 1124, 2002.

47a. Shaffer, D. et al., Increased U.S. prescription trends associated with the CDC *Bacillus anthracis* antimicrobial postexposure prophylaxis campaign, *Pharmacoepidermiol Drug Saf*, 12, 177, 2003.

48. Holland, J.J., Writing to Congress May Be Final Victim of Bioterror Attacks, *AP*, February 6, 2004.
49. Capitol Hill anthrax incident: EPA's cleanup was successful; opportunities exist to enhance contract oversight, General Accounting Office report, GAO-03-686, 2003.
50. Office of Management and Budget, Report to Congress on Combating Terrorism, September 2003.
51. U.S. Postal Service, Emergency Preparedness Plan, Board of Governors FY 2005 appropriations request, approved December 9, 2003 meeting, e-mail from USPS spokesman, February 26, 2004.
52. Hughes, J.M. and Gerberding, J.L., Anthrax bioterrorism: lessons learned and future directions, *Emerg Infect Dis*, 8, 1013, 2002.
53. Mott, J.A. et al., Call-tracking data and the public health response to bioterrorism-related anthrax, *Emerg Infect Dis*, 8, 1088, 2002.
54. Heller, M.B. et al., Laboratory response to anthrax bioterrorism, New York City, 2001. *Emerg Infect Dis*, 8, 1096, 2002.
55. Dworkin, M.S., Ma, X., and Golash, R.G., Fear of bioterrorism and implications for public health preparedness, *Emerg Infect Dis*, 9, 503, 2003.
56. Parks, D., Jeffco Spent $1 Million on Anthrax Responses, *Birmingham News* (Alabama), April 3, 2002.

57. Tengelsen, L. et al., Coordinated response to reports of possible anthrax contamination, Idaho, 2001, *Emerg Infect Dis*, 8, 1093, 2002.
58. Harris, S.H., *Factories of Death: Japanese Secret Biological Warfare, 1932–1945, and the American Cover-Up*, Routledge, New York; revised edition, 2002; chap. 5–9.
59. Kristof, N.D., Unmasking Horror — A Special Report; Japan Confronting Gruesome War Atrocity, *New York Times*, A1, March 17, 1995.
60. Nixon, R.M., Remarks announcing decisions on chemical and biological defense policies and programs, November 25, 1969.
61. Du Preez, J. and Korbyakov, D., Renewed efforts to strengthen the BTWC, Center for Nonproliferation Studies, Monterey Institute of International Studies, accessed February 26, 2004, at http://cns.miis.edu/pubs/week/021111.htm.
62. Biological weapons proliferation concerns, fact sheet, Henry L. Stimson Center, at www.stimson.org/cbw/?sn=CB2001121274.
63. Chemical and biological weapons: possession and programs past and present, chart from Center for Nonproliferation Studies, Monterey Institute of International Studies, 2002, at http://cns.miis.edu/research/cbw/possess.htm.
64. Miller, J., Engelberg, S., and Broad, W., *Germs: Biological Weapons and America's Secret War*, Simon & Schuster, New York, 2001, chap. 3.
65. Broad, W.J. and Miller, J., U.S. Recently Produced Anthrax in a Highly Lethal Powder Form, A1, *New York Times*, December 13, 2001.
66. Alibek, K. with Handelman, S., *Biohazard*, Random House, New York, 1999, chap. 3, chap. 12.
67. Cole, L.A., *The Eleventh Plague: The Politics of Biological and Chemical Warfare*, Henry Holt, New York, 1988.
68. Alibek, K. with Handelman, S., *Biohazard*, Random House, New York, 1999, chap. 20.
69. Christoff, J.A., Weapons of Mass Destruction: Observations on U.S. Threat Reduction and Nonproliferation Programs in Russia, GAO statement to the House Armed Services Committee, March 4, 2003.
70. Woolf, A.F., Nunn-Lugar cooperative threat reduction programs: issues for Congress, Congressional Research Service report 97-1027F, updated March 6, 2002.
71. Threat Findings of the Nunn, Lugar-Dominici Act, Appendix E, accessed February 18, 2004, at http://www.rand.org/publications/MR/MR1251/MR1251.AppE.pdf.
72. G8 Summit: Preventing the proliferation of weapons of mass destruction, fact sheet, the White House Office of the Press Secretary, June 27, 2002.
73. Murphy, D.E., Horrific Tales Emerge in Apartheid Hearings, *Los Angeles Times*, A1, June 19, 1998.
74. Beresford, D.S., Africa 'Killed with Anthrax,' *The Guardian* (London), 3, June 10, 1998.
75. Warrick, J. and Mintz, J., Lethal Legacy: Bioweapons for Sale; U.S. Declined South African Scientist's Offer on Man-Made Pathogens, *Washington Post*, A1, April 21, 2003.
76. Warrick, J., Biotoxins Fall into Private Hands; Global Risk Seen in S. African Poisons, *Washington Post*, A1, April 21, 2003.
77. Rissanen, J., The biological weapons convention, issue brief for Center for Nonproliferation Studies, 2003.
78. Zilinskas, R.A., Iraq's biological weapons. The past as future?, *JAMA*, 278, 418, 1997.
79. Smith, R.J., UN Says Iraqis Prepared Germ Weapons in Gulf War; Baghdad Balked, Fearing U.S. Nuclear Retaliation, *Washington Post*, A1, August 26, 1995.

80. Chandrasekaran, R., Iraq Lacks New Proof of Arms Destruction; U.S., UN Had Demanded Evidence for Claims, *Washington Post*, A16, December 9, 2002.
81. Transcript of George W. Bush's Remarks on the Security Council's Iraq Resolution, *New York Times*, A12, November 9, 2002.
82. Bumiller, E., In Blunt Words, Bush Threatens Hussein Again, *New York Times*, A1, November 21, 2002.
83. Comprehensive Report of the Special Advisor to the DCI on Iraq's WMD (the Duelfer report), Sept. 30, 2004, accessed at http://www.cia.gov/cia/reports/iraq_wmd_2004/.
84. Key Findings of the Comprehensive Report of the Special Advisor to the DCI on Iraq's WMD (the Duelfer report), Sept. 30, 2004, accessed at http://www.cia.gov/cia/reports/iraq_wmd_2004/.
85. Kay, D., Testimony to Senate Armed Services Committee hearing on Iraqi weapons of mass destruction and related programs, FDCH Political Transcripts, January 28, 2004.
86. Falkenrath, R.A., Newman, R.D., and Thayer, B.A., *America's Achilles' Heel: Nuclear, Biological, and Chemical Terrorism and Covert Attack*, MIT Press, Cambridge, MA, 1998, chap. 3.
87. Hoffman, B., *Inside Terrorism*, Columbia University Press, New York, 1998, chap. 4, chap. 7.
88. Johnston, D. with Van Natta, D., Jr., U.S. Officials See Signs of a Revived al Qaeda, *New York Times*, A1, May 17, 2003.
89. Slavin, Peter, Saudi Bombing Blamed on al Qaeda; Officials Point to Parallels with May 12 Attacks, *Washington Post*, 1, November 10, 2003.
90. Turkey Indicts 69 over Istanbul Suicide Bombings, *Agence France Presse*, February 25, 2004.
91. Hoge, W., Terror Suspects: Arrests Reported in Britain and Germany, *New York Times*, A13, February 7, 2003.
92. Frankel, G., London Mosque Is Raided in Toxin Case, *Washington Post*, A10, January 21, 2003.
93. The Worldwide Threat in 2003: Evolving Dangers in a Complex World, Director of Central Intelligence's briefing, as prepared for delivery, February 11, 2003, at www.cia.gov/cia/public_affairs/speeches/2003/dci_speech_02112003.html.
94. Thomas, J., Hate Groups: U.S. Groups Have Some Ties to Germ Warfare, *New York Times*, B8, November 2, 2001.
95. Lewin, T., Anthrax Is Familiar Threat at Nation's Abortion Clinics, *New York Times*, B7, November 7, 2001.
96. Clines, F.X, Man Is Arrested in Threats Mailed to Abortion Clinics, *New York Times*, A20, December 6, 2001.
97. Thomas, J., California Doctor's Suicide Leaves Many Troubling Mysteries Unsolved, *New York Times*, A28, November 3, 2002.
98. Paul R. Pillar, *Terrorism and U.S. Foreign Policy*, Brookings Institution Press, Washington, D.C., 2001, chap.2.
99. Pape, R.A., Dying to Kill Us, *New York Times*, A17, September 22, 2003.
100. Cronin, A.K., Terrorists and Suicide Attacks, Congressional Research Service Report for Congress, 2003.
101. Authors' analysis of data in the RAND-MIPT Terrorism Incident Database, January 1, 2000–March 8, 2003.
102. Authors' analysis of data in the RAND Terrorism Chronology (1968–1997) and in the RAND-MIPT Terrorism Incident Database (January 1, 2000–March 8, 2003).

103. Neumeister, L., Government Ends Case with Confession by Bombing's Alleged Mastermind, *AP*, October 22, 1997.
104. Fried, J.P., Sheik and 9 Followers Guilty of a Conspiracy of Terrorism, *New York Times*, A1, October 2, 1995.
105. Russakoff, D., 3 Convicted of Plotting to Bomb U.S. Jets; Trial Opened Window on High-Tech Terror, *Washington Post*, A1, September 6, 1996.
106. Wallace, C.P., Weaving a Wide Web of Terror; the Plan, Officials Say, Was To Blow Up 11 U.S. Airlines in One Day, *Los Angeles Times*, A1, May 28, 1995.
107. Gillespie, E.M., Judge Gets Assurances for Ressam, but Postpones Sentencing, *AP*, February 27, 2003.
108. Murakami, K., Seattle Center New Year's Eve Gala Canceled; Schell Cites Security Concerns; Midnight Fireworks Still On, *Seattle Post-Intelligencer*, A1, December 28, 1999.

2 Bioterrorism and the Public Health System

INTRODUCTION

The ability of hospitals to respond appropriately to the threat of bioterrorism is dictated to a large extent by the capabilities of state and local health departments and of the U.S. Centers for Disease Control and Prevention (CDC). This interdependence arises from several facts:

- Hospital clinical laboratories may lack the ability to rapidly identify specific pathogenic organisms used in an attack and typically lack the high-level containment facilities needed to process materials that contain highly contagious pathogens such as variola virus, which causes smallpox, or the plague bacillus. Local, state, and national laboratories are often utilized to provide these services.
- Public health authorities have access to broad reporting sources, including hospitals and other health care facilities, to monitor prevalence of various infections within a community.
- Departments of health in many areas conduct syndromic surveillance to promote the early identification of unexpected clusters of diseases such as pneumonia, skin rashes, and hemorrhagic fevers.
- Clinical, laboratory, and administrative staff of public health departments are more likely to possess the requisite expertise in outbreak control and resource allocation to contain and monitor a potential biological attack than hospital or hospital-network staffs.

Despite these inevitable areas of interdependence, local, state, and federal public health authorities represent a loose structure often fraught with ambiguous lines of authority. Approximately 3,000 local (municipal and county) health departments exist in the U.S.[1] Under normal circumstances, they are typically charged with such diverse activities as restaurant inspection, disease outbreak investigation, vaccination campaigns, and environmental testing.[2] The typical local department is small, with a median of 13 full-time employees, and most serve regions with fewer than 50,000 residents.[2]

The CDC, founded in 1946, currently has more than 8000 employees. It serves as a source of both funding and information to local and state health departments and provides assistance in evaluating outbreaks of disease and in dealing with many other health issues. The CDC, however, lacks authority over local departments except under exceptional circumstances in which outbreaks or other health issues cross state lines.

The limitations imposed by this national health infrastructure quickly become obvious in any discussion of nationwide bioterrorism preparedness. As the events of 2001 so clearly illustrated, communication and coordinated action among a loose amalgam of public health agencies with an unclear reporting structure could rapidly lead to confusion and inconsistent planning strategies. The fact that the attacks involved anthrax, a disease with which the public health and medical community were largely unfamiliar, only served to highlight deficiencies in the system.

THE PUBLIC HEALTH SYSTEM AT THE TIME OF THE 2001 ANTHRAX ATTACKS

Recent Enhancements

In the years before 2001, several important national measures had been instituted to enhance the nation's preparedness for biological attack. The CDC had developed the National Pharmaceutical Stockpile (since renamed the Strategic National Stockpile), a supply of critical antibiotics, vaccines, antidotes, and other supplies to be used in the event of a biological emergency. The Health Alert Network (HAN), a nationwide communications system linking the CDC with state and local health departments through the Internet, had been established and strengthened in the late 1990s. Epi-X, a secure Internet-based communication system, was also established to facilitate sharing of information by public health officials across jurisdictions. These entities are described in further detail in the text that follows. Finally, educational material had been provided by the CDC and the military in the form of courses, videotapes, and other modalities for medical providers, first responders, laboratory workers, and other key personnel.

Warnings of Weaknesses

Several analyses of hospital preparedness for mass casualties and terrorist events were carried out prior to the attacks of 2001, as were several national readiness exercises. In general, the findings indicated that public health authorities were poorly prepared to interact with hospitals during a variety of hypothetical incidents. Bioterrorism preparedness was singled out in several instances as especially inadequate.

TOPOFF

TOPOFF (for "Top Officials"), the first of a planned series of national readiness drills, was held in May 2000. It involved simulated attacks with a chemical weapon, mustard gas, in Portsmouth, NH, and with a biological weapon, aerosolized plague bacteria, covertly released in a performing arts theater in Denver, CO. The 3-day, $3 million exercise occurred in real time, involving real rescuers and local officials, as well as participation by the CDC and the U.S. attorney general, although only three of Denver's acute care hospitals participated. By the time the exercise ended,

3700 cases of plague had been "reported" from at least 11 states and several foreign countries, 950 people had "died,"[3] and the "outbreak" was still expanding.[3,4]

The exercise revealed a number of major problems in the response, including lack of surge capacity to handle patients and dispense antibiotic prophylaxis; difficulties in coordination and communication, with unclear lines of authority; difficulties with decision making, which was conducted through unwieldy mass conference calls; conflicts over who should get prophylaxis; and failure by public officials to move quickly and decisively to contain the spread of the disease.[3,5]

Dark Winter

The following year, in June 2001, a tabletop exercise called Dark Winter was staged to examine how senior level policymakers would handle a covert smallpox attack. Its 12 players were current or past public officials playing members of the National Security Council. Sam Nunn, a former senator from Georgia, filled the role of the president of the U.S.

In the Dark Winter scenario, smallpox was covertly released in three shopping malls in Oklahoma City, Philadelphia, and Atlanta on December 1, 2002, initially infecting 3,000 people. The outbreak came to the National Security Council's attention on December 9. By December 22, 25 states had reported 16,000 cases, with 1,000 deaths. Demands for vaccine sparked riots and looting, and 100,000 deaths were projected over the next few weeks, before vaccine stocks could be augmented.[6,7]

The basic lesson its developers drew from Dark Winter was that the U.S. was ill prepared to meet a biological attack, lacking adequate vaccine and antibiotic stockpiles, adequate means of distribution, strategies and plans for response, information systems and coherent protocols for decision making, and a vigorous public health infrastructure.[8,9] TOPOFF and Dark Winter are described in greater detail in Appendix C.

The Gilmore Commission Report of 2001

Between March and September 2001,[10] the RAND Corporation conducted a national survey of the heads of local response organizations, including fire and police departments, emergency medical services, hospitals and local and state public health agencies, as well as local and state offices of emergency management. The work was done for the Advisory Panel to Assess Domestic Response Capabilities for Terrorism Involving Weapons of Mass Destruction (known as the Gilmore Commission), a panel created by the secretary of defense in 1999. The data from this survey is particularly illuminating, as almost all the responses were received before September 11, 2001. More than 1000 agencies, approximately two thirds of those in the survey, responded.

The survey focused on preparedness for attacks on the scale of the Oklahoma City bombing of 1995 and requested responses covering four types of terrorist scenarios: biological, chemical, or nuclear attack, or large-scale bombings with conventional explosives. Particular aspects of planning received close attention in this survey. These included:

- Procedures for communication with other organizations
- Plans for mass decontamination
- Plans for isolation and quarantine
- Coordination of agencies across jurisdictions

The survey indicated that fewer than one third of the organizations had plans in place sufficient to handle a biological or chemical attack comparable in devastation to the bombing in Oklahoma City that resulted in fewer than 200 fatalities. Planning for chemical attacks was more likely to be adequate than that for biological attacks. In general, public health organizations were no more prepared to respond to biological attack than the other types of agencies surveyed, including hospitals.

Accentuating the overall poor results of the survey and the particularly low level of preparedness for biological attack was the limited scale of the biological scenario presented in the survey. The biological agent used in the hypothetical attack was *Brucella*, a bacterial pathogen that is not on the CDC's Category A list of dangerous pathogens likely to be used in an attack. Ultimately, the scenario projected only seven deaths.

Among agencies that had adequate plans in place (the minority), the extent of preparedness varied in the four key areas listed in the preceding text. The survey found the following:

- Communication procedures: Although appropriate procedures were generally in place (in 100% of Emergency Medical Services (EMS) agencies, for example), plans typically focused on communication among local response agencies. A relative deficiency within this category was found among law enforcement agencies, only 59% of which had plans addressing biological attacks.
- Mass decontamination: Only 50 to 65% of agencies with plans addressed mass decontamination for chemical attacks, and only 35 to 60% of these addressed this issue for biological attacks.
- Isolation and quarantine: Plans were found to be in place for isolation and/or quarantine of victims of a biological attack in 56% of hospitals' plans, and 35% and 19% of local and state health department plans, respectively.
- Coordination across jurisdictions: More than 90% of state and local offices of emergency management had plans, but only 78% of these agencies and 53% of law enforcement agencies had plans to address biological attacks.

Perhaps the most telling concern in this survey was the finding that only 7% had biological response plans in place and had tested those plans through tabletop exercises or drills within the 2 years preceding the survey. Furthermore, fewer than half of the exercises focusing on biological attacks that had been conducted by fire departments or law enforcement agencies had addressed communication with hospitals and public health departments. Only 25% of the exercises of hospital and public health agencies in this area addressed communication with law enforcement, fire departments, or emergency medical services.

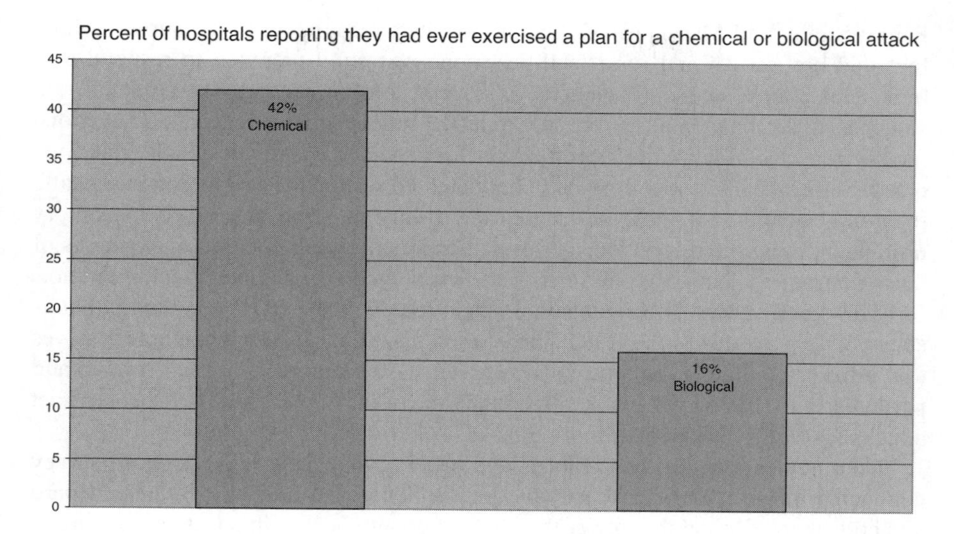

FIGURE 2.1 Chemical vs. biological exercises. (From Fricker, R.D., Jr., Jacobson, J.O., and Davis, L.M., RAND issue paper, 2002. www.rand.org/publications/IP/IP217/IP217/index.html.)

As in other aspects of this survey, preparedness for chemical attacks, although often inadequate, was more advanced than preparedness for biological attacks (Figure 2.1).

Similar findings were contained in Smithson and Levy's October 2000 report for the Henry L. Stimson Center, based in part on interviews with medical providers, first responders, and local officials in 30 cities around the country. When asked to rate their preparedness on a scale of 1 to 10 before and after having received assistance from a federal training program, local officials said their readiness for a chemical attack improved from an average "before" rating of 3.1 to an "after" rating of 5.9. For bioterrorism readiness, the average "before" rating was only 1.7; it rose to an "after" rating of 4.1. One of the chief worries of responders, Smithson and Levy found, was that they would be unable to diagnose an unusual disease such as smallpox or anthrax in a timely fashion. Other obstacles included lack of surge capacity, with many hospitals operating so close to capacity that they routinely had to go on "bypass" during the influenza season, diverting ambulances to other facilities. In addition, hospitals had relatively few intensive care unit beds and ventilators.[11]

Other Surveys

A number of other surveys and reports done before September 11, 2001, focused on gaps in preparation for bioterrorism, including providers' assessments that they lacked training and resources.

In a survey by Treat and colleagues,[12] an unselected group of 40 hospitals were surveyed within FEMA region III (District of Columbia, West Virginia, Virginia,

Pennsylvania, and Maryland). Of the 30 hospitals responding to the survey, which included both urban and rural facilities, none was fully prepared to respond to a biological attack, and only eight (27%) were considered partially prepared. No vaccines, other than tetanus, were stockpiled by any hospital surveyed, and only one facility reported stockpiling ciprofloxacin for a potential anthrax attack. Only one quarter of hospitals responding had conducted educational sessions for their staffs regarding weapons of mass destruction, and only one had developed mandatory training. Among the respondents, 20% had conducted drills focused on weapons of mass destruction, but only one facility had employed a biological attack scenario.

This small survey of hospitals in a single region of the country, although not as statistically powerful as the Rand Corporation's national survey, nonetheless serves to reinforce the finding that hospitals were remarkably unprepared for terrorism and particularly for biological attack around the time of the September 11, 2001, terrorist attacks and the subsequent anthrax attacks.

Communication gaps on the local level were also evident. In a telephone survey conducted in West Virginia shortly before the September 11, 2001, attacks, Hoard and colleagues[13] found that fewer than half of county health directors responding to the survey had provided contact information to local hospitals, and only 14% had attended training sessions for weapons of mass destruction preparedness in conjunction with hospitals.

The Anthrax Experience

Despite these warnings, the anthrax attacks of 2001 revealed gaps and flaws in the public health apparatus in the U.S. that had not been fully anticipated prior to that period. After the initial case of fatal pulmonary anthrax was diagnosed in Florida, initial announcements from the CDC did not acknowledge the high likelihood that an intentional release of anthrax spores had occurred.[1] As subsequent cases of pulmonary and cutaneous anthrax were seen in New York City, Washington, D.C., and Connecticut, and as it rapidly became clear that contaminated mail had been used to disseminate this highly unusual infection, local departments of health, particularly in New York City and in Washington, D.C., were rapidly flooded with requests to analyze suspicious packages and to test the environment in postal processing facilities and other buildings. Simultaneously, these departments, in conjunction with the CDC, were pressed to issue guidelines for screening and treatment of potential victims, and to keep medical professionals and the public informed of the status of the attack by means of almost daily press releases and announcements for weeks throughout late 2001. (Communication problems during the attacks are discussed in greater detail in Chapter 7.)

These activities became necessary during an especially confusing period shortly after both cities had been attacked by means of hijacked commercial airliners on September 11, when the immediate and long-term health effects of those attacks were unknown and the risk of further bioterrorist attacks could not be accurately estimated.

Planning efforts following the still-mysterious anthrax attacks were confounded by this uncertainty, and strategies to prepare for the possibility of further attacks, not only with anthrax but with other biological agents as well as chemical and nuclear weapons, had to be rapidly developed and coordinated by public health authorities.

In a report to Congress in October 2003, the U.S. General Accounting Office highlighted many of the specific obstacles that confronted the public health systems on the national, state, and local levels during the anthrax attacks.[14] Key findings of this report included the following:

- At the state and local level, prior planning activities proved helpful in responding to the anthrax attacks, but the extent of coordination needed across public and private entities was unanticipated.
- Difficulty was encountered in getting information into the hands of clinicians, even when communication among agencies was effective.
- At the federal level, the CDC was not fully prepared to coordinate a national response to the attacks and encountered difficulty in managing the rapidly accumulating data it was receiving.
- Despite the fact that the anthrax attacks had occurred in six "epicenters" (Florida, New York, Connecticut, the Washington, D.C. regional area, New Jersey, and Capitol Hill), all on the Eastern seaboard, the effects were felt nationally as local health departments in all areas of the country were asked to evaluate suspicious powders and mail. Contributing to the unprecedented strain on resources across the country was the fact that 60 sites, primarily postal facilities, were ultimately found to be contaminated with anthrax spores, raising the specter of a widening pattern of cases transmitted through the mail.

A post-anthrax survey by Gursky and colleagues,[1] (involving physicians, professionals working in state and local health departments and laboratories, CDC officials, representatives of the media, the postal workers' union, and several not-for-profit health organizations) amplified many of these issues. Among the observations in the survey were the following:

- Public health decision-making processes at the time of the attacks were not adequate in a number of ways. The CDC, having never been in the position of reacting to outbreaks in five regions in such rapid succession, was not prepared to analyze the attacks and simultaneously provide practical advice to local public health departments, hospitals, and physicians.
- Many health departments crafted advisories for the public and medical communities, whereas others sought guidance from the CDC first.
- In some jurisdictions, elected officials, rather than public health or medical authorities, intervened to make decisions regarding antibiotic prophylaxis.
- The initial position of the CDC that anthrax spores could not pass through unopened envelopes (later proven incorrect) resulted in divergent recommendations regarding antibiotic prophylaxis for postal workers.

THE CURRENT STATE OF PREPAREDNESS IN U.S. PUBLIC HEALTH SYSTEMS

Following the attacks of 2001, approximately $1 billion was allocated by the federal government to state health departments for the purpose of enhancing preparedness for bioterrorism and other types of disease outbreaks.[15] Although this funding resulted in an increase of 132% in the number of state health department workers assigned to terrorism and infectious diseases, significant gaps were demonstrated in a survey of all 50 state health departments conducted by the Center for Acute Disease Epidemiology of the Iowa Department of Public Health and Iowa State University's Department of Microbiology.[15] Results of the survey indicated that the total number of such workers rose from 366 to 848 nationally between 2001 and 2003, and that 47 states had increased staffing. Nonetheless, difficulties in hiring qualified epidemiologists as well as in establishing effective disease surveillance systems were reported by more than half of the states. Planning for smallpox vaccination and food security issues were highlighted as special obstacles in this survey.

A report by the GAO to the Congress in September 2003 summarized the results of interviews of state and local public health authorities conducted across the country in 2002.[16] The report concluded that improvements had been made in some areas, particularly disease surveillance systems, after the anthrax attacks, but said important gaps still existed in the public health infrastructure. Among these were:

- Many local health departments continued to rely on passive systems of disease reporting, counting on laboratories and/or providers to report certain infectious diseases under their own initiative. Because of inefficiencies and delays associated with such systems, they were felt to be suboptimal in their ability to rapidly detect the emergence and spread of new infections (such as the severe acute respiratory syndrome SARS) or biological attacks.
- All of the states surveyed reported deficiencies in laboratory facilities. In many cases, these weaknesses became apparent in the surge of activity following the anthrax attacks, when an estimated 70,000 samples were tested nationally for the presence of anthrax. Although federal funding had begun to provide for improvements in laboratory services and some jurisdictions were rapid-testing procedures for key pathogens, these developments were in their earliest stages at the time of the survey.
- Personnel shortages were widely reported, as well as concerns about surge capacity in laboratory and epidemiologic personnel. The potential exposure of field personnel to highly infectious agents was also acknowledged as a key factor in projecting workforce needs.
- A general absence of regional coordination (especially between hospitals and public health authorities and between governmental jurisdictions, across state lines, for example) was underscored.
- The report also concluded that the role of hospitals in the response to a biological attack or other infectious disease emergency had not been fully recognized prior to the events of 2001, and that means of training hospital personnel and providing drills and exercises were needed.

The Results of TOPOFF 2

A major national readiness exercise conducted in May 2003 also produced mixed results, with participants divided over how well it went.[17,18] The exercise, TOPOFF 2, was a 5-day, $16 million drill that involved the explosion in Seattle of a "dirty bomb," designed to disseminate radioactive material, and the release of pneumonic plague in Chicago. Unlike TOPOFF 1, mentioned in the previous sections, TOPOFF 2 was preceded by a year of planning, including preliminary exercises, and participants knew the nature of the weapons that would be used. The exercise involved 8500 people and 25 federal, state, and local agencies, as well as private relief organizations and the government of Canada. It was the first to be run by the recently created Department of Homeland Security. In Illinois, 64 hospitals participated, seeing a combination of in-the-flesh mock patients and paper patients, whose history and symptoms were faxed to emergency departments. By the end, 5000 people had been "infected" with plague, and almost 1100 had "died."[19]

The Department of Homeland Security's 14-page public report on the exercise (a 200-page assessment is classified) cited problems with communications, coordination, scarcity of resources, and allocation of prophylaxis, problems similar to those seen in TOPOFF 1.[20]

The agency's public report identifies two problems specific to hospitals:

- Hospitals relied heavily on regular telephone and fax lines, which were overwhelmed by volume. In one location, three HAM radio operators were used to maintain communications. Data transmission was slow and involved error-prone manual copying and collecting.
- Hospitals had to cope with shortages of staff and of isolation and negative pressure rooms.

There were problems in determining who among first responders and local residents should get prophylaxis from the National Strategic Stockpile. Different agencies gave conflicting information about prophylaxis as well as about the locations where the plague was thought to have been released.[20] One participant reported that disputes over antibiotic distribution strategy were "our greatest and biggest fight" during the drill.[18] A fuller description of TOPOFF 2 can be found in Appendix C.

MAJOR OBSTACLES TO PREPARING THE PUBLIC HEALTH SYSTEM FOR BIOTERRORISM

In addition to the difficulties outlined above, public health systems confront a number of obstacles in antibioterrorism planning efforts.

Accurately Assessing the Hazard

In traditional hospital emergency preparedness planning, emphasis is placed on hazard vulnerability. Standards of the Joint Commission on Accreditation of Heathcare Organizations (JCAHO) require that a hazard vulnerability analysis (HVA) be performed at regular intervals to assist in guiding health departments and hospitals in the tailoring of their preparedness measures to specific circumstances. Where earthquakes or hurricanes are frequent events, hospitals should plan for the effects of such potential disasters. If hospitals serve an area with a nuclear power plant or a large airport, accidents and disasters unique to such facilities should be anticipated and planned for.

The central challenge facing public health authorities and hospitals in planning for bioterrorism attacks is that pre-event risk assessment may be difficult or impossible. The diversity of potential biological attack scenarios, even with the most likely agents of attack, calls for a great variety of specific plans for decontamination, isolation and quarantine, special handling of clinical specimens, enhanced capacity for ventilatory support, and ready communication with public health authorities in addition to the first-responder sectors of police, fire departments, and emergency medical services. Further confounding the planning process is the fact that biological attack may not come as a single, dramatic event but rather as an ongoing crisis created by repeated limited attacks, as in the anthrax incidents of 2001, or by a self-perpetuating attack that spreads person to person.

Standard external disaster drills employing scenarios such as plane crashes with multiple casualties fail to address most of the unique challenges that would be encountered in a biological attack.

Finally, although catastrophic weather events, earthquakes, fires, and accidents are unusual, they occur regularly and predictably over long periods of time. This enables hospital planners to concentrate on becoming familiar with the demands created by these events, secure in the knowledge that their preparations may well be needed some day. The rarity of biological terror attacks so far — only two have been recognized in the U.S., both affecting limited geographical areas — provides little incentive for hospital emergency planners to focus on the diverse requirements they would impose.

Recognizing these obstacles, it may be prudent to regard specific planning for biological attack to be a component of other, more commonplace planning needs within a hospital or hospital network. These needs include:

- Ensuring adequate isolation procedures
- Developing algorithms to assist triage personnel and other staff at points of entry to the hospital in recognizing the signs of a contagious disease
- Improving methods of communication between hospitals and public health authorities

Throughout this book, we have endeavored to keep these obstacles in mind and to provide planning strategies for hospitals that are as convenient as is practical.

Unpredictable Needs for Crisis Response

The sudden appearance of West Nile virus infection in many states beginning in the late 1990s, and the SARS outbreak that began in Asia in late 2002 and spread to the Western Hemisphere in the spring of 2003, illustrate the potential for unpredictable but highly labor-intensive events regularly faced by the U.S. public health apparatus. This potential was reinforced in the fall and winter of 2003–2004 when an unexpectedly early influenza epidemic struck many areas of the country, resulting in a sudden shortage of influenza vaccine. Although such crises consume the resources of hospitals and public health agencies, they also may help these entities become more effective at recognizing and responding to infectious disease outbreaks, whether they represent natural occurrences or biological attacks.

Lack of Standards for Preparedness

Currently, accepted standards and protocols for many aspects of hospital preparedness do not exist. There is no consensus, for instance, about which medications and how many doses should be stockpiled by hospitals, or how many ventilators should be accessible to hospitals of various sizes. There are no standard protocols for running hospital drills and exercises, or for assuring backup communications capacity in the event of a crisis. The development of unified standards, evidence-based where possible, might be expected to help hospitals gain a minimum level of preparedness. This might be especially useful for smaller hospitals that may have less in-house expertise in infectious disease or emergency management.

Ongoing Responsibilities of Public Health Officials

Public health authorities on the local, state, and federal level are constantly involved in the tracking and controlling of less dramatic outbreaks, such as food poisoning, tuberculosis, sexually transmitted diseases, viral hepatitis, and clusters of nosocomial infections.

In many large cities, such as New York, public health authorities bear responsibility for monitoring the HIV/AIDS epidemic and for directing state and federal funding initiatives focused on care of HIV-infected individuals and testing of those engaged in high-risk behavior.

For these and many other reasons, federal, state, and local health authorities find themselves with variable and often limited time to devote to planning for the response to a bioterrorist attack that may never come.

Funding at the Local Level

Federal funding for preparedness has increased sharply since September 11, 2001. According to the Department of Health and Human Services, its total spending on bioterrorism preparedness rose from about $300 million in 2001 to $1.8 billion in 2002, to $3.5 billion in 2003. In 2003, $1.4 billion of this money went to the states and to three cities (New York, Los Angeles, and Chicago), including $870 million for improving public health preparedness and $498 million for developing surge capacity in hospitals.[21,22]

Nonetheless, lack of adequate funding remains a common theme among hospitals and other state and local organizations, according to a 2003 RAND Corporation survey of 918 state and local response agencies (including fire and police departments, hospitals, public health agencies, and emergency medical services), done for the Gilmore Commission. More funding was said to be needed in particular to support training, equipment procurement, and the conducting of risk assessments[23] (Figure 2.2).

ISSUES OF PUBLIC HEALTH INFRASTRUCTURE

A consensus exists that the terrorist events of 2001, especially the anthrax attacks, revealed major flaws in the level of preparedness of the public health apparatus. Funding was made available almost immediately to bolster state and local health departments and enhance their ability to respond to biological attacks. Strategies to improve response effectiveness have centered on several recurrent themes: enhanced syndromic surveillance; better communication between hospitals, public health authorities, and such first responders as fire departments and emergency medical services; and repeated drills and exercises. An appreciation of the potential vulnerability of the U.S. population to smallpox, a CDC Category A biological terror agent, resulted in a federal-level strategy to immunize health care workers, first responders, and, eventually, much of the general population to variola virus. Each of these strategies has been implemented to varying degrees in many locales. Each, however, also has been met with criticism and skepticism in some quarters.

SYNDROMIC SURVEILLANCE

Syndromic surveillance refers to a process by which public health authorities monitor the incidence of selected clinical syndromes (e.g., fever and cough, diarrhea, unexplained skin rashes, etc.) for the purpose of early identification of outbreaks of disease. This monitoring may be carried out passively or by gathering data on the syndrome under surveillance on a regular basis from key health care entry points, such as emergency departments, private physicians' offices, or health maintenance organizations. Syndromic surveillance had been an established strategy employed by health departments in many areas of the country prior to the 2001 attacks. Federal funding for bioterrorism preparedness made available since that time has been utilized in some areas to make such surveillance more widespread and effective. It has been pointed out, however, that such surveillance is, of necessity, more sensitive than specific for particular diseases.[24] For example, though many pathogens cause fever and cough, none, with the exception of *Bacillus anthracis,* have actually represented an intentional biological attack.

Furthermore, the two cases of pulmonary anthrax in New York City would not have been detected by syndromic surveillance of fever and cough.

The ability of a health department to respond to a sudden surge in a particular symptom complex is central to the potential value of syndromic surveillance. In the case of fever and cough, seasonal surges during the winter months resulting from a variety of common viral and bacterial pathogens are commonplace, and each such surge would have to be prioritized in order to correctly identify those requiring immediate action and intervention. Conversely, surveillance for syndromes more specific for pulmonary anthrax — for example, fever, cough, and widened mediastinum — might be too specific to detect the early stages of a biological attack with another respiratory pathogen, such as *Yersinia pestis.*

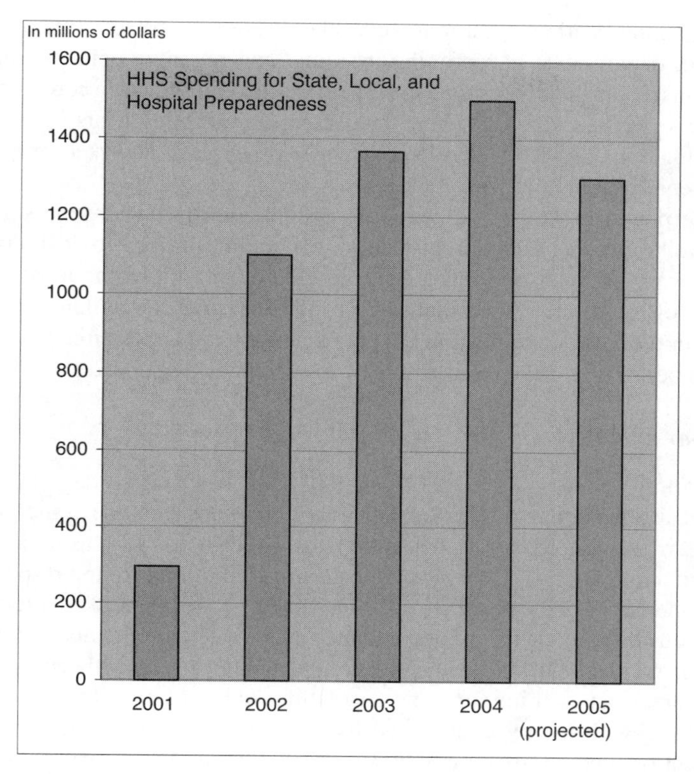

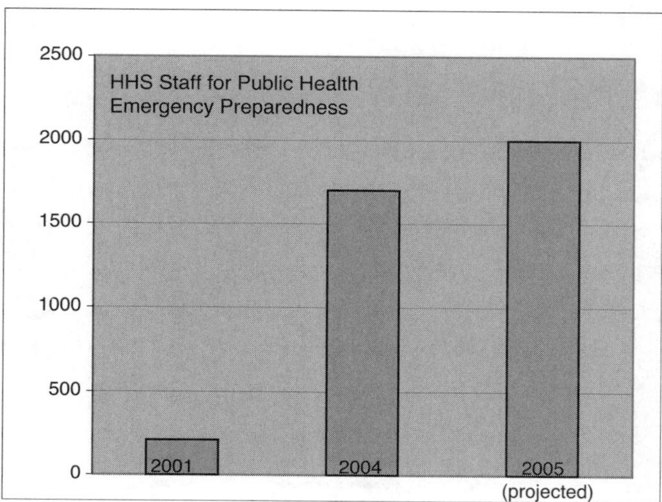

FIGURE 2.2 Federal resources for preparedness. (From Department of Health and Human Services, HHS provides $1.4 billion more to states and hospitals for terrorism preparedness, press release, September 2, 2003.)

Further complicating syndromic surveillance are the obstacles encountered by local health departments in recruiting, training, and retaining epidemiologists and laboratorians to adequately respond to surges in a specific symptom complex. Finally, syndromic surveillance has not been subjected to controlled trials in detection of actual biological attacks for obvious reasons and has been analyzed only in hypothetical scenarios.

On the positive side, it is a plausible assumption that syndromic surveillance might permit rapid identification of a target population for a biological attack, once the attack was underway and recognized. In fact, this might be the most significant advantage of syndromic surveillance. The use of such surveillance, of course, involves not the early identification but the response to an attack already in progress, and might be equally effective if reserved for postattack response.

Drills and Exercises

Surveys of preparedness prior to 2001 generally indicated a higher degree of planning for chemical attack than for biological attack, perhaps because issues raised by chemical terrorism more closely resemble real-life scenarios such as toxic spills and airborne contamination with toxic chemicals already familiar to first responders and hospital emergency personnel. In a 2003 survey, hospitals ranked preparing for chemical attacks as their top priority among unconventional threats, but gave such preparation relatively low priority.[23] Although public health authorities must frequently address issues of immunization, isolation, and, occasionally, even quarantine of individuals with highly contagious diseases, mass casualties occurring over a short period of time are extremely different from naturally occurring infections in the U.S. (Figure 2.3).

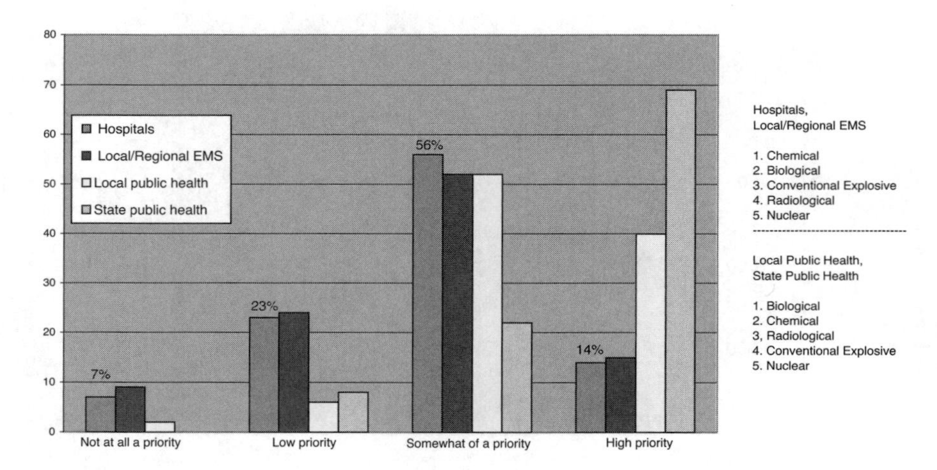

FIGURE 2.3 Hospital priorities in preparedness. (From Advisory Panel to Assess Domestic Response Capabilities for Terrorism Involving Weapons of Mass Destruction, fifth annual report to the President and the Congress, 2003, p. D-4.)

Preparedness for bioterrorism, for these reasons, must focus on drills, tabletop exercises, and other educational efforts designed to maintain the preparedness of entire cities for the unlikely event of a biological attack.

The Use of Quarantine Measures

Although the definition of the term quarantine has become somewhat ambiguous, it has been suggested that the term be applied to the practice of compulsory separation of healthy individuals or groups who have potentially been exposed to a contagious disease. This practice may include restriction of movement of individuals or populations or their segregation within defined geographic areas.[25] Thus, a distinction can be drawn between quarantine and the practice of isolation in which individuals with known or suspected contagious diseases are confined to prevent them from transmitting infection.

Quarantine, as defined above, has been suggested as an important strategy in the response to a biological attack in several well-publicized national drills and exercises, and was widely used during the SARS outbreak of 2003. However, the medical justification for liberal application of quarantine has been challenged,[25] and the legal and logistical difficulties in applying and enforcing quarantine are daunting, suggesting that the resources that would be needed to enforce such a measure during a biological attack might be better spent on other efforts. It should be noted that consideration of quarantine should occur only in response to a contagious disease, that is, infection that can be spread from person to person. It has also been pointed out that quarantine may unjustifiably expose uninfected individuals to the contagious disease if it does appear within the quarantined population.[25] Finally, the long incubation period of some of the most feared agents of bioterrorism, most notably smallpox, would undermine the effectiveness of quarantine, as many exposed individuals would have traveled outside the region of the attack before developing symptoms or themselves becoming contagious.

For these reasons, quarantine, although frequently suggested as an appropriate strategy in mock drills and exercises, may not be medically justifiable or logistically feasible in most circumstances.

Interagency Communication

The Health Alert Network

The Health Alert Network (HAN), inaugurated in 1999 by the CDC, is undergoing continuous expansion as part of the CDC's Public Health Emergency Preparedness and Response Program, which also coordinates the CDC's website in this area. By means of HAN, it is anticipated that the CDC and state and local health departments could use the Internet to communicate effectively and efficiently with one another. The system was not fully operational at the time of the anthrax attacks, with only 60% of local health departments possessing appropriate Internet access.[1]

At the time of this writing, HAN is connected to all 50 states, as well as three urban health departments, three county health departments, eight territories, and the

District of Columbia. Overall, 89% of U.S. counties are connected directly or indirectly to HAN.[26] HAN provides the capacity for urgent information to be communicated among public health authorities. Educational materials and presentations are also provided to assist in the training of local public health officials and clinical personnel.

Epi-X

Epi-X, created in 2000, is an electronic Internet-based system designed to facilitate communication of sensitive and urgent information regarding disease outbreaks.[27] By means of this system, state and local heath authorities, poison control centers, and public health practitioners can share information through a secure, encrypted process. Access is carefully controlled and currently limited to public health officials designated by their agency through their state health department. At the time of this writing, Epi-X has more than 1200 users and shares information regarding outbreaks within and across jurisdictions. It is staffed 24 hours per day.

As in the case of HAN, Epi-X was not well utilized during the anthrax attacks of 2001, according to the survey by Gursky and colleagues.[1]

The Smallpox Vaccination Campaign

In the winter of 2002–2003, a national smallpox vaccination campaign was launched. This effort was made feasible by the purchase and manufacture of substantial quantities of smallpox vaccine, which had been in short supply since the global eradication of smallpox in the 1970s. The details and outcome of this effort, which included both military and specific civilian personnel, are reviewed in Appendix B of this book.

The Strategic National Stockpile

In 1999, the CDC, in collaboration with the Department of Health and Human Services, established the National Pharmaceutical Stockpile (NPS).[28] This stockpile consisted of large quantities of essential medical materials that could be distributed to states within 12 hours of a decision to deploy them in the event of a national emergency. It was created because officials recognized that critical supplies might be rapidly exhausted or unavailable under certain emergency conditions. The NPS was renamed the Strategic National Stockpile (SNS) in 2003 and was placed under the jurisdiction of the Department of Homeland Security.

The SNS includes antibiotics, antidotes, antitoxins, and other pharmaceuticals required for life support, as well as equipment to provide for intravenous administration, airway maintenance, and surgery. Components of the SNS, called pushpacks, are distributed in strategic locations across the country to permit rapid deployment. Additional supplies, if needed, may be shipped within 24 to 36 hours after the pushpack.

SUMMARY

It is clear that the level of preparedness of the U.S. public health network has improved since the attacks of 2001. Educational efforts directed at the public and the medical communities have intensified. Syndromic surveillance and other strategies for the detection of and response to future attacks have been improved in many localities. At the national level, public health authorities have been brought into closer alliance with federal agencies involved in disaster management and law enforcement under the Department of Homeland Security. Nonetheless, as much of the data presented in this chapter suggests, coordination among various public health jurisdictions, adequate staffing of health departments with qualified personnel, and funding of laboratory and other public health needs remain issues to be addressed. Furthermore, the connection between planning at the hospital level and at the governmental level (local, state, and federal) has not yet been optimized, and communication with medical providers working outside the hospital setting remains a particularly difficult challenge.

References

1. Gursky, E., Inglesby, T.V., and O'Toole, T., Anthrax 2001: observations on the medical and public health response, *Biosecur and Bioterror*, 2, 97, 2003.
2. National Association of City and County Health Officials, Local Public Health Agency Infrastructure: A Chartbook, October 2001. www.naccho.org/general428.cfm.
3. Hoffman, R.E. and Norton J.E., Lessons learned from a full-scale bioterrorism exercise, *Emerg Infect Dis*, 6, 652, 2000.
4. O'Toole, T., quoted in "U.S. totally unprepared for bioterrorism," *UPI*, August 22, 2000.
5. Inglesby, T.V., Grossman, R., and O'Toole T., A plague on your city: observations from TOPOFF, *Clin Infect Dis*, 32, 436, 2001.
6. O'Toole, T., Mair, M., and Inglesby, T.V., Shining Light on 'Dark Winter,' *Clin Infect Dis*, 34, 972, 2002.
7. Final script, Dark Winter Bioterrorism Exercise — Andrews Air Force Base, June 22–23, 2001, accessed November 4, 2003, from http://www.hopkins-biodefense.org/DARK%20WINTER.pdf.
8. Dark Winter Lessons Learned, accessed November 4, 2003, from http://www.hopkins-biodefense.org/DARK%20WINTER.pdf.
9. Hamre, J., Transcript of testimony to the House Government Reform Subcommittee on National Security, Veterans Affairs and International Relations, July 23, 2001, Federal Document Clearing House Inc., accessed through Nexis, November 4, 2003.
10. Fricker, R.D., Jr., Jacobson, J.O., and Davis, L.M., Measuring and evaluating local preparedness for a chemical or biological terrorist attack, RAND issue paper, 2002. www.rand.org/publications/IP/IP217/IP217/index.html.
11. Smithson, A.E. and Levy, L.-E., Ataxia: The Chemical and Biological Terrorism Threat and the US Response, Report No. 35, The Henry L. Stimson Center, 2000.
12. Treat, K.N. et al., Hospital preparedness for weapons of mass destruction incidents: an initial assessment, *Ann Emerg Med*, 38, 1, 2001.

13. Hoard, M.L. et al., Preparing at the local level for events involving weapons of mass destruction, *Emerg Infect Dis*, 8, 1006, 2002. www.cdc.gov/ncidod/EIDvol8no9/01-0520.htm.
14. U.S. General Accounting Office, Bioterrorism: Public health response to anthrax incidents of 2001, report, GAO-04-152, 2003.
15. Centers for Disease Control and Prevention, Terrorism preparedness in state health departments — United States, 2001–2003. *MMWR*, 52, 1051, 2003.
16. U.S. General Accounting Office, Testimony before the Subcommittee on Emergency Preparedness and Response, Select Committee on Homeland Security, House of Representatives, Infectious diseases: Gaps remain in capabilities of state and local agencies, GAO-03-1176T, September 24, 2003.
17. Fessler P., Lessons learned from a national counterterrorism exercise conducted, *NPR Weekend Edition* transcript, December 20, 2003.
18. Fiorill, J., TOPOFF 2 participants recommend narrower drills, better dissemination of results, *Global Security Newswire*, accessed October 31, 2003. www.nti.org.
19. Sesno F. and Meserve, J., comments in *CNN Newsnight* transcript, May 16, 2003.
20. Department of Homeland Security, Top Officials (TOPOFF) Exercise Series: TOPOFF2 After Action Summary for Public Release, 2003.
21. Department of Health and Human Services, HHS provides $1.4 billion more to states and hospitals for terrorism preparedness, press release, September 2, 2003.
22. Department of Health and Human Services, The top twelve HHS highlights — 2003, press release, December 31, 2003.
23. Advisory Panel to Assess Domestic Response Capabilities for Terrorism Involving Weapons of Mass Destruction, fifth annual report to the President and the Congress, 2003, p. D-4.
24. Reingold, A., If syndromic surveillance is the answer, what is the question? *Biosecur and Bioterror*, 1, 77, 2003.
25. Barbera, J. et al., Large-scale quarantine following biological terrorism in the United States: Scientific examination, logistic and legal limits, and possible consequences, *JAMA*, 286, 2711, 2001.
26. CDC Health Alert Network website page. www.phppo.cdc.gov/HAN.
27. CDC Epi-X website page. www.cdc.gov/epix.
28. CDC Strategic National Stockpile website page. www.bt.cdc.gov/stockpile/index.asp.

Section II

Improving Hospital Readiness and Response

3 Hospital Preparations and Needs

INTRODUCTION

The obstacles confronted by hospitals in planning for bioterrorist attack are truly daunting. For reasons of financial survival, U.S. hospitals typically seek to operate with few empty inpatient beds; censuses tend to be high particularly in large urban hospitals. Supplies are often ordered on an "as needed" basis in an attempt to control costs. Physicians at voluntary and public hospitals often are not full-time employees and may, in fact, admit patients to and serve on administrative and planning committees of several hospitals within a large geographical area. Teaching hospitals often rely heavily on resident house staff to provide direct patient care. These young physicians, qualified as they may be, may have little or no training in responding to the circumstances they would face in a biological attack.

In such a setting, a sudden need for more resources — more clinical staff, more expertise in infectious diseases, more beds, ventilators, isolation rooms, or pharmaceutical supplies — would pose an immediate dilemma for virtually any hospital.

As discussed in the first chapter of this book, several large-scale exercises have illustrated the problem of inadequate "surge capacity" within U.S. hospitals, from the emergency departments to the intensive care units to the inpatient units and clinics. In a crisis the need for additional supplies, equipment, and staff in these areas may rapidly become overwhelming.

Of equal concern is the possibility that a substantial proportion of hospital staff would simply fail to report for duty in a terrorist attack or would refuse to treat bioterror victims, fearing for their own or their families' safety.[1,2] Those who do work would be expected to face prolonged shifts, confusion, large numbers of patients to triage and evaluate, all while dealing with their own emotional reactions to the attack and their own fears for the future. Mental health professionals within the hospitals would almost certainly be called upon to assist employees in addressing their fears and emotional reactions.

Beyond the clinical (physician and nursing) staffs, other resources upon which hospitals depend would be rapidly taxed in areas under direct biological attack. Clinical laboratories, transportation services, and technical personnel in areas such as radiology and respiratory therapy could be rapidly pressed beyond their limits. The need to maintain security within the hospital and communications with law enforcement agencies would pose an enormous challenge to hospital safety and security staff. Social services staff would be charged with discharge planning to rapidly vacate needed hospital beds and provide safe transportation home for discharged patients. Pharmacy staff would be placed under enormous pressure to procure and provide needed antibiotics and vaccines until federal or local emergency supplies were delivered.

The need to communicate effectively with the public would also rapidly become crucial in an area under direct attack, as was demonstrated in New York City and Washington, D.C., during the anthrax attacks of 2001. Inevitably, representatives of the print and broadcast media would seek information from hospitals with casualties, both about the nature and extent of the attack and about the risks to the public. For this reason, public affairs representatives and hospital administrators would likely be called upon to present updated information that they themselves may not possess.

In a large-scale attack, morgue facilities and mortuary workers may be rapidly pushed to their physical and emotional limits. Proper means of disposal of infected remains are not well-established and agreed upon. In one recent exercise,[3] confusing and conflicting instructions came from local medical examiner staff and the local and state health departments regarding the relative advantages of embalming or cremating victims.

In an area under attack or thought to be at risk of attack, hospitals not seeing casualties would likely be asked to provide resources (staff, equipment, pharmaceuticals, expertise) to other regional hospitals, nursing homes, and related health care facilities, as well as to schools. Private physicians' offices, like hospital-based clinics, would probably become a focal point for members of the public seeking information, reassurance, or care.

As happened during the anthrax attacks in New York City, community physicians may have no recourse but to refer their concerned patients to already overcrowded hospital emergency rooms.

Under normal circumstances, hospitals vary widely in the emergency services they offer. Those offering the most specialized services are designated Level I or trauma centers. Level II and Level III facilities are less well equipped to address mass casualties. Level I centers could be expected to treat the worst casualties in a terrorist attack in their region. But many areas do not have such centers[4] and, even in regions with a high concentration of hospitals, such facilities might be quickly overwhelmed in a substantial attack (Figure 3.1).

Several possibilities could make this general sense of chaos even worse. An intentional failure of electrical power or a "cyberattack" on a hospital's information system could greatly magnify the difficulties in dealing with a subsequent or simultaneous biological attack. Such "enabler" events could rapidly overwhelm the hospital system even if the attack itself was limited.

As can be readily concluded from this rather bleak portrait, there is no obvious strategy to address all of these problems simultaneously and efficiently. National and local exercises and drills have served to highlight some previously unrecognized issues (see Appendix C). Planning for attack must be carefully coordinated and exercises must be repeatedly conducted at every level, from hospital departments to entire hospitals to hospital networks, geographically linked facilities, municipalities, states, and the federal government. In numerous discussions with hospital-based physicians, administrative personnel, and public health authorities, we have learned that complacency about the actual risk of attack in any given locale and lack of funds to enhance response capabilities have remained major obstacles to planning.

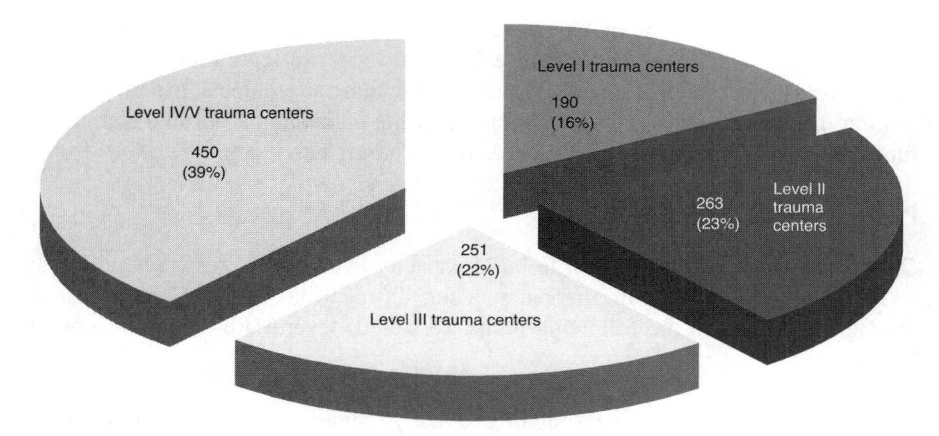

FIGURE 3.1 Types of U.S. Trauma Centers. Trauma centers are not evenly distributed. The number of Level I and II trauma centers per million population ranges from 0 (Arkansas) and 0.19 (Arizona) to 5.24 (District of Columbia) and 7.79 (North Dakota). (From MacKenzie, E.J. et al., National inventory of hospital trauma centers, *JAMA*, 289, 1515, 2003.)

In this chapter and the remaining chapters of Section II, we try to identify hospitals' basic needs and offer strategies that should be considered to meet those needs. The goal of this chapter is to familiarize the reader with emergency-management strategies that are specifically relevant in biological attack scenarios. A basic familiarity with general hospital emergency planning on the part of the reader is assumed.

A FRAMEWORK FOR HOSPITAL EMERGENCY PLANNING

To provide a framework for hospitals to assess their current level of preparedness and create a strategy for achieving their goals, it has been suggested that the elements of planning can be separated into mitigation, preparedness, response, and recovery.[5]

MITIGATION

Definition: Activities a health care organization undertakes in attempting to lessen the severity and impact a potential disaster or emergency might have on its operation.[5] Mitigation typically applies to emergencies, such as power failures, for which specific planning (i.e., provisions for emergency electrical generators) can be expected to reduce the impact on the functions of the hospital. It may be difficult to design strategies that would mitigate the impact of a biological attack. Obviously, making necessary personal protective equipment easily available, constructing high-level isolation rooms, building decontamination units, or enhancing biological safety levels for hospital laboratories are all measures that could serve to reduce the impact of an attack with a contagious agent. Given the relatively small probability of biological attack compared to the regular occurrence of power failures and weather emergencies, mitigation activities aimed solely at bioterrorism might not be cost effective. The steps listed above, however, would also mitigate more-likely emergency events (e.g., decontamination facilities for chemical accidents, isolation rooms to limit the spread of nosocomial pathogens) while enhancing a hospital's ability to function in the chaotic conditions inherent in a biological attack.

Preparedness

Definition: Activities undertaken to build capacity and identify resources that may be used should a disaster or emergency occur.[5] In regard to bioterrorism, preparedness should focus on the following items. As noted, several are explored in depth later in this book.

- Educating staff about responding to likely scenarios, with an emphasis on reducing the risk of spread of contagious agents (see Chapter 4 and Chapter 9)
- Conducting drills and tabletop exercises (see Chapter 8)
- Making contingency plans to boost surge capacity, such as keeping updated lists of retired personnel who might be called in, deciding how conference rooms might be converted to patient use, making advance agreements with supply vendors (see the section "Establishing Surge Capacity.")
- Maintaining an adequate supply of key equipment and supplies, including pharmaceuticals, personal protective equipment, ventilators, and backup communications equipment (see the sections "Infection Control" and "Establishing Surge Capacity" in this chapter).
- Arranging mutual aid and cross-credentialing agreements with nearby hospitals
- Establishing relationships and coordinating plans and drills with other organizations and public agencies in the community

Perhaps most important, given the relatively low risk of bioterrorism, hospitals need to stay alert to the possibility of such an event, updating their capacity for emergency communication with public health authorities, and ensuring the ability of their emergency department staff to recognize signs of biological terrorism in patients seeking care.

Response

Definition: The steps taken to manage an actual emergency. The response includes all steps from effective and efficient triage to prompt isolation or decontamination of victims as indicated; to safe and effective transport of patients and clinical specimens within the institution; to effective communication with public health and other civil authorities, as well as the press, the public, and health care workers. Obviously, effective clinical management of victims and minimization of the risk of contagion to staff, patients, and visitors are central to an effective response.

Recovery

Definition: The steps taken to return the hospital to normal levels of activity and readiness. The recovery phase of the hospital emergency plan represents a relatively recent addition to the standards set by the Joint Commission on Accreditation of Health Care Organizations (JCAHO).[4] The recovery phase involves the timing of decisions to return to normal levels of activity and readiness. Such decisions may be clear-cut in power failures, weather disasters, or multiple-casualty events such as airplane crashes where the duration of the event is limited and somewhat predictable. In a biological attack with contagious agents such as smallpox or the plague bacillus, victims may present in waves separated by days or weeks. Fear of unknown and possibly ongoing risk, as was seen in the anthrax attacks of 2001, would fuel the fears of the public and could result in successive waves of "worried well" seeking advice and care at the hospital. This phenomenon was especially crippling to hospitals in several of the national exercises described in Appendix C of this book. Close and frequent communications with public health authorities, and with other officials monitoring the local and national pattern of attack, will be vital in a hospital's decisions in the recovery phase.

THE EMERGENCY MANAGEMENT PLAN

The emergency management plan is designed to govern the hospital's activities during the response portion of an emergency. Typically, such plans cover a long list of items, including establishing a command structure to run the response; stipulating how, when, and by whom the plan can be activated or deactivated; establishing procedures for notifying and maintaining contact with personnel, public health authorities, and police; setting criteria for recalling staff, evacuating all or part of the hospital, isolating patients, and barring visitors.

Hospitals that developed their emergency management plans years ago, and have not updated them recently, would be wise to reassess their plan's suitability for a bioterrorism incident.

As applied to bioterrorism, the emergency management plan should focus on:

- Protecting staff, visitors, and other patients
- Safely handling patients and clinical specimens
- Adequate stockpiling of needed antibiotics and vaccines
- Interacting effectively with law enforcement and investigatory agencies
- Managing the "worried well"
- Helping staff, patients, families, and the public manage fear, uncertainty, and concern for their families
- Communicating effectively with the media

Emergency management plans should be flexible, accessible, and frequently reviewed and revised as necessary. In the realm of bioterrorism, the involvement of infection control and infectious diseases experts is highly desirable when such plans are created. It would be advisable to involve mental health, pediatric, and geriatric specialists as well, if possible. Plans that are ideally suited to point-in-time emergencies such as power failures may be inadequate to address the insidious and subtle challenges posed by the many possible agents and means of biological attack discussed in subsequent chapters.

JCAHO Standards

It is safe to say that, even before 9/11, virtually every U.S. hospital had an emergency management plan, if only because one is required by the Joint Commission on the Accreditation of Health Care Organizations (JCAHO), the U.S. accrediting body.

JCAHO does not have a specific standard about terrorism or bioterrorism. Instead, these subjects are among a wide range of emergencies for which the hospital must prepare, as outlined in the joint commission's Emergency Management Standards — Environment of Care.

Standard EC 1.4 requires that the hospital have an emergency management plan. Standard EC 2.9.1 requires that the plan be tested regularly. Each is a single short sentence, accompanied by a page or two of details elucidating the "intent" of the standard. Other Environment of Care standards require that the hospital implement its emergency management plan and that staff be educated about the hospital environment and know enough to fulfill their responsibilities within the environment.

As outlined in the "intent" portion of EC 1.4, JCAHO favors an "all hazards" approach, in which a comprehensive plan is developed that can apply to all types of likely emergency and disaster situations and that addresses all four phases of the emergency: mitigation, preparedness, response, and recovery.[5] The hazards covered can range from fires, floods, and power outages to plane crashes, toxic spills, epidemics, and terrorism. Hospitals are supposed to conduct a hazard vulnerability analysis to identify potential emergencies and set priorities for preparedness activities. In doing this, hospitals might consider the likelihood that the event will occur, the level of damage or injury should it occur, and the hospital's existing level of preparedness for the event. Compared to weather emergencies or other recurring events, bioterrorism could be expected to rank lower in likelihood but higher in both potential injury and lack of preparation, making it a candidate for a higher level of priority in planning.

The standard's "intent" elucidation includes more than a dozen areas of performance that should be addressed in the planning process.[6] Bioterrorism is mentioned explicitly only as an example of an event that would require notification to external authorities. In addition, it is said that the plan should identify facilities for chemical, biological, and radiological isolation and decontamination.

Standard EC 2.8.1. requires that the response portion of the plan be tested twice a year, either through drills or through activation in a real emergency. Drills are supposed to be conducted 4 to 8 months apart. Hospitals that offer emergency services are supposed to have at least one drill a year that includes volunteer mock patients or simulated individuals (cards or packets of information representing patients).[6,7] Tabletop exercises, while considered useful, do not count toward the required two drills a year.

During an onsite visit, JCAHO surveyors assess how a health care facility "plans, designs, implements, and improves its plan; how the plan applies to a variety of possible events; and whether staff at all levels have been trained in their roles and responsibilities in the plan."[7]

THE HOSPITAL EMERGENCY INCIDENT COMMAND SYSTEM (HEICS)

Developed by the San Mateo California Health Services Agency, HEICS represents a general framework for hospital response to various types of disasters. Many hospitals have adopted this system as the foundation of their emergency management plan. HEICS represents an adaptation of the incident command system (ICS) developed in the 1970s by the Firefighting Resource of Southern California Organized Against Potential Emergencies (FIRESCOPE).[8]

HEICS is a standardized format for emergency management designed to streamline communications within hospitals, between hospitals, and between hospitals and other agencies such as police and fire departments, by giving them a shared language and structure. This, it is hoped, will minimize chaos under emergency conditions in hospitals and make mutual assistance easier. At the heart of the system is an organizational chart of 49 jobs grouped into four sections: logistics, planning, finance, and operations.

Each section chief reports to the incident commander as do two other positions, public information officer and safety and security officer. Each job comes with a job action sheet, a written description of the mission and the tasks of the job, starting with those that should be performed immediately. The system also includes a series of documents, including patient tracking sheets, emergency credentialing forms, and activity logs.

HEICS' benefits are said to include the following:[9]

- A predictable chain of management
- A flexible organizational chart
- Prioritized response checklists
- Accountability of position function
- Improved documentation
- Common language to promote communication within the hospital and with outside agencies
- Cost effectiveness

In HEICS, job titles can be fairly specific. For instance, the treatment areas supervisor reports to the medical care director and supervises six jobs: triage unit leader, immediate treatment unit leader, delayed treatment unit leader, minor treatment unit leader, discharge unit leader, and morgue unit leader.

HEICS materials emphasize, however, that the system is flexible. Jobs are activated only if they are needed or probably will be needed. In a small facility, a single manager may have to take more than one role, or some roles may have to go unfilled.

Although not specifically designed for biological attack, the principles of HEICS are applicable to most bioterrorism scenarios. For further information on this detailed system the reader is referred to the Hospital Emergency Incident Command System, third edition, developed by the San Mateo County Health Services Agency, Emergency Medical Services.[9] The documents, including training materials, can be downloaded from a website of the California Emergency Medical Services Authority at www.emsa.ca.gov/Dms2/download.htm (Figure 3.2).

INFECTION CONTROL

Despite the complexity of the issues raised by planning for bioterrorism, most of the major tasks confronting hospitals can be considered as discrete issues that fall into one of two categories: infection control and surge capacity. Dividing the tasks in this way can simplify institution-wide planning and encourage cooperation by allowing key leaders and staff members to concentrate on limited, rather than global, responsibilities.

The protection of staff, visitors, and hospital patients from a biological attack must be among the highest priorities for a hospital, for practical as well as medical and ethical reasons. Reports[1,2] have indicated that a substantial proportion of hospital workers would be unwilling to report for duty in the event of such an attack. The disappointing acceptance of smallpox vaccination by health care workers so far appears to reflect not only fear of vaccine complications but also reluctance to become part of a "smallpox response team" because of fears for their own safety. Clearly, protection of staff in the event of an actual or expected attack goes far beyond the simple stocking of personal protective equipment to be used by first-line responders. Pre-event planning must take into account possible staffing shortages as well as the need both for education about the risk of contagion of suspected bioterrorism-related infections and a plan for providing emotional support to staff coping with fears for themselves and their families. (These issues are explored further in Chapter 6.)

CONTAGIOUS POTENTIAL OF SPECIFIC BIOLOGICAL AGENTS

Several of the biological agents that might be used in an attack are highly contagious and could easily spread within the hospital unless proper isolation and quarantine procedures are in effect. Of the Category A agents, variola virus, the cause of smallpox, and *Yersinia pestis*, the cause of plague, pose the greatest risk of person-to-person transmission. Both may be transmitted through aerosolization of respiratory secretions. Spores of *Bacillus anthracis* on the clothing of victims of an anthrax attack could, hypothetically, be reaerosolized inadvertently in the hospital, but this is thought to be unlikely. Person-to-person transmission of anthrax does not occur. Person-to-person transmission of *Franciscella tularensis*, the cause of tularemia, may conceivably occur through exposure to infected wounds, but person-to-person transmission of the respiratory infection is not considered a significant possibility. Nonetheless, respiratory tularemia has occurred among laboratory workers processing specimens contaminated with the organism. Botulism, because it requires ingestion of toxin or absorption of toxin through the respiratory tract, is not considered transmissible from person to person.

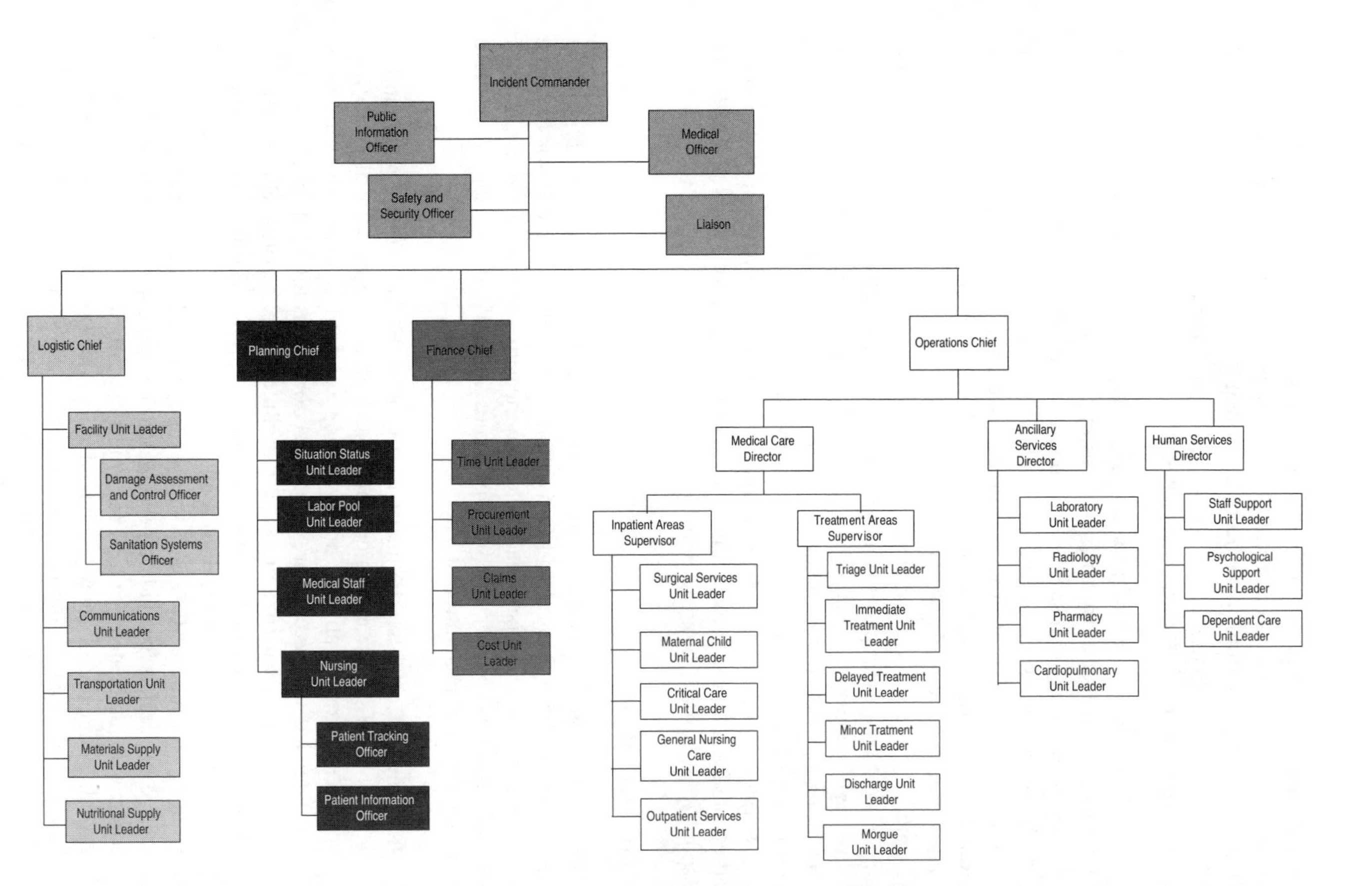

FIGURE 3.2 Hospital emergency incident command system organizational chart. (HEICS Manual Version 3, California Emergency Medical Services Authority.)

In the case of several of the hemorrhagic fever viruses (e.g., Ebola, Lassa), person-to-person transmission requires direct exposure to blood or secretions, although airborne precautions have been recommended for victims of these agents.[10]

General Elements of Infection Control

The issues involved in preventing a bioterrorist agent from spreading within the hospital are the same that every hospital faces in preventing hospital-acquired infection among patients and transmission of resistant hospital pathogens to staff and patients. If appropriate isolation and air-handling procedures are used routinely, and proper use of personal protective equipment is emphasized as it should be, the infection control issues posed by bioterrorism differ only in magnitude from those encountered in the day-to-day life of the hospital.

Hospitals are required to maintain strict and consistent strategies to prevent spread of infection among patients and between patients and staff. Nonetheless, the spread of highly contagious pathogens, especially those transmitted by the respiratory route, can prove very difficult to control within hospitals. A striking recent demonstration of this problem was seen in the worldwide outbreak of the severe acute respiratory syndrome (SARS) in 2003. In two of the epicenters of this unexpected event, Toronto and Taiwan, the vast majority of cases of SARS resulted from in-hospital (nosocomial) transmission.

Levels of Precaution

The Hospital Infection Control Advisory Committee (HICPAC) was established by the Centers for Disease Control and Prevention (CDC) in the early 1990s to create uniform environmental and personal protective measures to reduce the risk of such nosocomial transmission of disease. Guidelines formulated by that group have defined four levels of precautions:[11]

- Standard precautions. The health care worker (HCW) wears a gown and gloves. Face shield or surgical mask, and protective eyewear is worn if splashes or aersolization of body fluids is expected. Standard precautions are intended to prevent spread of infections transmitted through direct contact with the patient's blood or body fluids (e.g., hepatitis B or C, HIV infection). No environmental controls are required. The patient does not require isolation from other patients.
- Contact precautions. Gown and gloves are required. Face shield and protective eyewear as in standard precautions. The patient is placed in a private room with dedicated equipment. Transportation of the patient is minimized. Contact precautions are intended to reduce the risk of transmission of infections that require direct contact with the skin (e.g., scabies).
- Droplet precautions. Gown, gloves, and face shield or surgical mask with protective eyewear are required. The patient is placed in a private room and transportation is minimized. Droplet precautions are intended to prevent transmission of respiratory infections that are spread through large-particle droplets over short distances (e.g., influenza).

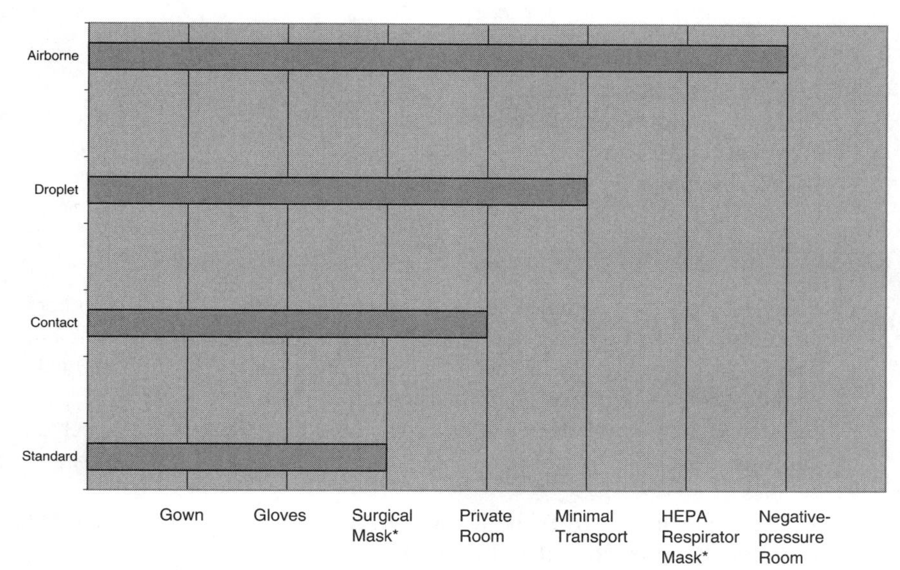

FIGURE 3.3 Levels of isolation precautions.

- Airborne precautions. Gown, gloves, and a high-efficiency mask (e.g., N95 respirator) with protective eyewear or a powered air-purifying respirator is worn. The patient is placed in a specially equipped negative-pressure room providing 6 to 12 air exchanges per hour with venting to the outdoors or through a high-efficiency filtration system. Transportation of the patient is minimized. Airborne precautions are designed to reduce the risk of transmission of infections spread by small droplet nuclei over distances greater than 3 ft (e.g., tuberculosis, measles) (Figure 3.3).

Personal Protective Equipment

The Occupational Safety and Health Administration of the U.S. Department of Labor has categorized personal protective equipment into several levels depending on the degree and type of protection required by various types of exposures.[12] The applicability of these standards to health care environments is under debate at the time of this writing.

Level A equipment (provides the greatest level of skin, respiratory, and eye protection):

- Positive-pressure, full face-piece self-contained breathing apparatus (SCBA), or positive pressure supplied air respirator with escape SCBA, approved by the National Institute for Occupational Safety and Health (NIOSH)
- Totally encapsulating chemical-protective suit
- Coveralls*

---

* Optional, depending on circumstances.

- Long underwear*
- Outer gloves, chemical resistant
- Inner gloves, chemical resistant
- Boots, chemical resistant, steel toe and shank
- Hard hat (under suit)*
- Disposable protective suit, gloves, and boots

Circumstances requiring Level A equipment:

- Entry into poorly ventilated areas is required and the absence of other conditions requiring Level A protection has not been determined.
- The hazardous substance has been identified and requires the highest level of protection of skin, eyes, and the respiratory tract.
- Substances with a high degree of hazard to the skin are known or suspected and skin contact is possible.

Level B equipment (provides the highest level of respiratory protection, but a lesser degree of skin protection than Level A):

- Positive-pressure, full face piece, self-contained breathing apparatus (SCBA) or positive-pressure-supplied air respirator with escape SCBA (NIOSH approved)
- Hooded, chemical-resistant clothing (including overalls, long-sleeved jacket; coveralls; one- or two-piece chemical splash suit; disposable chemical-resistant overalls
- Coveralls*
- Outer gloves, chemical resistant
- Inner gloves, chemical resistant
- Outer boots, chemical resistant, steel toe and shank
- Outer boot covers, chemical resistant*
- Hard hat*
- Face shield*

Circumstances requiring Level B equipment:

- The types of toxic substances and concentrations have been determined and require a high level of respiratory, but not skin, protection.
- The atmosphere contains less than 19.5% oxygen.
- The presence of incompletely identified gases has been detected, but the suspected substances are not thought to contain high levels of chemicals harmful to the skin or capable of being absorbed through the skin.

---

* Optional, depending on circumstances.

Level C equipment:

- Full-face or half-mask air-purifying respirators (NIOSH approved)
- Hooded chemical-resistant clothing (overalls; two-piece chemical-splash suit; disposable chemical-resistant overalls
- Coveralls*
- Outer gloves, chemical resistant
- Inner gloves, chemical resistant
- Outer boots, chemical-resistant steel toe and shank*
- Outer boot covers, chemical resistant (disposable)*
- Hard hat*
- Escape mask*
- Face shield*

Circumstances requiring Level C equipment:

- All criteria for the use of air-purifying respirators are met.
- The atmospheric contaminants, liquid splashes, or other direct contact will not adversely affect or be absorbed through exposed skin.
- The atmospheric contaminants have been identified, concentrations determined, and an adequate air-purifying respirator is available.

Level D equipment (provides protection only against nuisance contamination): A work uniform which may include, as appropriate:

- Coveralls
- Gloves*
- Boots/shoes, chemical-resistant steel toe and shank
- Boots, outer, chemical resistant, disposable*
- Safety glasses or chemical splash goggles*
- Hard hat*
- Escape mask*
- Face shield*

Isolation of Patients Known To Be Infected

Various recommendations have been promulgated by infectious disease and occupational health specialists for the design and maintenance of isolation rooms within hospitals and other health care facilities. Key among these features are negative pressure and adequate venting and filtering of air from the room:

* Optional, as needed.

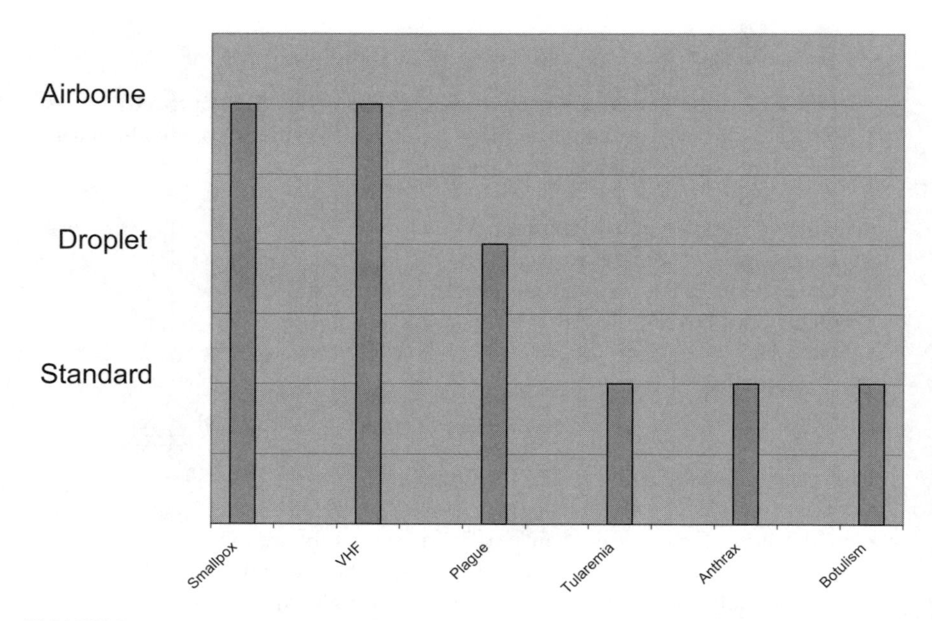

FIGURE 3.4 Isolation procedures: Category A agents.

- Negative pressure: To prevent the escape of airborne or droplet-borne pathogens, a lower air pressure must be maintained in the isolation room than in the adjacent rooms and corridors.
- Air filtering: Prior to venting of air from the isolation room, it should pass through a high-efficiency particle filter to prevent escape of airborne pathogens.
- Air exchanges: To reduce the concentration of airborne pathogens within the isolation room, air from the room must be vented such that there are at least six full air exchanges per hour (Figure 3.4).

Laboratory Roles and Safety Levels

The Laboratory Response Network (LRN), established through collaboration among the Federal Bureau of Investigation, the Association of Public Health Laboratories, and the Centers for Disease Control and Prevention, is composed of local, state, and federal public health laboratories. It was created in 1999 to facilitate coordination of the processing of laboratory specimens to rapidly and safely identify biological agents used in an attack. The LRN has established a stratification system to better define the role of each type of laboratory in responding to a biological attack.

- Level A laboratories: rule out specific pathogens and forward suspicious organisms to a higher-level laboratory.
- Level B: perform limited confirmation of bioterrorism agents and maintain the capacity to isolate the agent, perform preliminary testing, and transport suspicious pathogens safely.

- Level C: possess the capability of performing molecular assays for rapid identification.
- Level D: possess the capability to contain the highest level of organisms and have expertise in the diagnosis of rare and dangerous pathogens (federal laboratories).

Laboratories are also classified into four biosafety level (BSL) categories by the CDC[13] according to their capacity to contain highly contagious pathogens. In the following list are given the minimum standards for laboratories at each level. Successive levels represent degrees of protection of personnel and the community from infectious pathogens. Each level assumes that standards of the previous levels are also met.

- BSL 1. Practices, safety equipment, and facility design and construction appropriate for undergraduate and secondary educational training and teaching laboratories and for other laboratories in which work is done with defined and characterized strains of organisms not known to consistently cause disease in healthy humans. Standard microbiological practices with no special barriers are recommended. A sink for handwashing is recommended.
- BSL 2. Applicable to clinical, diagnostic, teaching, and other laboratories in which work is done with indigenous moderate-risk agents that are present in the community and are associated with human disease of varying severity. Standard microbiological practices should be followed and work can be conducted on an open bench if the risk of aerosolization of specimens is low. BSL 2 is applicable to work done with any human-derived blood, body fluids, tissues, or primary human cell lines where the presence of an infectious agent may be unknown. BSL 2 is not applicable to work with organisms known to be transmissible by the aerosol route.
- BSL 3. Practices, safety equipment, and design and construction are appropriate for clinical, diagnostic, teaching, research, or production facilities in which work involves indigenous or exotic organisms that may cause serious infection and that have a potential for respiratory transmission. Examples of such pathogens include *Mycobacterium tuberculosis* and *Coxiella burnetii*. Emphasis in BSL 3 facilities is placed on preventing transmission of potentially infectious aerosols to staff and to the community. All laboratory manipulations should be performed in a biological safety cabinet or other enclosed equipment. Access to the laboratory should be controlled and ventilation should be such that the release of infectious aerosols is minimized.
- BSL 4. Practices, safety equipment, facility design, and construction appropriate for work with dangerous and exotic pathogens that pose a high risk of life-threatening disease that may be transmitted by the aerosol route and have no effective vaccine or therapy. Precautions are designed to prevent respiratory, cutaneous, or mucous-membrane exposure to such agents. Work with specimens must be conducted in a high-level biological

safety cabinet or in a full-body air-supplied, positive-pressure suit. Specialized ventilation and waste disposal procedures are required.

Special Infection Control Issues in Bioterrorism

General guidelines such as those detailed above are designed to minimize risk of contagion to hospital patients and staff. In a biological attack, however, special issues are likely to arise.

Need To Intensively Educate Staff

Because the likely bioterrorist agents are rarely seen in nature in the U.S., and because they generate an aura of fear, extra efforts may be needed to educate hospital staff about these agents and the ways transmission can be prevented. Such educational activities should be conducted not only before a crisis but repeatedly during a crisis, through meetings, rounds, videos, and e-mail. During the 2003 SARS epidemic in Toronto, hospitals found that daily e-mail communication with staff, including those in home quarantine, was useful.[14,15] The daily e-mail bulletin was also used to answer employees' questions.

The anthrax attacks of 2001 and the subsequent smallpox vaccination campaigns served to illustrate the need for education of key personnel. During the anthrax attacks, stores of antibiotics such as ciprofloxacin were rapidly depleted in the Northeast. In many instances this surge in prescriptions for such agents reflected health care workers seeking to obtain supplies for themselves and their families. The appropriate use of nasal swab surveillance among postal workers to identify areas where anthrax exposure had occurred, so that workers in those areas could be offered preventive therapy, led many clinicians to mistakenly believe that this technique was an essential tool in diagnosing individual cases. In fact, a negative nasal swab result does not exclude either exposure to anthrax or infection. Education of staff is discussed in detail in Chapter 4 and in the tabletop exercises in Section IV of this book.

Expedited Triage in the Emergency Department

Under normal circumstances, patients seeking care in hospital emergency rooms are processed through a triage mechanism to assign them according to clinical indicators so that urgent care is provided where most needed. This process normally involves the creation of a medical record, the assignment of an identification number, and other "paperwork" activities that can slow the process of triage at times of high volume. Under attack conditions, the need for express triage would rapidly become apparent. Hospitals should include, in their pre-event planning, processes by which this process can be quickly streamlined. Preassigned medical record numbers and abbreviated assessment forms may be created for implementation under such circumstances.

In a truly extreme situation, it is possible that mass-casualty triage systems would be needed. These systems, such as START (Simple Triage and Rapid Treatment) and JumpSTART (a pediatric version), generally are intended for prehospital use in disasters in which medical resources are swamped by victims.[16] Such systems generally do not attempt resuscitation of apneic patients and usually prioritize victims in this order: urgent (critically ill but probably salvageable with minimal treatment); delayed (serious, but can wait without dying); nonurgent; and unsalvageable or expectant (likely to die despite significant treatment). The last group is, in effect, left to die. This is an approach so far from the standard of care for infectious disease patients under normal circumstances that its use in the hospital would reflect a catastrophe that had dwarfed all the health system's preparations.

Decontamination of Victims

Decontamination of victims of biological attack should rarely be necessary. In general, the biological agents anticipated as potential weapons would require aerosol dissemination or distribution through contaminated food or drinking water (see Chapter 9 and Chapter 10). For this reason, decontamination (showering) of victims would be expected to accomplish little under most circumstances.

Nonetheless, the availability of decontamination showers that can be deployed and put into operation rapidly may become crucial under certain attack conditions. The absence of adequate decontamination facilities or the lack of appropriately trained and protected staff to care for patients through the decontamination process could represent a bottleneck that could completely disrupt the functions of the emergency department, despite otherwise adequate preparations.

In some locales, decontamination of victims could be largely accomplished in the field by first responders employing portable or transportable decontamination units. In areas where such capacity is absent or at a minimum, or in a sizable attack or an attack directly involving the hospital, the task of decontamination of victims could fall primarily on the hospital emergency department and its staff.

Decontamination in biological attack scenarios may be required by physical, mechanical, or chemical methods. Physical decontamination may involve removal of aerosolized infectious agents from contaminated air (through the use of specialized isolation rooms in which air is circulated through high-efficiency particulate filters) or through removal of infectious material from skin. Skin decontamination may be as simple as washing skin exposed to biological agents with soap and water. Under most circumstances this form of decontamination is adequate. Gross contamination of skin may require decontamination with disinfectants such as sodium hypochlorite (0.5% solution to minimize skin irritation).

Decontamination with soap and water is recommended for victims of anthrax and of ricin poisoning. It may also be needed to remove or inactivate contagious agents (e.g., plague bacillus or smallpox virus) if gross contamination of skin has occurred.

Some hospitals, particularly in large urban areas, have permanent decontamination units or temporary units that can be deployed rapidly if indicated. These units typically are designed as tunnels with multiple showerheads through which victims can be moved rapidly. Logistical issues raised by such units may be substantial and include the need to protect staff working in the unit from aerosolized biological agents; the separation of males and females who must disrobe for effective decontamination; the handling and disposal of contaminated clothing and other personal belongings; and maintenance of privacy and comfort for individuals undergoing decontamination.

Decontamination of vulnerable individuals, including children, the frail elderly, nonambulatory patients, and especially individuals who have sustained significant trauma, poses a challenging dilemma. Speed, warmth, and emotional support may be helpful. The safe disposal of contaminated runoff water must also be addressed. The reader may find detailed information regarding decontamination procedures elsewhere.[5,17]

Unaccustomed Legal Issues

Hospital legal and risk management staffs, accustomed to addressing issues of malpractice and misconduct by staff, may suddenly face novel questions about patient privacy and the hospital's proper relationship with both public health and law enforcement agencies.

Complicating these issues are the recent enactments of the Health Insurance Portability and Accountability Act (HIPAA) and the Uniting and Strengthening America by Providing Appropriate Tools Required to Intercept and Obstruct Terrorism (USA PATRIOT) Act. The former enhances the safeguards on the confidentiality of patient medical records, whereas the latter broadens the authority of law enforcement agencies to conduct surveillance of individuals. Both have provisions dealing with such issues as access to medical records and obtaining a patient's or provider's consent for disclosure of records.

These two federal laws, in addition to local health codes and traditional relationships between agencies, may result in confusing situations that hospital legal advisors may be pressed to resolve. For example: Under what circumstances does a patient, an apparent victim of a biological attack, become a suspect in that attack? What impact does this change in status have on the hospital's responsibility to safeguard confidential medical information? What authority do hospitals, under the direction of local public health agencies, have to enforce involuntary quarantine? Where can legal staffs and advisors turn for additional insight into these issues?

According to the HHS Office of Civil Rights, HIPAA allows covered entities to disclose an individual's protected health information without the individual's authorization to a public health authority acting as authorized by law in response to a bioterrorism threat or public health emergency, or to public officials who are reasonably able to prevent or lessen a serious and imminent threat to public health or safety related to bioterrorism. In addition, according to the HHS guidance, disclosure of protected health information, without the individual's authorization, is permitted where the circumstances of the emergency involve law enforcement activities, national security and intelligence activities, or judicial and administrative proceedings.[18]

Nonetheless, according to Rothstein and colleagues at the Institute for Bioethics, Health Policy, and Law at the University of Louisville, there is much confusion over the rules, and some covered institutions might engage in "defensive practices" and not report public health information for fear of incurring potential serious penalties for violating the Privacy Rule.[2]

In view of the far-reaching effects and relative novelty of the legal issues, an indepth discussion is beyond the scope of this text. Nonetheless, hospital legal consultants should be aware of the public health issues likely to arise in a bioterrorist event and should seek guidance on the hospital's legal rights and obligations.

Home Quarantine

Asymptomatic patients who may have come into close contact with the biological agent of attack or with a contagious victim may be quarantined at home pending the onset of symptoms. With the involvement, if possible, of public health authorities, such individuals could be monitored by means of telephone contact and instructed where, when, and if they should seek medical evaluation. Such evaluation could be provided not only by hospital emergency rooms and clinics if necessary but by a predetermined cadre of community providers.

Protection of Visitors

Under circumstances where risk of contagion exists or when the patient flow or the operations of the hospital are disrupted by the presence of the visitors, the hospital may be forced to restrict access even to normally public areas. As discussed in Chapter 4, security staff require specific education to function effectively under such conditions. Specifically, they must be assured that their own risk has been minimized and that protective equipment, if required for their use, is readily available.

Coordination with Other Facilities and Organizations

Hospitals within close geographical proximity or hospital networks, even if they span a larger area, should consider pre-event collaboration over such issues as pharmacy inventory, cross-credentialing of staff, and planning for transfer of victims or of other inpatients, if conditions warrant. Traditional rivalries and conflicting missions among hospitals can present substantial obstacles to effective planning, and such efforts should be among the first missions of emergency planning committees within hospitals.

ESTABLISHING SURGE CAPACITY

Surge capacity, as it applies to hospitals, refers to the ability to respond to the needs of a much larger number of patients than are normally evaluated, treated, and housed. The importance of surge capacity was demonstrated in the TOPOFF and Dark Winter exercises (see Appendix C) as well as in the immediate aftermath of the September 11, 2001, attacks on the World Trade Center and Pentagon. In both the real and hypothetical circumstances, large numbers of patients, most of whom did not need hospital care, flooded local emergency rooms. The anthrax attack of 2001 similarly resulted in an enormous number of excess emergency room visits, primarily by the "worried well." In any future attack, the needs of the worried well and the needs of the sick or injured will undoubtedly confront hospitals.

Surge capacity is most critical for victims or potential victims of a biological attack in these areas: isolation rooms, decontamination areas, and intensive care unit beds. In a typical hospital, only a small number of rooms fit the criteria for isolation rooms. Although many hospitals have increased their isolation capacity in the last several years, no facility could be expected to provide full isolation for more than a few dozen patients at a time. Sufficient numbers of victims could overwhelm even the most well-planned strategies for sudden surges in isolation needs. In parallel, a surge in the need for ventilators, disposable personal protective equipment, and key pharmaceuticals and vaccines will have to be met.

For the worried well, the challenge will be in providing humane strategies for reassurance, dissemination of accurate information, and physical areas where these individuals can be evaluated with minimal disruption of normal hospital functions, as well as those new needs imposed by the direct victims of an attack.

In addition to facilities for the care of the victims and space for the management of the worried well, a need for establishing surge capacity in the staffing of the hospital will be paramount. While hospitals typically have procedures under which staff can be prevented from leaving at the end of their shift if a disaster situation is declared, the need for additional clinical and nonclinical staff may become acute within hours of an attack. Hospitals receiving victims of a biological attack with a contagious agent such as plague or variola (smallpox) virus, or any facility attempting to respond to an apparent biological attack nearby with an unknown agent, may encounter difficulty in identifying staff willing to work regardless of the availability of personal protective equipment.

No strategy for adequately addressing these needs has been established to be effective and no single approach will be appropriate for all hospitals and all localities. In preparing for bioterrorism, however, discussion of potential surge capacity should, at a minimum, focus on several key questions. The way the hospital chooses to answer these questions should be written into the hospital's emergency management plan.

Mobilizing Additional Staff

What resources for additional staff can be rapidly mobilized?

Suggested strategies: Hospitals within close geographic proximity to one another may create pre-event systems of cross-credentialing to permit physicians and nurses to work where they are most needed. Medical students, recently retired health care workers, and former housestaff now employed elsewhere may also represent potential sources of additional help in caring for victims. Part-time workers may be induced to work full time. Contract agencies may be hired to supply nurses or other workers, either to work directly with biological victims or, perhaps preferably, to relieve hospital staff members of their usual work so they can care for biological victims. Physicians affiliated with the hospital may be asked to work outside their specialties. Trained members of the hospital's existing volunteer corps may be able to help with social support, transportation, and clerical duties.

Experience suggests that the need for quick infusions of professional and nonprofessional staff is the most urgent need in a contagious epidemic.[15] This is a matter of high importance in that inadequate staffing patterns early in an outbreak may not only lead to poorer outcomes for patients but can lead to lapses that spread and intensify the epidemic, making it harder to contain. As with creation of extra space, advance planning is necessary to maximize the chances of securing the needed staff quickly. This includes arranging mutual aid agreements, keeping updated lists of backup personnel and contract agencies, and possibly making advance agreements with contract agencies.

Once an event has occurred or is suspected, added personnel, especially epidemiologists, may be available from local, state, or federal public health agencies; their response is likely to depend on how wide the attack is and how intense the competition is for additional staff. In a major emergency, the National Disaster Medical System could be activated. This system, run by the Department of Homeland Security's Federal Emergency Management Agency (FEMA), sends in Disaster Medical Assistance Teams (DMATs), units of volunteer doctors, nurses, and others that are supposed to supplement local medical efforts with rapid-response aid until other resources can be mobilized or the situation comes under control. Although DMATs usually work at the scene of disasters, triaging patients to hospitals, they could be used to assist overworked hospital staff in a crisis.[19]

Given that the scope of a potential outbreak cannot be predicted, however, hospitals should make their own plans and not assume that public health agencies will be able to help them with staffing.

The Needs and Contributions of Nonclinical Departments

How does the need for surge capacity affect the nonclinical departments?

A bioterrorist emergency may place extraordinary demands on many nonclinical employees of the hospital, including security, housekeeping, clerical, supply, and inventory staffs. In all those areas, hospitals may need to augment staffs. In addition, the emergency will affect how these staff members do their jobs, as described below, and will require close supervision to ensure that all staff members are protected from contagion.

Hospital police: Hospital police should be trained in procedures of hospital lockdown, crowd control, communication with other facilities, and enforcement of external and internal disaster procedures. In the event of a terrorist attack, hospital security personnel would likely be called upon to communicate with law enforcement agencies and to assist in assuring that potential evidence is retained. Hospital police might also be involved in the early stages of involuntary quarantine or isolation of potential victims and, with the cooperation of local law enforcement agencies and public health officials, with taking potential perpetrators of the attack into custody if they are present on hospital premises.

Social services: Social services personnel should have pre-event training in the facilitation of rapid discharge of patients and in providing counseling and supportive services to the worried well as well as to coworkers.

Admitting: The admitting office should have established pre-event procedures for locating empty beds rapidly and tracking patients in isolation. Specific procedures for distinguishing attack victims from other patients should be established pre-event.

Escort and transportation services: Escort and transport personnel may be at high risk of contagion if an agent such as variola virus or plague bacillus is used in an attack. For this reason, they should receive adequate pre-event training in the use of personal protective equipment. Specific supervision of the use of equipment by these staff members should be assigned to a senior-level administrator if possible. Pre-event routes of evacuation of patients and of transport of victims with highly contagious conditions should be established and emphasized in drills and exercises.

Engineering and maintenance: Maintenance of adequate isolation facilities should be an ongoing responsibility of engineering and maintenance personnel. Several such personnel should receive specific training in the use of personal protective equipment in preparation for maintenance needs arising during an attack. Engineering staff should also participate in drawing up contingency plans for expansion of isolation or other clinical space.

Central supply: Central supply personnel are at risk of exposure to used instruments and other materials that have come into contact with potentially infectious material. Personnel from this area should be involved in pre-event planning as well as drills and exercises.

External affairs: External affairs personnel should be prepared to communicate with the press. Questions regarding the crisis, victims, etc., should be referred to adequately prepared external affairs representatives to avoid conflicting and confusing information reaching the public. Personnel with these responsibilities should be included in pre-event exercises and drills. (For a fuller discussion, see Chapter 7.) External affairs may also be assigned to aid in coordinating resources with other local hospitals and health care facilities.

Making Space for an Influx of Patients

Clearing the Emergency Room

How can the emergency room be rapidly cleared of nonacute patients to allow for a large number of victims of a biological attack?

Suggested strategies: At the first notification of a terrorist attack, rapidly triage nonacute patients and discharge them whenever possible. Promptly admit patients likely requiring admission to noncritical-care beds. Cohort patients awaiting critical-care beds, if possible, in a critical-care area of the emergency department until details of the attack are clear. Evacuate some patients to other hospitals as stipulated in pre-event mutual-aid agreements.

Making More Beds Available

How can inpatient beds, especially isolation and intensive care unit beds, be made available in a prompt and efficient manner?

Suggested regional strategies: Designate certain facilities within geographical areas to serve as the primary hospitals for victims or possible victims of highly contagious diseases. Form regional networks of hospitals to maximize the use of available isolation rooms within a reasonable geographical area.

Suggested hospital strategies: Cancel all elective surgery. Cohort isolated patients when possible, with the guidance of infection control staff, to empty isolation rooms for victims of the attack. Transfer patients from intensive care units to nonintensive-care areas if possible; if needed, create new nonintensive-care wards in meeting rooms, office areas, etc. Create new temporary intensive care areas if possible in the recovery room, pediatric ICU, and emergency room. Involve social services in arranging pickup of discharged patients. Create temporary discharge lounge in the hospital lobby or other suitable location for discharged patients to wait for pickup.

Each of these strategies presents logistical obstacles, and some may actually enhance the likelihood of transmission of contagious diseases if not applied according to specific guidelines.

Cohorting

One way to increase isolation-room capacity in a facility is to cohort patients with contagious diseases such as smallpox or plague, placing two patients together in an isolation room designed for single occupancy.

A mechanism must be in place to ensure that only persons already exposed to or infected with the agent in question are grouped together. This requirement mandates that definitive clinical or microbiological diagnoses have been made in both cases before the patients are placed together. Even so, if merely exposed patients are cohorted with ill ones, the uninfected individuals are being put at risk in order to reduce broader transmission within the facility. For these reasons, cohorting of victims would be unlikely to provide an immediate solution during the first day or two of an attack when diagnoses may not be clear. Later, however, it may be workable. Because loneliness and anxiety frequently accompany isolation, cohorting patients, perhaps including children and family members, may ease the emotional burdens on ill patients in some cases.

Designating Contagion Hospitals

Designating certain facilities to be the primary points of care for patients with contagious diseases such as smallpox or plague would require evacuating other patients from those facilities. In addition, this strategy would be expected to result in longer transport times for certain victims who live far from the designated hospital and could thereby result in delay in treatment, as well as an exacerbation of transportation problems within a community under attack. Issues of stigmatizing an institution, community, or staff would have to be addressed by community leaders. Nonetheless, this strategy would enable a concentration of isolation and decontamination equipment and capacity in the designated facilities. Other hospitals in the area, relieved of caring for attack victims, could provide appropriate care for patients evacuated from the designated facility. Staff working in the designated hospitals could receive specialized training in caring for victims, potential victims, and contacts. They might also receive special social and perhaps financial support that could serve as an incentive for working with attack victims.

Using Regional Networks

Forming networks in which hospitals would share information about available isolation rooms, as well as relevant equipment and pharmaceuticals, would seem to be a logical step regardless of other strategies employed. Cost and effort would, of necessity, be expended in maintaining these lines of communications and periodically testing their effectiveness in drills and mock exercises.

Creating New Space

In an emergency, hospitals have shown ingenuity in carving out treatment areas on short notice. During the 2003 SARS epidemic in Toronto, the provincial government requested that a hospital caring for SARS patients establish a clinic to assess members of the public with symptoms. The clinic was built within a week in an ambulance bay of about 1800 square feet. It included eight negative-pressure isolation rooms made of pipe framing and plastic walls and ceilings, along with office space, staff changing areas, a lead-lined x-ray room, and rooms for x-ray viewing and case review. A waiting area at the clinic entrance was provided by erection of a 40 by 20-foot tent.[15]

Such quick responses require skilled engineering staff and readily accessible blueprints and other information about the hospital infrastructure, especially ventilation systems. The hospital's emergency management plan could include a plan and timeline for constructing extra space that would be needed under a few different emergency scenarios.

An option to consider would be purchase of a large rapid-assembly tent, of the type used in refugee missions and wilderness camps, to create space for triage, care of noncritical patients, or the worried well. With lighting, heating, ventilation systems, cots, and a portable generator, such a tent might cost about $20,000.[16]

Making Room for the Worried Well

Where can large numbers of worried well individuals be placed for evaluation, education, reassurance, and any other needs that arise?

Suggestions: Make pre-event plans to establish an external triage area so that the worried well may be triaged to be sent home without entering the emergency room or hospital when possible. Make plans to stabilize, care for, or transfer physically well persons who are too psychologically distraught to be released. For well patients reporting because of potential exposure to the biological agent, make pre-event arrangements to designate an appropriate nonclinical area of the hospital (e.g., auditorium, cafeteria, etc.) where such individuals can be interviewed.

Diverting Potential Patients

Under what circumstances would the public be advised not to come to emergency rooms for evaluation?

Suggestions: In consultation with public health authorities, hospitals receiving large numbers of victims or unable to create sufficient surge capacity as above should make efforts to enlist the aid of other local hospitals, as well as community health centers, extended care facilities, and possibly even schools. Ideally, such arrangements should become part of pre-event planning and drills, with arrangements made in advance. If nonacute facilities are enlisted, they will need supply and medication stocks, as well as training.

Ensuring Adequate Supplies and Equipment

How Can Hospitals Ensure They Have Necessary Medications?

Suggested strategy: The pharmacy should be directed to maintain a certain minimum inventory of antibiotics and antidotes that might be needed in a biological attack. The size and components of this inventory should be established with the advice of local public health officials and, ideally, coordinated among hospitals serving the same region. The hospital should consider whether its normal stores of other medications should be increased as well, to prevent shortages if it should have difficulty getting deliveries in an emergency. Stockpiling medications requires a pharmacist's supervision to make sure stores are rotated and that adequate levels are maintained without waste.

Antibiotics critical to the management of the Category A agents of bioterrorism are catalogued in Appendix A of this book. Maintaining expanded inventories of a limited number of such agents may be critical for hospitals without rapid access to public health supplies of these agents.

As discussed in Chapter 2, a national stockpile of such key drugs, as well as antidotes to likely chemical terrorism agents and vaccines, and equipment and supplies to care for victims of a terrorist attack are maintained for rapid deployment.

In a terrorist attack, however, transportation might be disrupted and a hospital might have to rely for several days on its own stock of pharmaceuticals to treat or provide prophylaxis for patients, staff, the public, and possibly staff families. Hospitals may also have difficulty immediately replenishing supplies of the medications needed by other patients in the hospital. In addition, as was seen in the early stages of the anthrax attacks of 2001, antibiotic shortages may occur quickly as physicians come under pressure to prescribe these agents to potential victims and the worried well alike.

In California, a state bioterrorism plan suggests that hospitals establish caches of several antibiotics containing enough medication for 50 persons for 72 hours.[20] Similarly, a consensus conference in 2003 on pediatric issues in preparedness recommended that hospitals maintain a 48-hour supply of relevant medications and equipment to treat children for the typical hospital pediatric census plus 100 additional pediatric patients. This recommendation was predicated on the idea that hospitals that normally treat few if any children could suddenly have a surge of pediatric patients in an emergency.[21]

Communications Equipment

How can the hospital preserve essential communications capacity?

Communications between the hospital and other health care facilities or key governmental agencies may be disrupted during a terrorist attack. Following the attacks on the World Trade Center in 2001, telephone communications, including by cellular systems, were impeded for a variety of reasons. A catastrophic destructive event may cause direct damage to telephone equipment and lines. Bioterrorism as an isolated form of attack would be more likely to create an overload of telephone and Internet communications as a concerned public sought to obtain information and contact loved ones. Some hospital networks have developed dedicated radio communications systems permitting contact to be maintained despite a loss of telephone service.

Loss of communications within hospitals (paging systems, internal wireless telephone systems, computerized medical records, and pharmacy interfaces) may also occur in an attack affecting electrical power. Although unlikely in an isolated biological attack, the possibility of a combined attack should be taken into account in general emergency preparedness planning. Hospitals that have adopted state-of-the-art computerized paperless information technology systems may find themselves more vulnerable in the event of a power failure or deliberate "cyberattack" than others if adequate backup systems are not in place. Hospitals should develop strategies enabling them to rapidly return to paper communication and, if necessary, to the use of runners to transmit vital information within the hospital.

REFERENCES

1. Shapira, Y. et al., Willingness of staff to report to their hospital duties following an unconventional missile attack: a state-wide survey, *Isr J Med Sci*, 27, 704, 1991.
2. Rothstein, M.A. et al., Quarantine and Isolation: Lessons Learned from SARS, report to the CDC, Institute for Bioethics, Health Policy and Law at the University of Louisville, KY, 2003.
3. Personal communication.
4. MacKenzie, E.J. et al., National inventory of hospital trauma centers, *JAMA*, 289, 1515, 2003.
5. Joint Commission on Accreditation of Healthcare Organization (JCAHO), *Guide to Emergency Management Planning in Health Care*, Joint Commission Resources, Oakbrook Terrace, IL, 2002.
6. JCAHO, Emergency Management Standards — EC 1.4 and EC 2.9.1, Revisions to intents to provide for better emergency preparedness, accessed at Joint Commission Resources website, originally published as Emergency Management Standards clarified, *Perspectives*, 22, 6, 2002.
7. JCAHO, Facts about the Emergency Management Standards, fact sheet, accessed at JCAHO website: www.jcaho.org/accredited+organizations/hospitals/standards/ems+facts.htm.

8. Auf der Heide, E., Principles of hospital disaster planning, in *Disaster Medicine*, Hogan, D.E. and Burstein, J.L., Eds., Lippincott Williams & Wilkins, Philadephia, 2002, chap. 8.
9. The San Mateo County Health Services Agency, Emergency Medical Services, Hospital Emergency Incident Command System, 3rd ed., San Mateo, CA, 1998.
10. Weinstein, R.S. and Alibek, K., *Biological and Chemical Terrorism: A Guide for Healthcare Providers and First Responders*, Thieme, New York, 2003.
11. Grow, R.W. and Rubinson, L., The challenge of hospital infection control during a response to bioterrorist attacks, *Biosecur and Bioterror*, 1, 215, 2003.
12. Occupational Safety and Health Administration Regulations, Part 1910, Standard 1910.120, Appendix B.
13. U.S. Department of Health and Human Services: Public Health Service, Centers for Disease Control and Prevention, and National Institutes, Biosafety in Microbiological and Biomedical Laboratories, U.S. Government Printing Office, Washington, D.C., 1999.
14. Maunder, R. et al., The immediate psychological and occupational impact of the 2003 SARS outbreak in a teaching hospital, *CMAJ*, 168, 1245, 2003.
15. Loutfy, M.R. et al., Hospital preparedness and SARS, *Emerg Infect Dis*, 10, [serial on the Internet], 2004.
16. Hogan, D.E. and Lairet, J., Triage, in *Disaster Medicine*, Hogan, D.E. and Burstein, J.L., Eds., Lippincott Williams & Wilkins, Philadephia, 2002, chap. 2.
17. Couch, D., *The U.S. Armed Forces Nuclear, Biological, and Chemical Survival Manual*, Basic Books, New York, 2003.
18. HHS Office of Civil Rights, Guidance Explaining Significant Aspects of the Privacy Rule — December 4, 2002, FAQs on Public Health Uses and Disclosures, accessed at www.hhs.gov/ocr/hipaa/privacy.html.
19. National Disaster Medical System, What is a Disaster Medical Assistance Team (DMAT)?, fact sheet, accessed at http://www.oep-ndms.dhhs.gov/dmat.html.
20. State of California Emergency Medical Services Authority, Hospital Bioterrorism Preparedness Program, 2003, Implementation Plan, accessed at EMSA website: www.emsa.cahwnet.gov./hbppc/hbppc_imp_plan2003.asp.
21. Markenson, D. and Redlener, I., Pediatric Preparedness for Disasters and Terrorism: A National Consensus Conference, executive summary of Mailman School of Public Health's National Center for Disaster Preparedness consensus conference, 2003.

4 Targeting Staff Education

INTRODUCTION

Hospitals are complex organizations. They combine the services of hotels, pharmacies, laboratories, restaurants, social service agencies, and a host of other businesses with the complex demands of providing up-to-date medical care and, often, education of student doctors, nurses, and pharmacists. They serve diverse types of populations requiring carefully targeted health services. In addition, they must be conscious not only of their community image and competitive position but remain in compliance with a host of regulatory standards involving virtually all of their functions. The day-to-day operation of a hospital, unlike most organizations, must take into account the regular occurrence of extraordinary surges in the need for beds, pharmaceuticals, and services.

Hospital staffs consist of individuals with diverse educational and economic backgrounds as well as ethnic diversity. Many basic training requirements are imposed on hospital staffs. These range from instruction on safety, environmental issues, and prevention of transmission of infections to patient privacy. The task of maintaining an adequate base of knowledge in such diverse areas across a broad spectrum of employees is truly daunting. Most hospitals provide standard education in key areas to all employees by means of "inservice" sessions, either in the form of live lectures or videotapes. All staff members are typically required to undergo periodic (often annual) refresher sessions in areas relevant to their specific jobs.

In this climate of constant training and retraining, hospitals must now seek to develop means of effectively preparing their staffs for bioterrorism. As discussed in Chapters 2 and 3, the current level of such preparedness does not appear to be adequate in the majority of U.S. hospitals. Some of the obstacles to effective training for bioterrorism are obvious:

1. The likelihood that any given hospital will become involved in a bioterrorism event is, thankfully, small. As a result, however, efforts to train large numbers of employees ranging from housekeepers to mortuary workers to physicians to laboratory technologists and others could seem to carry a low priority.
2. The great variety of potential biological attack scenarios (see Chapter 9 and Section IV, Tabletop Exercises) seem simply to require too much education.
3. Accrediting bodies, specifically the Joint Commission on Accreditation of Healthcare Organizations (JCAHO), place little emphasis on specific preparation for bioterrorism, despite their established standards for general emergency preparedness (see Chapter 3).

Given the seemingly impossible task of adequate preparation of all hospital staff for biological attack, it is tempting to relegate such planning to outside authorities, such as health departments. However, as detailed in Chapter 2, the public health infrastructure in many localities faces its own almost insurmountable problems in this area and can provide little in the way of useful strategies for hospitals to educate their staff prior to an attack.

STRATEGIES FOR EDUCATING AND PREPARING HOSPITAL STAFF

ESTABLISHING THE EDUCATIONAL MISSION

The JCAHO, among other organizations, mandates that hospital personnel be oriented to and educated about the environment of their hospital and possess the knowledge and skills to perform their duties within the environment.[1] To provide education to the entire staff regarding bioterrorism, although difficult, is an unavoidable responsibility of a hospital's clinical and administrative leadership. The levels of expertise required by physicians and by public affairs officers would, for example, differ greatly. The director of safety may require knowledge of the legal aspects of crowd control, lockdown, and the safety of his staff during a biological attack. The chief medical officer, in contrast, may require in-depth understanding of clinical staffing needs and capacity. Thus, the specific elements of a response plan may be divided into targeted curricula that can be readily presented and repeated without providing unnecessary information irrelevant to an individual staff member's daily activities. A general, admittedly somewhat arbitrary, division of curricular needs might separate along the following professional lines:

1. *The emergency room clinical staff:* Important areas of emphasis would include decontamination and isolation procedures; rapid identification of potential victims especially in the early stages of the attack; communication with internal and external consultants; transfer of information to public health authorities; use of personal protective equipment and employment of strategies to protect themselves as well as patients and visitors from avoidable exposure to contagious agents.
2. *The inpatient clinical staff, including those working in critical care areas:* Detailed familiarity with decontamination procedures is less important than it is for the emergency department staff. Areas of emphasis would involve effective isolation procedures, including the proper use of limited personal protective equipment (especially particulate respirators, protective eyewear, and the proper use of negative-pressure rooms). Clinical staffs in all areas should be aware of basic management issues involved in the care of patients exposed to the likeliest agents of biological attack (see Chapter 10).
3. *Laboratory staff:* Little information regarding decontamination procedures may be required, but the use of adequate personal protective equipment (particulate respirators, protective eyewear) and the appropriate

processing of clinical specimens should be emphasized. Laboratorians (physicians as well as technologists) should be completely familiar with the precautions to be taken in the processing of specimens in specific attack scenarios. In some instances — for example, a smallpox attack — there may be little purpose and substantial risk in processing respiratory specimens in the hospital laboratory. Therefore, laboratorians must, among other issues, understand the situations in which proper packaging of specimens for transport to public health laboratories would be critical.

4. *Hospital security staff:* Hospital security staff may be involved in biological attack scenarios in several key ways. In the event of an external disaster, they would bear responsibility for maintaining order and controlling the security of the hospital environment while arranging the rapid deployment of the hospital's incident command structure. Because of their diverse potential roles, an understanding of the risk of contagion of key potential agents of biological terror is required, both to help in informing the public and controlling panic and, importantly, in properly protecting themselves. A basic understanding of the risk represented by each of the key pathogens will greatly help the hospital security staff in confidently performing their duties without exposing themselves or their families to unnecessary risks.
5. *External affairs staff:* As was seen in the anthrax attacks of 2001, the flow of information during a biological attack can become confusing and contradictory. The external affairs personnel of individual hospitals within an area experiencing an attack would be abruptly placed in the position of answering questions posed by a diverse media and the public. Issues faced by such personnel are addressed in detail in Chapter 7. Pre-event educational efforts could be focused on the means by which accurate information could be obtained either from internal or external authorities. Control of the dissemination of information should have as its goal accurate provision of information and clear statements of advice to the public, when appropriate. Although a basic understanding of the likely agents of biological attack would be of great value to the beleaguered information officer, education regarding the means of obtaining timely and accurate information may be of even greater importance. The approach to the education of staff who would be dealing directly with the news media and the public should emphasize an understanding of the needs of both in crisis situations. In addition, a basic familiarity with the hospital's emergency plans would be invaluable. These purposes might be best accomplished through targeted informational sessions for these individuals and, perhaps, a working understanding of the type of information being provided to the rest of the hospital staff.
6. *Senior clinical and administrative leaders:* During a biological or other terrorist attack, a calm and informed approach by individuals in senior leadership positions could greatly facilitate the ability of the hospital to respond in the most efficient manner possible. Individuals in such positions of authority must remain current in the basic disaster-preparedness

measures in place. They must understand and accept the responsibilities and the latitude that they possess in allocating resources and establishing useful contacts with other area hospitals and public health authorities. A basic familiarity with the issues likely to arise in event of a biological attack with the Category A agents would be a valuable asset to such individuals.

Obviously, there are many other job categories in modern hospitals than those listed above. However, it seems sensible to divide the hospital staff into a relatively small number of distinct categories and provide targeted educational efforts accordingly. In this chapter, we present a suggested curriculum to be offered to individuals in specified job categories. We recognize that opinions may differ on the content of the curriculum and the means by which we suggest categorizing the staff. Hospitals should designate specific working groups to develop curricula and other educational strategies that reflect their unique environment. Nonetheless, we hope that this framework will provide at least a starting point to be adapted to the circumstances unique to each hospital.

Elements of the Curriculum

The necessary elements of a curriculum in bioterrorism for health care workers can be divided into discrete, although somewhat overlapping, categories. The elements listed below are separated in a manner that can lead more readily to the development of specific educational needs for the disparate categories of employees working at an acute- or chronic-care hospital. Some staff members require a comprehensive understanding of a particular area, whereas others need little or no specific education in the same area. By focusing the curricular needs in this way, it is hoped that educational activities may be relatively brief and adaptable to a variety of formats.

Not every topic is addressed in detail in this book, although the majority are. Because of the rapidly changing nature of our understanding of the bioterrorism threat, we have provided direction in using the Internet to access the most current information to guide planning activities (Chapter 13). Inevitably, many planning activities must be conducted in cooperation with local public health authorities and law enforcement agencies. We mention several such activities here, but encourage hospital leaders to take the initiative in establishing effective communication with the relevant agencies serving their communities. As indicated in Chapter 2, the public health apparatus in the U.S., although robust, varies in structure, function, and mission from state to state and among communities.

1. **Clinical Recognition of Syndromes Associated with Biological Attack Scenarios**
   The ability to diagnose and effectively manage infections caused by biological terrorism includes an understanding of natural history, physical findings, laboratory patterns, isolation procedures (when applicable), and the approach to diagnosis and therapy. Embodied in this knowledge base is an understanding of the role of personal protective equipment and the

proper means of obtaining and processing laboratory specimens, as well as an understanding of the methods for evaluating contacts and potential contacts of victims. (See Chapters 5, 9, 10, and Appendix C)

2. **Medical Management of Likely Diseases To Be Encountered**
   This similar but slightly reoriented knowledge base would include the ability to manage complications of diseases of biological attack that might not be manifest on initial presentation. (See Chapters 9, 10, and Appendix C)
3. **Understanding the Role of Decontamination and Isolation of Victims and Contacts**
   This knowledge element requires an understanding of the uses of decontamination in biological attack. Because most agents of biological terror would not require extensive decontamination, the employees needing this education should also understand why unnecessary mass decontamination procedures may represent an impediment to the response to biological attack. Specific topics include the following: the means of deploying decontamination equipment and effectively staffing decontamination areas within the hospital; the use of personal protective equipment; and the means of identifying those patients and staff members who require decontamination. (See Chapters 3 and 10)
4. **Understanding Uses of Personal Protective Equipment**
   This component of the curriculum would focus on the proper uses of personal protective equipment (PPE), including indications for the various levels of PPE, as well as the means of locating and deploying equipment in the event of an attack. (See Chapters 3 and 10)
5. **Understanding How Clinical Specimens Should Be Handled**
   The proper means of collecting, packing, and transporting clinical specimens would be covered in this component of the curriculum. Included would be the specific use of PPE by the clinical, transport, and laboratory staff involved in handling and processing such specimens. (See Chapter 3)
6. **Understanding Hospital Plans for Establishing Surge Capacity**
   The management of patient flow such that the emergency department and other clinical areas do not become overwhelmed with patients not needing acute care would be addressed in this component of the curriculum. A knowledge of space limitations and availability within the hospital or at predesignated locations outside the hospital would be emphasized. Strategies for holding potentially exposed individuals not requiring evaluation by public health authorities or medical care would be addressed. Other appropriate topics would include the means of obtaining additional equipment and supplies, the processes for rapidly discharging or transferring hospital patients, and limiting access of individuals seeking elective care. (See Chapter 3)
7. **Understanding Likely Security Concerns**
   Issues to be addressed include the procedures for strictly enforcing existing security procedures and, if appropriate, limiting access to public areas of the hospital. In addition, the potential interactions and means of com-

munication between hospital security staff and law enforcement agencies should be discussed.

8. **Understanding Communication Issues with News Media**
A pre-event procedure for effective communication with print and broadcast news media should be established. All hospital staff should be aware of the general procedures for responding to inquiries from the press. Such inquires are best handled through a coordinated effort directed by the hospital's senior leadership and, if available, public affairs staff. (See Chapter 7)
9. **Recognizing and Understanding the Psychological Impact of a Terrorist Attack on Health Care Workers**
The emotional impact of a terrorist attack on the hospital's staff should not be underestimated. The stress and fear associated with the dual roles of hospital employee and member of the general public in a community under attack should be anticipated and provisions for addressing the emotional needs of the staff developed. (See Chapter 6)
10. **Familiarity with Regulations Governing Quarantine**
The need for quarantine (confinement of individuals who may have been exposed to a contagious agent) would presumably be determined by public health authorities. Hospital staff, however, would be required to assist in enforcing quarantine procedures when necessary. All clinical, administrative, and security personnel would require a basic understanding of quarantine procedures set forth by local departments of health and their individual roles in putting these procedures into practice. (See Chapters 2 and 3)
11. **Familiarity with Regulations and Guidelines Governing Reporting of Suspected or Proven Cases to Public Health Authorities**
Clinic and emergency department physicians and nurses as well as hospital laboratory staff typically have an understanding of general requirements for reporting contagious diseases to local public health authorities. Under circumstances of a biological attack, suspected cases of infection with the unusual pathogens anticipated would also require a vigilant system of reporting. Responsibility for such enhanced reporting and communication with health departments would likely become the province of laboratory directors, emergency department staff, and infection control personnel.
12. **Understanding Job-Specific Measures To Be Observed To Minimize Risk to Employees and Their Families**
All employees who have direct contact with patients or with clinical specimens should be familiar with the use of particulate respirator masks and be properly fit-tested. (See Chapter 3)
13. **Understanding the Role of the Hospital and the Health Care Worker in a Biological Attack**
General orientation regarding the likely role that the hospital would play in the event of a biological attack should be provided to all employees. All hospital-based health care workers should be instructed on the general

procedures that might be undertaken in such an event (e.g., lockdown, emergency call-in of off-duty workers, etc.).

In a larger sense, all hospital workers must understand the special role that they and their institution would play in a bioterrorist attack. Similar to the way they are held to high standards in areas such as patient confidentiality, personal hygiene, and sense of service and responsibility, much would be expected of hospital workers in the event of an attack. As was witnessed in the very limited anthrax attacks of 2001, the public would expect the hospital and its workers to remain available and accessible not only to treat victims but to provide reliable information and a safe sanctuary when necessary. It is important that all hospital workers understand that these expectations would impact their work lives in many ways. The hospital must take responsibility for preparing its workers for such an environment.

14. **Identifying Reliable Sources of Information To Be Consulted in the Event of an Attack**
The hospital worker, whether on duty or not, would likely receive information regarding an attack from the usual news sources that the general public depends upon. A system of rumor control may be necessary within a hospital so that employees could rapidly confirm the validity of information received regarding the attack and its effects on the hospital. This type of strategy would most likely come under the direction of the hospital's administrative and public relations staff.
15. **Understanding the Chain of Command and How It Would Operate in the Event of an Attack**
All hospital employees should be thoroughly familiar with their position in the hospital chain of command.
16. **Understanding How Equipment and Supplies Relevant to the Individual's Duties Would Be Obtained**
Department-specific instructions on how to obtain personal protective equipment and other key materials relevant to a biological attack should be provided to all employees working in patient-care and public areas of the hospital. The circumstances under which they would be advised or required to use such equipment should be made clear and the means by which this information would be communicated to them emphasized.
17. **Understanding the Unique Needs of Special Populations Served by the Hospital**
Each hospital serves unique patient populations (e.g., geriatric patients, children, disabled, mental health, etc.). Particularly on inpatient units, the special needs of geriatric, pediatric, and mental health patients require special attention. In the area of surge capacity, for example, it may be difficult or impossible to discharge such patients on short notice to create the space required to treat victims of an attack. Hospitals must give particular attention to strategies needed to address such issues.

18. **Engineering Issues: Heating, Ventilation, and Air-Conditioning**
Clinical, administrative, and engineering staffs should be familiar with the ventilation issues raised by isolation procedures. Specifically, a basic understanding of the functioning and testing of rooms designed for airborne isolation would be appropriate. Obviously, engineering personnel would require specific knowledge regarding maintenance and repair of such equipment.

SUGGESTED CATEGORIZATION OF STAFF BY EDUCATIONAL REQUIREMENTS

The above list can be used to establish educational goals according to employment categories within the hospital. A suggested scheme is as follows:

1. **Emergency department clinical staff (physicians, nurses, physician's assistants, nurse practitioners, respiratory therapists, etc.)**
Educational priorities: 1, 2, 3, 4, 5, 6, 7, 8, 10, 11, 12, 13, 14, 15, 16, 18
2. **Outpatient clinical staff**
Educational priorities: 1, 2, 3, 4, 5, 6, 7, 8, 10, 11, 12, 13, 14, 15, 16
3. **Inpatient clinical staff**
Educational priorities: 1, 2, 3, 4, 5, 6, 8, 9, 10, 11, 12, 13, 14, 16, 17
4. **Senior administrative leadership**
Educational priorities: 3, 4, 6, 7, 8, 9, 10, 11, 12, 13, 14, 15, 16, 17, 18
5. **Senior clinical leadership**
Educational priorities: 1, 3, 4, 6, 7, 8, 9, 10, 11, 12, 13, 14, 15, 16, 17
6. **Security personnel**
Educational priorities: 3, 4, 6, 7, 8, 10, 12, 13, 14, 15, 16
7. **Laboratory and pathology personnel**
Educational priorities: 1, 4, 5, 7, 8, 11, 12, 13, 14, 15, 16, 18
8. **Housekeeping personnel**
Educational priorities: 3, 4, 12, 13, 15, 16
9. **Transport personnel**
Educational priorities: 3, 4, 5, 6, 12, 13, 15, 17
10. **Social services**
Educational priorities: 4, 6, 7, 8, 9, 10, 12, 13, 15, 16, 17
11. **Office, nonclinical staff**
Educational priorities: 6, 7, 8, 9, 12, 13, 15, 16
12. **Volunteers, students, per diem personnel**
Educational priorities: 7, 8, 12, 13, 14, 15, 16
13. **Pharmacy staff**
Educational priorities: 6, 7, 8, 9, 12, 13, 14, 15, 16
14. **Human resources staff**
Educational priorities: 6, 7, 8, 9, 12, 13, 15, 16
15. **Vendors**
Educational priorities: 6, 7, 8

EDUCATIONAL STRATEGIES AND FORMATS

By identifying the specific educational needs of various types of health care personnel, it is our hope that the task of providing up-to-date information can be simplified. Information of importance is often communicated to hospital staff through large-scale lectures, videotape or web presentations, or electronic or paper memos. Any of these avenues of communication can be effective. Such efforts may not reach all workers, however. Furthermore, certain information that may be vitally important to those performing some tasks may have little or no relevance to other workers. As can be seen in the suggested strategy given in the preceding text, some knowledge is sufficiently important to the entire organization, and all categories of employees should be provided specific education in those areas, whereas other facts may be relevant to a smaller group of senior leaders and those working in narrowly defined areas or job categories.

In Section IV, a series of suggested tabletop exercises, the issues relevant to specific job categories are again emphasized. It is our assumption that limited, intensive education confined to information relevant to the specific worker is more easily and efficiently communicated than more massive curricula to which all workers must be exposed.

It is our hope that, with guidance from these exercises and the specific curriculum topics identified in this chapter, hospitals can develop focused training programs for their employees.

Reference

1. Joint Commission on Accreditation of Healthcare Organizations, *Guide to Emergency Management Planning in Healthcare*, Joint Commission Resources, Oakbrook Terrace, IL, 2002.

5 Psychological Factors in Patients and the Public

Terrorism is about psychology .... Terrorism is about making ordinary people feel vulnerable, anxious, confused, uncertain, and helpless.

Philip G. Zimbardo, former president of the American Psychological Association, February 26, 2003[1]

INTRODUCTION

It is a truism, and a truth, that terrorism is a psychological weapon.[2–5] Besides the physical damage done to direct victims, it can affect the thoughts, feelings, and behavior of millions of survivors, witnesses, and family members, along with far-off observers who know of it only through media reports. Shortly after 9/11, surveys indicated that many, if not most, Americans suffered some degree of stress.[6] For most people who are not direct victims, terrorism's psychological effects will not be intense or long lasting.[6–8] But in the short and middle term, they could make it more difficult for hospitals to deal with an unfolding crisis. As data presented in this chapter demonstrate, a hospital's ability to address the psychological impact of bioterrorism may be a key determinant of its level of preparedness.

Any terrorist attack can be frightening, but a biological attack could be expected to be especially terrifying, causing high levels of psychological stress and trauma.[9,10] "The microbial world is mysterious, threatening, and frightening to most people," Holloway and colleagues state. "The stressors associated with a biological terrorist attack could create high numbers of acute and potentially chronic psychiatric casualties who must be recognized, diagnosed, and treated to facilitate triage and medical care."[11]

In fact, despite the dramatic terrorism seen in recent years, the only widely reported instances of mass panic — breakdowns in social norms leading to flight or disorder — have occurred in response to two naturally occurring outbreaks of infectious disease. Those outbreaks — of pneumonic plague in Surat, India, in 1994 and severe acute respiratory syndrome (SARS) in China in 2003 — were poorly managed by medical and political authorities.

In both Surat and Beijing, hundreds of thousands of people fled the city. In Surat, an impoverished city of 1.8 million, most of the city's private physicians left even though the infection responded to antibiotics. Clinics and pharmacies were boarded up, leaving the overworked staff of the city's Civil Hospital to cope with thousands of cases. In China, many violated quarantines, and thousands of people in a rural town rioted and trashed a school that they thought would be used to house SARS patients.[12–17]

Overview of Likely Reactions

Panic, however, is a rare reaction.[18,19] Health care facilities need to prepare for common, predictable reactions that could affect the willingness and ability of staff to work and of patients to cooperate and recover:

- Large numbers of nonexposed people are likely to seek treatment for what they fear is exposure or infection. Even in places far from the scene of an attack, patients may present with psychogenic symptoms or exacerbation of existing illness, including psychiatric illness.
- People who are exposed or ill can be expected to feel fearful, isolated, angry, guilty, anxious, and depressed. Some may suffer organic psychiatric conditions stemming from their illness or treatment, which could affect their compliance with treatment and infection control measures.
- Staff reactions may range from anxiety and fatigue to a worst-case scenario of widespread absenteeism if personnel fear infection or stay home to care for their families. Underlying resentments may be amplified, but so may underlying collegiality and altruism.
- Stringent infection control procedures may increase stress on staff, patients, and families.
- Patients and staff alike may be desperate to find missing family members or may be grieving over lost loved ones.
- Patients hospitalized for unrelated reasons may feel fearful, isolated, and neglected.
- Large numbers of people, including professionals and untrained people, may contact the hospital volunteering to help.

The Need for Planning and Training

As part of its overall disaster plan, every hospital should include steps to mitigate and manage the psychological impact of terrorism on patients and staff.

Social workers, psychiatric crisis nurses, psychiatrists, and other relevant personnel should be involved in developing the psychosocial components. A team should be identified that could take the lead in this area should a bioterrorism event occur. The team members may need to educate themselves first in disaster mental health issues because many mental health professionals may not be knowledgeable or experienced in this area.[4]

Unlike psychiatric practice, disaster mental health consists largely of providing comfort, coping skills, and practical assistance to people who do not have underlying psychiatric problems and have not sought psychological therapy. Some of its functions can be filled by well-trained and supervised volunteers who are not mental health professionals; in many hospitals, volunteers already perform some of this work.

Careful planning to meet psychosocial needs is particularly important because resources in this area are likely to be stretched extremely thin, and a high-stress situation could last for weeks or months.

One of the recurring themes of hospital preparedness is that bioterrorism preparations, costly and time-consuming as they are, can provide benefits even if the feared event never occurs. This model applies well to psychological preparations, which ideally can strengthen a sense of community, help staff cope with the normal stresses of life, and encourage psychological growth.

It can also better prepare staff to help patients with the psychosocial concerns that are so common in medical practice. In the absence of terrorism, substantial numbers of patients who seek care for physical complaints appear to suffer from undiagnosed anxiety and depressive disorders.[20,21] In addition, naturally occurring severe illness, as well as the invasive medical procedures often used to treat it, have psychological sequelae for many patients and their families.[22,23] Given these facts, greater attention to psychological considerations may prove helpful in everyday practice.

The Fundamentals of Response

This chapter will describe the possible psychological impact of a bioterrorist attack on adult survivors, families, and witnesses. (Special considerations concerning hospital staff are dealt with in Chapter 6. Special issues concerning children are addressed in Chapter 11.) This chapter will outline measures that seem likely to minimize psychosocial damage and allow individuals' and communities' natural resilience to do its healing work. Given a lack of research on the efficacy of various mental health interventions in a bioterrorist event, the suggestions here reflect expert consensus and what we believe are reasonable assumptions based on evidence from related events.

One of those assumptions is that minimizing physical casualties will minimize psychological casualties as well. For hospitals, that means making adequate preparations for bioterrorism and, in the event of an attack, acting wisely and swiftly to prevent death and treat illness, as described in other sections of this book. "A well-organized, effective medical response instills hope and confidence and reduces fear and anxiety," according to Hall and colleagues.[9]

The same could be said of effective communication, as described in Chapter 12. Health and safety preparations "may reduce psychological casualties by increasing the public's confidence and sense of mastery and reducing fear through communicating convincingly to the public that the community is ready in the event of a bioterrorism event," according to a report by the Institute of Medicine's Committee on Responding to the Psychological Consequences of Terrorism.[7]

Finally, the emphasis in this chapter on psychological problems should not obscure the reality that most people exposed to trauma recover over time, relying largely on their own family and friends and their own well-developed coping mechanisms. An entire popular literature of suffering and recovery attests to the fact that many people use trauma as a path to psychological growth and spiritual insight, and feel their life is better for it.

POTENTIAL SHORT-TERM ADVERSE EFFECTS

Psychological Distress Following Disaster

A wide range of psychological symptoms are likely to be seen among patients, families, and the public at large in the event of a widespread biological attack.

Such symptoms are commonly seen among survivors and rescue workers after the trauma of a disaster, whether natural, accidental, or intentional. Specialists in disaster mental health typically refer to these as "normal responses to abnormal events."[24,25] Symptoms can include alienation, anger, confusion, decreased appetite, decreased libido, decreased self-esteem, despair, disbelief, dissociation, distortion of thoughts, fatigue, grief, guilt, helplessness, hyperarousal, increased substance use, insomnia, intrusive thoughts, irritability, loss of pleasure in regular activities, self-blame, sleep disturbances, social withdrawal, somatic complaints, and terror.[7,23,26]

Immediately after trauma, individuals also may be especially suggestible and quick to respond to emotional tone, changing circumstances, and rumors.[27] Those tendencies can facilitate or complicate attempts to provide health care, making a well-organized response particularly important.

After a major terrorist incident, symptoms of psychological distress — including anger, fear, depression, disturbed sleep, and hypervigilance — have been reported by large segments of the population that were not personally involved in the event. In a national survey of 560 adults done 3 to 5 days after September 11, 2001, 44% reported having one or more substantial symptoms of stress and 90% had at least one symptom to some degree.[6]

In most cases such symptoms are normal emotional reactions that should not be considered pathological. According to Shalev, medicalizing these responses can interfere with normal healing processes, which are aided by family, friends, and other nonprofessional sources of comfort and support. "Expressions of distress are often appropriate at this stage, and one should be very careful not to classify them as 'symptoms' in the sense of being indicative of a mental disorder," Shalev writes.[27] In most people, as studies of 9/11 reactions suggest, these symptoms resolve without intervention, typically within weeks or months.[7,8,25,28–30]

In some cases, as described below, psychological problems persist. In addition, in any large group of persons seeking emergency care, there may be individuals with active psychiatric illness whose condition may deteriorate in the face of trauma or chaos. Should a bioterrorist attack occur, distinguishing such patients, who may require psychiatric hospitalization, from the "normally distressed" will be one of the challenges of triage (Table 5.1).

Psychological Distress Linked to Illness

Because it causes illness rather than injury, and may act insidiously rather than through high-impact events, bioterrorism differs from the kind of disasters whose psychological impact has been studied most. But even absent terrorism, serious illness can be expected to cause psychosocial distress as well as psychiatric abnormalities in some patients.

TABLE 5.1
Psychic Impact of Terrorism on Adults

Study	Subjects	Postevent	Event-Related Effects
After Oklahoma City Bombing			
North, 1999	182 survivors	6 months	45% psychiatric disorder 34.3% PTSD
North, 2002	88 male victims	34 months	23% PTSD
	181 rescue workers	34 months	13% PTSD
After September 11, 2001, Attacks			
Schuster, 2001	560 U.S. adults	3–4 days	44% one or more significant stress symptoms
Galea, 2002	1008 Manhattan adults	5–8 weeks	7.5% symptoms consistent w/PTSD 9.7% symptoms consistent w/major depression
Schlenger, 2002	2273 U.S. adults	1–2 months	Probable PTSD: 11% NYC, 2.7% DC, 4% other U.S.
Silver, 2002	933 U.S. adults	2 months	17% symptoms posttraumatic stress
	787 U.S. adults	3 months	5.8% symptoms posttraumatic stress
Chen, 2003	555 NYC Chinatown residents (near WTC)	5 months	17% four or more emotional symptoms
Galea, 2003	2752 Manhattan adults	6 months	0.6% symptoms consistent w/PTSD

Under normal conditions, anxiety, depression, irritability, posttraumatic stress symptoms, and social isolation have been reported in a wide range of seriously ill patients, both adult and pediatric, with conditions that include myocardial infarction, Legionnaires' disease, adult respiratory distress syndrome, meningococcal disease, cancer, and conditions requiring surgery.[22–23,31–35]

In addition, patients in critical care units may experience temporary confusion, delirium, anxiety, depression, delusions, and audiovisual hallucinations, sometimes called Intensive Care Unit psychosis.[36]

Families of seriously ill patients also commonly have high levels of stress. They may eat and sleep less, while increasing their smoking, drinking, and use of over-the-counter and prescription medications in increased amounts.[37] Stress levels are especially extreme among the parents of critically ill children, reaching near-panic levels initially upon emergency admission. As a result, parents may have difficulty concentrating, remembering, or even asking questions.[38] Such "normal" stress from illness could be expected to be heightened in a biological attack, especially if the cause, treatment, prognosis, and transmission routes of the agent are not clear (Table 5.2).

Examples from the 2003 SARS Outbreak

A report from the 2003 epidemic of SARS (severe acute respiratory syndrome) suggests the complications possible in an infectious disease outbreak. Cheng and

TABLE 5.2
Psychic Impact on Adults of Illness or Injury

Study	Subjects	Postevent	Event-Related Effects
Clarke, 1997	37 surgical patients	At discharge	27% had high levels of posttraumatic stress symptoms
Shalev, 1998	211 ER trauma patients	1 month	29.9% met PTSD diagnosis 19% met major depression diagnosis
	(same)	4 months	17.5% met PTSD diagnosis 14.2% met major depression diagnosis
Cuthbertson, 2004	78 ICU survivors	3 months	14% met PTSD diagnosis
Jones, 2004	104 ICU survivors' relatives	6 months	49% had elevated distress ("cause for concern" level)
Lettinga, 2002	122 Legionnaires' disease survivors	17 months	15% met PTSD diagnosis
Kapfhammer, 2004	46 ARDS (acute respiratory distress syndrome) survivors	At discharge median 8 years later	43% met PTSD diagnosis 24% met PTSD diagnosis
Schelling, 1998	80 ARDS survivors	2–11 years	28% had symptoms of PTSD

colleagues, psychiatric consultants at a Hong Kong hospital, were called to assess and manage 10 SARS patients, none of whom had a psychiatric history. In most cases, patients were interviewed by telephone for infection control reasons. Five were diagnosed as having adjustment disorder, marked by anger, anxiety, suicidal ideas, and depression. The patients attributed these reactions to the severity of their symptoms, their isolation, and other specific effects of SARS. Two were a married couple depressed by the sudden decline of their daughter who also had SARS.

Two were diagnosed with organic hallucinosis and two with organic manic disorder, including one patient who left the hospital for several hours. The organic disorders were linked to large doses of corticosteroids used to treat SARS. The tenth patient received no psychiatric diagnosis. She was angry and feared her family would get SARS because a physician had earlier misdiagnosed her as not having the disease.[39]

In another case, a teacher in Singapore underwent many tests and months of treatment with antipyretics and antibiotics because her body temperature repeatedly exceeded 37.5°C in the mandatory temperature monitoring imposed on teachers as a SARS control measure. (The cutoff point was later revised to 37.9°C.) Despite no evidence of infection, she was agitated and concerned that she might be harboring the SARS virus. After giving a fuller history, she was diagnosed as depressed over a marital breakup, was started on paroxetine, and referred to counseling.[40]

The "Worried Well" and Somatic Symptoms

In the event of a major biological or chemical attack, health institutions can expect to be deluged with patients seeking care, including many who have no injury. When Israel was attacked by Iraqi SCUD missiles during the 1991 Gulf War, 232 people were admitted to emergency rooms for injuries from the attacks, most minor, while 544 people were admitted to emergency rooms for acute anxiety, and 40 were injured rushing for shelter.[41] After sarin was released in the Tokyo subway in 1995, about 5500 people sought medical care; more than 4000 of them showed no sign of exposure to the nerve gas.[42] During the anthrax attacks of 2001, many patients came into emergency departments in New York City, a locus of the attacks, concerned that they had seen or touched substances they thought might contain anthrax.[43]

Many such patients will have no symptoms and will be successfully reassured. But others may have stress-related somatic symptoms, which can include elevated heart rate, elevated blood pressure, shortness of breath, faintness or dizziness, fatigue, flushing, headaches, heartburn, nausea, rash, sweating, tightness in the chest or throat, and tremors.[9,10,43,44] Medical staff will need to differentiate these symptoms from those of biological or chemical weapons, which they can resemble.

Conversely, some possible biological agents can cause symptoms that might be attributed to psychiatric illness. Q fever and many viral agents can cause encephalitis, with symptoms of lethargy, confusion, and mood alteration. Brucellosis can cause depression, anorexia, irritability, and many somatic complaints, with relatively few physical abnormalities.[43,45] An outbreak of botulism, eventually linked to consumption of chopped garlic, caused six patients to be mistakenly diagnosed with myasthenia gravis, four with psychiatric disorders, and three with stroke.[46]

A Note on Terminology

Some practitioners consider the term "worried well" to be disparaging and counsel against its use.[9,47] Hall and colleagues suggest labeling triage patients as "high risk," "moderate risk," and "minimal risk." Because the term "worried well" is widely used and universally understood among clinicians, we think it plays a useful role, preventing confusion that might arise from less direct terminology. It does not seem to us intrinsically demeaning, especially if used in a respectful context. We note the objections here in case clinicians want to consider not using the term with patients.

Outbreaks of Medically Unexplained Symptoms

Somatic symptoms may present in mass form as outbreaks of medically unexplained symptoms. This phenomenon, sometimes called mass or epidemic psychogenic illness or hysteria, often involves respiratory or gastrointestinal symptoms that, depending on the circumstances, might be attributed to prodromal infectious illness, a chemical weapon, toxic exposure, or even acute radiation sickness.[48] Such outbreaks have been seen in schools, factories, sports facilities, and other group settings. Often they begin with perceived noxious odors, false reports of toxic gas, or a dramatic emergency response to a single report of illness. Typically they spread quickly and resolve quickly.[49–52]

Mass Panic

The term "panic" is often used loosely to describe any public sign of fear or concern. During the fall of 2001, the term was sometimes used to describe the conduct of people who called their doctor with questions about anthrax, who got prescriptions for antibiotic prophylaxis against public health authorities' advice, or who called the police about mysterious white powders at a time when authorities were soliciting such calls.

Traditionally, however, the word has meant a sudden, overpowering, and often contagious terror that leads to abandonment of social roles and concerns, often with disorganized flight. Mass panic of this type is rare after terrorism or disaster in general.[18,19] It did not occur after the sarin attack in the Tokyo subways in 1995, the SCUD missile attacks on Israel in 1994, the Oklahoma City bombing in 1995, the bombing of the World Trade Center in 1993, or the destruction of the World Trade Center and the attack on the Pentagon on September 11, 2001. It did not occur during the anthrax attacks in 2001. Disasters often evoke adaptive, helping behavior, which was seen in all these terrorist events.[19,48]

As noted earlier, panic did occur to some degree in two recent natural disease outbreaks, of SARS in China and plague in India, that resembled possible bioterrorist scenarios and that were poorly managed by public authorities. The mistakes included concealing and dishonestly underestimating the problem, failing to act promptly, and failing to inform the public in a credible fashion.

The risk factors for panic are said to include perception that the risk of death is high, the chance of escape is small or fleeting, the treatment resources are limited, the response by authorities is ineffective, and the credibility of authorities is lacking. It is believed that training and simulation before the event, and providing accurate credible information during the event, can help reduce risk of mass panic.[10]

POTENTIAL DELAYED ADVERSE EFFECTS

For those who experience it, a biological attack may combine features of warfare, disaster, and serious illness. All those kinds of traumatic events have been linked to the development of psychiatric illness, such as acute stress disorder, posttraumatic stress disorder, depression, and substance use disorder, in some survivors and witnesses.[7,53,54] Others may develop problems that have features of posttraumatic stress disorder but do not meet all the diagnostic criteria in the *Diagnostic and Statistical Manual of Mental Disorders*, Fourth Edition (DSM-IV).

Increases in unhealthy behaviors may follow terrorism or other stressful situations. In random-digit-dial surveys of Manhattan residents, 30.8% reported increased use of cigarettes, alcohol, or marijuana 1 month after September 11. The figure fell only slightly, to 27.3%, at 6 months after the disaster. The stability of the results, the authors note, suggest potential long-term health consequences.[55]

Lingering Effects on the Anthrax Survivors

A study of 15 of the 16 adult survivors of the 2001 anthrax attacks found that 1 year later they had more unexplained somatic complaints, higher levels of psychological distress and lower health-related quality of life indices than referent populations. Eight of the 15 had not yet returned to work; all of these were receiving psychiatric services. Nine of the 15 had scores consistent with clinically relevant psychological distress. Depression, anxiety, obsessive–compulsive behavior, and hostility were the most frequently reported symptoms.[57]

Posttraumatic Stress Disorder

Of the posttrauma disorders, the most heavily studied has been posttraumatic stress disorder (PTSD). Study has focused largely on combat veterans or vehicle accident victims rather than people exposed to terrorism or illness.

Posttraumatic stress disorder and acute stress disorder are both anxiety disorders that follow exposure to an event that involves risk of death or physical injury and that provokes intense fear or horror. Both involve significant distress with symptoms that include:

- Persistently reexperiencing the event through intrusive images, thoughts, dreams, or flashbacks
- "Numbing," avoiding reminders of the trauma, or feeling detached or estranged from others
- Persistently experiencing symptoms of increased arousal, such as difficulty sleeping, outbursts of anger, increased vigilance, difficulty concentrating

For a diagnosis of acute stress disorder, a person must also have at least three dissociative symptoms (such as detachment, absence of emotional responsiveness, feeling dazed and out of touch with one's surroundings, feeling that events or oneself are not real). Acute stress disorder occurs within a month of the trauma. PTSD is diagnosed after a month. PTSD is considered chronic if it persists for 3 months or more; delayed if it begins more than 6 months after the event.[57] PTSD is often seen in conjunction with depression or substance abuse. About half of PTSD cases remit within 6 months. In a substantial number of cases, however, the disorder persists for years and can dominate the sufferer's life.[25,53,58–61]

An estimated 8 to 9% of Americans will experience PTSD at some point in their lives.[7] Nationally, the prevalence of PTSD within the previous year has been estimated to be 3.6%.[57]

According to the Institute of Medicine's Committee on Responding to the Psychological Consequences of Terrorism, "There is some evidence that children, survivors of past traumatic events (including refugees), ethnic minority populations, and those with preexisting psychiatric illness may be especially vulnerable to psychological consequences, although some of these data are contradictory. Events of closer proximity, longer duration, and greater intensity might be expected to result in increased psychological consequences."[7]

Risk among Individuals Directly Affected by Trauma

The risk of developing PTSD is elevated in those who have been victims of traumatic events, especially those who suffered injury, felt threatened with violent death, or lost a loved one. Longer, more intense exposure to grotesque or horrific scenes may exacerbate the effect.[62]

PTSD was seen in about 30% of male Vietnam veterans and persisted chronically in more than a third of those affected veterans.[63]

In civilian life, a study of 2181 adults in the Detroit area found that 9.2% of those exposed to trauma developed probable PTSD. The highest risk was found in those who had been the victims of violent assault, 20.9% of whom developed probable PTSD. But the most common precipitating event was the sudden, unexpected death of a loved one. This accounted for 31% of the cases, although it carried a risk of 14.3%, lower than that for violent assault.[65]

Elevated rates were seen among both victims and rescuers after the Oklahoma City terrorist bombing. In a study 34 months later, North and colleagues found 23% of male primary victims and 13% of male rescue workers had PTSD related to the bombing.[65]

Elevated rates of PTSD also have been seen among other survivors of critical illness:

- Among survivors of acute respiratory distress syndrome (ARDS), 22 out of 80 patients in one study had evidence of PTSD.[33] In another study, 20 out of 46 ARDS survivors had PTSD upon discharge; 11 still had it at follow-up, a median 8 years later.[66] Of 200 Legionnaires' disease patients, 15% had PTSD at 17 months after diagnosis.[34]
- Of 78 survivors of a general ICU, 14% met the full diagnostic criteria for PTSD, 3 months after discharge.[67] Approximately 6 to 12 months after discharge from a pediatric intensive care unit, 4 of 19 children had PTSD, as did 9 of their 33 parents.[68]

A review of PTSD following medical illness found that poor social support and negative interactions with health care staff seemed to predispose patients to the development of PTSD symptoms.[54]

Risk to the General Population

Terrorism may cause serious psychological effects among people who were far from the scene and suffered no direct loss. It is not clear how widespread such effects may be. Evidence indicates serious effects are likely to last only a few months.

In a national study, 17% of those outside New York City reported high levels of PTSD symptoms related to September 11 two months after the attack. At 6 months, this fell to 5.8%, still above the estimated national baseline 3.9% prevalence of PTSD. (Because the researchers did not assess such diagnostic criteria as functional impairment or duration of symptoms, they did not characterize the respondents as having PTSD.)[25]

In a separate national survey, done 1 to 2 months after September 11, an elevated level of probable PTSD (11.2%) was found only in the New York metropolitan area. Levels were 2.7% in Washington, D.C., although it also saw terror on September 11 through the attack on the Pentagon, 3.6% in other major metropolitan areas, and 4% in the rest of the country.[8]

In a random-digit-dial survey of Manhattan residents 1 month after September 11, 7.5% reported symptoms consistent with current posttraumatic stress disorder and 9.7% reported symptoms consistent with current depression. Overall, 13.6% reported symptoms that met the criteria for one of those disorders, and 3.7% reported symptoms that met the criteria for both. But 6 months after the attack, the percent reporting PTSD symptoms had fallen to 0.6%.[60]

Risk Factors for PTSD

Many factors have been linked to elevated risk of developing PTSD. Being aware of these factors can help health care providers target psychological resources to individuals who may be most vulnerable (Box 5.1).[61]

BOX 5.1
Posttrauma Warning Signs

These features have been linked to an increased risk of developing serious problems after a traumatic event.

Since the Event:

Feeling numb, disconnected, unreal, or dreamlike
Withdrawing from other people
Avoiding places, people, or activities that are reminders of the trauma
Keeping excessively busy to avoid thinking about what has happened
Blaming oneself
Feeling like one has given up
Feeling continuous distress with no relief
Spending many hours a day watching or reading reports about the event

During the Event:

Suffered injury
Lost a loved one or friend
Had extensive or intense exposure to trauma, especially dead bodies or graphic suffering
Had to deal with children dying

Before the Event:

Was diagnosed with a psychiatric illness
Suffered trauma, especially personal assault, repeated trauma, or assaults during childhood
Grew up in a family with psychopathology

Personal Circumstances:

Has little social support
Has low socioeconomic status
Is female
Is young

Dissociative Reactions

People who show dissociative symptoms at the time of trauma are more likely than others to develop PTSD later.[69,70] In a study of 182 survivors 6 months after the Oklahoma City bombing, 94% who met avoidance and numbing criteria had a full PTSD diagnosis.[71] A meta-analysis of 68 studies dealing with predictors of PTSD found peritraumatic dissociation yielded the largest effect.[71]

In several studies, most accident and assault survivors who met the diagnosis for Acute Stress Disorder within 1 month of their trauma went on to develop PTSD.[72] The acute stress disorder diagnosis includes dissociative symptoms.

Several studies have found that trauma survivors whose heart rate was elevated in the emergency room or at time of hospital discharge (about 95 beats per minute) were more likely than others to develop PTSD.[73,74]

Disengaged Coping Styles

A national survey on the aftermath of September 11 found that PTSD symptoms were likelier among those who coped by "giving up" or disengaging, as well as by denial, self-distraction, self-blame, and seeking social support. The researchers reported that "active coping" in the immediate aftermath was the only strategy linked to lower levels of PTSD.[25] Active coping in this context included such steps as giving blood or attending memorial services. It is not clear whether active coping was itself protective or reflected psychic factors that made individuals more resistant to stress.

Similarly, in a study of surgical patients upon admission and discharge, coping styles of avoidance and acceptance–resignation were associated with a poorer psychiatric outcome.[32]

Demographic Factors and Personal History

The following groups have an elevated risk of developing PTSD:

- Women. Studies have found that women are twice as likely as men to report symptoms of PTSD.[25,65,75] In a survey of Manhattan residents 5 to 8 weeks after September 11, most of the gap disappeared when the data was adjusted for previous trauma, previous psychological disorders, social responsibilities, and emotional reactions at the time of the event.[75] In another study, women who had been violently assaulted were far more likely than men to develop PTSD; this difference accounted for most of the overall 2:1 gender gap.[76]
- Individuals with a history of experiencing trauma, especially rape, torture, or other personal assaults. Those who have endured multiple traumatic events or who experienced trauma in childhood may be at particular risk.[77] Childhood trauma is quite common: In a survey of more than 8000 New York City schoolchildren after September 11, 64% reported having been exposed to at least one traumatic event before 9/11; 39% said they had seen a killing or a serious injury.[78]
- Individuals with a family history of psychopathology or a personal history of psychiatric illness.[7,25,70]
- People with low levels of social support,[25,30,79] including those experiencing marital separation.

In post–September 11 studies in New York City, people of Hispanic ethnicity were also more likely to report symptoms consistent with PTSD.[30] Other reported risk factors include youth and lower socioeconomic level.[7] Some studies have found higher levels of PTSD symptoms in people who had heavier exposure to media accounts.[6,17] As with coping styles, it is not clear whether high media exposure promotes psychic distress, reflects it, or plays roles that vary with the individual and the situation.

EARLY INTERVENTION MEASURES

Reasons for Caution on Interventions

Little scientific evidence exists to indicate which mental health interventions, if any, can reduce psychological distress from disasters in general or bioterrorism in particular. Nor is it clear how different approaches may affect different segments of the population.

Much of the research on preventing or treating the psychological damage of trauma is drawn from experiences involving military combat, natural disasters, motor vehicle accidents, or sexual assault, situations that may bear little resemblance to a bioterrorist episode.

Psychological First Aid

The concept of providing posttrauma psychological first aid — nontherapeutic measures designed to bolster a person's sense of safety, well-being, and empowerment — has become a staple of immediate postdisaster mental health services.[27,81,82]

Psychological first aid is based on the idea that most patients with psychological symptoms will be healthy people who have endured extraordinarily stressful experiences.

The goal is to encourage — and emphasize — patients' natural resilience and ability to recover, to help them understand that their reactions are normal and appropriate, and that they can expect to feel better in the future. Disaster mental health experts caution against pathologizing normal responses, fearing it may promote feelings of helplessness in some people and may make others less likely to use support services.

For 3 weeks after the Oklahoma City bombing, for instance, families of the missing waited in a Compassion Center, attended by mental health professionals. These staff were termed "escorts," not counselors or therapists, in order to avoid "stigmatizing mental health labels" and to emphasize "active outreach and empowerment of the individual."[83]

This approach resembles but goes beyond the traditional military medical response to combat stress: remove soldiers to a safe place nearby; give them food and rest; tell them they will be fine — and then send them back to the front as soon as possible. (This military approach is sometimes known by the acronym PIE, for proximity, immediacy, expectancy.)[84]

Ideally, a range of supportive and educational services should be provided as part of psychological first aid.[9,18,27]

- Provide a safe place that prevents exposure to more stress, if possible, with appropriate comforts such as food, hot drinks, showers, and blankets.
- Console and comfort, offering a warm and empathetic human connection. Ideally, patients should not be left alone.
- Provide support for the bereaved.
- Help restore patients' sense of control. Staff should identify themselves, explain what patients can expect, provide accurate information, safeguard patients' dignity.
- Reunite patients with family or friends. If quarantine or isolation prevents direct contact, phone or e-mail contacts should be arranged. According to the report of the Institute of Medicine's Committee on Responding to the Psychological Consequences of Terrorism, "The inability of people to be with loved ones who may be ill or dying will create significant psychological distress. People may choose not to bring sick family members to the hospital for fear of separation, which may lead to spread of contamination or contagion."[7] In addition, family and friends serve as natural caregivers, providing many other aspects of psychological first aid. It is especially important, of course, to reunite parents and children.
- Help patients with real-world problems, such as tracking down family members or getting care for pets. The problems need not be big ones: During the 2003 SARS outbreak, staff in one Toronto hospital went to a drugstore to get hygiene items for a patient in isolation and arranged for a pizza delivery to a house in quarantine.[85]
- Provide opportunities for patients to talk about their experiences and feelings if they choose to, but without encouraging or forcing disclosures.
- Provide opportunities for patients to talk with clergy or spiritual mentors. For many people, clergy — not mental health professionals — are a main source of guidance and sympathy in times of crisis, and prayer is an important part of a coping response, especially for many seriously ill people. In the weeks after September 11, attendance increased at houses of worship around the country, and mental health workers in New York and Washington, D.C., said that even some of their secular clients felt a need to pray.[86]

In addition, as part of psychological first aid, providers should:

- Educate patients about the range of normal reactions to stress, encouraging them to view their own reactions as normal.
- Educate patients about symptoms or feelings that would warrant them seeking care in the future.
- Instruct patients in basic self-care measures, such as eating well, getting plenty of sleep, restoring routines as much as possible, getting aerobic exercise, and connecting with family and friends.

- Provide opportunities for "active coping," such as volunteer activities or participation in memorial services.
- Connect patients with support or counseling resources they can use if they feel the need.
- Identify patients who may be at particular risk of suffering serious psychological problems, as described earlier, and make appropriate arrangements for counseling or follow-up.

If persons are undergoing extremely intense or psychotic reactions that do not respond to such techniques, or have severe insomnia, short-term use of benzodiazepines or antipsychotic or other medications may be needed.

Humane as it may be, does psychological first aid (PFA) prevent psychological damage? According to the Institute of Medicine committee report, "No evidence is yet available to assess its efficacy. PFA can be used to deal with the daily stresses of life (e.g., family strife, job stress, the academic and interpersonal challenges faced by schoolchildren). It is in these developments that the skills are tested, practiced, refined, and generally maintained as an active part of daily life. In this way, PFA may provide daily benefit, whether there are terrorism events or not."[7]

Psychological Debriefing

Psychological debriefing is generally understood to be a 2- to 4-hour intervention that happens shortly after a traumatic event, within days or a week. Its aim is to get people to talk about their experiences, vent their feelings, and learn stress-management techniques, as a way of alleviating distress, assessing the need for follow-up, and preventing long-term consequences. Psychological debriefing has become a staple of Employee Assistance Programs, often offered along with group or individual counseling. After September 11, debriefings were apparently used with thousands of New Yorkers, including survivors, witnesses, and employees with no direct involvement.[81] The best-known form of psychological debriefing, called Critical Incident Stress Debriefing (CISD) or "the Mitchell model," is a small-group discussion with a trained leader or facilitator.[87,88] Originally intended for firefighters, police officers, emergency medical technicians, and other rescue workers, it is now used in one-on-one sessions and with direct trauma victims as well.

Psychological debriefing starts with an introduction, emphasizing that the session is not psychotherapy and it is confidential. In steps 2 to 5, the facilitator asks each person to describe what he or she saw or did during the event (the facts stage); recall his or her thoughts about what happened (thoughts stage); describe emotional reactions and current feelings about what happened (reaction stage); and discuss any physical or psychological symptoms noticed (symptoms stage). In Step 6, the teaching phase, the facilitator explains that the symptoms are normal and offers suggestions for stress management. In the final stage, the facilitator sums up, shares referral resources, and answers questions.[89]

The program is part of a wider array of services offered by the International Critical Incident Stress Foundation, based in Maryland. These include, among others, pre-incident preparedness training for rescue workers, and "defusing," a three-stage version of CISD that occurs within 12 hours of the event, as needed.[91] The foundation trains more than 30,000 people a year in its system, called Critical Incident Stress Management (CISM).[92] Public agencies and corporations around the country have CISM teams ready to respond to trauma; in March 2004, the foundation's website listed more than 300 teams for which current information was available.

Recent Recommendations on Early Intervention

In studies, most people who have undergone debriefing said it was helpful and that they would recommend it to others; some are enthusiastic advocates of it.[90,93] The evidence on whether it works to prevent PTSD is unclear. Various studies have suggested debriefing reduces PTSD symptoms, has no effect, or even promotes PTSD, but the studies have been flawed and the results difficult to interpret.[89] Recent reviews of the evidence have produced calls to cease compulsory debriefing of victims of trauma.[93]

A workshop of 58 disaster mental health experts, convened in Washington, D.C., in 2001 to consider the impact of early psychological interventions for mass trauma victims, concluded there was some evidence that "early intervention in the form of a single one-on-one recital of events and expression of emotions evoked by a traumatic event (as advocated in some forms of psychological debriefing) does not consistently reduce risks of later developing PTSD or related adjustment difficulties." It added, "Some survivors (e.g., those with high arousal) may be put at heightened risk for adverse outcomes as a result of such early interventions."[82]

The workshop recommended that participation in early intervention sessions, whether administered in groups or individually, should be voluntary. (It also recommended dropping use of the term "debriefing" in this context.)

Discussing another approach that has gained some popularity, eye-movement desensitization and reprocessing (EMDR), the consensus statement found "no evidence" that it is a treatment of choice as an early mental health intervention.

Litz and colleagues conclude that the blanket use of single-session psychological debriefing is inappropriate. They suggest that exposed persons, whether survivors, witnesses, family members, or rescue workers, be screened for the magnitude of their exposure and the appropriateness of their emotional response, with multisession intervention of demonstrated efficacy offered to those who seem to need it.[81]

A report by the American College of Neuropsychopharmacology took a similar position. It stated: "An emerging response to traumatic events, including the events of 9/11, is to provide emergency mental health treatments, such as debriefing, to everyone directly exposed. In some settings debriefing has become mandatory. Research suggests that debriefing is at best ineffective and possibly harmful. For the present, interventions should only be offered to those at highest risk, especially those demonstrating serious symptoms. The interventions must have been found effective in well-designed clinical trials."[5]

Bisson and colleagues suggest that while one-time group or individual debriefing cannot be advocated as preventing development of PTSD, debriefing may have benefits, especially as part of a comprehensive management program. They note that it is well-received by most people and may be useful for screening, education, and support. If psychological debriefing or any similar intervention is used, they say, it should not be mandatory, providers must be experienced and well-trained, and participants should be clinically assessed.[94]

LONGER-TERM TREATMENT

COGNITIVE–BEHAVIORAL THERAPY

Evidence suggests that cognitive–behavioral therapy, provided in several therapy sessions beginning a few weeks after the event, is effective in treating PTSD among accident and assault victims, either speeding up the rate of recovery or reducing the prevalence of the disorder.[5,27,44,95–98]

Cognitive–behavioral therapy takes a problem-solving, symptom-oriented approach, seeking to help people change their view of the event and to adapt their behavior. It often includes exposure therapy, in which patients repeatedly imagine and describe the traumatic event in a safe context to bring their fear under control. This may be followed by gradual exposure to places or situations associated with the event.

Marshall and Suh describe using this process with several patients, including an artist who had been working in her studio near the World Trade Center the morning of the attack. She suffered nightmares and intrusive memories and could not bring herself to go back to the studio, where her paintings and possessions lay covered in ash. Her first "*in vivo*" exercise was walking by her building with a friend who acted as coach. Eventually, she was able to clean up her studio and return to work there.[4]

Cognitive–behavioral therapy for trauma can also include learning ways to cope with anxiety, such as breathing techniques; deal with negative thoughts ("cognitive restructuring"); manage anger; prepare for stress reactions ("stress inoculation"); deal with urges to use alcohol or drugs when stress occurs; relate better with people (social skills or marital therapy); realistically appraise the risk of future terrorism relative to everyday risks; identify the specific elements in a given situation that cause distress; identify different ways of dealing with problems, such as seeking help, changing goals, and postponing decisions.

PHARMACOLOGICAL TREATMENT

Along with therapy, antidepressants are often used, generally with selective serotonin reuptake inhibitors (SSRIs) as the first-line choice.[96] Tricyclic antidepressants (TCAs) and monoamine oxidase inhibitors (MAOIs) have also been found effective.[99]

Benzodiazepines, useful in some other anxiety disorders, have not proven effective in PTSD. They are sometimes used for a few days shortly after a traumatic event for patients who otherwise are unable to get adequate sleep, but long-term use as treatment of PTSD is not generally recommended.[27,100]

FEATURES OF A HOSPITAL PSYCHOLOGICAL PREPAREDNESS PLAN

As mentioned earlier, every hospital should have a plan to mitigate and manage the psychological impact of terrorism on patients and staff. The following list includes basic features of a plan. Measures to alleviate distress among hospital staff in particular are covered in greater detail in Chapter 6. Social workers, psychiatric nurses, psychiatrists, and other relevant personnel should be involved in the planning, and a team should be identified to take the lead in this area should bioterrorism occur.

BEFORE THE EVENT

- Educate and train mental health professionals in issues of disaster mental health care. Training and information is offered by many agencies and professional groups, including the American Red Cross, the Substance Abuse and Mental Health Services Administration (SAMHSA) of the U.S. Department of Health and Human Services, and professional organizations. Education of emergency, infectious disease, and primary care staff should also be considered.
- If possible, include a mental health professional in the command group that will lead the hospital's response to terrorism.
- Be sure staff are well trained in use of protective gear and procedures and that adequate equipment is available.
- Prepare or acquire materials on normal reactions to psychologically traumatic events and ways of alleviating stress, for distribution to patients, staff, and the public in the event of an incident. Sources of materials are listed in Chapter 11.
- Encourage staff, outpatients, and discharged patients to make family emergency plans, emphasizing the need to make backup arrangements for care of children, dependent parents, and pets. Materials outlining such planning, and including samples of written family plans, should be distributed. The hospital could also hold informational meetings for staff and patients on these issues.
- Consider what role, if any, existing or additional volunteers, including clergy, would play in helping with practical and social support. Organize and train volunteers, if they will be used.
- Become familiar with local or regional arrangements for tracking patients so as to be effective in helping staff and patients locate their loved ones.
- Encourage staff in self-care/stress-reduction activities, such as exercise, nutrition, smoking cessation, meditation, and "active coping" skills.
- Ensure that internal communications are adequate. Arrange for staff to have access to hospital e-mail and intranets from home as well as office.

DURING THE EVENT

- Involve mental health staff in triage of patients in whom exposure is unclear.

- Make provisions for dealing with unexposed but concerned persons (the "worried well") who do not accept negative physical findings, who are distraught, or who have troubling psychogenic symptoms. As noted in Chapter 3, space needs to be set aside for care of these patients. For reasons of both infection control and stress reduction, the space should be separate but not far from the emergency department. It should also be away from the area where media will congregate, so patients can leave without having to encounter reporters. Hall and colleagues recommend establishing a clinical registry to follow up distressed patients. This in itself can serve as a "psychological intervention, assuring patients that their concerns are being taken seriously."[9]
- Communicate promptly and clearly with staff, responding to concerns and questions.
- Provide psychological support for staff, inpatients, and their families, including patients who were hospitalized for other reasons. Measures could include a set schedule of initial and follow-up visits or phone interviews by mental health professionals with inpatients; referrals to mental health hotlines for families; distribution of materials about normal reactions to stressful situations and means of self-care; and establishment of family networks or phone trees. Special attention should be paid to ensuring that staff are getting adequate sleep.
- Provide practical support for staff, inpatients, and their families. Measures could include ensuring means of communication between staff and patients and their respective families, especially if isolation is imposed; supplying recreational materials (books, magazines, recordings); supplying a relaxed space for staff socializing, if infection control permits; making contacts with public or private agencies that could help with care of children, elderly parents, or pets; and providing staff to work on locating missing family members.
- Act promptly to procure staff reinforcements if they are necessary to avoid overwork.
- Encourage and, if necessary, force staff to take breaks and leave at the end of their shifts.

After the Event

- Continue to provide confidential psychiatric services for staff and psychiatric follow-up for patients, if needed.
- Hold memorial or commemorative services, if appropriate.
- Consider holding psychological debriefing sessions.

REFERENCES

1. Zimbardo, P.G., The Political Psychology of Terrorist Alarms, essay posted on APA Online, February 26, 2003, accessed at www.apa.org/about/division/terrorism.html.

2. Susser, E.S., Herman, D.B., and Aaron, B., Combating the terror of terrorism, *Sci Am,* 287, 70, 2002.
3. Saathoff, G. and Everly, G.S., Jr., Psychological challenges of bioterror: containing contagion, *Int J Emerg Ment Health*, 4, 245, 2002.
4. Marshall, R.D. and Suh, E.J., Contextualizing trauma: using evidence-based treatments in a multicultural community after 9/11, *Psych Q*, 74, 2003.
5. American College of Neuropsychopharmacology, The Impact of Terrorism on Brain and Behavior: What We Know and What We Need To Know, executive summary, accessed May 12, 2004, at www.acnp.org.
6. Schuster, M.A. et al., A national survey of stress reactions after the September 11, 2001 terrorist attacks, *NEJM*, 345, 1507, 2001.
7. Committee on Responding to the Psychological Consequences of Terrorism, Institute of Medicine, in Butler, A.S., Panzer, A.M., and Goldfrank, L.R., Eds, *Responding to the Psychological Consequences of Terrorism: A Public Health Strategy*, National Academies Press, Washington, D.C., 2003.
8. Schlenger, W.E. et al., Psychological reactions to terrorist attacks: findings from the National Study of Americans' Reactions to September 11, *JAMA*, 288, 581, 2002.
9. Hall, M.J., Norwood, A.E., Ursano, R.J., and Fullerton, C.S., The psychological impacts of bioterrorism, *Biosecur and Bioterror*, 1, 139, 2003.
10. Lacy, T.J. and Benedek, D.M., Terrorism and weapons of mass destruction: managing the behavioral reaction in primary care, *South Med J*, 96, 394, 2003.
11. Holloway, H.C. et al., The threat of biological weapons: prophylaxis and mitigation of psychological and social consequences, *JAMA*, 278, 425, 1997.
12. Garrett, L., *Betrayal of Trust: The Collapse of Global Public Health*, Hyperion, New York, 2000, chap. 1.
13. Pomfret, J., Thousands Flee Beijing, Fearing SARS; Schools are Closed as Toll in Capital Rises to 35 Dead, *Washington Post*, A20, April 24, 2003.
14. Garrett, L., China's Epidemic Discord; Warring SARS Strategies Afflict Politics, Public Health, *Newsday*, A3, April 27, 2003.
15. Eckholm, E., SARS Is the Spark for a Riot in China, *New York Times*, A1, April 29, 2003.
16. Pomfret, J., A Mistrust of Government Undercuts China's Effort, *Washington Post*, A1, April 29, 2003.
17. Liang, W. et al., Severe acute respiratory syndrome, Beijing, 2003, *Emerg Infect Dis*, 10, 25, 2004.
18. Raphael, B., *When Disaster Strikes: How Individuals and Communities Cope With Catastrophe*, Basic Books, New York, 1986, chap. 3.
19. Glass, T.A. and Schoch-Spana, M., Bioterrorism and the people: how to vaccinate a city against panic, *Clin Infect Dis*, 34, 217, 2002.
20. Kroenke, K., Jackson, J.L., and Chamberlin, J., Depressive and anxiety disorders in patients presenting with physical complaints: clinical predictors and outcome, *Am J Med*, 103, 339, 1997.
21. Stein, M.B., Attending to anxiety disorders in primary care, *J Clin Psychiatry*, 64, 35, 2003.
22. Stuber, M.L., Shemesh, E., and Saxe, G.N., Posttraumatic stress response in children with life-threatening illnesses, *Child Adolesc Psychiatr Clin N Am*, 12, 195, 2003.
23. Jones, C., Providing psychological support for patients after critical illness, *Clin Intensive Care*, 5, 176, 1994.

24. Young, B.H. et al., *Disaster Mental Health Services: A Guidebook for Clinicians and Administrators*, National Center for PTSD, Washington, D.C., 2002, accessed May 4, 2004, at www.ncptsd.org//publications/disaster/index.html.
25. Silver, R.C. et al., Nationwide longitudinal study of psychological responses to September 11, *JAMA*, 288, 1235, 2002.
26. Lacey, T.J. and Benedek, D.M., Terrorism and weapons of mass destruction: managing the behavioral reaction in primary care, *South Med J*, 96, 394, 2003.
27. Shalev, A.Y., Treating survivors in the acute aftermath of traumatic events, in *Treating Trauma Survivors with PTSD: Bridging the Gap Between Intervention Research and Practice*, Yehuda, R., Ed., American Psychiatric Press, Washington, D.C., 2002, chap. 7.
28. Masten, A.S., Ordinary magic: resilience processes in development, *Am Psychologist*, 56, 227, 2001.
29. DeLisi, L.E. et al., A survey of New Yorkers after the September 11, 2001, terrorist attacks, *Am J Psychiatry*, 160, 780, 2003.
30. Galea, S. et al., Psychological sequelae of the September 11 terrorist attacks in New York City, *NEJM*, 346, 982, 2002.
31. Kucharski, A., Psychologic stress in myocardial infarction, *Am Fam Physician*, 17, 154, 1978.
32. Clarke, D.M. et al., Psychiatric disturbance and acute stress responses in surgical patients, *Aust NZ J Surg*, 67, 115, 1997.
33. Schelling, G. et al., Health-related quality of life and posttraumatic stress disorder in survivors of the acute respiratory distress syndrome, *Crit Care Med*, 26, 651, 1998.
34. Lettinga, K.D. et al., Health-related quality of life and posttraumatic stress disorder among survivors of an outbreak of Legionnaires' disease, *Clin Infect Dis*, 35, 11, 2002.
35. Lesko, L.M., Psychiatric aspects of bone marrow transplantation, *Psycho-Oncology*, 2, 161, 1993.
36. Dyson, M., Intensive care unit psychosis, the therapeutic nurse–patient relationship and the influence of the intensive care setting: analyses of interrelating factors, *J Clin Nurs*, 8, 284, 1999.
37. Halm, M.A. et al., Behavioral responses of family members during critical illness, *Clin Nurs Res*, 2, 414, 1993.
38. Huckabay, L.M. and Tilem-Kessler, D., Patterns of parental stress in PICU emergency admission, *Dimens Crit Care Nurs*, 18, 36, 1999.
39. Cheng et al., Psychiatric complications in patients with severe acute respiratory syndrome (SARS) during the acute treatment phase: a series of 10 cases, *Brit J Psychiatry*, 184, 359, 2004.
40. Tan, Y.S. and Cheong, P.Y., Fever attribution in the SARS outbreak, *Singapore Med J*, 44, 590, 2003.
41. Karsenty, E.J. et al., Medical aspects of the Iraqi missile attacks on Israel, *Israeli J Med Sci*, 27, 603, 1991.
42. Smithson, A.E. and Levy, L.-A., Ataxia: The Chemical and Biological Terrorism Threat and the US Response, Henry L. Stimson Center Report No. 35, 2000, chap. 3.
43. DiGiovanni, C., Jr., Domestic terrorism with chemical or biological agents: psychiatric aspects, *Am J Psychiatry*, 156, 1500, 1999.

44. U.S. Department of Health and Human Services, Mental Health: A Report of the Surgeon General — Executive Summary, Rockville, MD: U.S. Department of Health and Human Services, Substance Abuse and Mental Health Services Administration, Center for Mental Health Services, National Institutes of Health, National Institute of Mental Health, 1999, chap. 2.
45. Mandell, G.L., Bennett, J.E., and Dolin, R., *Mandell, Douglas, and Bennett's Principles and Practice of Infectious Diseases*, 5th edition, Churchill Livingstone, Philadelphia, 2000.
46. St. Louis, M.E. et al., Botulism from chopped garlic: delayed recognition of a major outbreak, *Ann Intern Med*, 108, 363, 1988.
47. Smith, R.C., Minor acute illness: A preliminary research report on the "worried well," *Journ Fam Pract*, 51, 24, 2002.
48. Pastel, R.H., Collective behaviors: mass panic and outbreaks of multiple unexplained symptoms, *Mil Med*, 166, 44, 2001.
49. Jones, T.F. et al., Mass psychogenic illness attributed to toxic exposure at a high school, *NEJM*, 342, 96, 2000.
50. Small, G.W., A sudden outbreak of illness suggestive of mass hysteria in schoolchildren, *Arch Fam Med*, 3, 711, 1994.
51. Struewing, J.P. and Gray, G.C., An epidemic of respiratory complaints exacerbated by mass psychogenic illness in a military recruit population, *Am J Epid*, 132, 1120, 1990.
52. Engels, C.C., Outbreaks of medically unexplained physical symptoms after military action, terrorist threat, or technological disaster, *Mil Med*, 166, 47, 2001.
53. Kessler, R.C., Posttraumatic Stress Disorder in the National Comorbidity Survey, *Arch Gen Psychiatry*, 52, 1048, 1995.
54. Tedstone, J.E. and Tarrier, N., Posttraumatic stress disorder following medical illness and treatment, *Clin Psychol Rev*, 23, 409, 2003.
55. Vlahov, D. et al., Sustained increased consumption of cigarettes, alcohol, and marijuana among Manhattan residents after September 11, 2001, *Am J Public Health*, 94, 253, 2004.
56. Reissman, D.B. et al., One-year health assessment of adult survivors of *Bacillus anthracis* infection, *JAMA*, 291, 1994, 2004.
57. American Psychiatric Association, Diagnostic and Statistical Manual of Mental Disorders — Fourth Edition (DSM-IV), American Psychiatric Press, Washington, D.C., 1994.
58. U.S. Department of Health and Human Services, Mental Health: A Report of the Surgeon General, Rockville, MD: U.S. Department of Health and Human Services, Substance Abuse and Mental Health Services Administration, Center for Mental Health Services, National Institutes of Health, National Institute of Mental Health, 1999, chap. 4.
59. Galea, S. et al., Trends of probable posttraumatic stress disorder in New York City after the September 11 terrorist attacks, *Am J Epidemiol*, 158, 514, 2003.
60. Shalev, A.Y. et al., Prospective study of posttraumatic stress disorder and depression following trauma, *Am J Psychiatry*, 155, 630, 1998.
61. Norris, F.H., Risk factors for adverse outcomes in natural and human-caused disasters: a review of the empirical literature, National Center for PTSD fact sheet, accessed May 15, 2004, from www.ncptsd.org/facts/disasters/fs_riskfactors.html.

62. Kulka, R.A. et al., Trauma and the Vietnam War Generation: Report of Findings from the National Vietnam Veterans Readjustment Study, Brunner/Mazel, New York, 1990, as reported in Epidemiological Facts about PTSD, a National Center for PTSD fact sheet, accessed May 15, 2004, at www.ncptsd.org/facts/general/fs_epidemiological.html.
63. Breslau, N. et al., Trauma and posttraumatic stress disorder in the community: The 1996 Detroit Area Survey of Trauma, *Arch Gen Psychiatry*, 55, 626, 1998.
64. North, C.S. et al., Psychiatric disorders in rescue workers after the Oklahoma City bombing, *Am J Psychiatry*, 159, 857, 2002.
65. Kapfhammer, H.P. et al., Posttraumatic stress disorder and health-related quality of life in long-term survivors of acute respiratory distress syndrome, *Am J Psychiatry*, 161, 45, 2004.
66. Cuthbertson, B.H. et al., Posttraumatic stress disorder after critical illness requiring general intensive care, *Intensive Care Med*, 30, 450, 2004.
67. Rees, G., Psychiatric outcomes following paediatric intensive care unit (PICU) admission: a cohort study, *Intensive Care Med*, 2004. {Epub ahead of print}
68. Birmes, P. et al., The predictive power of peritraumatic dissociation and acute stress symptoms for posttraumatic stress symptoms: a three-month prospective study, *Am J Psychiatry*, 160, 1337, 2003.
69. North, C.S. et al., Psychiatric disorder among survivors of the Oklahoma City bombing, *JAMA*, 282, 755, 1999.
70. Ozer, E.J. et al., Predictors of posttraumatic stress disorder and symptoms in adults: a meta-analysis, *Psychol Bull*, 129, 52, 2003.
71. Harvey, A.G. and Bryant, R.A., The relationship between acute stress disorder and posttraumatic stress disorder: a two-year prospective evaluation, *J Consult Clin Psychol*, 67, 985, 1999.
72. Shalev, A.Y. et al., A prospective study of heart rate response following trauma and the subsequent development of posttraumatic stress disorder, *Arch Gen Psychiatry*, 55, 553, 1998.
73. Bryant, A.R. et al., Acute psychological arousal and posttraumatic stress disorder: a two-year prospective study, *J Trauma Stress*, 16, 439, 2003.
74. Pulcino, T. et al., Posttraumatic stress in women after the September 11 terrorist attacks in New York City, *J Women's Health* (Larchmont), 12, 809, 2003.
75. Breslau, N., Gender differences in trauma and posttraumatic stress disorder, *J Gender Specif Med*, 5, 34, 2002.
76. Breslau, N. et al., Previous exposure to trauma and PTSD effects of subsequent trauma: results from the Detroit Area Survey of Trauma, *Am J Psychiatry*, 156, 902, 1999.
77. Applied Research and Consulting LLC, Columbia University Mailman School of Public Health and New York State Psychiatric Institute, Effects of the World Trade Center Attack on NYC Public School Students: Initial Report to the New York City Board of Education, 2002.
78. Brewin, C.R., Andrews, B., and Valentine, J.D., Meta-analysis of risk factors for posttraumatic stress disorder in trauma-exposed adults, *J Consulting Clin Psychol*, 68, 748, 2000.
79. Pfefferbaum, B. et al., Television exposure in children after a terrorist incident, *Psychiatry*, 64, 202, 2001.
80. Litz, B.T. et al., Early intervention for trauma: current status and future directions, *Clin Psychol*, 9, 112, 2002.

81. National Institute of Mental Health et al., Mental Health and Mass Violence: Evidence-Based Early Psychological Intervention for Victims/Survivors of Mass Violence, a Workshop to Reach Consensus on Best Practices, NIH Publication No. 02-5138, U.S. Government Printing Office, Washington, D.C., 2002.
82. Sitterle, K.A., Mental health services at the Compassion Center: the Oklahoma City bombing, *NCP Clinical Q*, 5, 20, 1995.
83. Stretch, R.H., Follow-Up Studies of Veterans, in *Textbook of Military Medicine, War Psychiatry*, the Office of the Surgeon General, Department of the Army, Borden Institute, Walter Reed Army Medical Center, 1995, chap. 18.
84. Maunder, R. et al., The immediate psychological and occupational impact of the 2003 SARS outbreak in a teaching hospital, *CMAJ*, 168, 1245, 2003.
85. Rosin, H., In Terror's Wake: "God, You Around?"; For Many Who Have Avoided Churches and Religion, a Need to Pray Emerges from Attacks, *Washington Post*, A3, September 27, 2001.
86. Mitchell, J.T. and Everly, G.S., Jr., The scientific evidence for critical incident stress management, *JEMS*, 22, 86, 1997.
87. Everly, G.S., Jr., and Mitchell, J.T., The debriefing "controversy" and crisis intervention: a review of lexical and substantive issues, *Int J Emerg Ment Health*, 2, 211, 2000.
88. McNally R.J., Bryant R.A., and Ehlers A., Does early psychological intervention promote recovery from posttraumatic stress? *Psychological Science in the Public Interest*, 4, 45, 2003.
89. Statements on website of International Critical Incident Stress Foundation, accessed May 15, 2004, at www.icisf.org.
90. Groopman, J., The Grief Industry; How Much Does Crisis Counselling Help — or Hurt?, *New Yorker*, 30, January 26, 2004.
91. Mitchell, J.T., Crisis intervention and critical incident stress management: a defense of the field, article accessed May 15, 2004, on website of International Critical Incident Stress Foundation, www.icisf.org/articles.
92. Wessely, S., Rose, S., and Bisson, J., Brief psychological interventions ("debriefing") for trauma-related symptoms and the prevention of post traumatic stress disorder, Cochrane Database Syst Rev, 2, CD000560, 2000.
93. Bisson, J.L., McFarlane, A., and Rose, S., Psychological debriefing, National Center for PTSD fact sheet, accessed May 11, 2004, at www.ncptsd.org/facts/disasters/fs_debriefing_disaster.html.
94. Ballenger, J.C. et al., Consensus statement on posttraumatic stress disorder from the International Consensus Group on Depression and Anxiety, *J Clin Psychiatry*, 61, 60, 2000.
95. Foa, E.B., Davidson, J.R.T., and Frances, A., Eds., *The Expert Consensus Guideline Series: Treatment of Posttraumatic Stress Disorder, J Clin Psychiatry*, 60 (suppl 16), 1999.
96. Bryant, R.A. et al., Treatment of acute stress disorder: a comparison of cognitive-behavioral therapy and supportive counseling, *J Consult Clin Psychol*, 66, 862, 1998.
97. Bryant, R.A. et al., Cognitive therapy of acute stress disorder: a four-year follow-up, *Behav Res Ther*, 41, 489, 2003.
98. Davidson, J.R., Treatment of posttraumatic stress disorder: the impact of paroxetine, *Psychopharmacol Bull*, 37, 76, 2003.
99. Gelpin, E. et al., Treatment of recent trauma survivors with benzodiazepines: a prospective study, *J Clin Psychiatry*, 57, 390, 1996.
100. Davidson, J.R., Use of benzodiazepines in social anxiety disorder, generalized anxiety disorder, and posttraumatic stress disorder, *J Clin Psychiatry*, 65, 29, 2004.

6 Managing Stress on Hospital Staff

INTRODUCTION

In a bioterrorism event, hospital workers and others who care for victims have many potential sources of stress. As members of the public, they and their families have the same fears and responsibilities as any other people. As hospital workers, they may be at heightened risk for contracting the disease. As caregivers, they may experience "vicarious trauma" from empathetic listening to patients' tales of grief, fear, and loss. As rescuers, they may face guilt and confusion if they are unable to save victims.

First responders to disasters appear to face an intermediate risk of psychiatric distress and illness, higher than uninvolved people but lower than primary victims.[1] Distress can be expected to be particularly high if there are many deaths or if the victims include many children. Although studies have tended to involve firefighters or other rescue workers who were at the scene of disasters, in a bioterrorism attack, doctors and nurses may play the role of first responders. They are likely to be the first to see the victims; they will save or fail to save the most desperately injured; they may face unknown risks and labor in dangerous conditions. In addition, like first responders at the World Trade Center on 9/11 or hospital staff during the 2003 SARS outbreak, they may be struggling to save colleagues and friends.

At the very least, staff members are likely to experience fatigue and worry. At worst, they may feel such fear of infection, lack of confidence in authorities, and conflict over family priorities that they refuse to work with infected patients or even to show up for work.

Hospital staffers generally can be expected to be psychologically resilient, like the public in general, with effective coping skills honed to deal with the normal stresses of their work. For most of them, as for the public in general, psychological distress from a terrorist event can be expected to be temporary.[1–4] However, during the height of a crisis, it can make doing a difficult job much harder.

Every hospital's disaster plan should include steps to minimize the adverse psychological impact of terrorism on staff and patients. (Psychological issues concerning patients and the public are addressed in Chapter 5; related media issues are covered in Chapter 7.) Social workers, psychologists, psychiatric nurses, psychiatrists, and other relevant hospital personnel should be involved in developing the psychosocial components of the disaster plan. A team knowledgeable about disaster mental health should be ready to act should a bioterrorism event occur.

Disaster mental health consists largely of providing emotional support, practical assistance, and help with coping skills to people who do not have underlying psychiatric problems and have not sought psychological therapy. Based on hospitals' experiences during disease outbreaks and disasters, a few elements seem most crucial in helping staff. These are:

- Information during a crisis: It should be accurate and ample; disseminated in different forums (by e-mail, in meetings, on paper), and distributed promptly and repeatedly because people under stress may have difficulty absorbing what they are told. Hospital leaders should answer staff questions quickly and fully. Listening to staffers' concerns can be therapeutic in itself.
- Rest and relief: Fatigue and overwork make coping with stress harder. Staffers need reasonable shifts and breaks, particularly if they are burdened with wearing personal protective equipment and complying with stringent infection-control procedures. They may also need help with insomnia.
- Help with taking care of family: They should be assured of their family's safety and other personal issues.
- Efforts to manage psychological distress can be expected to work best if there is a foundation of trust and goodwill among the staff and leaders of the hospital; if the medical response to the incident is swift and competent; and if staffers can see that the hospital was well prepared.

THE 2003 SARS EXPERIENCE

Despite much speculation, few data are available regarding the psychological impact of a biological attack on hospital workers. Important lessons, however, can be learned from the 2003 outbreak of severe acute respiratory syndrome (SARS). Although the outbreak occurred naturally, it had many of the features feared in a bioterrorist attack: It was caused by a novel agent (a previously unknown coronavirus) for which there was no vaccine and no specific treatment; the agent spread readily from person to person, spreading among hospital patients and staff; it was dangerous, killing almost 10% of the 8098 cases worldwide; it had nonspecific symptoms, such as fever, cough, and malaise; and its containment required onerous and costly measures, including the quarantine of thousands of people.

The 2003 outbreak was concentrated in China, Hong Kong, and Toronto. In Toronto, 40% of the cases occurred in health care workers, and accounts emerging from Toronto hospitals and health officials paint a vivid picture of the stresses and fears that beset patients, families, and especially staff dealing with SARS.

Patients and staff alike felt angry, guilty, anxious, depressed, fearful, and upset that their family and friends would be quarantined. Health care workers' families were stigmatized or shunned in some instances. Patients with mild symptoms felt bored and lonely. Patients hospitalized for other reasons worried about infection and endured frustration from delays, cancellations of procedures, transfers, and lack of family visits.[5–8]

The amount of anger, guilt, anxiety, and fear among both patients and staff was "incredible," according to a doctor who worked in two Toronto hospitals during the outbreaks. Two factors heightened these emotions: early uncertainty about the nature of the virus caused fear, and spread of the virus within the hospital angered patients and staff, who felt hospital authorities were not doing enough to protect them.[9]

In a survey of employees at a large tertiary care hospital in Toronto during the 2003 SARS outbreak, 29% of the respondents — including 45% of the responding nurses — had scores indicating probable emotional distress on a questionnaire. Factors significantly associated with distress included being a nurse, part-time employment status, lifestyle affected by SARS outbreak, and ability to do one's job affected by the precautionary measures. Two thirds of the respondents reported SARS-related concern for their own or their family's health. Associated factors were: perception of a greater risk of death from SARS, living with children, personal or family lifestyle affected by SARS outbreak, and being treated differently by people because of working in a hospital.[10]

Hospitals offered nurses double pay to work SARS units but were unable in some cases to fill all the needed slots, requiring mandatory assignments, with pregnancy the only exemption. In a small number of cases doctors, nurses, and nonprofessional staff either refused to work in such units or to care for SARS patients on general wards.[5,7,11,12]

Recurring Problems

In accounts of the outbreak, some psychosocial problems are repeatedly mentioned.

- Problems over children at home: Patients who were single parents were stressed about getting care for their quarantined children at home. Staffers with children at home felt torn between their desire and duty to serve professionally and their fears about infecting their children.

This was eloquently described in the report of the Canadian National Advisory Committee on SARS and Public Health:

Unlike HIV or hepatitis, SARS "could be transmitted to a health care worker's children by a goodnight kiss," the report said. "Hundreds of health care workers isolated themselves from their families during the outbreak, wearing masks at home, sleeping in the basement, taking meals alone, and waiting to see if they would develop tell-tale symptoms. The Committee would like to salute each and every one of them for their courage and commitment."[7]

"While most [employees] also noted a heightened sense of pride, teamwork, and solidarity, others experienced post-traumatic stress disorder, and a minority felt they needed to change careers," according to the report.[7]

- Fatigue and isolation: Staff meetings at hospitals were ended or scaled back; daily e-mail messages were used to communicate with their staff, including, where possible, those at home.[5,6,8] Staffers with possible contact were quarantined for 10 days, raising the burden on the remaining staff.

At times, "half the staff has been quarantined," forcing others to constantly work overtime, Dr. James Brunton, chief of infectious diseases at the University of

Toronto, told a reporter. "They're not getting enough sleep, they struggle with putting on the protection gear, and they are worried about getting infected themselves."[12]

The burden was so great that Canada recruited U.S. infectious disease specialists, offering them the equivalent of U.S. $1400 a day for 2 weeks' work, to provide relief for Canadian colleagues.[12]

- Practical obstacles to doing the job: They had to wait in line to be screened before they could enter the building each day. Working in full infection-control garb was exhausting and required frequent breaks. Masks were isolating.[11] To enter a SARS patient's room, staff also donned goggles, face shield, hair net, gown over scrubs, and two pair of gloves. Upon leaving, staff followed a precise sequence of disrobing that included washing the hands four times at different points in the process.[6]

In May, when the outbreak seemed to be ending in Toronto, it was learned that nosocomial transmission had been going on for weeks on one ward at North York General Hospital. All staff there went on a 10-day work quarantine: They had to wear N95 respirators at all times in the hospital and had to stay home in quarantine when not at work.[6]

- Caring for colleagues or other medical personnel as patients: Staff members emotionally identified with these patients, suffered heightened fears, or were anxious about their own skills.[6] In some cases, hospitalized staff sought a high level of information and input in medical decision making. Cheung, a physician who contracted SARS, describes taking part in "an almost surreal academic discussion" about his suddenly deteriorating condition at a time when he thought death might be near. He survived to write about it.[13]
- Tensions over pay and respect: Nurses' reactions reflected long-standing concerns that their input is not taken seriously by decision makers, the report of the National Advisory Committee on SARS and Public Health said. "Nurses and support staff expressed frustration with communication delays, impractical or unrealistic directives, and the inconsistent application of rewards and incentives for those working in high-risk situations …. At North York General Hospital, nurses alleged that administrators ignored their warnings of an impending second SARS outbreak."[7]

In addition, many nurses were working part-time in several institutions, a practice that was halted to prevent spread of the virus. Some nurses lost income, but doctors were compensated for all or most of their lost income. Critical-care nurses supplied by a company under contract to the province were paid up to three times as much as other critical-care nurses. There was resentment over these and other perceived inequities.

Several hospitals and front-line focus groups said the heavy use of part-time nurses to cover peaks in demand at lower cost was a problem in terms of planning and levels of commitment in an emergency.[7]

Measures To Deal with the Impact

Hospitals took various measures to deal with the psychological impact of the outbreak.[5,6,8,9]
For patients, steps included:

- One or more visits by mental health personnel, who emphasized the range of normal emotions the patient might be experiencing and helped dealing with practical concerns
- Supportive psychotherapy, if needed
- Psychiatric crisis phone lines
- An outpatient psychiatry service to deal with problems after discharge

For staff, steps included:

- A lounge for relaxing or a quiet staff room for discussion with members of a SARS psychological team
- Informal conversation with psychiatrists who were on the unit to see patients
- Debriefing sessions after the outbreak run by an outside company
- A confidential telephone support line staffed by psychiatric nurses
- Memorials for the three Toronto health care workers who died

Maunder emphasizes the importance of keeping staff well informed, supporting them practically and emotionally, and responding promptly to their questions and suggestions[5]: In the view of Maunder and colleagues, "Most people cope very well in their own way and benefit a great deal from a relatively small quotient of shared concern, good information and support."[8]

NORMAL REACTIONS

After traumatic events, a wide range of psychological symptoms are considered normal among survivors and rescue workers.[14,15] These include alienation, anger, confusion, decreased appetite, decreased libido, decreased self-esteem, despair, disbelief, dissociation, distortion of thoughts, fatigue, grief, guilt, helplessness, hyperarousal, increased substance use, insomnia, intrusive thoughts, irritability, loss of pleasure in regular activities, self-blame, sleep disturbances, social withdrawal, somatic complaints, and terror.[2,16,17]

Some people may experience stress-related somatic symptoms such as elevated heart rate or blood pressure, shortness of breath, dizziness, flushing, headaches, nausea, rash, sweating, tightness in the chest or throat, and tremors.[8,9,18,19] It may be difficult to differentiate these symptoms from nonspecific symptoms of a biological agent.

Medical workers may also show warning signs of burnout, including excessive exposure to trauma, inability to disengage from work, irritability, inability to relax, and difficulties communicating with others.[20]

In most people, as studies of 9/11 reactions suggest, posttrauma stress reactions resolve without intervention, usually within weeks or months.[6,7,25,28–30]

In some cases, as described in the following text, psychological problems persist and individuals may develop psychiatric illness such as acute stress disorder, post-traumatic stress disorder (PTSD), depression, and substance use disorder.[2,21,22] A fuller discussion of PTSD can be found in Chapter 5.

In brief, people are more likely to get PTSD if they were injured or faced violent death; if their exposure to trauma was prolonged and intense; if their immediate coping reaction was dissociative (marked by detachment, absence of emotional responsiveness, feeling dazed and out of touch, feeling that events or oneself are unreal); if they experienced trauma earlier in their life, especially violence, repeated trauma, or trauma in childhood; or if they were diagnosed with a psychiatric illness before the event.[15,23–30]

Elevated rates of PTSD were seen among both victims and rescuers after the Oklahoma City terrorist bombing. In a study 34 months later, North et al. found 23% of male primary victims and 13% of male rescue workers had posttraumatic stress disorder related to the bombing. The rescue workers, 181 firefighters, also had a high rate of alcohol disorders (24%), but virtually no new cases occurred after the disaster.[1]

In a bioterrorist scenario, all employees of hospitals that are treating cases might be reasonably regarded as directly affected individuals at elevated risk of PTSD.

MINIMIZING DISTRESS AMONG HOSPITAL STAFF

With relatively little scientific evidence to guide us, these suggestions about how to minimize staff distress in a bioterrorist episode are based on expert opinion, personal experience, and accounts of hospital performance in natural disease outbreaks.

Measures To Take before the Event

Training and Equipment

Dealing with the psychological effects of terrorism in a hospital, as in any workplace, should begin before the event with building trust and confidence so that the hospital is prepared and equipped for a bioterrorist event. That includes providing adequate training for employees and planning ways to minimize risk to them. The hospital should feel morally obligated to do its utmost to ensure the safety of workers and should communicate this to them. Psychological preparedness for a traumatic event may afford some protection from stress, another reason to bolster hospital training and preparedness.[1,31]

In planning for surge capacity, which may necessitate unorthodox assignments, hospital leaders should try to assign people to tasks for which they are prepared. Feeling overwhelmed, confused, or incompetent can be extremely stressful even in an objectively low-stress situation; feeling that one is performing well can redeem a high-stress situation.

Family and Professional Responsibilities

In planning, explore ways of easing family concerns. The hospital should encourage employees, especially those with children, dependent parents, or pets, to make concrete plans for their care in the event of an emergency or quarantine. What happens if school is released early? If neighborhoods are quarantined? Talking with their families and making written arrangements may help individuals come to terms with these issues and become more comfortable with their answers.

Depending on circumstances and the community, the hospital may want to make contingency planning for forms of family support that could be activated in an emergency. These might include planning emergency daycare services; setting up a phone tree network to check on families; facilitating a family "buddy" system, or making contacts in community or faith-based organizations that could work with families.

The Institute of Medicine's Committee on Responding to the Psychological Consequences of Terrorism suggests that if many workers, especially nonprofessional employees, lack adequate insurance, the hospital may want to consider establishing an insurance fund that would supplement workers' compensation coverage for those who get sick or die because of a bioterrorist event. The committee report also suggests that the military can be a model for providing services to families while soldiers are deployed.[2]

In addition, the hospital, in consultation with staff and their representatives, would be wise to formulate or reaffirm a policy that clarifies the responsibilities of staff to work despite personal risk and that outlines any exceptions. It is a measure of the difficulty of this question that a working group of bioethicists and others, formed to look at ethical questions after the 2003 SARS outbreak in Toronto, was unable to reach a consensus on this issue.[32]

Resilience and Coping

Before there is a crisis, the hospital should consider what it can do to strengthen the baseline mental health, coping skills, and community ties of its staff. This might include offering education or support groups on self-care, coping, relaxation techniques, and smoking cessation, or providing accessible and comfortable areas where employees can relax and talk. Activities that allow employees to build personal relationships with colleagues in their own and other areas of the hospital may be helpful.

Staff can also be encouraged to develop a "buddy" system with a coworker or to work in teams to provide mutual support.[33]

Measures To Take During the Event

There seems to be a consensus that during and immediately after a traumatic event, the most appropriate psychosocial intervention is "psychological first aid" — nontherapeutic measures aimed at providing emotional and practical support.[20,34,35] The goal is to bolster individuals' natural resilience, to assure them that their reactions are normal, appropriate, and temporary.

Prompt and Accurate Communication

During the event, accurate and honest risk communication and sharing of information are crucial. Personal protection and infection-control training needs to be reinforced. Employees' concerns need to be investigated and addressed quickly, not only for the peace of mind of employees but also for the proper functioning of the hospital and optimal provision of care. Accurate communication should include encouragement and praise, both directly from hospital leaders and through the sharing of supportive messages from patients or others.

During the 2003 SARS outbreak in Toronto, several hospitals relied heavily on daily e-mail communication with staff in the hospital and those quarantined at home. The daily e-mail can also be used to respond quickly to staff questions.[5,6] Giving employees access from home to hospital e-mail and intranets is desirable.

Countering Fatigue and Isolation

Supervisors should emphasize the importance of getting adequate sleep for proper professional and emotional functioning, especially if a state of emergency persists for days or weeks. Arrangements should be made to treat insomnia, if necessary.[5]

If possible, staffers should not work extremely long shifts with heavy patient loads for days on end. Breaks are needed, especially if staff are working in protective gear. Especially early in a crisis, when adrenaline and altruism may run high, workers may need to be given explicit permission, or even ordered, to stop working and take care of themselves.

To make reasonable workloads possible, hospital leaders may need to act early and effectively to get staff reinforcements committed from other hospitals or from public health agencies.

If possible, staff should be rotated through higher and lower stress assignments. Working in teams or as partners may be helpful.

If possible, there should be a comfortable place where staff can relax and talk during breaks. It should be equipped with phones and e-mail resources so staff can stay in touch with family and friends.

Leaders and managers of staff need to set an example of appropriate responses to stress.

Practical and Emotional Support

To the extent possible, the major elements of psychological first aid described in Chapter 5, Section "Psychological First Aid," should be provided for staff as well as patients.

As with patients, staff should be assisted, when possible, with practical problems, especially those that affect their ability to do a good job in an emergency. Adequate supplies and equipment need to be made readily available.

Mental health personnel should be present in the high-stress areas, offering formal and informal services, including empathetic listening for staff in an informal context and reminders about the range of normal reactions that may be common, such as anger, irritability, and insomnia. As with patients, psychological first aid should be presented as emotional and practical support rather than as psychotherapy, although psychotherapy should be available if needed.

Mental health personnel may want to consider offering voluntary "defusing" sessions, short sessions held as soon as a need is felt — after a hospital shift ends, for instance — at which affected individuals can discuss their feelings about what they have experienced and are given coping information.

Because employees may hesitate to discuss psychosocial problems at work, the hospital should arrange for an accessible confidential psychological service that can be contacted outside the workplace.[2]

After the Event

After the crisis, providers often are eager to get back to normal and move on. After a sense of normalcy has been regained, reflection about what occurred can help staff gain strength and confidence from their performance and a greater appreciation of their colleagues and the bonds between them.[36]

The hospital may want to consider holding psychological debriefing sessions for members of various departments as part of a comprehensive psychological care program. Debriefing, which has become widely used in Employee Assistance Programs, is generally thought of as one or several 2- to 4-hour small-group sessions with rescue workers or other people who have had similar experiences.[37,38] Led by a trained facilitator, participants are supposed to describe their experiences during the crisis, discuss their thoughts and feelings, and get advice about stress management and follow-up referrals, if necessary.

As described in Chapter 5, the efficacy and desirability of debriefing, especially when done one-on-one with direct victims, have been called into question, and there is a consensus that it should never be mandatory. Some studies indicated it had no effect on PTSD or suggested it had a counterproductive effect. Most of the studies that showed a counterproductive effect dealt with direct victims such as survivors of motor vehicle accidents, burns, and rape. One study involved peacekeepers in Bosnia, a group with some similarity to emergency or medical workers. In that study, the debriefed group had higher PTSD levels at 6 months but scored lower on anxiety, depression, and alcohol problems.[39]

Bisson and colleagues suggest although while one-time group or individual debriefing cannot be advocated to prevent development of PTSD, debriefing is well received by most people and may be useful for screening, education, and support, as part of a comprehensive management program. If psychological debriefing or any similar intervention is used, they say, providers should be experienced and well trained, and participants should be clinically assessed.[39]

The hospital should continue providing access to confidential off-premises psychiatric services for employees who may need them weeks or even months after the event. It should also consider setting up a system for long-term follow-up.

Hospital leaders should find a forum to give recognition and appreciation for the work that was done and the sacrifices made.

Once the event is over, consider holding a ceremony at which employees can express their grief, voice their appreciation, and affirm their bonds. If colleagues or patients were lost, this could take the form of a memorial, with families invited, and music, commentary, and prayer provided by employees or former patients, if they so desire. During the early years of the AIDS epidemic, when patient deaths were heartbreakingly frequent, collective memorial services held periodically in an urban hospital helped the hospital's AIDS staff honor their patients, affirm the value of their work, and form strong bonds that benefited patients for years to come.[40]

References

1. North, C.S. et al., Psychiatric disorders in rescue workers after the Oklahoma City bombing, *Am J Psychiatry*, 159, 857, 2002.
2. Committee on Responding to the Psychological Consequences of Terrorism, Institute of Medicine, Butler, A.S., Panzer, A.M., and Goldfrank, L.R., Eds., *Responding to the Psychological Consequences of Terrorism: A Public Health Strategy*, National Academies Press, Washington, D.C., 2003.
3. Schuster, M.A. et al., A national survey of stress reactions after the September 11, 2001 terrorist attacks, *NEJM*, 345, 1507, 2001.
4. Schlenger, W.E. et al., Psychological reactions to terrorist attacks; findings from the National Study of Americans' Reactions to September 11, *JAMA*, 288, 581, 2002.
5. Maunder, R. et al., The immediate psychological and occupational impact of the 2003 SARS outbreak in a teaching hospital, *CMAJ*, 168, 1245, 2003.
6. Loutfy M.R. et al., Hospital preparedness and SARS. *Emerg Infect Dis*, 10 [serial on the Internet], 2004.
7. National Advisory Committee on SARS and Public Health, Learning From SARS: Renewal of Public Health in Canada, 2003, chap. 2 and chap. 8.
8. Maunder, R., Stress, coping and lessons learned from the SARS outbreak, *Healthcare Q*, 6, 4, 2003.
9. Loutfy, M., personal communication, May 18, 2004.
10. Nickell, L.A. et al., Psychosocial effects of SARS on hospital staff: survey of a large tertiary care institution, *CMAJ*, 170, 793, 2004.
11. Schull, M.J. and Redelmeier, D.A., Infection control for the disinterested, *CMAJ*, 169, 122, 2003.
12. Altman, L.K., Behind the Mask, the Fear of SARS, *New York Times*, F1, June 24, 2003.
13. Cheung, C.M., My experience with SARS, *CMAJ*, 169, 1284, 2003.
14. Young, B.H. et al., *Disaster Mental Health Services: A Guidebook for Clinicians and Administrators*, National Center for PTSD, Washington, D.C., 2002, accessed May 4, 2004, at www.ncptsd.org//publications/disaster/index.html.
15. Silver, R.C. et al., Nationwide longitudinal study of psychological responses to September 11, *JAMA*, 288, 1235, 2002.
16. Jones, C., Providing psychological support for patients after critical illness, *Clin Intensive Care*, 5, 176, 1994.
17. Lacey, T.J. and Benedek, D.M., Terrorism and weapons of mass destruction: managing the behavioral reaction in primary care, *South Med J*, 96, 394, 2003.
18. DiGiovanni, C. Jr., Domestic terrorism with chemical or biological agents: psychiatric aspects, *Am J Psychiatry*, 156, 1500, 1999.

19. U.S. Department of Health and Human Services, Mental Health: A Report of the Surgeon General — Executive Summary, Rockville, MD: U.S. Department of Health and Human Services, Substance Abuse and Mental Health Services Administration, Center for Mental Health Services, National Institutes of Health, National Institute of Mental Health, 1999, chap. 2.
20. Shalev, A.Y., Treating survivors in the acute aftermath of traumatic events, in *Treating Trauma Survivors with PTSD: Bridging the Gap Between Intervention Research and Practice*, Yehuda, R., Ed., American Psychiatric Press, Washington, D.C., 2002, chap. 7.
21. Kessler, R.C., Posttraumatic stress disorder in the National Comorbidity Survey, *Arch Gen Psychiatry*, 52, 1048, 1995.
22. Tedstone, J.E. and Tarrier, N., Posttraumatic stress disorder following medical illness and treatment, *Clin Psychol Rev*, 23, 409, 2003.
23. Norris, F.H., Risk factors for adverse outcomes in natural and human-caused disasters: a review of the empirical literature, National Center for PTSD fact sheet, accessed May 15, 2004, from www.ncptsd.org/facts/disasters/fs_riskfactors.html.
24. Breslau, N. et al., Trauma and posttraumatic stress disorder in the community: The 1996 Detroit Area Survey of Trauma, *Arch Gen Psychiatry*, 55, 626, 1998.
25. Birmes, P. et al., The predictive power of peritraumatic dissociation and acute stress symptoms for posttraumatic stress symptoms: a three-month prospective study, *Am J Psychiatry*, 160, 1337, 2003.
26. North, C.S. et al., Psychiatric disorder among survivors of the Oklahoma City bombing, *JAMA*, 282, 755, 1999.
27. Ozer, E.J. et al., Predictors of posttraumatic stress disorder and symptoms in adults: a meta-analysis, *Psychol Bull*, 129, 52, 2003.
28. Breslau, N. et al., Previous exposure to trauma and PTSD effects of subsequent trauma: results from the Detroit Area Survey of Trauma, *Am J Psychiatry*, 156, 902, 1999.
29. Brewin, C.R., Andrews, B., and Valentine, J.D., Meta-analysis of risk factors for posttraumatic stress disorder in trauma-exposed adults, *J Consult Clin Psychol*, 68, 748, 2000.
30. Galea, S. et al., Psychological sequelae of the September 11 terrorist attacks in New York City, *NEJM*, 346, 982, 2002.
31. Basoglu, M. et al., Psychological preparedness for trauma as a protective factor in survivors of torture, *Psychol Med*, 27, 1421, 1997.
32. Singer, P.A. et al., Ethics and SARS: lessons from Toronto, *BMJ*, 327, 1342, 2003.
33. National Center for PTSD, Disaster Rescue and Response Workers, fact sheet, available at www.ncptsd.org/facts/disasters/fs_rescue_workers.html.
34. Litz, B.T. et al., Early intervention for trauma: current status and future directions, *Clin Psychol*, 9, 112, 2002.
35. National Institute of Mental Health et al., Mental Health and Mass Violence: Evidence-Based Early Psychological Intervention for Victims/Survivors of Mass Violence, a Workshop to Reach Consensus on Best Practices, NIH Publication No. 02-5138, U.S. Government Printing Office, Washington, D.C., 2002.
36. Butler, L.D. et al., Fostering resilience in response to terrorism: among primary care providers, fact sheet from the American Psychological Association Task Force on Resilience in Response to Terrorism, accessed May, 2004 from www.apa.org/psychologists/resilience.html.

37. Mitchell, J.T. and Everly, G.S., Jr., The scientific evidence for critical incident stress management, *JEMS*, 22, 86, 1997.
38. Everly, G.S., Jr. and Mitchell, J.T., The debriefing "controversy" and crisis intervention: a review of lexical and substantive issues, *Int J Emerg Ment Health*, 2, 211, 2000.
39. Bisson, J.L., McFarlane, A., and Rose, S., Psychological debriefing, National Center for PTSD fact sheet, accessed May 11, 2004, at www.ncptsd.org/facts/disasters/fs_debriefing_disaster.html.
40. Author's experience.

7 Communicating through the Media

INTRODUCTION

In preparedness planning for bioterrorism, it is essential for medical institutions to have a plan for dealing with the media and public communication. Yet, when health professionals and officials think about how they would deal with mass casualties — how they would find the necessary staff, space, equipment, medications, energy, and mental fortitude — it can be easy to shunt public communications to the end of the list, a nicety to be attended to when resources allow.

Not surprisingly, large-scale federal bioterrorism exercises, such as TOPOFF and TOPOFF 2, have tended to focus on decision making, paying relatively little attention to public communication. Participants in such drills typically include thousands of real medical workers, rescuers, and public officials, but few if any real journalists.[1,2] The Department of Homeland Security's after-action summary on TOPOFF 2 notes that many participants wanted "additional challenges in the area of public information" and suggests that future exercises should include "a more aggressive mock-media element with a more aggressive news-gathering function that includes mock-press conferences."[3]

Physicians, who might be expected to communicate with the public should bioterrorism occur, generally have little experience in dealing with the media. They typically are used to talking with patients one-to-one, and even in that familiar mode, many lack the skills, time, or inclination to communicate as effectively as possible.[4–7] Emergency planners sometimes view the media as sensationalistic fear-mongers whose desire to "get the story" knows no bounds and could spur panic.[2,8]

Still, there has been growing recognition that effective communication with the media and the public during a crisis can play an important part in containing and managing unusual outbreaks of disease, and that communication flaws can hinder those efforts and multiply the disruptive effects of terrorism.[8,9]

Jeffrey P. Koplan, director of the Centers for Disease Control and Prevention (CDC) during the 2001 anthrax occurrences, wrote:

> During the anthrax crisis as in no other, it became obvious that public communication had become in some sense fully as important as — if not more important than — the line duties of senior decision makers. If this lesson was not totally clear during those harrowing October days, it has become indelibly apparent in subsequent 'crises' involving mass preemptive vaccination for smallpox, West Nile virus outbreaks, and the recent eruption of SARS (Severe Acute Respiratory Syndrome).[10]

This chapter will look at ways to communicate effectively through the media.

Lessons of the Anthrax Crisis

In handling the anthrax attacks of 2001, health officials faced many difficulties and pressures that helped lead to important errors in communicating with the public. These errors included:

- Suggesting that the first case of inhalational anthrax in Florida might have been contracted naturally, perhaps by drinking from a stream, whereas medical personnel at the scene knew immediately that a natural origin was extremely unlikely[11]
- Having nonmedical officials, rather than the CDC, handle medical questions at initial news conferences[11,12]
- Announcing "facts" about anthrax, such as the expected mortality rate and the number of spores needed to cause infection, that turned out to be inaccurate, based as they were on the limited data available from past outbreaks and animal studies[11,12]
- Failing to quickly and clearly resolve or explain conflicting or confusing information on a number of topics, including the role of nasal swab testing, the need for prophylaxis, and the proper regimen for prophylaxis[13]
- Engaging in a distracting and confusing debate over whether the anthrax sent to Senator Thomas Daschle's office, which was finely powdered and easily aerosolized, could properly be described as weaponized[14]
- Offering reassurances to postal workers and to the public that anthrax spores would be unable to escape a sealed envelope. This turned out to be untrue, an error that has been blamed in part for the death of two postal workers in the Brentwood Mail Processing and Distribution Center in Washington, D.C.[15]
- Failing to adequately explain why potential exposures of workers were handled differently in the Brentwood postal facility and the Hart Senate Office Building,[16,17] and failing to respond convincingly to charges that the differences in treatment reflected racial and other social inequities[18]

Some of these errors — including the most serious, the inaccurate reassurances about postal workers' safety — reflect the lack of knowledge at the time. But their impact might have been lessened if federal officials had adhered to a common precept of risk communication: when scientific facts are unknown or uncertain, authorities should not over-reassure their audience. In this case, if federal health officials had felt unable to voice reassurance on that point, they might have been forced by public pressure to act more promptly to protect the Brentwood postal workers.

It is not surprising that authorities did not speak with a credible, consistent voice. According to a study of the medical and public health response to the anthrax attacks, many public health agencies were not prepared to meet the demands of the media, which they found burdensome and time consuming. Participants reported they had disputes over who should release information, they were afraid to speak in a fast-changing situation, and they lacked prepared materials, communication plans, and media skills. The federal media effort took weeks to achieve some level of effectiveness. The confused messages, according to this assessment, damaged government credibility and promoted "an increasingly aggressive media feeding frenzy."[13]

Efforts To Improve Communication

Since the 2001 anthrax attacks, emergency risk communication (ERC), sometimes called crisis and emergency risk communication (CERC), has increasingly emerged as a discipline in itself. According to the CDC, "Crisis and emergency risk communication is the attempt by science or public health professionals to provide information that allows an individual, stakeholders, or an entire community to make the best possible decisions about their well-being, under nearly impossible time constraints, and to communicate those decisions, while accepting the imperfect nature of their choices."[19] This communication approach builds on the well-established field of risk communication, which involves explaining and discussing risk and uncertainty, often in cases when environmental hazard or pollution is an issue. Principles of risk communication are explained in the later sections of this chapter.

Since 2001, the CDC has stepped up its efforts to improve communications by its own staff members and by others around the country who might be involved should biological terrorism occur. The CDC offers a program called ERC (Emergency Risk Communication) CDCynergy that includes training sessions for potential spokespeople, as well as training manuals and CDs, many available at the program's website, www.cdc.gov/cdcynergy/emergency.

Journalism institutes and programs, such as the Poynter Institute, Fred Friendly Seminars, and the Cantigny Conference Series, have begun to hold bioterrorism seminars, at which reporters, producers, editors, and news executives discuss issues of coverage with public health officials and emergency medical professionals or contemplate "what if" scenarios. The Radio and Television News Directors Foundation, with support from the Carnegie Foundation of New York, has published "A Journalist's Guide to Covering Bioterrorism."

In this chapter, we draw on some of these materials, as well as on first-hand knowledge from our many years of working as a hospital-based infectious disease specialist and a newspaper editor, respectively.

THE ROLE OF THE MEDIA

The terms "the media," "the press," and "journalism" are often used as if they were synonyms, but it is worth remembering that not all media outlets practice journalism. Journalism involves collecting information from varied and often competing sources; attempting to weigh its accuracy, importance, and relevance; trying to reconcile or at least acknowledge factual conflicts; preparing reports that aspire to be accurate, interesting, fair, and easily understood; and delivering the reports. These tasks may not always be performed fully or well, but they are the basic elements of journalism, just as taking a history, doing a physical examination, and running diagnostic tests are the basic elements of medical diagnosis.

In general, journalism is found in newspapers, magazines, broadcast television, and radio news programs. Nonjournalistic media include many radio and television talk shows; web logs or "blogs," journals posted by individuals or small groups on the Internet; e-mail lists; and many kinds of websites. The cable news networks offer a mix of journalism and nonjournalistic reporting, in which reporters and "experts," who are sometimes self-interested parties, sit around talking loosely. Nonjournalistic media often present opinion, speculation, rumor, or narrowly sourced information as though it were fact.

It is commonly said, by journalists and by their critics, that the standards of journalism have been eroded by the rise of the nonjournalistic media.[2,8] With round-the-clock instant reporting on cable television and the Internet in a fiercely profit-driven environment, some media outlets have engaged in excessive coverage, sensationalism, and careless reporting. Speed and brevity have become the premier values for many, and issues may be presented with cartoon-like simplicity and overheated language. Yet, with the exception of the events leading up to the impeachment of President Bill Clinton, most recent media excesses have involved matters that are not central to the life of the nation, such as unsolved crimes and bizarre or poignant behavior by celebrities or other individuals.

In times of national crisis, the media generally has moderated its tendency to hype the facts and has shown little inclination to adhere to its supposed adversarial role toward government. In part for that reason, the public's estimate of media patriotism, accuracy, and morality rose after 9/11.*

At times, the media has hastened to reassure, even when reassurances may be unrealistic, and has been slow to challenge official actions or statements that seem dubious on their face. Although reporters and outlets vary widely, the mainstream media generally respect expertise and authority, particularly in specialized fields like medicine, and in many cases, reporters see their job largely as reporting what experts say.

For instance, in reporting the first announcement of a case of inhalational anthrax in Florida in 2001, the media gave ample coverage to officials' statements that there was no evidence of terrorism, that it appeared to be an isolated case, and that it was not contagious. Also widely reported was an official's implausible statement implying that the patient might have contracted anthrax by drinking water from a stream, and others' speculation that naturally acquired cases may have occurred unnoticed for years before increased vigilance led to the reporting of the current case.[20–23]

Media Behavior in a Crisis

Based on the media's response to 9/11, to the anthrax attacks, and to recent outbreaks of SARS, West Nile virus, and other illnesses, the media response to a bioterrorist incident could be expected to have three predictable stages.

---

* According to polling by the Pew Research Center for the People and the Press, the percentage of respondents who said the news organizations "stand up for America" rose from 43% in early September 2001 to 69% in November 2001. Estimates of the media's accuracy and morality also rose, by lesser amounts. Pew Research Center for the People and the Press, "Terror Coverage Boosts News Media's Images," survey report, November 28, 2001; accessed at www.people-press.org/reports.

Trying To Find Out if Something Newsworthy Is Happening

If a pathogen were covertly released, the media might get wind of a problem at about the same time medical authorities do, before any official statement has been made. With many potential biological agents, initial symptoms might be difficult to distinguish from common illnesses, including flu. The media and public health officials might be simultaneously seeking answers to these questions:

- Are unusual or excess cases of illness occurring?
- If so, how many people are sick? Where are they? How many, if any, have died?
- What is causing the illness?
- Is the outbreak natural or intentional?
- If intentional, where and when was the pathogen released? Who is at risk? What should they do?

If it seemed possible or likely that an unusual and dangerous outbreak of disease was occurring, local media would act aggressively to find out more about it. Reporters would try to question a wide variety of sources that might have seen evidence of it, from local doctors and health officials to politicians, school and police officials, the CDC, acquaintances who happen to work in the local hospital, and perhaps even funeral directors. The reporters' calls would trigger speculation and spread concern, as the politicians and others tried to find out what was going on. Rumors would start to spread. Media outlets might send reporters to stand outside emergency department entrances and interview patients, families, and employees as they leave. This is the stage at which the media is often deemed to be sensationalistic and engaged in fear-mongering.

If the situation remained unclear, the questions for journalists would become: Is this a story? Do we have enough information to report it? How good are our sources? If something important is happening, we do not want to get beat on the story. But we do not want to go with a story and be wrong. If we do report it, how should we characterize it, and how big should we play the story?

While such questions were being asked by the traditional press, the story might well break in a less traditional forum, such as a web log, and quickly be picked up by the traditional media.

At some point during this process, local hospital officials would almost certainly be called by the media. In such a situation, it is best to answer questions honestly. For the hospital, the truth might be: "We have seen a higher than expected number of people with flulike symptoms. Although there is no reason to expect it is anything other than the flu, we have reported it to the state health department and they are investigating."

Or the truth might be: "We have seen more people this week than last with flu-like symptoms, but the numbers are within the range we typically see. Although there is no reason to think it is anything other than the flu, we are watching the situation closely and will call in the state health department (or other appropriate agency) if there is any sign it is anything other than normal flu."

Both these answers are likely to trigger many questions, which too can be answered honestly. Rather than emphasizing what is not known, it is better to emphasize the efforts that are being made to find the answers and to otherwise protect public health. It is important to communicate, if true, that the hospital is awake, alert, and oriented to the situation.

Even if everything is completely normal, it is appropriate and reassuring to address the questions seriously and to emphasize the ongoing vigilance that should be a part of the hospital's normal operations.

Of course, if the hospital has noted any unusual pattern of illness, the appropriate public health and municipal officials should be alerted first, before any statement is given to the media. These officials should also be told that the hospital has been called by reporters and intends to answer their questions. Depending on the circumstances, the officials may choose to make a statement or have a joint press conference. It is best to coordinate statements so as to reconcile any factual conflicts that may exist and present information consistently.

If there is evidence of a biological attack, an official press conference is almost certain to be held quickly. Communication experts agree that it is best if authorities can announce such news themselves, because once a story breaks in the media, it is difficult to correct errors or false impressions.[24]

Covering the Story

Once officials say they know or suspect a biological attack has occurred, the media can be expected to flood the story. The official statements will be extensively reported, with transcripts printed and video clips repeated nonstop on websites and television. The media will do many explanatory stories about the pathogen and its symptoms, and how illness can be prevented or treated. They will do many public service stories about who should go where for prophylaxis, which schools or businesses are open or closed, and how children's questions should be answered. These stories are likely to include maps, charts, and hotline numbers. They will do many heartrending "human interest" stories about individuals who have been infected; about residents who are terrified and want to leave town; and about heroic volunteers, rescue workers, and medical personnel. If there are deaths, they will memorialize the dead.

Such stories will be in addition to reports on the main news: what has happened, how many are how sick, what the public generally should do, who released the pathogen and how they are being hunted or dealt with, and how the authorities are reacting at all levels of government.

It is in this phase that the media is often said to be at their best.[25] Much of the public is eager for the information the media can provide, and the authorities are eager to use the media to disseminate information widely and quickly. However, after the obvious stories have been covered, some may feel that such blanket coverage is overkill and that its sheer volume heightens public concern to unnecessary levels.[26,27]

In this stage, if the hospital is located in an area where the outbreak is occurring, its communications are likely to be coordinated by federal and regional authorities, and its energies are likely to be consumed by the day-to-day demands of the crisis. In terms of communications, this may mean giving frequent updates about the number and kind of patients the hospital is seeing, their condition, and how the hospital is dealing with the situation. These updates might go directly to the media by a variety of means described in the later sections of this chapter, or to a regional crisis operations center that would handle media communication.

Outside the outbreak area, the media's main need will be for expert voices. Hospitals can use their resources to educate the press and the public by providing accurate background materials and access to knowledgeable sources who can give interviews for broadcast and print media.

Assessing Performance

If the episode is limited in time and casualties, as it was in the anthrax attacks, the third stage is likely to arrive quickly. In this stage, the media focuses on attempts to assess the handling of the crisis, focusing on the performance of public officials. Public and private agencies, as well as members of the public and academics, may try to lay blame for inadequacies and identify ways to do better in the future. The media may serve as a conduit for the criticisms and assessments by others, as well as point the finger directly.

In a worst-case scenario — a contagious pathogen that is resistant to treatment, with wide and ongoing dissemination by parties unknown – the operations of the media could be profoundly affected by casualties, absenteeism, travel restrictions, and economic dislocation. In such an unprecedented situation, it is impossible to predict how the media would react. But it seems plausible that nontraditional media, including e-mail networks and web logs, might become increasingly important.

How the Media Can Help

In planning for communications, it helps to understand the principal ways the media can be helpful to medical providers in a crisis, based on past performance.

Serving as an Early Warning System

At times, the media can uncover and disseminate information more quickly and more widely than any other sector of society. News crews commonly monitor emergency frequencies and often get to the scene of emergencies before most first responders. Their on-air and online reports can provide an early warning of the likely extent and nature of casualties.

When the Alfred P. Murrah Federal Building was attacked in 1995, continuous live coverage began 12 minutes after the bombing.[28] In the first minutes of the World Trade Center attack on September 11, 2001, when it was not clear whether the plane's collision with the north tower was accidental or intentional, a New York radio station broadcast accounts from witnesses who said the plane had headed straight for the building, without any apparent attempt to avoid hitting it.

It has been suggested that news personnel should be regarded as first responders and should receive appropriate training.[29,30] However, such a designation may be unsuitable in that journalists do not rescue victims or restore order; moreover, their role requires independence from government control. These distinctions may have been blurred, at least temporarily, by the practice of embedding reporters with U.S. troops during the 2003 war in Iraq. Still, it seems best to regard the media as first responders only in a metaphorical sense.

Providing a Backup Communications Network

In emergency situations, such as the 9/11 attacks, direct communication among emergency and medical workers typically is difficult or impossible, as both individuals and technology get overloaded past the point of failure. In this setting, television and radio stations' ability to broadcast can be a useful, if imperfect, way of sharing information among emergency workers.

Hours after the sarin attack in the Tokyo subway in 1995, doctors at St. Luke's Hospital, which received the most casualties from the attack, learned from watching television news reports that police had confirmed sarin as the toxic agent in the incident. The police did not inform the hospital directly.[31] Although St. Luke's physicians had suspected as much, based on information from medical personnel outside the hospital, and had begun to treat the most critically ill for sarin exposure, the confirmation led them to initiate treatment for those with moderate and mild symptoms.[32]

Similarly, in a study of the public health response to the 2001 anthrax attacks, which was plagued with communication problems, many participants said the media was the most consistent and timely source of information for physicians and public health practitioners.[13]

Serving as a Conduit for Official Information and Direction

In an intentional outbreak of a contagious disease, effective communication could become as much a lifesaving tool as vaccination or isolation by teaching and motivating the public to take actions that would help contain the outbreak. Who should go to the hospital? Who should stay home? Who needs to get vaccine or prophylaxis? Where can they get it and when? What symptoms should they watch for? How can transmission be prevented? Should children go to school? Would it not be best to just get out of town? Underlying these and a thousand other questions is the fundamental one that effective communication can help answer: Are the authorities doing everything possible to bring this under control and save lives, including mine?

Assuming that authorities are working hard to do the right thing, accurate information about their efforts, promptly and calmly presented by credible and knowledgeable people, can be expected to reassure at least some people that the authorities are doing all that can be done.[9] Research is lacking on how the credibility of public health sources affects the public's behavior.[33] But it seems reasonable to expect that prompt and accurate communication may decrease anxiety, thereby helping to reduce hospital visits and demands for treatment by unaffected people.[34]

Such demands by the "worried well" have been among the most taxing features of terrorist episodes and disease outbreaks. In a wide range of situations, including the Oklahoma City bombing, the Tokyo subway sarin attack, the 1993 Hanta virus outbreak in the Four Corners area, and the anthrax mail attacks of 2001, the bulk of the burden on medical resources has come from people who were not physically injured or sickened by the event. In the Tokyo sarin attack, for instance, of some 5500 people who swamped local hospitals, only 54 were critically or severely injured, and about 1000 had mild symptoms.[34]

Lifting some of this burden from hospitals would, in effect, multiply hospital staffing and space resources instantly and at relatively little cost. It could save lives by freeing resources for people who need them. Such people include patients whose illnesses are unrelated to the attack but whose care is likely to suffer if hospitals are swamped.

THE ROLE OF HOSPITALS IN CRISIS COMMUNICATION

If an intentional outbreak of a contagious disease were to occur, the need for early, effective, and sustained communication would be paramount. In such a case, federal officials would almost certainly coordinate and run the communications strategy, as they did during the anthrax attacks of 2001, with the participation of involved local medical and political personnel. Local health authorities might be called upon to limit independent contacts with the media.

In many cases, however, knowledgeable local medical authorities might be able to play useful roles in communicating with the media, with the public, and with local physicians who may not be well informed on bioterrorism topics. Local communication efforts might be especially helpful in localities that have not yet experienced an outbreak. In such places, federal communication resources may be scarce while public concern may be mounting.

Local hospitals' roles could involve:

- Explaining and elaborating on official announcements.
- Helping to channel fear in useful directions by explaining how members of the public can protect themselves, how the public or medical professionals can help through volunteer activities (if any), and how parents can explain the situation to children.
- Providing information about what the local hospital is doing to diagnose and treat patients or to prepare for possible patients. This might include explaining or defending the hospital's actions if they were to come under attack.
- Answering residents' and local physicians' questions about risk, symptoms, treatment, and prophylaxis.
- Receiving information about possible cases that may not have come to official attention.

- Debunking bogus cures, unnecessary protective measures, and unfounded rumors.
- Correcting factual errors if they appear in the local media.
- Providing background materials and educational information to the media to promote better coverage.

It is worth remembering that when hospital spokespeople communicate with the public through the media, they are also communicating with their own workers. A well-run communications program can help reassure workers who are not medical professionals that the hospital is doing what needs to be done. This, in turn, might help reduce the fears that could lead to widespread absenteeism among workers. The same materials that are prepared for the public can serve as educational tools for the nonprofessional staff within the hospital.

The Importance of Local Experts

In a crisis, the demands of the broadcast media, in particular, can be draining and distracting. Even when nothing new is known, round-the-clock coverage demands that something fill the void. In this setting, the media may turn to "experts" whose opinions are poorly founded or to human interest stories that center on fear and speculation. Local medical authorities can do a public service simply by filling up broadcast time that otherwise might be filled by less responsible or knowledgeable "talking heads." It may not be true that good information always drives out bad, but it can at least keep bad information from going unchallenged.

The participation of local experts may be particularly potent in that many people say they would turn to local physicians and local media for information in a crisis. Asked which information sources they would use if a bioterrorism event were suspected, respondents in a large national survey in 2002 chose "local television and radio," "own physician, health care professional, or HMO," and "local or state health department" as their top three choices.[35] The "own physician" response had been ranked No. 4 in the 2001 version of the survey, taken before September 11 and the anthrax attacks. That it rose to No. 2 may indicate that people's experiences during the 2001 attacks increased their faith in their own doctors, at least relative to other sources.[35]

In a separate 2001 survey, respondents were asked about sources they would trust a great deal in a bioterrorism event. If the event were national, the top choice was the director of the CDC, with 48%, followed by the U.S. Surgeon General with 44%. If the event were local, the top answer was "your own doctor," with 77%, compared to 66% for the next highest source, "director of your local fire department."[35]

Similarly, in a simulated episode of bioterrorism, a Rift Valley fever outbreak in a southern U.S. community, responders, their spouses, members of the media, and residents all expressed a preference for information from local sources, especially early in the outbreak[36] (Figure 7.1).

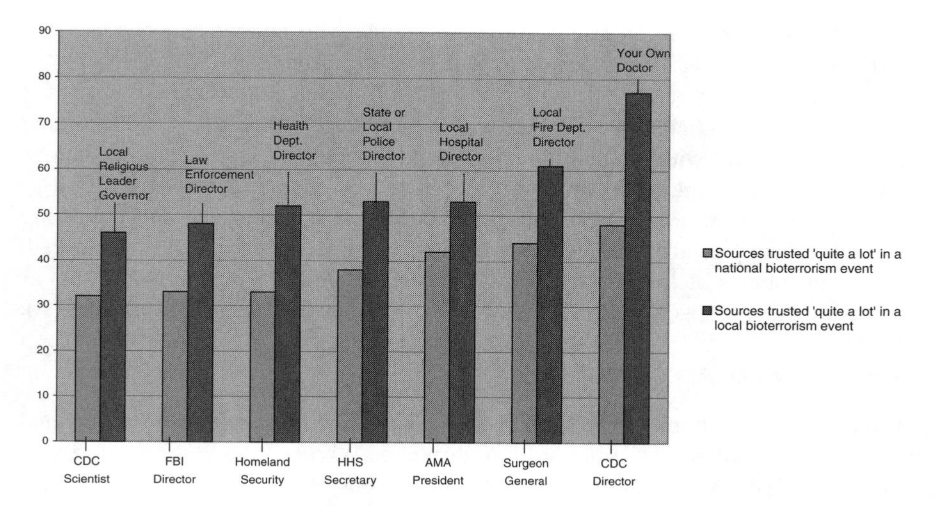

FIGURE 7.1 Trust in local vs. national sources. A survey of Americans done during the 2001 anthrax attack found local sources on bioterrorism were trusted more than national sources, with the highest level of trust reserved for "your own doctor." (From Pollard, W.E., Public perceptions of information sources concerning bioterrorism before and after anthrax attacks: an analysis of national survey data, *J Health Commun*, 8, 97, 2003.)

CREATING A CRISIS MEDIA PLAN

Most hospitals have a public communication plan or at least a set of traditional practices for dealing with the media in normal times. This may include rules on who may talk with the press, how public statements will be approved, and how patient confidentiality will be safeguarded. Many of these elements can remain useful in times of crisis, but others must be adjusted for abnormal circumstances. One major difference is in timing — the hospital may need to react much more quickly than usual; it may need to get out information earlier and later in the day than usual. Here are some major steps in planning for effective media communication in a crisis.

ASSIGN RESPONSIBILITY

Make it someone's job to plan for communications with press and public; do not let it become an afterthought. The planner should be an integral part of all preparedness activities. Hospital public relations or community relations officials could fill this role. If they are relatively low ranking or lack experience in dealing with the press in stressful circumstances — if their job consists largely of placing notices of meetings in the press and appearing at friendly community forums — the job might be better given to a more senior administrator. The planner need not be a physician.

Identify at least two potential spokespersons. In most cases, these should be physicians who have been involved in the planning process and who could be expected to play a major role in a crisis. The spokesperson might be, for instance, a senior infectious diseases specialist, the head of the emergency department, or the chief of medicine. It is important to choose people who neither fear nor hate the media, who have a calm demeanor, a clear style of speech, and who consider the role important. They should be willing to accommodate the press even when it is inconvenient. Potential spokespeople need to prepare for their roles by becoming and staying current with the literature, including federal and state recommendations to the public. Training in dealing with the press is available through the CDC, as noted earlier. At the least, spokespersons should train by preparing and practicing delivery of simple, accurate answers to the questions most likely to be asked. Suggested sources include Chapter 8 of this book (Frequently Asked Questions) as well as many of the websites listed in Chapter 13 (Internet Sources of Information).

Plan To Ensure Accuracy

Hospital planners should decide in advance how they will ensure the accuracy and appropriateness of the information they dispense. Who will have the authority to approve or issue statements or postings on the hospital website? The hospital's normal procedures may be too slow and time consuming to be useful in a crisis.

Hospital officials also should decide whether and how they want to prevent or limit comments to the media by staff members other than the spokespeople. It may be better to have one voice speaking for the institution, to prevent confusing or mixed messages, which tend to undermine credibility. In some situations, however, other staff members may make a valuable contribution without officially representing the institution. Whatever is decided, the policy should be known to all whom it affects.

Make Physical and Technical Arrangements

Make sure the communication operation is physically integrated into the hospital's disaster plan. Whether or not the hospital has set up an emergency operations center, there should be space and sufficient phone lines, e-mail connections, and wireless means of communication to deal with extremely high numbers of calls. In the TOPOFF 2 training exercise, which involved a simulated release of plague in Chicago, the phone system in at least one hospital was overwhelmed, and HAM radio operators were needed to help.

In a mass casualty situation, you may plan to use off-site facilities for the "worried well," family members, and others who do not need emergency medical care but might flock to the hospital. If there is likely to be a large media presence in your hospital, it may be better to locate facilities for them at the offsite locale, not in the hospital, as part of your efforts to reduce overload and chaos. In any case, they should be located away from the emergency department or other main receiving area, so patients and families are not forced to confront them, whether they want to or not.

Get To Know the Media

It is important to make contacts with the local media and compile up-to-date contact lists before an incident occurs. Like preexisting relationships with security and emergency officials, preexisting relationships with the media can save time and missteps later by fostering trust. Yet, making such contacts and keeping them up to date can be troublesome and time consuming because local reporters have high turnover and the internal organization of media outlets can be difficult to discern (occasionally, even to those who work in them).

In peaceful times, hospitals tend to deal with reporters who specialize in health topics or human interest features. In planning for bioterrorism, however, hospitals should try to make contact with high-level news executives at each local radio, television, and print outlet. These producers and editors play key roles in deciding what will be covered, who will cover it, and how it will be presented. In many cases, reporters, who deal firsthand with knowledgeable sources, may understand the story better and want to take a cautious or nuanced approach. But in a competitive business, editors and producers may pressure reporters to match or top the competition's coverage even if it is not well founded. Especially in a crisis, individual reporters may not know, let alone control, how their work is used. The final product may blend the work of many reporters, with seasoned police or political reporters in the lead roles and familiar health reporters in secondary roles. For these reasons, it is important to have direct relationships with editors and producers and to provide them with background and contextual information.

Members of the media who already deal with the hospital are a good source on how their newsroom is organized and which editors or producers should be approached.

In many cases, one or two news outlets or a few particularly talented reporters tend to shape coverage in a geographic area or media market. Their original stories are picked up and echoed by others, through wire services or directly, often without attribution. Experts counsel against playing favorites in the release of information in the early days of a crisis.[37] But it is worth expending extra time and effort to form working relationships with reporters, editors, and producers at influential outlets. Where they lead, others will follow.

In one large city, emergency operations personnel met with broadcast journalists regularly, four times a year, to keep them apprised of emergency plans. That helped them when an outbreak of West Nile virus occurred.[30]

Contact lists should include multiple ways of reaching recipients, including office and home phone, fax, and e-mail, as well as cell phones. Copies of the list and of any necessary software should be kept in several places, including at least one set held off-site. Periodically using these lists for the distribution of routine information will help keep them up to date.

Plan Ways To Distribute Information

Plan ways of communicating that are appropriate to your situation. The main methods available include the well-known techniques of public relations: in-person news conferences, telephone news conferences, fax and e-mail networks, and websites updated daily or better. Several of these methods are appropriate for communicating with local physicians as well as the media.

In the month after the first anthrax case was announced in October 2001, the CDC headquarters in Atlanta received an average of 900 press calls a week, with hundreds of others received by CDC staff in the field.[38] To handle this tide of queries, communications staff eventually developed several tools:

- A form was used in the field to provide daily updates of information the media wanted, such as numbers of patients. The daily updates were faxed to a large number of people.
- A telephone briefing with senior CDC scientists was held most days at noon, with reporters who called in from around the country. The transcript of each session was posted within hours on the CDC website.
- A cumulative question-and-answer list was compiled to serve as a record of the best available answers to questions asked by the media or other sources. Such a ready reference could prove especially useful in a continuing crisis, when many different hospital employees may have to deal with the media over time and many different reporters may be covering the story. It can help the institution maintain consistency, which fosters public confidence, and can help communications staffers explain necessary changes in policy or information.[38]

Although such measures may be excessive for a single hospital, a more modest form of regular daily communication may be helpful. In a crisis, reporters may be assigned to call health departments, hospitals, and other relevant institutions each day to check what is new. Releasing information at a set time each day can relieve the hospital staff of having to answer many of these calls, while satisfying the media's need for fresh information.

What if nothing is new? In a crisis, the fact that nothing new has happened — no new cases seen, no pathogenic sources identified — is often news in itself. A daily statement could also restate important points of information or advice. Framing the statement with fresh quotes or a different perspective can make it more likely to be used by the media. In such a case, however, the release should make it clear that the substance of the comments has been previously released. Failure to spell that out may not only be deceptive but may confuse reporters, leading to inaccurate and ominous stories about plans being "stepped up" or advice "shifting."

Releases can include direct quotes from individuals in written and audio versions, posted on the facility's website. An e-mail alert can let those on your e-mail list know the high points of the information being posted that day.

A daily statement — or any other comments — can also be distributed by fax. If the distribution list is large — for instance, if it includes local physicians — it may require a blast fax distribution, in which a document is faxed to a large number of recipients in a short period of time. Commercial "blast fax" companies exist to handle such distributions.

One state health department found that blast faxes were a better way to communicate with primary health care providers than e-mail or dedicated websites, because fax machines were used for normal business in nearly all their offices, whereas office e-mail might go unchecked. This health department used faxes to disseminate information after the anthrax attacks to primary care providers in hospitals and offices.[39]

Plan To Track the Media

During a crisis, it can be important to know what is being said in the media. The media sometimes reports information before official networks do. Media reports may shape patient concerns and generate specific questions that physicians should be prepared to answer; coverage may be inaccurate or distorted and need correction. Hospital communications staff should decide in advance which outlets or programs are important to monitor. The job might be divided among a wide range of staffers, with individuals asked to monitor, at least sporadically, a given TV station or a popular radio call-in show. Staffers need to know what kind of information they should report, how they should report it, and to whom.

Reach Non-English Speakers

Hospitals in areas where many residents are not fluent in English should plan ways to communicate adequately with this part of the public. Contact should be made with the foreign-language media, if any, and they should be included in all distributions of information. If educational forums for the media are conducted, as suggested in the following text, the foreign-language media should be included. If the foreign-language media are numerous, separate sessions for them might be warranted. During the 2003 SARS outbreak, which was focused in Asia, the New York City health department met separately with Chinese-American community leaders and the Chinese language press in New York to improve the dissemination of information.[40]

It would be highly desirable if at least one of the hospital's spokespeople were bilingual in the area's predominant non-English language, with enough fluency to do telephone and radio interviews. To the extent possible, documents being prepared in advance should be translated into the major languages spoken in the community. Arrangements should be made to secure translation services in the event of a crisis.

Practice during Peaceful Times

If the spokespeople are inexperienced with the press, it would be wise for them to practice. The hospital could seek to get media coverage of a related subject, such as its bioterrorism planning activities. It could offer its spokespeople to discuss flu vaccination in the fall or to comment on ways of containing SARS.

A more ambitious course would be to offer periodic educational forums for the local media on general bioterrorism topics or on specific issues, such as a pathogen that has been in the news recently. These updates could fill many functions, providing:

- Useful education for media people who might be involved in coverage.
- Incentives for the spokespeople to update their own knowledge and to prepare effective ways of discussing the issue.

- Incentives for the hospital to produce or gather useful materials for handouts. These materials could form the basis for flyers or website posting should a biological attack occur.
- An opportunity for hospital spokespeople and others to get to know media people who might be involved in coverage were an incident to occur.

Similar meetings could be held to educate local physicians, pharmacists, and other medical personnel.

Prepare Materials

Since 2001, a great deal of material suitable for the public has been prepared on anthrax and other possible biological agents. Some reliable sources are listed in Chapter 11. It may be worth preparing drafts of leaflets and of a web page that could be quickly revised if necessary and released in the event of a biological incident. Such materials could consist of basic information on various agents and on hospital procedures, with links to the CDC and Department of Homeland Security websites and to relevant local or state agencies.

Consider compiling lists of medical experts outside your institution to whom you could refer reporters if media demands became too taxing. Securing advance permission from these experts would, of course, be necessary.

APPLYING PRINCIPLES OF RISK COMMUNICATION

This chapter has focused largely on methods of communication. As for content, we favor the open approach advocated by experts in the field of risk communication. This discipline emphasizes understanding and addressing the public's concerns in an honest and empathetic way; acknowledging uncertainty, fear, and danger; emphasizing the steps that are being taken to deal with the problem; and imparting accurate information that allows the public to make informed decisions and reasonably anticipate what is to come.

Risk communication typically comes into play in public situations in which hazards exist or are suspected and decisions must be made amid uncertainty. But clinicians skilled in delivering serious diagnoses will find that many of its features are similar to those they employ every day with individual patients.

This discussion of risk communication draws largely on the writings of Vincent T. Covello and his colleagues at the Center for Risk Communications, and of Peter M. Sandman. These specialists in risk communication were contributors to the CDC's risk communications training program.

Trust and Reassurance

The need to establish or maintain trust is paramount. The qualities in a spokesperson or an institution that foster trust are openness, honesty, competence, empathy, dedication, and commitment.[41] Trust is undermined by unrealistic reassurance;

unwillingness to acknowledge danger, error, or suffering; and unwillingness to disclose information without good reason.

Inconsistency and conflicts among experts are also generally seen as eroding trust, especially if authorities make definitive-sounding pronouncements they later must withdraw or hedge.[41] In some cases, however, conflicts among experts may be intentionally aired without damaging trust if they are presented in the context of explaining scientific uncertainties to the public. Such public airing may give the public a more realistic appreciation of the difficulties in decision making that officials face.[18] Risk communication experts counsel that over-reassurance is among the most common failings of authorities in a crisis.[9,42] Sometimes this reflects flaws in the state of scientific knowledge. In the anthrax crisis of 2001, for instance, the CDC said that anthrax could not escape from sealed envelopes, a judgment that turned out to be wrong.[13,14] Sometimes, however, over-reassurance seems to reflect an almost automatic tendency to console and placate the public, bolstered by a fear of setting off panic. When the first case of inhalational anthrax was announced, for instance, some officials seemed to bend over backward to make it seem plausible that the case might be a natural occurrence.[20,22,43] Such over-reassurance may make health authorities seem dishonest or incompetent and may paradoxically increase fear,[42,44] possibly eroding the public's willingness to follow authorities' directions about self-protection, prophylaxis, and the like.

Sandman argues that a seesaw effect exists: If authorities are too reassuring, the public balances them by worrying. If authorities seem appropriately concerned, the public is reassured and its concern eases.[45] Sandman goes so far as to advise expressing reassuring information in a subordinate manner, as if the point were to express concern. He gives this example: "Even though we haven't seen a new case in 18 days, it is too soon to say we're out of the woods yet."[46]

When ricin was found on a letter-opening machine in a Senate mailroom in 2004, that was the tack taken by Dr. John Eisold, the Capitol physician. He was quoted as saying, "Although we have no evidence that anybody has received a significant exposure to make them sick at this 12-to-24-hour mark, we remain vigilant."[47]

One goal of effective risk communication is to demonstrate to the public that competent, dedicated people are doing what can be done to handle the situation. That is thought to be inherently reassuring.[9] Spokespeople should emphasize what is being done to meet the challenges that exist. In addition, by imparting information about what people can do, and warnings about what may happen in the future, such communication may restore some sense of control.

To communicate effectively in a crisis:

- Speak up early. You are better off setting the terms of a story than trying to correct it later.
- Do not over-reassure. Resist the temptation to say more than you know.
- Acknowledge uncertainty, but communicate that a process is underway to learn more, if true.
- Tell the public what steps, if any, they can take to protect themselves and their families or to help others.

- Give anticipatory guidance if you can, even if the information is grim. If deaths are likely to occur, they may be easier to accept if the public expects them and is mentally prepared.[44] Feelings of anxiety and uncertainty may be less troublesome if people have been warned they are likely to occur and have been given suggestions for dealing with them.
- Openly express sympathy, regret, grief, and loss, if appropriate. At one point on September 11, 2001, New York Mayor Rudolph W. Giuliani was asked about the number of casualties. Giuliani, who has been widely praised for his performance that day, lacked information but did not try to minimize the loss. Instead, he memorably expressed the common suffering, saying: "The number of casualties will be more than any of us can bear."[48]
- Know the main points you want to make, and repeat them. In a pressured situation, people often have difficulty absorbing information.
- In interviews, as in press releases, know what you want to communicate, rather than simply responding to questions. Do respond to questions, but if reporters do not ask the questions you want to answer, ask them yourself. (For instance: "You might be asking — how can I tell the difference between anthrax and the flu?")
- If you make an error or give erroneous information, correct the mistake as soon as possible and apologize for it.

Fear and Panic

Outrage Factors

Risk communication experts have identified aspects of a threat situation that tend to heighten public concern. These are often called "outrage factors." People are more likely to be concerned about a threat if it is:

- Involuntary
- Inequitably distributed
- Unfamiliar
- Controlled by others
- Mysterious or poorly understood
- Caused by humans, rather than nature
- Without any potential benefit
- Irrevocably harmful
- Harmful in a particularly dreadful way
- A cause of identifiable individual casualties, rather than overall increased risk
- A threat to oneself, family, or friends, directly and personally[41,49]

These factors help account for situations in which the public and the media appear to be more anxious about unproven or extremely rare health risks than about well-established hazards that kill thousands of Americans each year, such as smoking or influenza.

Medical professionals may tend to characterize such heightened concerns as irrational and attempt to dismiss them by pointing out that far more Americans die each year of heart disease or cancer than are killed by the potential hazard of the moment. But such arguments are often perceived as condescending and unconvincing.[50] Moreover, they may be irrational themselves, in that they seem to imply that only the most lethal hazard should merit concern or trigger preventative action.

To be trusted as a spokesperson, it helps to acknowledge people's fears in a respectful way. This could be particularly important in a bioterrorist incident, when many of the outrage factors might come into play. A spokesperson who speaks slightingly of those fears or who fails to acknowledge the gravity of any loss of life, even a single death, is not well-suited to winning public trust.

Panic

Officials often talk of the need to prevent panic, sometimes implying that talking openly about a biological hazard will spur this phenomenon. But the likelihood of panic may be exaggerated.[9,42]

During the terrorist attacks of 9/11, panic was not evident. Under the most difficult circumstances, thousands of people evacuated the World Trade Center in an orderly fashion, with many instances of individuals helping others rather than getting out as quickly as possible, including two men who carried a woman in a wheelchair down 68 flights to safety.[51,52] Soon afterward, volunteers in large numbers turned out to help in appropriate ways, even when it still seemed possible that more acts of terrorism might follow.[9]

During the anthrax attacks the following month, many people called the police or went to emergency departments with a wide array of harmless white powders, and thousands got prescriptions for ciprofloxacin against official recommendations.[53] These behaviors caused difficulties for police and medical personnel and were sometimes characterized as panic in newspaper stories. Yet, reporting suspicious powders was a step that authorities had asked the public to take. And the quest for antibiotics, although contrary to public health recommendations, was neither irrational nor pursued in extreme ways, as far as was reported.[42] Surveys done in November and December 2001 by the Harvard School of Public Health found that most Americans thought there was little risk they would get anthrax and most were taking few, if any, precautions.[54,55]

More than 2 years later, in 2004, a letter containing ricin was found in a Senate mail room, and it was revealed that ricin had been mailed to the White House a few months earlier. The public and media response was subdued, bordering on blasé. In part, that may reflect differences between ricin, a little-known poison that would be difficult to distribute widely, and anthrax, which had been widely discussed as a possible terrorist agent for years before 2001. It may also reflect the fact that the ricin caused no illness, as far as is known. But it also seemed to reflect post-anthrax public acceptance. The idea of a biologically based hazard sent through the mail was no longer new or shocking, and it was easy to assume that harm, if any, would be limited, as it had been in the anthrax event.[56]

Fear, false alarms, and a surge of "worried well" would seem to be inevitable features in most bioterrorist attacks. Medical and other authorities need to prepare for these phenomena, but fear of provoking them should not prevent honest, though measured, communication with the public.

SELECTED MEDIA ISSUES

As in any field, some members of the media are more trustworthy, intelligent, well-informed, and hardworking than others. No one likes a lazy, careless reporter, of course, but sometimes the best reporters can be the most troublesome, asking hard questions, finding sources who dispute the hospital's assertions, and declining to write the story officials may have in mind. With reporters of all kinds, certain issues and areas of confusion commonly arise in dealings with medical personnel. Here are some guidelines for productive dealings with the media.

MEET THE MEDIA'S TECHNICAL NEEDS

To get the most out of your dealings with the media, it pays to accommodate their technical needs:

- Return phone calls quickly. If you cannot answer the reporter's questions, explain briefly why. If you are not the appropriate person to comment, try to refer them to the right source. Try to avoid a curt "no comment."
- Try to work within their deadlines. For broadcast media, this may mean getting information out before dawn and late in the evening. Today, even newspapers may have round-the-clock deadlines if they have active news websites. Such websites may function much like wire services, and stories posted there may be picked up by other media before they ever appear on paper.
- If you are releasing information, provide written or taped versions of your most important points, ideally with direct quotes that can be used.
- Practice speaking briefly and directly, in "sound bites" that use language easily understood by the public. Specific suggestions on such language appear in the later sections of this chapter.

STICK TO WHAT YOU KNOW

You should not allow yourself to be pushed further than you want to go when it comes to content. With the media, as with the public, it is best not to go beyond what you know for sure. One veteran editor likes to say there are things you know, and then there are things you know well enough to put in the newspaper. If things are unclear or uncertain, it is best to state this plainly. Do not feel obliged to keep talking to fill up a silence during an interview.

If you disagree with the assumptions or tenor of a question, restate the question before answering it or else your answer may be interpreted as endorsing the thrust of the question. The question may be phrased judgmentally: "As the police are overwhelmed and unable to deal with all the suspicious substances being reported, what do you advise people to do if they see something suspicious?" If you answer that question, you may be cast as having said that the police were overwhelmed.

If information new to you is presented in a question, make it clear in your answer that you do not know if this information is true. Otherwise, your answer may be interpreted as confirmation. Do not go out on a limb and make sweeping statements based on information a reporter tells you. Better to check and get back to the reporter.

Resist pressure to be more definitive than you can be. If you do not know, you do not know, even if the question gets asked six times. One of the major ways that news stories err is by dropping out the qualifiers and hedging clauses (sometimes deemed "weasel words" by reporters) when they paraphrase a source's answer. If the qualifiers are an essential part of your answer, you must make that clear.

You can encourage accurate reporting by making your comments succinct, clear, and energetic, or at least nonbureaucratic, even when what you are saying is not definitive.

Be cautious, however, about using humor. In a grave situation, it can seem insensitive. Irony and sarcasm are particularly risky; they are easily mistaken for serious comment, especially when they appear in print.

Speaking "Off the Record"

In general, do not say anything you do not want to see in print or hear reported. Sometimes, for instance, as a reporter is packing up after an interview, a source will chat or joke, saying things he never would have said when the reporter's notebook or tape recorder were out. This chattiness may represent an attempt to seem friendly or simply an upwelling of relief that the interview is over. It could involve subjects, such as internal disputes, that have nothing to do with the subject of the interview. To the reporter, however, anything that is said is fair game even if the official interview is over.

If you do want to speak in private with a media representative, get specific agreement in advance as to how your comments will or will not be used. Saying something is "off the record" is not enough, because the phrase has no fixed meaning. Sources may think it means their statements cannot be used at all. But the reporter may think they can appear in print as long as they are not attributed to the source by name. Sources who want to speak privately should negotiate their terms in advance. They might specify exactly the kind of nameless attribution they want. For instance, "a medical source" is so general an attribution that it is unlikely to lead to identification. "A local physician involved in bioterrorism planning" is less blind. "A spokesperson at the local hospital" is almost certainly identifiable.

A source may get a reporter's agreement that the source's comments will not be reported, even without attribution. But if the information is interesting, the reporter probably will attempt to get the information from other sources and then use it. In the course of approaching other sources, reporters may reveal the original source's identity, if only inadvertently.

Any arrangement with a reporter should be made before the source comments. Retroactive requests for anonymity are favors; reporters may grant them, but generally do not feel obliged to do so. On the other hand, reporters who agree to a source's terms in advance generally do respect them. It is standard practice for reporters to refuse to reveal sources even under court order.[57,58] A few have gone to jail as a result, although authorities usually relent before that point.*

Speaking To Be Understood

In recent years, realization has grown that many Americans have difficulty understanding the language commonly used by medical professionals. As a result, increased effort has gone into making medical communication simpler, clearer, and more comprehensible to lay people.[59–61]

Studies have shown problems with both general literacy and health literacy, the latter being the ability to read and comprehend health-related material, such as instructions on taking medication. A 1992 federal survey estimated that about 21% of U.S. adults (more than 40 million people) had no more than a rudimentary reading ability, including 8 million who were completely illiterate.[62] In another study, done in an urban public hospital, more than 80% of patients aged 60 or older were deemed to have inadequate or marginal health literacy.[63] Several studies have linked low health literacy to poorer health in people with a chronic disease.[64,65]

Reporters can be assumed to be more health literate than the average American if only because most journalists are college educated. But except for health and science reporters, they can be expected to have no special knowledge of medicine, public health, epidemiology, or statistical concepts. Many reporters do not understand the idea of statistical significance and have only a shaky grasp of such a rudimentary mathematical tool as percentages.

Not surprisingly then, after anthrax was first reported in Florida, stories in major newspapers and wire services referred to it as a virus.[66–68] One story referred to it as both a virus and "bacterial spores."[69] Several newspapers, including the *New York Times*, quoted without demurral a U.S. attorney who announced that someone had "tested positive for presence of the virus."[70] It seems clear that the distinction between bacteria and viruses is not meaningful to many generally literate Americans.

Yet, at the time, the CDC's definition of anthrax in its website's Frequently Asked Questions (FAQ) was laden with technically sophisticated language: "*Bacillus anthracis*, the etiologic agent of anthrax, is a large, Gram-positive, nonmotile, spore-forming bacterial rod. The three virulence factors of *B. anthracis* are edema toxin, lethal toxin, and a capsular antigen ..."[71]

By 2004, the CDC's website FAQ definition had grown less technical, although it remained somewhat challenging: "Anthrax is an acute infectious disease caused by the spore-forming bacterium *B. anthracis*. Anthrax most commonly occurs in

* Among reporters who have been jailed for refusing to reveal a source are Bill Farr of the *Los Angeles Herald Examiner* in 1971, Paul William Corsetti of the *Boston Herald American* in 1982, and freelance writer Vanessa Leggett in 2001.

wild and domestic lower vertebrates (cattle, sheep, goats, camels, antelopes, and other herbivores), but it can also occur in humans when they are exposed to infected animals or to tissue from infected animals or when anthrax spores are used as a bioterrorist weapon ..."[72]

To be widely understood, especially at a time of stress, it is important to communicate clearly, simply, and nontechnically. This is true whether you are speaking directly to the public or indirectly, through the media. Advocates of such simple communication, sometimes called the "plain language" movement, advise simple measures like the following:[73]

- Use short sentences with simple structures. Avoid multiple clauses, especially at the start of sentences because they may obscure the subject of the sentence.
- Use short, common English words — "give" rather than "administer," "see" rather than "perceive" or "apprehend."
- Avoid use of medical or bureaucratic terms and abbreviations. If you must use them, define them immediately. Common medical terms, like "morbidity," "etiology," and "MI," are not meaningful to large numbers of Americans. Talking about "Title III money" or "HIPAA rules" makes you sound as if you do not care whether regular people can understand you.
- Before using an analogy, comparison, or anecdote, test it on lay people to make sure it conveys the desired message and nothing more.
- Avoid use of words that can have different meanings in medical and colloquial English. Phrases like "positive test results" or "progressive illness" can make bad news sound like good news. In normal English, patients go to a doctor with symptoms or problems; they do not "present with complaints."
- Use a term consistently, rather than switching among synonyms, and define it at the start. That's true even with a word as common as "children." Does that mean people under 18? Under 16? Under 13? Be specific.
- Use the active voice.
- State your main points early in the communication, and do not hesitate to repeat them, even several times.
- In written material, use large-enough type, wide-enough margins and line spacing, and frequent-enough headings to make reading easy.
- In written matter, use questions as headings when appropriate.

Correcting Media Errors

If you notice a substantive factual error in the media, especially in information about or from your institution, move quickly to correct it by calling an editor or producer, or the media outlet's ombudsman or "public editor," if there is one. (The ombudsman or public editor generally investigates readers' complaints.) If the error is in a newspaper, do not assume that nothing can be done until the next day's issue. The story may also have been posted on the newspaper's website, where it can be immediately corrected or removed.

In a bioterrorism event, media outlets may be so busy that getting through takes more time than you have. If you leave messages on voicemail, fax, or e-mail, explain the error in detail, and specify the corrective action you would like to see. Make it as easy as possible for the editor to comply.

Many newspapers routinely run corrections or clarifications; broadcast sources sometimes correct errors on the air, at least can avoid repeating the mistake, and can correct print archives. In our experience, the subjects of stories often do not report factual errors they notice. This is unfortunate in that the longer an error goes unchallenged, the harder it will be to get a correction, as the entire matter comes to seem irrelevant. Yet, the error will live on in electronic databases, often to be picked up and repeated months or years later.

In most cases, the media will consider a story wrong only if it is factually inaccurate. Sources and other involved parties, however, often perceive errors not of fact but of emphasis or interpretation. If you report a conceptual error, or allege that your comments were taken out of context, media outlets generally will not run a correction, but will suggest writing a letter to the editor. This is worth doing if the matter is important to you, as the letter will be electronically archived and is likely to be retrieved along with the background for future stories. In any case, it may be worth discussing your objections with a responsible editor or producer to try to avoid similar conceptual errors in the future.

In discussions of error, try to remain calm and polite. In the best of times, errors in the mainstream media are almost always unintentional, although they may reflect laziness or ignorance. During a bioterrorism crisis, news people, like medical professionals, are likely to be overworked and highly stressed. In this context, insults and accusations may be especially counterproductive.

REFERENCES

1. Ethiel, N., Ed., *Terrorism: Informing the Public*, Cantigny Conference Series report, McCormick Tribune Foundation, Chicago, 2002, 95.
2. Garrett, L., Understanding media's response to epidemics, *Public Health Reports*, 2, S87, 2001.
3. Department of Homeland Security, Top Officials (TOPOFF) Exercise Series: TOPOFF 2, After Action Summary Report for Public Release, 2003.
4. Frymoyer, J.W. and Frymoyer, N.P., Physician–patient communication: a lost art? *J Am Acad Orthoped Surg*, 10, 95, 2002.
5. Ferguson, W.J., and Candib, L.M., Culture, language, and the doctor–patient relationship, *Fam Med*, 34, 353, 2002.
6. Ravdin, P.M., Siminoff, I.A., and Harvey, J.A., Survey of breast cancer patients concerning their knowledge and expectations of adjuvant therapy, *J Clin Oncol*, 16, 515, 1998.
7. Braddock, C.H., III et al., How doctors and patients discuss routine clinical decisions, Informed decision making in the outpatient setting, *J Gen Intern Med*, 12, 339, 1997.
8. Smithson, A.E. and Levy, L.-A., Ataxia: The Chemical and Biological Terrorism Threat and the US Response, Henry L. Stimson Center Report No. 35, 2000, 274–6, 212.

9. Glass, T.A. and Schoch-Spana, M., Bioterrorism and the people: how to vaccinate a city against panic, *Clin Infect Dis*, 34, 217, 2002.
10. Koplan, J.P., Communication during public health emergencies, *J Health Commun*, 8, 144, 2003.
11. Altman, L.K. and Kolata, G., Anthrax Missteps Offer Guide To Fight Next Bioterror Battle, *New York Times*, 1A, January 6, 2002.
12. Hobbs, J. et al., Communicating health information to an alarmed public facing a threat such as a bioterrorist attack, *J Health Commun*, 9, 67, 2004.
13. Gursky, E., Inglesby, T.V., and O'Toole, T., Anthrax 2001: Observations on the medical and public health response, *Biosecur and Bioterror*, 1, 97, 2003.
14. Thompson, M.W., *The Killer Strain: Anthrax and a Government Exposed*, Harper-Collins, New York, 2003, chap. 9.
15. Thompson, M.W., *The Killer Strain: Anthrax and a Government Exposed*, Harper-Collins, New York, 2003, chap. 12.
16. Vanderford, M.L., Communication lessons learned in the emergency operations center during CDC's anthrax response: a commentary, *J Health Commun*, 8, 11, 2003.
17. Robinson, M.B., Public Health Experts Criticize Bush Administration over Early Anthrax Messages, *AP*, November 29, 2001.
18. Sandman, P., Dilemmas in emergency communication policy, chapter in Emergency Risk Communication CDCynergy, CD-ROM, 2003; accessed February 16, 2004, at www.cdc.gov/communication/emergency/features/Dilemmas.pdf.
19. CDC, Emergency and risk communication overview, at www.cdc.gov/cdcynergy/emergency.
20. Weiss, R., Florida Anthrax Case Not a Result of Terrorism, Officials Say, *Washington Post*, A15, October 5, 2001.
21. Susman, E., Investigators Hunt for Anthrax Cause in Florida, *UPI,* October 5, 2001.
22. Ricks, D., Anthrax Found in Florida Man but Case Is Called Isolated, *Newsday*, A24, October 5, 2001.
23. Avery, S., Anthrax Victim Visited NC; Bioterrorism Connection Uncertain, *News and Observer* (Raleigh, NC), A17, October 5, 2001.
24. Ethiel, N., Ed., *Terrorism: Informing the Public*, Cantigny Conference Series report, McCormick Tribune Foundation, Chicago, 2002, 158.
25. Sesno, F., Comments Made at Terrorism: A Fred Friendly Seminar, New York, 2004.
26. Tubbs, S., Friend or Foe: the News Media Under Siege, *St. Petersburg* (FL) *Times*, 1F, December 2, 2001.
27. Goodman, T., The Endless News Cycle of Fear; CNN, MSNBC, and Fox News Drop Other Stories to Dwell on Terrorism, *San Francisco Chronicle*, 48, November 25, 2001.
28. Alfred P. Murrah Federal Building Bombing, April 19, 1995: Final Report, Fire Protection Publications, Oklahoma State University, Stillwater, OK, 366, 1996, as cited in Smithson, A.E. and Levy, L.-A., Ataxia: The Chemical and Biological Terrorism Threat and the US Response, Henry L. Stimson Center Report No. 35, 2000, 274–6, 212.
29. Ethiel, N., Ed., *Terrorism: Informing the Public*, Cantigny Conference Series report, McCormick Tribune Foundation, Chicago, 2002, 174.
30. Hauer, J., comments made at Reporting on Terrorism: A Fred Friendly Seminar, New York, 2004.
31. Okumura, T. et al., The Tokyo subway sarin attack: disaster management, Part 2: hospital response, *Acad Emerg Med*, 5, 618, 1998.

32. Smithson, A.E. and Levy, L.-A., Ataxia: The Chemical and Biological Terrorism Threat and the US Response, Henry L. Stimson Center Report No. 35, 2000, 97.
33. Blendon, R.J. et al., Opinion surveys to track the public's response to a bioterrorist attack, *J Health Commun*, 8, 87, 2003.
34. Smithson, A.E. and Levy, L.-A., Ataxia: The Chemical and Biological Terrorism Threat and the US Response, Henry L. Stimson Center Report No. 35, 2000, chap. 3.
35. Pollard, W.E., Public perceptions of information sources concerning bioterrorism before and after anthrax attacks: an analysis of national survey data, *J Health Commun*, 8, 97, 2003.
36. DiGiovanni C. Jr. et al., Community reaction to bioterrorism: prospective study of simulated outbreak, *Emerg Infect Dis*, 9, 708, 2003.
37. CDC, Helping the media help you during a public crisis, Emergency and Risk Communication Training, feature excerpt 6, accessed February 16, 2004, at www.cdc.gov/communication/emergency/features/f006.htm.
38. Robinson, S.J. and Newstetter, W.C., Uncertain science and certain deadlines, *J Health Commun*, 8, 17, 2003.
39. Rhode Island Department of Health, Fax communication with primary care providers during public health emergencies, Best Practice Initiative, U.S. Department of Health and Human Services, accessed January 19, 2004, at www.phs.os.dhhs./ophs/Best Practice/RI.htm.
40. Virasami, B., Setting the Record Straight on SARS; Fearing Fallout from Media Coverage, Local Chinese Business and Health Officials Gather, *Newsday* (New York), A35, June 5, 2003.
41. Covello, V.T. et al., Risk communication, the West Nile virus epidemic, and bioterrorism: responding to the communication challenges posed by the intentional or unintentional release of a pathogen in an urban setting, *J Urban Health*, 78, 382, 2001.
42. Sandman, P.M., Beyond panic prevention: addressing emotion in emergency communication, chapter in CDCynergy Emergency Risk Communication, accessed at www.psandman.com.
43. Associated Press, Anthrax Scare: Florida Man 'Critically Ill' with Rare Inhaled Form of Deadly Disease; U.S. Officials Say No Evidence Points to Terrorism, *Houston Chronicle*, A4, October 5, 2001.
44. Schwartz, J., The Truth Hurts; Efforts to Calm the Nation's Fears Spin Out of Control, *New York Times*, A1, October 28, 2001.
45. Sandman, P.M., Anthrax, bioterrorism, and risk communication: guidelines for action, accessed January 15, 2004, at www.psandman.com/col/part1.htm, 5, 2001.
46. Sandman, P.M. and Lanard, J., Risk communication recommendations for infectious disease outbreaks, prepared for the World Health Organization SARS Scientific Research Advisory Committee, 2003, accessed January 15, 2004, at www.psandman.com/articles/who-srac.htm.
47. Johnston, D. and Hulse, C., Finding of Deadly Poison in Office Disrupts the Senate, *New York Times*, 1A, February 4, 2004.
48. Barry, D., Hospitals; Pictures of Medical Readiness, Waiting and Hoping for Survivors to Fill Their Wards, *New York Times*, A9, September 12, 2001.
49. Fischhoff, B. et al., *Acceptable Risk*, Cambridge University Press, Cambridge, MA, 1981, as cited in Agency for Toxic Substances and Disease Registry, A Primer on Health Communication Principles and Practices, accessed February 16, 2004, at www.atsdr.cdc.gov/HEC/primer.html.

50. Mullin, S., The anthrax attacks in New York City: the "Giuliani Press Conference Model" and other communication strategies that helped, *J Health Commun*, 8, 15, 2003.
51. NY men honored for September 11 heroism, *AP*, October 29, 2001.
52. Murphy, D.E. and Levy, C.J., The Evacuation That Kept a Horrible Toll from Climbing Higher, *New York Times*, B10, September 21, 2001.
53. Ricks, D., 32,000 NYers Were Prescribed Cipro; Survey: Anthrax Fears Spurred 600% Rise, *Newsday*, A8, December 13, 2001.
54. Harvard School of Public Health, Survey Shows Americans Not Panicking over Anthrax, but Starting To Take Steps To Protect Themselves Against Possible Bioterrorist Attacks, press release, November 8, 2001.
55. Harvard School of Public Health, Survey Shows Anthrax Incidents Have Impact on People's Worries and Behaviors in Three Cities Where Bioterrorism Reported, press release, December 17, 2001.
56. Reel, M., For Many on Hill, It's Wait and See; This Time Around, Fear More Contained, *Washington Post*, B1, February 4, 2004.
57. Liptak, A., Leaks and the Courts: There's Law, but Little Order, *New York Times*, Section 4, Page 33, October 5, 2003.
58. AP Reporter Declines to Reveal Sources for Wen Ho Lee Stories, *AP*, January 7, 2004.
59. Rudd, R.E., Comings, J.P., and Hyde, J.N., Leave no one behind: improving health and risk communication through attention to literacy, *J Health Commun*, 8, 104, 2003.
60. Parker, R.M. and Gazmararian, J.A., Health literacy: essential for health communication, *J Health Commun*, 8, 116, 2003.
61. Center for Health Care Strategies, Inc., Resources for Health Literacy Information and Publication, fact sheet accessed January 16, 2004, at www.chcs.org/resource/hl.html.
62. National Assessment of Adult Literacy, Overview of 1992 results, accessed January 16, 2004, at www.nces.ed.gov/naal/resources/92results.asp.
63. Williams, M.V., Inadequate functional health literacy among patients at two public hospitals, *JAMA*, 274, 1677, 1995.
64. Schillinger, D. et al., Association of health literacy with diabetes outcomes, *JAMA*, 288, 475, 2002.
65. Kalichman, S.C. and Rompa, D., Functional health literacy is associated with health status and health-related knowledge in people living with HIV-AIDS, *J Acquired Immune Defic Syndr*, 25, 337, 2000.
66. Kidwell, D., Garcia, M., and Lebowitz, L., Anthrax Case May Be Linked to Iowa Strain from 1950s; Match Would Confirm Virus Was No Accident; 770 Await Test Results, Knight Ridder, *Charlotte Observer* (NC), 1A, October 10, 2001.
67. Gribbin, A. and Seper, J., Anthrax Cases Spur FBI Probe, Concern, *Washington Times*, A1, October 9, 2001.
68. Dowd, M., Where Are You, Mrs. Miniver? *New York Times*, A19, October 10, 2001.
69. Langford, T., Anthrax Found in 2nd Man in Florida; FBI Investigating, but Experts Say Public Health Risk Is Small, *Dallas Morning News*, 1A, October 9, 2001.
70. Canedy, D. and Yardley, J., Florida Inquiry Finds Anthrax in Third Person, *New York Times*, A1, October 11, 2001.
71. As quoted in Zarcadoolas, C., Pleasant, A., and Greer, D.S., Elaborating a definition of health literacy: a commentary, in *J Health Commun*, 8, 119, 2003.

72. CDC, Frequently Asked questions (FAQ) on Anthrax, accessed January 17, 2004, at www.bt.cdc.gov/agent/anthrax/faq/index.asp.
73. The Plain Language Action & Information Network, Writing user-friendly documents, accessed January 16, 2004, at www.plainlanguage.gov.

8 Frequently Asked Questions

INTRODUCTION

Since the anthrax attacks of 2001, a large number of questions have been raised by the medical and public health communities, governmental officials, unions representing health care workers, the postal service, representatives of "first responders" such as police and fire department personnel, and emergency medical personnel regarding preparations for potential future attacks. In addition, the news media and the public have sought answers to many of the same questions. In this chapter, we have identified what we believe to be the central frequently asked questions regarding bioterrorism and have attempted to provide answers as well as direction in obtaining further information. The critical question "How likely is a bioterrorism attack" remains largely unanswerable. The probability of an attack, if calculable, would dictate much more precisely the most productive steps to be taken to minimize casualties and respond effectively. At present, however, the answers to the following frequently asked questions must represent "best guess" responses based on previous experience, exercises and drills that have been conducted, and common sense. We have divided this chapter into questions that any member of the public might have to assist in guiding health care providers in answering them. In addition, we have included questions of particular relevance to health care workers themselves, the primary intended readership of this book.

In the answers to these questions we recapitulate information found elsewhere in this book for the convenience of the reader. Where appropriate, we have included references to other chapters in this book in which additional information can be found relevant to each question.

QUESTIONS OF CONCERN TO THE PUBLIC, INCLUDING HEALTH CARE WORKERS

How Likely Is a Bioterrorism Attack?

The answer to this question is unknown and undoubtedly changes with time in ways that even the most effective intelligence apparatus may not detect. As is summarized in several chapters of this book, particularly Chapter 1, agents of biological warfare have been developed by numerous governments over the past century. The potential for mass casualties has been demonstrated in mathematical models of various modes of release of infectious agents. Large-scale drills and exercises have indicated that biological attack remains a potentially effective means of terrorism. The future undoubtedly will bring genetically engineered organisms that might prove to be effective as weapons of mass destruction. Nonetheless, despite these obvious concerns, neither governments nor traditional terrorist organizations have employed biological agents in large-scale attacks since World War II till the time of this writing.

As the new century unfolds, the place of bioterrorism may become clearer. The failure, at this point, to identify biological weapons stocks in Iraq represents a compelling example of how the perception of risk and the presence of an imminent threat may diverge at times. For now, it must be considered, along with other forms of terrorism, as a possibility that requires a unique form of planning.

What Are the Most Likely Agents To Be Used in an Attack?

Speculation about potential agents of biological attack has centered on those organisms considered Category A agents by the U.S. Centers for Disease Control and Prevention (CDC). These are *Bacillus anthracis*, the cause of anthrax; variola virus (smallpox); *Yersinia pestis* (plague); *Franciscella tularensis* (tularemia); the toxin of *Clostridium botulinum* (botulism); and various hemorrhagic fever viruses, including Ebola, dengue, and eight others. These agents have received the most attention for a variety of reasons. All can cause either high rates of mortality or morbidity. Some have been developed for or actually used in biological warfare, and most may be relatively easily transmitted. Unfortunately, however, many other organisms could potentially be used in an attack (see Chapter 9 and Chapter 10), and fears exist that some of the Category A agents could be genetically altered and thereby rendered less amenable to therapy or prevention.

The most feared agents are those that cause infection by means of the respiratory tract (e.g., anthrax, smallpox, plague) and could thus infect large numbers of victims through airborne dissemination. However, foodborne pathogens, such as salmonella or botulism toxin, also carry this potential. (See Chapter 9 and Chapter 10)

Why Are These Considered Likely?

The previously mentioned biological agents are considered to be the likeliest to be effectively weaponized at this time because they are known or suspected of being available and could potentially cause large numbers of casualties. Effective vaccination is currently available only for smallpox, and the vast majority of civilians have little or no immunity to any of the agents. (See Chapter 9, Chapter 10, Appendix A, and Appendix B)

How Can I Best Protect Myself and My Family?

Should I Own a Gas Mask or Other Type of Personal Protective Equipment?

Privately owned personal protective equipment (PPE) such as gas masks, mask respirators, and surgical masks would be unlikely to offer any advantage in a biological attack. Health care workers and first responders with such equipment are aware that proper use requires training and practice. Improper use could result in a false assumption of protection against a highly contagious pathogen even if one were known to be present in the immediate environment. Perhaps a larger issue in this area is the fact that infection by one of the airborne agents likely to be used in a biological attack requires sustained exposure at close range to an infected individual if the agent is highly contagious (plague, smallpox) or exposure to an airborne (presumably, initially undetected) release over a community. In each of these scenarios, it is highly unlikely that an individual would realize that exposure was occurring and could use such protective equipment effectively to prevent contagion.

Should I Designate a "Safe Room" in My House?

The effectiveness of a safe room seems questionable. If the intent of such a room is to prevent the entry of airborne pathogens during an aerosol attack over a community, it should be recognized that minute amounts of certain pathogens (anthrax, plague, bacillus) or toxins (botulinum) can cause devastating disease. Such a room, therefore, would require an independent, clean air supply to be used for any sustained period and would have to be essentially airtight otherwise. Leaving aside the cost of creating such a room, and the fact that apartment dwellers might encounter additional difficulties in establishing one, it is unlikely that household members would be aware of an airborne attack in time to make use of it.

The potentially false sense of security created by the establishment of a safe room could, conceivably, increase the level of risk. Evacuation of an area or relocation to a predetermined facility designated by public safety authorities may represent a more sensible strategy in many, if not most, types of attacks. In other circumstances, simply remaining indoors, without an elaborate safe room, may be preferable.

What General Supplies Would Be Appropriate for Me To Keep at Home?

Despite the dubious effectiveness of a safe room, establishing a single location within a home where typical emergency equipment can be easily located seems sensible. The equipment should include flashlights, radio, fresh batteries and, perhaps, a first aid kit, drinking water, and easily stored foods. This type of supply room (or closet or cabinet) would be of potential use in the event that "home quarantine" was recommended by public health authorities (see Box 8-1).

Under What Circumstances Might Quarantine Be Imposed?

If a highly contagious agent such as smallpox virus or the plague bacillus were used in an attack, human-to-human spread of infection would cause significant "second wave" casualties. Household contacts of known cases of diseases such as this might be asked to remain at home and be monitored by telephone for early symptoms of infection. If symptoms developed, they could then be transported to designated

BOX 8.1
Federal Readiness Advice to the Public

For general emergency preparedness, not specifically bioterrorism, the Department of Homeland Security recommends that members of the public stock:

At least one gallon of water per person per day for at least 3 days

At least a 3-day supply of nonperishable foods that require no cooking or water, such as canned food, protein bars, dry cereal, peanut butter, canned juice

Supplies for infants, as needed

Battery-powered radio and extra batteries

Flashlight and extra batteries

Whistle

Dust mask to help filter air

Moist towelettes

Wrench or pliers to turn off utilities

Plastic sheeting and duct tape to shelter-in-place

Garbage bags and ties for personal sanitation

A first aid kit, which should include:

- Two pairs of sterile gloves
- Sterile dressings
- Cleansing agent
- Antibiotic ointment
- Burn ointment
- Eyewash solution
- Thermometer
- Prescription medications, as needed
- Prescribed medical supplies, such as glucose monitoring equipment, as needed

The kit may also include cell phone, scissors, tweezers, petroleum jelly or other lubricant, potassium iodide (in case of radiation release), aspirin or non-aspirin pain reliever, antidiarrhea medication, antacid, syrup of ipecac, laxative, and activated charcoal.

Source: www.ready.gov.

hospital emergency rooms. Obviously, plans such as this would vary according to local public health authorities' policies. In even more extraordinary circumstances, areas of a city or other geographical region in which cases of a contagious agent have been diagnosed might be subject to quarantine rules under which travel into or out of the area is restricted. (See Chapter 2)

Under What Circumstances Might Travel Restrictions Be Imposed?

Travel restrictions would very likely be advisable if a locality reported an attack with a highly contagious agent such as smallpox virus or plague bacillus. In several federally run exercises, most notably TOPOFF 1, the late imposition of travel restrictions barring out-of-state travel after a mock plague release led to widespread dissemination of infection to other states and internationally. The legal authority to impose travel restrictions was unclear in that and several other exercises and would most likely vary from state to state. Despite such complexities and the obvious inconvenience and potential chaos that would accompany travel restrictions, such measures could represent one vital component of an effective response to a biological attack. The daunting practical obstacles to the institution of effective travel restrictions are discussed elsewhere in this book. (See Chapter 2)

What Is the Most Reliable Source of Information during an Attack?

The general public will be almost completely dependent on their usual sources of news information in the event of a bioterrorist attack (see Chapter 7). Hospitals and public health officials, as well as other governmental and emergency management personnel, will depend upon information received directly from sources such as the CDC and other national and local government agencies. For this reason, the potential for conflicting information as well as confusion among members of the public will be great. The impact on hospitals of public fears was seen dramatically after the attacks of 9/11 and the subsequent anthrax attacks. News agencies, print, broadcast, and the Internet scrambled to obtain accurate information from public health authorities and, often, from independent experts without direct knowledge of events and planning activities. Public affairs officers at hospitals in New York City were left scrambling for information to provide to their own hospital staffs, the press and a concerned public, and patient population. The degree of confusion was high. Regarding the anthrax attacks, efforts to reassure the public that the initial case in Florida was naturally acquired infection proved premature.

The CDC website (www.cdc.gov) has frequent updates regarding bioterrorism for both the professional and lay public and, in the event of an attack, represents the most dependable source of information. Local and state health department websites typically provide access to similar information and links to the CDC and other relevant governmental websites. Chatrooms and private websites are probably best avoided when accurate information and operational guidelines are sought. (See Chapter 13)

What Do the Various National Levels of Alert (the Colors) Mean and What Should My Family Do if the Alert Status Is Raised?

Following the attacks of 2001, the newly formed Department of Homeland Security developed a system to aid in publicizing the perceived level of threat of terrorist attack. This system, in which five levels of threat are described by color codes, is designed primarily to advise local, state, and national government agencies, as well as hospitals about general and specific measures to be enacted under various threat conditions. Nonetheless, when the national threat alert level is raised, as occurred during the Christmas and New Year's holidays of 2003–2004, news media attention is attracted and the public quickly becomes aware. Patients as well as health care workers may inquire as to the specific measures they should take to protect themselves and their families when the threat level is changed. Concerns have been expressed that announcements and reports of the threat level may serve more to confuse than to clarify these issues for the general public.

The threat levels as currently defined have the following implications (www.dhs.gov):

1. Low condition (Green): A low risk of terrorist attack exists. Federal departments and agencies should consider refining and exercising previously planned measures; continuing the training of appropriate personnel; and maintaining a system by which vulnerabilities can be assessed.
2. Guarded condition (Blue): A general risk of terrorist attack exists. In addition to the above measures, it is recommended that federal agencies consider checking communications with key emergency response and command facilities; reviewing and updating emergency response procedures; and providing the public with any information that may be helpful in preparing to respond appropriately to an attack.
3. Elevated condition (Yellow): A significant risk of terrorist attack exists. In addition to the above measures, it is recommended that federal departments and agencies consider increasing surveillance of critical locations; coordinating emergency plans among various jurisdictions; assessing the precise nature of the threat and refining protective plans accordingly, and implementing, as needed, contingency and emergency response plans.
4. High condition (Orange): A high risk of attack exists. In addition to the above, it is recommended that federal departments and agencies consider coordinating security efforts with state and local law enforcement, National Guard, and military organizations, as needed; canceling public events, changing their location, or taking additional security precautions at such events; preparing to execute contingency plans, including moving to alternate sites or dispersing their workforce, and restricting access to threatened facilities to essential personnel only.
5. Severe condition (Red): A severe risk of attack exists. Federal agencies and departments should consider increasing or redirecting personnel to critical emergency needs; assigning emergency response personnel and prepositioning and mobilizing specially trained teams or resources; monitoring, redirecting, or constraining transportation systems and closing public and government facilities.

At the time of this writing, the national alert level has remained at yellow except for brief periods at orange at the beginning of the Iraq war and during the 2003–2004 holiday season.

It is clear from this that threat level designations are intended to alert governmental agencies and suggest specific measures that they should take. No specific advice for the general public is included in these national guidelines.

Should I Discuss Bioterrorism with My Children? If So, How Should I Do This?

The answer to this question cannot be a generalization. Each family must decide whether to discuss the potential for terrorist attacks with their children, on the basis of their own ability to do so and their opinion as to the appropriateness of this topic for their children. However, some general advice can be provided to parents seeking an answer to these questions:

1. Children's fears of bioterrorism may be influenced and exaggerated by their exposure to television, radio, and other sources of information designed for adults.
2. The general level of concern about terrorist attacks at the present time has become, to varying degrees, the background music of our children's lives.
3. Children's fears generated by what they hear and read may be complex and extend to their own safety as well as that of their parents and other loved ones.
4. Anxiety about terrorism may underlie symptoms of depression in children, as it has been shown to, in some instances, in adults.
5. Children may think that bioterrorism attacks have occurred frequently.
6. The attitude of parents toward terrorism in general may influence their children's feelings in ways that are not necessarily obvious.
7. Young children might be unable to comprehend complex issues such as bioterrorism and react to any discussion with exaggerated anxiety or with confusion.

With these issues in mind, parents can feel free to communicate to their children certain undisputed facts that can serve to reassure them:

1. Attacks with biological agents have been extremely rare in modern times and almost all have occurred between opposing armies within war zones.
2. At the time of this writing, as far as has been determined, no biological attack on civilians in the U.S. has been successfully carried out by foreign governments or foreign terrorist organizations.
3. There are many individuals in our country who are carefully preparing to keep us all safe in the unlikely event of any future attack.
4. Schools are safe places to be.
5. There are certain dangers in the world that children must all be aware of (crossing the street, riding a bicycle without wearing a helmet, using a seat belt, and, for younger children, a car seat or booster seat, etc.). Because of the real risks of serious injuries resulting from carelessness

in these areas, it is much more important that children concentrate on them and let adult experts and their parents take care of risks such as bioterrorism. (See Chapter 11)

How Afraid Should I Be? How Can I Deal with My Fears?

Fear of bioterrorism is fear of the unknown. A public informed of the basic steps to be taken in the event of an attack would likely result in a more orderly response were such an attack to occur. Actual fear of an attack should be placed in the broader context of fear of death or injury from any cause. It should be reiterated, as is pointed out in Chapter 1 of this book, that the number of individuals in the U.S. who died of influenza and its complications in the month of October 2001 exceeded deaths in the anthrax attack by many hundredfold. Nonetheless, many individuals each year fail to receive the highly effective influenza vaccination. Similarly, automobile accidents, disproportionately associated with alcohol consumption, continue to claim tens of thousands of lives in the U.S. annually.

Assessing one's personal risk of becoming the victim of a biological or other terrorist attack is possible within certain broad parameters:

1. Statistically, the likelihood of being a victim of a biological attack is extremely small.
2. The risk is likely greater in certain locations. Terrorist groups have often targeted symbolic targets, such as government buildings, religious facilities, and, as in the case of the 9/11 attacks, financial institutions. Working or living near such facilities presumably increases the risk of being within the perimeter of a biological attack.
3. The risk may be dictated by occupation. Government officials, police, and fire department personnel as well as other first responders are at higher risk of exposure to an unknown agent of biological attack than members of the general public. As the anthrax attacks of 2001 illustrated, individuals associated with the government or with news outlets may be singled out as targets.
4. Specific activities, including travel to likely target areas in the U.S. and abroad, may raise the risk of becoming a victim.

What Changes in My Lifestyle Should I Consider?

A variety of recommendations can be found regarding lifestyle changes in anticipation of biological and other types of terrorist attacks. Most often, governmental officials have advised the public to go about their usual activities while maintaining increased vigilance for suspicious activity around them. The effectiveness and consequences of such general advice have not been established. Nonetheless, it is likely that an informed public is more likely to respond appropriately in the event of an actual attack. As has been demonstrated in national exercises such as TOPOFF and Dark Winter (see Chapter 2), measures that affect the entire population of a region, such as travel restrictions, may have to be communicated broadly and quickly in the event of an actual attack. For this reason, it is sensible to have access to the usual means of dissemination of information (e.g., radio, television) on a daily basis. In a more general sense, however, interested members of the public should consult reliable sources of information regarding terrorism prior to any attack so that advice given during an attack may be more easily understood. As noted, the websites of the CDC (www.cdc.gov) and the office of homeland security (www.dhs.gov) may be the most appropriate sources of such information. Numerous books addressed to the general public and providing appropriate background information on all forms of terrorism have also been published in recent years. (See Chapter 13)

What Has the Government Done since 9/11 To Protect U.S. Citizens from Biological Attack?

The federal government has provided additional funding to state and local governments to raise their abilities to respond to biological attack. This support has come in a variety of forms, including funding to enhance syndromic surveillance, upgrade public health laboratories, train key personnel, purchase personal protective equipment, and conduct drills and exercises. A number of such drills have been conducted on a national level following the 2001 attacks. In addition, the CDC and the Department of Homeland Security have provided educational materials for the general public as well as first responders and medical personnel. The national smallpox vaccination campaign initiated in 2003 was also a direct result of additional federal funding for bioterrorism preparedness. Research funding has also been provided from the federal government under a variety of initiatives in order to improve our general understanding of key potential agents of biological attack and to seek improved means of detecting, treating, and preventing diseases caused by these agents.

The federal government has also issued advice in a variety of areas related to terrorism (see Box 8.2). This advice has included, among other points, the following:

1. Families should establish a means of locating each member in the event of a terrorist attack. This may be accomplished by planning for every family member to contact an individual who does not live with the family by telephone. This contact individual can then take a "roll call" of family members and keep everyone informed as to the whereabouts of each individual. It has been suggested that, if feasible, an individual living in another area should be enlisted for this purpose.
2. Be suspicious of unexpected packages arriving through the mail.
3. Maintain a means of accessing public information announcements by radio, television, or the Internet. In a biological attack, the decision to leave one's residence or workplace or to remain would be largely dictated by public health and other civil authorities who would communicate such recommendations through these channels.
4. Advice regarding air travel safety, precautions to be taken while traveling abroad, when to consider establishing a safe room, and other practical matters may be found on various federal government websites, including some listed in Chapter 13 of this book.

BOX 8.2
Federal Bioterrorism Advice to the Public

In the event of a biological attack, the Department of Homeland Security advises the public to watch TV, listen to the radio, or check the Internet for official news including information about these issues:

- Are you in the group or area authorities consider in danger?
- What are the signs and symptoms of the disease?
- Are medications or vaccines being distributed?
- Where? Who should get them?
- Where should you seek emergency medical care if you become sick?

A potentially exposed person is advised to follow instructions of doctors and other public health officials, and be prepared to be kept away from others or even be quarantined.

People who get sick during a biological emergency should not assume that they should go to a hospital emergency room or that their illness is a result of the attack. If their symptoms match and they are in a group considered at high risk, the advice is to immediately seek medical attention.

Reference: www.ready.gov

What Have Local Governments Done?

As discussed in Chapter 2, the steps taken by local governments and health departments since the attacks of 2001 have varied widely. Some localities have placed great emphasis on educating both the medical community and the public regarding bioterrorism. In others, laboratory facilities have been upgraded to better respond to the sudden demands that would accompany an act of terrorism. Civilian smallpox vaccination campaigns have received emphasis in some areas. By and large, communication between public health agencies and particularly between the federal CDC and state and local authorities has been enhanced. (See Chapter 2)

To Whom Should I Express Any Concerns I Have about Bioterrorism?

Widespread concerns regarding all forms of terrorism have, of course, already triggered a broad public discussion. From the standpoint of an individual citizen, whether employed in health care or emergency response sectors or not, expressing specific concerns may be difficult. It is appropriate for parents to inquire about emergency preparations in place at their children's schools. Similarly, large employers likely have established procedures that may be readily accessible from company or union sources. Ultimately, it is important to remain informed about general preparedness for terrorism. Questions or concerns involving planning beyond the schools and the workplace should be addressed to local government officials. Public forums conducted by health departments and legislative representatives may serve to address specific questions and concerns.

How Can I Get Further Information?

As noted in the preceding text, there are many excellent sources of information regarding bioterrorism both for health care professionals and the general public. In Chapter 13 of this book, we have identified a number of reliable sources of information and indicated the intended audience as well as the nature of the information provided.

Besides the Anthrax Letters in 2001, What Other Bioterrorism Attacks Have Taken Place in the U.S. or Abroad?

Proven biological attacks have been extremely unusual. In various chapters of this book (especially Chapter 1 and Chapter 9), the historical pattern of biological warfare and of terrorism related to specific pathogens are discussed. Much insight into the actual circumstances that might prevail in an attack can be gained by reviewing the tabletop exercises presented in Section IV and the results of large-scale exercises and drills that have been conducted in recent years. Details of several major exercises can be found in Appendix C.

QUESTIONS SPECIFIC TO HEALTH CARE WORKERS

Hospital-based health care workers would be faced with challenges and concerns beyond those of the general public. In this section, answers to several anticipated questions are provided. These answers are intentionally general and somewhat generic because hospitals vary in specific procedures regarding emergency management and various types of hospital employees (trauma surgeons vs. infectious-diseases physicians; nurses in triage areas of the emergency room vs. nurses working on an obstetrical ward; mortuary workers vs. engineering personnel) would have markedly differing risks, questions, and concerns.

How Would Health Care Personnel Learn of an Attack?

Whether victims of a biological attack were seen in the worker's hospital or elsewhere, health care personnel on duty would most likely hear of an attack through the hospital's command structure and would rapidly gain additional information through radio and television reports.

What Would Be the Most Appropriate Course of Action for a Health Care Worker Who Is at Home When an Attack Is Announced?

A biological attack anywhere in the world may be the prelude to an attack affecting the service area of a particular hospital. For this reason, health care workers in all job categories should be aware of emergency call-in procedures in effect at their hospital and anticipate that they may be asked or required to report to supervisors in the event that an attack is detected. However, following the terrorist attacks on the World Trade Center in 2001, confusion was created by well-intentioned health care workers and first responders reporting to ground zero or nearby hospitals to offer their assistance. Disorganized staffing situations without clear command structures may exacerbate an already chaotic situation. For this reason, unless previously informed that they are required to report for duty in the event of an attack or specifically asked to report at the time of an attack, health care workers in most job categories should attempt to reach their supervisors prior to reporting for extra duty. For this reason, it is vitally important that hospital-based workers provide their supervisors with up-to-date contact information prior to any attack. (See Chapter 3)

What Strategies Have Been Suggested To Protect Health Care Workers in the Event of an Attack?

Efforts to protect hospital-based health care workers have focused on more extensive training in the use of personal protective equipment as well as national and local drills to determine potential areas of vulnerability. OSHA and CDC standards (see Chapter 3) that have been established for the containment of nosocomial infections are largely applicable to protection against the agents of bioterrorism. Complacency, however, may pose the greatest risk to health care workers. Because a biological attack is unlikely and hospitals and individual health care workers at all levels contend with much more common problems each day, familiarity with specific protective procedures to be used in such an attack may rapidly wane. For this reason, repeated exercises and drills as suggested at the federal level (see the preceding text) and as required by JCAHO (see Chapter 3) should be conducted to aid health care workers in maintaining an appropriate level of knowledge. The tabletop exercises included in this book are designed to be of use to health care workers in a variety of job categories and may form the basis of a repeated curriculum to be provided, in modified form as necessary, to help in accomplishing this. (See Chapter 3 and Section IV)

What Are the Earliest Signs of Each of the Category A Agents?

The pathogenesis, clinical and laboratory manifestations, epidemiology, and treatment of the following conditions are addressed in much greater detail in Chapter 9 and Chapter 10. However, the early signs of infection with the so-called Category A agents of bioterrorism are listed here for convenience to assist in answering questions of health care workers. (See Chapter 9 and Chapter 10)

Smallpox

Smallpox typically begins with a high fever and body aches — an illness indistinguishable from many common viral infections, particularly influenza. Within 2 to 3 days, the characteristic rash appears, including sores in the mouth and then rapidly progressive vesiculonodular lesions on the extremities. It is only at this stage, after the appearance of the characteristic rash, that smallpox would likely be recognized, unless other cases had already occurred in the setting of an attack. Because naturally occurring smallpox has not existed anywhere in the world since 1978, any case of smallpox would be regarded as an intentional attack and the beginning of an epidemic.

Anthrax

Anthrax occurs in three forms: cutaneous, pulmonary, and gastrointestinal. The most feared type and that most likely to be seen in a terrorist attack is pulmonary anthrax, although several cases of cutaneous infection were also seen during the 2001 attack. Although not as rare as smallpox, naturally occurring anthrax, particularly pulmonary infection, is extremely uncommon in the U.S. Unfortunately, the early symptoms of anthrax are nonspecific and include fever, muscle aches, and other influenza-like symptoms. The patient with pulmonary anthrax, however, rapidly (usually within 24 hours) manifests signs of progressive bacterial infection, including shock, respiratory distress and, in some cases, disseminated intravascular coagulation. Because pulmonary anthrax infection rapidly involves the mediastinal lymph nodes, widening of the mediastinum on chest x-ray may be a characteristic feature of the infection.

Cutaneous anthrax appears as a pustular lesion or cluster of such lesions, which over several days coalesce to form an ulcerating lesion that subsequently develops a characteristic black eschar. Features of sepsis, as typically seen in pulmonary infection, are rare in cutaneous anthrax.

Plague

As discussed in Chapter 9, plague may present in two distinct forms: bubonic and pneumonic. Pneumonic plague caused by aerosol release of the plague bacillus is of the greatest concern. Early manifestations of pneumonic plague are brief because progression to severe hemorrhagic pneumonia generally occurs within hours to a day or two. Patients with pneumonic plague are most likely to present with rapidly progressive, diffuse pneumonia manifested by cough (productive in many cases of bloody sputum) accompanied by high fever and hypoxemia. Chest x-ray is likely to demonstrate multilobar infiltrates, possibly with necrosis and pleural effusion.

Botulism

Unlike the other Category A agents, botulism produces an insidious illness characterized by weakness and often cranial nerve palsies. An intentional release of botulinum toxin may be carried out by aerosol or through contamination of food. In either case the illness presents with these neurological features. Weakness may involve the muscles of respiration, and patients may present with signs of hypoventilation such as bradypnea or shallow respirations. Typical features of infection (fever, leukocytosis, etc.) are absent, and the diagnosis of botulism may be obscured.

Tularemia

As indicated in Chapter 9, although tularemia would most likely be spread by means of aerosolization in a biological attack, the infection that would follow would begin as a nonspecific febrile illness followed by progressive pneumonia. Depending on the season of the year, a single case would likely be confused with influenza, an atypical pneumonia such as Legionnaire's disease or, perhaps, the severe acute respiratory syndrome (SARS). Respiratory symptoms in tularemia progress more slowly than in inhalational anthrax or plague and, for this reason, the urgency of precise diagnosis may not initially be recognized. In the setting of an established outbreak or attack, of course, tularemia would be suspected much earlier in such cases.

Viral Hemorrhagic Fever

The various viral hemorrhagic fevers may be indistinguishable from each other or from other infectious or noninfectious diseases. High fever and signs of an unexplained bleeding diathesis would likely raise suspicion of sepsis with disseminated intravascular coagulation or disseminated noninfectious vasculitis at first. Even if an unusual infection was suspected, meningococcemia or rickettsial infection (particularly Rocky Mountain spotted fever) would be considered before viral hemorrhagic fevers unless a cluster of cases presenting simultaneously was recognized or viral hemorrhagic fever had already been diagnosed in a region.

What Health Care Jobs Put Me at the Greatest Risk of Coming into Contact with a Bioterrorism Agent?

Jobs that involve direct contact with patients, blood, or other laboratory specimens pose the greatest risk of contagion. Of particular concern are emergency room or walk-in-clinic staff, especially those working in areas (such as registration and triage) where patient encounters occur before medical evaluation has taken place. Physicians and nurses working at such acute hospital-entry points are also at risk, as are individuals working in respiratory therapy, housekeeping, transport, x-ray, laboratory and pathology accessioning and processing areas, and mortuary workers. Engineering and maintenance workers who might be called upon to test or repair isolation or decontamination equipment during an attack should also be presumed to be at higher risk. Specific types of medical providers, including specialists in infectious diseases, dermatology, pathology, critical care, and trauma care may also, under certain circumstances, be at high risk. Hospital security personnel may also be at increased risk.

The potential risk to health care workers was demonstrated dramatically in the global outbreak of SARS seen in 2003. In China, where the largest number of cases were seen, health care workers, primarily physicians and nurses, were among the most frequent victims of this highly contagious respiratory infection.[1,2,3]

What Workplace Safety Issues Should Be of Concern?

Health care workers should be familiar with OSHA and JCAHO standards as they apply to specific work areas and job titles (see Chapter 3). Employees likely to come into contact with patients with contagious respiratory conditions are typically trained in isolation procedures and the use of respirator masks. However, hospital-based employees who do not routinely receive such training (secretarial, administrative staff, etc.) may be at added risk. If unsuspected circulation of such highly contagious respiratory pathogens as anthrax and plague were to occur within a hospital, all employees would, of course, be at risk. Maintaining the safety of hospital staff if the hospital is itself the target of an attack would be a massive challenge under such circumstances and, in all likelihood, public health authorities in collaboration with hospital safety and security personnel would direct employees in evacuation, isolation, and other potentially necessary procedures. (See Chapters 2 and 10)

What Are My Responsibilities in General in Preparing for the Possibility of an Attack?

Hospital-based workers in all job categories should be familiar with general emergency procedures and with specific actions that they are expected to take in the event of an internal or external disaster. Many hospitals follow the Hospital Emergency Incident Command Center (HEICS) system (see Chapter 3). Of paramount importance for each worker is an understanding of the chain of command within his or her department and the best means of communicating with department leadership in the event of a terrorist attack. Although hospitals vary in such procedures, several bodies have created standards that all hospitals must meet. (See Chapter 4)

Should I Be Immunized to Smallpox? To Anthrax?

The answer to this question lies primarily in your specific job category and your daily functions (see the preceding text). Immunization to smallpox became a priority in the spring of 2003, after the Advisory Council on Immunization Practices recommended staged immunization of health care workers in high-risk jobs, followed by all first-responders and ultimately followed by most of the U.S. population. Despite the large-scale production to provide smallpox vaccination for this effort, fears of vaccine side effects and other factors impeded efforts to immunize even the individuals at highest risk in the event of an attack. Given this somewhat unexpected situation, some hospitals proceeded to offer voluntary immunization to employees in key areas in order to form smallpox response teams. The effectiveness of this approach has not been established. The decision to undergo smallpox immunization at this point remains at the discretion of the individual health care worker or employee. Procedures and side effects relevant to the smallpox vaccine may be found in Appendix B of this book.

At the time of this writing, anthrax vaccination has not been recommended for health care workers. (See Appendix A)

REFERENCES

1. Emanuel, E.J., The lessons of SARS, *Ann Intern Med*, 139, 589, 2003.
2. Maunder, R. et al., The immediate psychological and occupational impact of the 2003 SARS outbreak in a teaching hospital, *CMAJ*, 168, 1245, 2003.
3. Zhou, G., Qi, Y., and Li, L., Investigation report on the SARS infection rate of the second medical team of Peking University First Hospital, *Beijing Da Xue Xue Bao*, 35 Suppl., 59, 2003.

Section III

Prevention, Diagnosis, and Treatment of Likely Biological Agents

9 Likely Agents of Biological Attack

INTRODUCTION

The U.S. Centers for Disease Control and Prevention (CDC)[1] classifies biological agents that could potentially be used in terrorist attacks into three categories: A, B, and C. Although the categories are somewhat arbitrary, they serve the purpose of focusing discussion and strategies on key features of various pathogens. This chapter provides a review of specific bioterrorism-related issues, including, when available, historical data or data from drills and exercises relevant to each agent. The discussion focuses on Category A agents and several other likely pathogens. In the chapter that follows, Chapter 10, medical aspects of these and a number of additional likely agents are discussed. These include routes of transmission, incubation periods, clinical features, and diagnostic and therapeutic issues. Although this organization of the material is somewhat arbitrary and results in some degree of repetition, it is hoped that separating the discussions in this fashion has resulted in chapters that serve both the immediate needs of clinicians (Chapter 10) and the needs of planners who seek to understand the place that each agent holds in the current concept of the threat of biological attack (this chapter). It will be noted that several agents — those causing brucellosis, Q fever, and melioidosis, for example — though discussed in Chapter 10, are omitted from this discussion. This reflects the relative paucity of information regarding their potential use in bioterrorism. They are included in the clinical discussion because they are agents of concern for which clear-cut diagnostic and treatment guidelines can, nonetheless, be provided.

Treatment regimens for the most likely agents of biological terror are also provided, for convenience, in more detail in Appendix A of this book.

CLASSIFICATION OF POTENTIAL AGENTS OF BIOTERRORISM

Category A agents are of greatest concern and meet the following criteria:[1]

1. They can be readily disseminated and, in some cases, spread person to person. For this reason they pose the greatest threat of a deleterious effect on public health.
2. They may spread across a large area and require a high degree of public awareness.
3. They may necessitate a great deal of specific planning to protect the public health.

   Examples: smallpox, anthrax, plague, tularemia, botulism, hemorrhagic fever viruses

Category B agents are of somewhat less concern and meet the following criteria:

1. Dissemination is relatively easy, although more difficult than for Category A agents.
2. They cause moderate morbidity and low mortality.
3. They require increased surveillance and diagnostic capacity on the part of public health authorities.
   Examples: brucellosis, Q fever, foodborne bacteria (see the following text)

Category C agents are of still less concern but meet the following criteria:

1. They are readily available and/or easily produced.
2. They are easily disseminated.
3. They have the potential for causing significant morbidity and mortality and would have a substantial public health impact.
   Example: Drug-resistant tuberculosis

A great number of other organisms might also have a potential role in bioterrorism. Among these are the foodborne bacteria shigella, salmonella, brucella, *E. coli*, and cholera, as well as a variety of other pathogens such as *Chlamydia psittaci*, the agent of psittacosis. In addition, substances obtained from biological sources, such as ricin toxin, an extract of castor beans, are considered potential biological weapons (see Box 9.1, Box 9.2, Box 9.3, and Box 9.4).

CATEGORY A AGENTS

What follows is a summary of key features of the Category A agents focusing on issues related to their potential use in bioterrorism. As noted, clinical features of each of the diseases caused by these agents as well as strategies for diagnosis, containment, and therapy are reviewed in more detail in the next chapter. As can be seen from this discussion, several of these agents have been the subject of mock drills. Outcomes of these exercises, some of which have been held at the highest levels of government, are also reviewed elsewhere (Appendix C). Finally, specific tabletop exercises are provided in this book (Section IV) employing data regarding each of these agents. These exercises repeat and amplify some of the information included in this and the following chapter.

SMALLPOX

Why It Is Considered Likely

Smallpox (variola) has several features that may serve to make it a likely agent of biological attack. These include:

BOX 9.1
Category A Agents

Bacillus anthracis
Clostridium botulinum
Yersinia pestis
Variola major and other pox viruses
Hemorrhagic fever viruses
- Arenaviruses
  - Lymphocytic choreomeningitis virus
  - Junin virus
  - Machupo virus
  - Guanarito virus
  - Lassa fever virus
- Bunya viruses
  - Hantaviruses
  - Rift Valley fever virus
- Flaviviruses
  - Dengue virus
- Filoviruses
  - Ebola virus
  - Marburg virus

Contagiousness: Smallpox has an attack rate of approximately 30% in nonimmune populations.

Case fatality rate: Approximately one third of victims die.

Susceptibility of the population: After global eradication was declared in 1980, immunization of civilian populations was rapidly curtailed all over the world. Military personnel in various countries continued to receive the vaccine into the 1980s, but with the exception of Israel, this too was discontinued by 1990. Supplies of this apparently unnecessary vaccine subsequently fell to low levels. Because the vaccine confers protection for approximately 10 years on average, it is assumed that essentially the entire human population lacks effective immunity to smallpox. Vaccination programs were reinstituted among selected health care workers in the U.S. and elsewhere in 2002 and 2003, and vaccine production was greatly accelerated during this period.

Evidence exists that orthopox viruses might be rendered relatively resistant to the immune response elicited by the current smallpox vaccine by means of genetic engineering.

Vaccination, if administered within 3 days of exposure, remains the only effective therapy for smallpox. No antiviral agent is currently known to be effective against human smallpox.

BOX 9.2
Category B Agents

Burkholderia pseudomallei
Coxiella burnetti
Brucella specis
Burkholderia mallei
Ricin toxin (from *Ricinus communis*)
Epsilon toxin of *Clostridium perfringens*
Staphylococcus enterotoxin B
Rickettsia prowazekii
Food and Waterborne Pathogens
- Bacteria
  - Diarrheagenic *Escherichia coli*
  - Pathogenic vibrios
  - *Shigella species*
  - *Listeria monocytogenes*
  - *Campylobacter jejuni*
  - *Yersinia enterocolitica*
- Viruses
  - Caliciviruses
  - Hepatitis A
- Protozoa
  - *Cryptosporidium parvum*
  - *Cyclospora cayatanensis*
  - *Giardia lamblia*
  - *Entameba histolytica*
  - *Toxoplasma gondii*
  - *Microsporidia*

Other encephalitis viruses
- West Nile virus
- LaCrosse virus
- California encephalitis virus
- Venezuelan equine encephalitis virus
- Eastern equine encephalitis virus
- Western equine encephalitis virus
- Japanese encephalitis virus
- Kyasanur Forest virus

BOX 9.3
Category C Agents

Tickborne hemorrhagic fever viruses
Crimean-Congo hemorrhagic fever virus
Tickborne encephalitis viruses
Yellow fever virus
Multi-drug-resistant *Mycobacterium tuberculosis*
Influenza virus
Other Rickettsiae
Rabies virus

BOX 9.4
Category A Agents: Approximate Case-Fatality Rates (Untreated)

Smallpox	33%
Anthrax (inhalational)	86%*
Plague	
Pneumonic	90%
Bubonic	50–60%
Tularemia (inhalational)	35%
Botulism	5%
Viral hemorrhagic fevers	15–90%**

* Based on Sverdlovsk incident (see text).
** Varies with specific agent.

Availability

The availability of variola virus for potential use in bioterrorism is not fully known. After global eradication of smallpox was confirmed in 1980, it was determined that limited stocks of the virus would be maintained at the CDC in Atlanta, Georgia, and at a virological laboratory in the Soviet Union. Since that time, and especially since the breakup of the Soviet Union in the early 1990s, concerns have been expressed that supplies of the virus originally kept in the Soviet Union have been studied for potential weaponization for use in biological warfare.[2] For this reason, smallpox remains perhaps the most feared of the category A agents, despite the fact that there have been no documented cases of the disease for over a quarter of a century (see Table 9.1).

TABLE 9.1
Status of Category A Agents

Agent	Availability	Previously Weaponized?
Variola virus	No natural sources, restricted laboratory sources	Yes
Bacillus anthracis	Environmental, laboratory sources	Yes
Yersinia pestis	Environmental, laboratory sources	Yes
Francisella tularensis	Environmental, laboratory sources	Unknown
Botulinum toxin	Environmental, laboratory sources	Presumed
Viral hemorrhagic fever viruses	Environmental, laboratory sources	Unknown

Means of Weaponizing

Aerosolization: As a disease that was naturally transmitted by airborne droplet, smallpox can presumably be weaponized if viable virus can be effectively aerosolized over a population center or within a closed environment. Some evidence has been put forth that the Soviet Union experimented with "bomblets" to study the feasibility of this mode of transmission.[2] The results of the studies and the current understanding of how variola virus could be effectively weaponized in this fashion are unknown.

Person to person: As discussed in the next chapter, smallpox is a highly contagious disease. Despite this fact, there is no evidence in modern times that variola virus has been intentionally released into a population by means of human-to-human spread. Historically, however, the potential effectiveness of this means of distribution was demonstrated by the Spanish conquest of the Aztec empire in the 16th century, which has been attributed by many authors to the spread of smallpox from infected Spanish soldiers to the nonimmune Aztec population.

Fomites: Variola virus has historically been "weaponized" through the distribution of blankets contaminated with body fluids from smallpox victims[2] (see Table 9.2).

TABLE 9.2
Potential Means of Transmission in Biological Attack Scenarios: Category A Agents

Smallpox	Person-to-person, aerosol fomites
Anthrax	Aerosol, contaminated food, water
Plague	Person-to-person, aerosol
Tularemia	Aerosol
Viral hemorrhagic fever	Aerosol, person-to-person
Botulism	Aerosol, contaminated food, water

Potential Consequences of an Attack

The potential consequences of a smallpox attack are a cause of great concern among civil defense planners and public health authorities. As a contagious disease that spreads readily from person to person, smallpox would affect more individuals than those exposed during the initial phase of an attack. These primary victims would soon become capable of infecting others. Secondary, tertiary, and subsequent waves of infection would be likely. Of course, if large numbers of individuals were infected during a single attack, the medical needs of the primary victims alone might cripple the hospital system and overwhelm the capacity to adequately vaccinate and quarantine patients and contacts. Even a limited attack in a single location, however, could rapidly lead to a worldwide epidemic of smallpox (see the following text). Only effective measures to isolate victims, protect health care workers, and quarantine known and suspected contacts of the initial and subsequent victims would provide a brake to spread of the epidemic.

Because postexposure vaccination is the only effective means of treating smallpox that is currently established, the availability and means of rapid distribution of vaccine would be an immediate challenge to public health and other civil authorities.

Health care workers in hospitals would rapidly be confronted with large numbers of individuals seeking reassurance that they did not have smallpox and that they could safely leave their homes.

Both the emotional impact of a smallpox attack as well as the very legitimate fears of contagion and death could produce chaos in hospitals, schools, workplaces, public buildings, and a host of other venues where people gather in large numbers. Effective quarantine of a region, such as a city or state, would require enormous law enforcement resources at a time when public fears would be at a maximum.

Historical Information

Smallpox stands as one of the greatest killers in human history, perhaps the greatest. It has been recognized for 10,000 years.[3] It is estimated that population centers of at least 200,000 are required to sustain the presence of a disease within a community.[2] With the growth of population and the formation of cities in the ancient world came epidemics of smallpox. Among many recorded were those in India in 1500 B.C., China in 1122 B.C. and in Athens (in which one third of the population succumbed) in 437 B.C.[2] Throughout the Dark and Middle Ages, smallpox epidemics continued to ravage and to dictate the course of human civilization. Outbreaks continued to occur well into the 20th century until global eradication of smallpox was accomplished in 1979.

The use of variola virus as an agent of biological warfare is also well documented. British soldiers distributed contaminated blankets of smallpox victims to Indians in North America during the French and Indian wars, resulting in the death of 50% or more of some tribes.[4]

Insights Gained from Exercises and Mock Drills

The Dark Winter exercise, conducted in 2001 prior to the September 11 and anthrax attacks, demonstrated the challenges that would be presented by a smallpox attack.[5] In this exercise (detailed in Appendix C of this book), which involved a simulated release of smallpox in three states, it was concluded that key leaders were unprepared, the chain of command was unclear, information on vaccine supply and distribution was confusing, and hospitals were overwhelmed by concerned, but uninfected, individuals seeking information and reassurance. Projections from this exercise indicated that smallpox would spread to 25 states and 15 foreign countries within 13 days with a predicted 16,000 cases and 1,000 deaths within that time period. It was clear, also, that insufficient surge capacity existed with the hospital system as well as the pharmaceutical industry to rapidly respond to such a crisis. Legal and jurisdictional issues were also raised, particularly regarding the authority to impose quarantine and travel restrictions on large numbers of individuals.

Mathematical modeling of a hypothetical smallpox release has also been used to estimate the potential impact on public health. In an analysis by Meltzer and colleagues[6] it was estimated that 100 persons initially infected and 3 secondary cases for each would lead to an outbreak that would require extensive quarantine measures. Effective quarantine in such a scenario was estimated to require the removal of at least 50% of infected individuals from the general population daily. Such quarantine accompanied by prompt vaccination would eventually contain the outbreak after 1 year and would require 9 million doses of vaccine. During this time 4200 cases of smallpox would occur, according to this model.

ANTHRAX

Anthrax is often considered to be the most likely agent to be used in a large-scale bioterrorist attack.[7]

Why It Is Considered Likely

It causes devastating disease: As discussed in the next chapter, anthrax, particularly when it occurs as a respiratory infection, is a rapidly fatal disease. Only prompt administration of appropriate antibiotics and supportive measures can prevent death.

It is relatively easily obtained: Unlike variola virus, *Bacillus anthracis*, the bacterium that causes anthrax, exists naturally in the environment. Soil from a variety of agricultural regions around the world contains viable spores of the organism. The organism is easily cultivated in the laboratory, and transformation from the vegetative (noninfectious bacillary) form to the infectious spore form is also easily accomplished. Anthrax spores are remarkably resistant to degradation and are of a caliber (3 to 6 microns) that makes them suitable for aerosol distribution. Unlike many of the putative agents of bioterrorism, *B. anthracis* causes substantial human disease in its natural state. Worldwide, it is estimated that 20,000 to 100,000 human cases of anthrax occur annually, primarily in Asia, Africa, the Middle East, and Latin America.[7,8] Nonetheless, anthrax is exceedingly rare in the U.S. and in the developed world in general. Only 18 cases of inhalational anthrax were reported in the U.S. during the 20th century.

There is lack of an effective vaccine: Vaccination against anthrax, while available, is not as effective and not nearly as convenient as vaccination against smallpox. As discussed in the next chapter, the anthrax vaccine must be administered several times over a period of 18 months and then followed by an annual booster injection to maintain its effectiveness.

It has already been effectively used: Unlike the other category A agents, anthrax has already been effectively used in a bioterrorist attack: the so-far mysterious sequence of mailings laced with a highly infectious type of anthrax spore in October and November of 2001. Although the relationship between that attack and the September 11, 2001, attacks on the World Trade Center and the Pentagon is unknown, the temporal link between these events has made the danger of bioterrorism seem more real to the public as well as public health and other civil authorities.

There is persistent contamination: As was learned after the 2001 attack, anthrax spores may persist on environmental surfaces for prolonged periods. Postal processing facilities as well as congressional office buildings remained unusable for months to years after those limited attacks because of the persistence of these spores.

Means of Weaponizing

The anthrax spore is the infectious form of the organism. As indicated above, the spore size renders it suitable for aerosolization, resulting in lower respiratory tract infection. Further "weaponization" can be accomplished by processing of the spores such that the tendency of individual spores to clump together is reduced and penetration deep into the distal airways is facilitated. This process results in a detectable coating of the spore that was seen in organisms recovered during the 2001 attack. Because of the small size of individual spores, cases of inhalational anthrax occurred among individuals who had simply handled unopened mail during that attack. The capacity of anthrax spores to pass through microscopic pores in paper was not previously recognized.

Potential Consequences of Attack

A large-scale release of aerosolized, weaponized anthrax spores over a heavily populated area would result in almost unimaginable devastation. The World Health Organization (WHO) has estimated that a release of 50 kg of spores upwind of a city of 500,000 would result in 125,000 cases of inhalational anthrax and 95,000 deaths.[8] In addition, as was learned in the 2001 attack, even a small number of actual victims of a much more limited release resulted in large numbers of "worried well" individuals reporting to emergency rooms with symptoms that they suspected represented anthrax. Because the spores settle on inanimate objects, the need for decontamination of clothing and monitoring of environmental surfaces and air supplies presented extremely difficult obstacles to public health and law enforcement authorities.

The hospital resources that would be required to effectively treat thousands of actual victims of anthrax are currently unavailable. The need for antibiotics effective against the specific strain of the organism employed in a large-scale attack would immediately result in supply and distribution problems that might be insurmountable. Beyond this, the consumption of other critical hospital resources, such as ventilators, intensive care unit beds, diagnostic facilities, and clinical personnel would be staggering.

Historical Information

One does not have to look far for a historical perspective on the potential of anthrax as an agent of biological terror and warfare. Two recent events deserve close evaluation in order to better confront the potential challenges faced by the public health and health care systems if a large-scale attack were to occur.

The 2001 Attack

Beginning several weeks after the attacks on the World Trade Center and Pentagon, an attack in which anthrax spores were transmitted by means of posted letters to Boca Raton, Florida, New York City, and Washington, D.C., was first detected. The first victim was a newspaper photo editor working in Boca Raton. Although no letter was ever found, it was eventually assumed that this individual had contracted inhalational anthrax after being exposed to a powder contained in a letter that had been opened in the office in which he worked. Between September 22 and October 25, 2001, a total of 22 individuals contracted anthrax (11 inhalational and 11 cutaneous). Contaminated letters postmarked September 17 and October 9 were mailed to news organizations and political figures in New York City and Washington, D.C., respectively. Mail processing facilities in both cities were subsequently found to be contaminated with anthrax spores. Nine of the inhalational cases and all of the cutaneous cases were linked directly to the handling of contaminated mail. Two of the inhalational cases — a nurse working in New York City and an elderly woman living in suburban Connecticut — were never fully explained because no direct link to contaminated letters was ever identified. Ultimately, 5 of the 11 inhalational patients died of their infection. All of the patients with cutaneous anthrax recovered. The attacks appeared to end as mysteriously as they had begun. A variety of individuals working in postal facilities in the two cities were found to be colonized with anthrax spores on surveillance nasal cultures and were treated with prolonged courses of antibiotics to prevent infection. All of these preventive measures appeared to have been successful. It was estimated that 250,000 prescriptions for preventive antibiotics had been written in October. Environmental contamination of postal facilities and Congressional office buildings remained detectable for many months after the attacks. For several days after the initial case in Boca Raton was diagnosed, confusing statements from public health authorities resulted in rising fears among the general public. Guidelines for screening and disposing of "suspicious packages" arriving through the mail were developed by public health and law enforcement authorities, and postal workers justifiably demanded additional surveillance and protection.

In the affected cities, hospital emergency rooms became the focal point of public anxiety. Concerned individuals fearing exposure or infection, desiring surveillance cultures, or simply wishing to turn in suspicious packages disrupted normal functions of the emergency departments and hospitals, especially during the first few weeks of the attacks.

Sverdlovsk Accident in 1979

In March 1979, an accidental release of anthrax spores into the atmosphere occurred at a biological weapons plant in Sverdlovsk in the Soviet Union. Over the next 43 days, 79 (68 fatal) cases of inhalational anthrax were seen among individuals in the vicinity of the plant.[9]

These incidents, both involving very limited releases of spores, which have been described in much greater detail elsewhere,[9] serve to assist in designing response measures to an anthrax attack.

Insights Gained from Exercises and Mock Drills

Neither the Dark Winter nor TOPOFF exercises examined the impact of an anthrax attack. Nevertheless, the above incidents probably offer sufficient insight into the potential impact on hospitals and public health authorities of an anthrax attack.

Plague

Why It Is Considered Likely

Contagiousness: Infection with the plague bacillus (*Yersinia pestis*) may follow a clinical course that makes it particularly well suited to the bioterrorist's armamentarium. If introduced directly into the respiratory tract via aerosolization, it causes a rapidly fatal pneumonia/sepsis syndrome (pneumonic plague). It may also be introduced, however, via the bite of the flea vector and cause localized infection of regional lymph nodes (bubonic plague) before ultimately spreading, through the blood, to the lungs. After arrival in the lungs, it produces a devastating form of pneumonia and, at the same time, renders the victim contagious to others. Thus person-to-person spread can result in a secondary wave of plague pneumonia within a population whether it is introduced by aerosol, by insect vector, or even through its animal reservoir — rodents. In any case, after plague has been introduced into a community, the rodent population may become infected and represent an ongoing source of the organism that may be especially difficult to eradicate. Because of this unfortunate pathogenesis, plague shares the "advantages" of anthrax (in that it may be distributed in a wide area by aerosolization) and smallpox (in that it results in a highly contagious disease).

Rapidly fatal: Unless treated promptly, pneumonic plague is essentially uniformly fatal within several days of the onset of symptoms.

Potential persistence in the environment: As indicated above, plague can establish an ongoing source of infection within a community through the infection of rodent reservoirs. These animals, if infested with fleas, can then become a persistent source of contagion for humans exposed to the flea vectors.

Difficulty in diagnosis: Pneumonic plague, the form that ultimately kills most of those who succumb to infection with *Y. pestis*, presents as a devastating hemorrhagic pneumonia with rapid respiratory failure and features of the sepsis syndrome. This scenario occurs within days of exposure. Any cluster of such cases would likely be recognized as suspected plague quickly by public health authorities monitoring reports from emergency rooms through syndromic surveillance mechanisms. However, bubonic plague would likely be misdiagnosed outside the epidemic setting. Because the illness presents in a manner comparable to other bacterial lymphadenitis syndromes initially, it would likely be mistaken for streptococcal or staphylococcal infection. As bubonic plague would very likely be seen only in the second wave of an aerosol attack, within several weeks after rodent infections became prevalent in the community, it would most likely be suspected locally. However, travellers from areas presenting far from the location of the original attack and, in the case of bubonic plague, weeks or months afterward, might very well be initially misdiagnosed.

Availability

The plague bacillus exists in a variety of animal vectors in endemic areas of the world and can be readily cultured in large quantities. For this reason, it may also be available from clinical and research laboratory sources.

Means of Weaponizing

Aerosolization: Intentional release of the plague bacillus into the atmosphere and, thereby, into communities was demonstrated through the use of infected fleas by the Japanese military during the 1930s and 1940s.[10] Estimates of the devastation produced by direct aerosol distribution of *Y. pestis* over a community of several million inhabitants indicate the potential for hundreds of thousands of cases of pneumonic plague (see Chapter 1).

Person to person: Transmission of pneumonic plague from person to person is highly efficient. With an incubation period of 1 to 4 days, the infection is essentially uniformly fatal in untreated cases. The susceptibility of populations where plague is not endemic is extremely high. Bubonic plague, which untreated carries a case-fatality rate of 50 to 60%, leaves only partial immunity in its survivors. The duration of that immunity has not been characterized.

Infection of rodents and other animals: As indicated above, the rodent population is susceptible to plague and could form an ongoing source of human infection within the community. Although the plagues of the Middle Ages were largely attributed to carriage of the organism by the rat population and transmission to humans by fleas, a large number of mammals are capable of serving as reservoirs in a similar fashion. Among these are ground squirrels, rabbits and hares, wild carnivores, and even domestic cats.

Potential Consequences of Attack

Rapid spread: The highly contagious nature of pneumonic plague and the short incubation period (1 to 4 days) create the possibility of remarkably rapid spread of this deadly infection through a community. Although victims rapidly become ill and incapacitated and are soon rendered incapable of traveling, even relatively advanced cases of plague, if unrecognized, pose great danger to first responders, including ambulance staff, triage officers, and other staff involved in initial care at hospitals, as well as other patients in the waiting areas of emergency departments or other facilities.

Need for high-level quarantine surge capacity: Suspected plague victims would require prompt isolation in negative pressure rooms. Potential contacts of known cases would require quarantine, close medical observation for early symptoms of disease and, very likely, preventive antibiotic therapy. Quarantine at home might be feasible for large numbers of such individuals if effective telephone monitoring could be maintained and rapid transport to appropriate isolation and care facilities arranged on short notice.

Need for travel restriction: As was suggested by mathematical modeling in the TOPOFF exercise (see Appendix C), the need to restrict travel of early victims of plague and potential and known contacts of cases would be essential in containing the attack within a limited geographical area. This would be necessary not only to prevent widespread human-to-human transmission (which occurred within days in the TOPOFF scenario) but to prevent spread to animal reservoirs in previously nonendemic areas and subsequent "second wave" outbreaks.

Historical Information

Plague has caused some of the most notorious pandemics in human history. The first recorded occurred in the 6th century A.D., killing between 50 and 60% of the combined population of North Africa, Europe, and Asia. The second and third great plague pandemics occurred in 1346 and 1855, respectively, spread largely by infected rodents and in each case killing tens of millions and eventually affecting all areas of the known world. Occasional outbreaks of plague continue to occur in the developing world.

It has been reported that the Japanese army experimented with plague as an agent of biological warfare by dropping infected fleas over China, successfully sparking outbreaks in populated areas.[10]

Insights Gained from Exercises and Mock Drills

In May 2000 the first so-called TOPOFF exercise was conducted to evaluate the response capabilities to chemical, nuclear, and biological attack. This exercise is discussed in detail in Appendix C of this book, but the essentials bear repeating here. The biological agent modeled in this hypothetical attack was the plague bacillus. In the scenario created, a release of plague bacillus occurred in a performing arts center in Denver, Colorado. Modeling indicated that within 2 days after the release victims would begin to be seen at local hospitals. By the fourth day after the release, 500 (including 25 fatal) cases had occurred and only then was the point of release clear based on epidemiologic investigation. During the first week after the attack began, antibiotic shortages were reported and hospitals were overwhelmed with cases and concerned individuals seeking reassurance. Over 80% of individuals entering hospital emergency rooms were the so-called "worried well." Because of delays in the imposition of travel restrictions and secondary spread (person to person) of pneumonic plague, this single release ultimately would have resulted in 4000 cases of pneumonic plague and 2000 deaths worldwide.

TULAREMIA

Why It Is Considered Likely

Infectivity: *Franciscella tularensis*, the etiologic agent of tularemia, is one of the most highly infectious bacteria known. Although it is not transmitted from person to person, it is estimated that an inoculum of as few as 10 organisms is sufficient to cause human disease.[11] Although a vaccine against tularemia exists, it is only partially protective against inhalational disease and does not produce protective immunity rapidly enough to be used in postexposure prophylaxis.[12] As naturally occurring tularemia is exceedingly rare in the U.S., vaccination is currently recommended only for individuals working in occupations likely to bring them into contact with the organism. As a result, very few persons in the U.S. are immune to tularemia.

Availability

Because the organism is prevalent in a variety of animals in many parts of the world (including areas of the U.S.) and can be recovered from water and soil in endemic areas, it can be assumed to be available through natural sources as well as, potentially, through microbiology laboratories in endemic areas.

Means of Weaponizing

Aerosolization: Although, as discussed in the next chapter, tularemia is typically transmitted to humans by direct contact with infected animals, it is assumed that aerosolization represents the most effective means of biological attack.[12]

Potential Consequences of Attack

On the basis of published estimates calculated by the WHO in the late 1960s, the effects of an aerosol release of the tularemia bacillus over a populated area would be devastating. About 50 kg of organisms distributed over a city of 5 million would be expected to result in 250,000 major casualties and 19,000 deaths.[13] Although direct human-to-human transmission of tularemia does not occur, prolonged bouts of illness marked by repeated relapses would sustain the effects of such an attack over weeks or months. In addition to the massive medical impact of such an attack, the financial impact would be proportionately devastating. Based on this model, it has been estimated that a tularemia epidemic would cost over $5 billion for every 100,000 victims.[14]

Need for isolation and ICU surge capacity: Since person-to-person transmission of tularemia has not been documented, respiratory isolation, although advisable if available, would not be strictly necessary. The risk to laboratory workers of acquiring the organism during processing of respiratory or other secretions would be high, however. Intensive care monitoring capacity could be rapidly exceeded in the event of a large-scale attack. The respiratory infection associated with inhalational tularemia, however, is not as rapidly progressive as that seen with pneumonic plague.

In addition, there would be a need for antibiotics that are not commonly stocked in large supply (e.g., gentamicin) and can only be given by injection.

Historical Information

F. tularensis has long been recognized as a potential agent of biological warfare. It, along with the plague bacillus, was studied by the Japanese in Manchuria before and during the second world war.[15] Prior to the elimination of its biological warfare program in the early 1970s, the U.S. also maintained a stockpile of the organism for potential military use.[16] It has been suggested that the Soviet Union maintained a similar stockpile, including genetically engineered antimicrobial-resistant strains of the organism, into the 1990s.[9]

Insights Gained from Exercises and Mock Drills

Large-scale mock exercises of bioterrorism preparedness measures have not employed tularemia as a model. However, similarities with plague, in that it produces a severe respiratory/sepsis syndrome, has a short (1 to 14 days) incubation period, and can infect a variety of animals leading to "second wave" cases, are relevant in response planning. Aerosolization of *F. tularensis* from environmental sources was described as a potential source of human infection in a recent outbreak of pulmonic tularemia in Martha's Vineyard, Massachusetts.[17] Of five cases that occurred in July 2000 in this small geographical area, lawnmowing and brush-cutting were found to be risk factors for infection among individuals who did not report direct animal contact. Thus tularemia, like anthrax, may pose a risk of second wave infections from environmental sources.

Botulism

Why It Is Considered Likely

The neurotoxin produced by the bacterium *Clostridium botulinum* is among the most lethal substances known; a few nanograms of the toxin can produce fatal paralysis. The disease caused by these toxins, botulism, occurs in three distinct varieties. The classic form of botulism is a foodborne illness in which preformed toxin is ingested in foods contaminated by the bacterium. Most often this is seen in home-canned foods and rarely in commercially prepared products. The other two forms of botulism are the so-called wound botulism, in which a wound becomes contaminated by the organism that then produces its toxin leading to systemic absorption, and infant botulism, in which the organism exists in the intestinal tract of the infant, produces its toxin, and releases it into the systemic circulation. In all three clinical forms of botulism, therefore, it is the toxin rather than the organism itself that results in disease. This fact has elevated botulism as a bioterrorism concern because toxin can be manufactured and stored in large quantities.

Availability

Spores of *C. botulinum* are ubiquitous in nature and, for example, are commonly found in honey. In recent years, type A botulinum toxin has come into increasing use as a neuromuscular paralyzing agent used pharmaceutically in cosmetic surgery and pain management. This toxin is manufactured from a specific strain (the Hall strain) of *C. botulinum*, and is available by prescription. This preparation of botulinum toxin is felt to be an unlikely tool for terrorism because the concentration of toxin is extremely low.[18]

Means of Weaponizing

In a terrorist attack, toxin could be disseminated either through food sources or as an aerosol release from which it could be absorbed directly through the mucosa of the respiratory and gastrointestinal tracts. The botulinum toxins are designated by letter A–G, with most human cases caused by A, B, E, or F.

Potential Consequences of Attack

Botulinum toxins cause paralysis by blocking neuromuscular transmission and inhibiting release of acetycholine. Depending on the size of the innoculum of toxin, the resulting paralysis begins 12 to 36 hours after exposure. Death is caused by respiratory paralysis and its complications. Unlike the other Category A agents (anthrax, plague, smallpox, etc.) botulinum toxin, if appropriately delivered in sufficient quantities, would cause massive numbers of cases of paralysis and quickly overburden the health care system with the need for ventilatory support for those patients requiring it. Antitoxin is currently available for types A, B, and C, but is in limited supply and is effective only if administered promptly. Perhaps the greatest obstacle to an effective response in the initial phases of an attack employing botulinum toxin would be difficulty in establishing and confirming the diagnosis of botulism among the victims. Other paralytic conditions, such as Guillain–Barre syndrome, polio or polio-like illnesses caused by echoviruses or Coxsackie viruses, or metabolic causes of paralysis such as hypokalemia, hyperthyroidism, or various poisonings might all be considered in isolated cases of botulism.

Historical Information

Efforts to develop botulinum toxin as a biological weapon began during the Japanese occupation of Manchuria prior to World War II.[19,20] Cultures of *C. botulinum* were administered orally to prisoners, with fatal outcomes.[18] In more recent times, the Soviet Union conducted research on weaponization of botulinum toxin, including attempts to splice the toxin gene in other bacteria,[9] and Iraq admitted to UN inspection teams after the 1991 Gulf war to having produced large amounts of botulinum toxin, some of which had been inserted into military weapons.[21,22]

Unlike several of the other Category A agents, botulinum toxin has already been used as an agent of bioterrorism, although unsuccessfully. The Japanese cult Aum Shinrikyo dispersed aerosols of the toxin on at least three occasions in the 1990s, directed at sites in Tokyo as well as U.S. military installations. Toxin was obtained from organisms in soil.[23,24]

Insights Gained from Exercises and Mock Drills

Large-scale exercises that have been described in the medical literature have not employed botulism toxin release scenarios. Nonetheless, as has been demonstrated in these exercises, surge capacity for large numbers of victims to be rapidly screened and either reassured, treated, or quarantined is a frequent obstacle to effective response. A large-scale attack employing botulinum toxin would create, in addition to these issues of surge capacity, a genuine need for a rapid increase in the ability of the health care system to provide ventilatory support and critical care for large numbers of patients in the absence or very limited supply of effective specific therapy. However, once botulism was recognized as the biological weapon being employed, quarantine and isolation would be of little importance because no person-to-person transmission occurs.

Hemorrhagic Fever Viruses

Why They Are Considered Likely

The term hemorrhagic fever viruses embodies many different pathogens. They are considered high-priority agents in planning the response to bioterrorism because many produce severe, rapidly fatal illness and some pose the risk of secondary spread through person-to-person contact or insect vectors. Because infection with these agents (see Chapter 10) is unusual in developed countries, delay in diagnosis of viral hemorrhagic fever syndromes would be likely.

Availability

The availability of agents in the category is largely unknown, although research laboratories may represent a potential source.

Means of Weaponizing

The means of weaponization would vary with the agent used (see Chapter 10).

Potential Consequences of Attack

Because of the inherent delay in clinical diagnosis and laboratory confirmation of viral hemorrhagic fevers, the potential for confusion regarding the need for isolation and quarantine, vaccination, and therapy would likely be high (see the following text).

Historical Information

No intentional releases of viral hemorrhagic fever viruses have been recognized.

Insights Gained from Exercises

The large-scale national exercises described elsewhere in this book have not employed mock attacks with hemorrhagic fever viruses. A study of a simulated release of one such agent, Rift Valley Fever virus (RVFV), focused on the community reaction, specifically the psychological impact on first responders, their families, and journalists. This study, by DiGiovanni and colleagues,[25] involved a simulated aerosol release of RVFV over a community of 300,000 in a semirural area. Fictitious news reports describing the attack were shown to four groups of individuals in the above categories, who subsequently answered questions about their reactions. All participants knew that the attack was simulated and not real. In the scenario as presented, confusion emerged over the appropriate treatment of RVFV, indications for immunization, and strategies of mosquito control because mosquitoes are the insect vector of the agent. The scenario appropriately also included jurisdictional conflicts and questions from health officials in neighboring states as to the adequacy of control measures.

The results of the survey indicated that the majority of participants incorrectly believed that RVFV could be transmitted from person to person. This misconception was especially common among first responders. More than half would attempt to be immunized. This reaction was especially common among the journalists involved. When rumors of a quarantine were raised, a majority (but only 59% of journalists) indicated that they would comply with a quarantine order. All participants preferred to receive information from local, rather than federal, sources. A majority of the journalists indicated that they would use local medical experts or their own physicians as sources in their stories. The vast majority of responders and journalists indicated that they would continue to work, and the majority of their spouses and domestic partners agreed with this decision.

This study is uniquely valuable in that it examines the response of journalists and family members of responders, rather than government officials or medical experts. It, unlike most mock exercises that have been described in the literature, reveals the potential for confusion within the journalism community and the heavy reliance that the public would, nevertheless, have on local reporting for accurate information.

Other Key Pathogens and Biological Agents

Foodborne Pathogens

Several important human pathogens are typically spread by means of contaminated food or from person to person via the fecal–oral route. Among these are *Salmonella* species, *Shigella dysenteriae, Brucella* species, *Escherichia coli*, and *Listeria monocytogenes.*

The potential for bioterrorism to come in the form of foodborne infections has long been recognized. In addition to intentional contamination of food products with botulism toxin (see the preceding text), there exists the possibility that conventional agents of food poisoning could be employed by terrorist groups to cause widespread morbidity and mortality. In fact, as discussed in the first chapter, a religious cult in Oregon caused illness in over 700 individuals in 1984 by contaminating restaurant salad bars with *Salmonella typhimurium* in the only significant attempt at bioterrorism to occur in the U.S. prior to the anthrax attacks of 2001. Accidental contamination of foods, particularly meats and dairy products, has occurred regularly with *Salmonella* species, invasive *E. coli*, and *L. monocytogenes*.

Concerns about foodborne terrorism focus on the ready availability of these organisms from the environment, clinical microbiology laboratories, and commercial sources of biological agents, as well as the ease with which they could be distributed. The likelihood of death from any of these agents is small, but if a large population were affected, significant numbers of deaths and, perhaps, overwhelming numbers of cases of severe illness might be seen. Many of these agents, most dramatically *S. dysenteriae* and related species, pose a great risk of person-to-person transmission and could readily overwhelm institutions, such as hospitals, nursing homes, and other long-term care facilities, through nosocomial spread to patients and staff. Such an occurrence would not only inflict substantial suffering on the victims, but would limit the capacity of the facility to respond to other forms of terrorist attack.

RICIN

Why It Is Considered Likely

Ricin is a normal chemical constituent of castor plants and is particularly concentrated in castor beans. Although not an organism, ricin is often considered a potential agent of bioterrorism because of its biological origin. It is considered a likely agent of attack because it is easily available and highly lethal. Ricin poisoning has occurred, although rarely, naturally through the chewing of castor beans. It accumulates as a by-product of the processing of castor plants and beans into castor oil and is thus relatively easily manufactured or acquired by terrorists.

Means of Weaponizing

Ricin poisoning may be by the inhalational or gastrointestinal route. It is assumed that inhalational ricin intoxication would be the likeliest means of attack with this substance. However, no human cases of inhalational ricin poisoning, either accidental or intentional, have been documented at the time of this writing. For this reason, animal data and speculation form the basis for the recommendations to respond to a ricin attack. For example, a very small particle size (approximately 5 μm) appears to be necessary for inhalational ricin poisoning, and it is unknown if the technology for creating such small particles, thus weaponizing ricin for inhalational spread, is within the capability of current terrorist groups. Unlike many of the other putative agents of bioterrorism, ricin has been used in several cases of intentional poisoning by the gastrointestinal route and, in one instance, by injection of the compound subcutaneously.

Potential Consequences of an Attack

The impact of a ricin attack is difficult to predict. If an effectively weaponized powdered preparation of the toxin could be distributed through the mail, a large number of cases, occurring in small or large clusters, could appear simultaneously or sporadically over a wide geographical area. The syndrome associated with inhalational ricin intoxication could be easily confused with a large variety of more likely illnesses (influenza, congestive heart failure, sepsis, etc.) until the attack was recognized and its scope determined.

Availability

Ricin is considered widely available because it is a constituent of castor beans and other components of the castor plant. The means by which ricin could be effectively weaponized to be used in a large-scale attack are currently unknown.

Historical Information

At the time of this writing, the source and significance of ricin detected on mail-processing equipment in the mail room of the U.S. Senate is under investigation. However, a more clear-cut use of ricin in a terrorist event occurred in October 2003 when a letter threatening contamination of the local water supply was received, accompanied by a sealed container, at a mail processing and distribution center in Greenville, SC.[26] Testing at the CDC confirmed the presence of ricin in the container. Surveillance of environmental surfaces at that facility revealed no further evidence of ricin and no facility employees reported symptoms of ricin poisoning. Statewide monitoring of emergency departments, clinicians, public health departments, and other postal facilities was carried out over the following month and revealed no cases of ricin-associated illness. The source and perpetrator of the "attack," if known, have not been made public.

Insights Gained from Exercises and Mock Attacks

Ricin has not been employed as an agent of terror in published mock exercises to date.

References

1. Centers for Disease Control and Prevention, Biological and chemical terrorism: strategic plan for preparedness and response, Recommendations of the CDC Strategic Planning Workgroup. *Morbid Mortal Weekly Rep,* 49(RR-4), 1, 2000.
2. Tucker, J.B., *Scourge: The Once and Future Threat of Smallpox,* Atlantic Monthly Press, New York, 2001.

3. Breman, J.B. and Henderson, D.A., Poxvirus dilemmas — monkeypox, smallpox, and biological terrorism. *N Engl J Med,* 339, 556, 1998.
4. Henderson, D.A. et al., Smallpox as a biological weapon: Medical and public health management. *JAMA,* 282(22), 2127, 1999.
5. O'Toole, T., Mair, M., and Inglesby, T.V., Shining light on "Dark Winter." *Clin Infect Dis,* 34(7), 972, 2002.
6. Meltzer, M.I. et al., Modeling potential responses to smallpox as a bioterrorist weapon. *Emerg Infect Dis,* 7(6), 959, 2001.
7. Inglesby, T.V. et al., Anthrax as a biological weapon: medical and public health management. *JAMA,* 281,1735, 1999.
8. Cieslak, T.J. and Eitzen, E.M.J. Clinical and epidemiologic principles of anthrax. *Emerg Infect Dis,* 5, 552, 1999.
9. Alibek, K. *Biohazard,* Random House, New York, 1999.
10. Inglesby, T.V. et al., Plague as a biological weapon: medical and public health management. *JAMA,* 293(17), 2281, 2000.
11. Saslow, S. et al., Tularemia vaccine study, II: Respiratory challenge. *Arch Intern Med,* 107, 134, 1961.
12. Dennis, D.T. et al., Tularemia as a biological weapon: Medical and public health management. *JAMA,* 285(21), 2763, 1998.
13. *Health Aspects of Chemical and Biological Weapons,* World Health Organization, Geneva, Switzerland, 105, 1970.
14. Kaufman, A.F. et al., The economic impact of a bioterrorist attack: are prevention and post-attack interventions programs justifiable? *Emerg Infect Dis,* 2, 83, 1997.
15. Harris, S., Japanese biological warfare research on humans: a case study of microbiology and ethics. *Ann NY Acad Sci,* 666, 21, 1992.
16. Christoper, G.W. et al., Biological warfare: a historical perspective. *JAMA,* 278, 412, 1997.
17. Feldman, K.A. et al., An outbreak of primary pneumonic tularemia on Martha's Vineyard. *N Engl J Med,* 345(22), 1601, 2003.
18. Arnon, S.S. et al., Consensus Statement: Botulinum toxin as a biological weapon. Medical and public health management. *JAMA,* 285(8), 1059, 2001.
19. Geissler, E. and Moon, J.E. (Eds.), *Biological and Toxin Weapons: Research, Development, and Use from the Middle Ages to 1945*. Oxford University Press, New York, 1999, Sipri Chemical and Biological Warfare Studies No. 18.
20. Smart, J.K., History of chemical and biological warfare: an American perspective. In: Sidell F.R., Takafuji E.T., and Franz D.R. (Eds.), *Medical Aspects of Chemical and Biological Warfare, Textbook of Military Medicine,* part I, vol. 3, Office of the Surgeon General, Washington, D.C., 1997, 9–86.
21. United Nations Security Council, Tenth Report of the Executive Chairman of the Special Commission Established by the Secretary-General Pursuant to Paragraph 9(b)(I) of Security Council Resolution 687 (1991) and Paragraph 3 of Resolution 699 (1991) on the Activities of the Special Commission, United Nations Security Council, New York, S1995, 1038, 1992.
22. Zilinskas, R.A., Iraq's biological weapons: the past as future? *JAMA*, 278, 418–424, 1997.
23. Tucker, J.B. (Ed.). *Toxic Terror: Assessing the Terrorist Use of Chemical and Biological Weapons,* MIT Press, Cambridge, MA, 2000.
24. WuDunn, S. and Broad, W.J. How Japan Germ Terror Alerted World. *New York Times*, May 26, 1998, A1, A10.

25. DiGiovanni, C. et al., Community reaction to bioterrorism: prospective study of simulated outbreak, *Emerg Infect Dis,* June 2003. Available from www.cdc.gov.ncidod/EID/vol9no6/02-0769.htm.
26. Centers for Disease Control and Prevention: investigation of a ricin-containing envelope at a postal facility — South Carolina, 2003. *Morbid Mortal Weekly Rep,* 52(46), 1129–1131, 2003.

10 Diagnosis and Management of Agents of Bioterrorism

INTRODUCTION

This chapter provides a concise overview of clinical and laboratory features of key pathogens with the potential for use in terrorist attacks.

A thorough discussion of pathogenesis of infection for each of these agents is beyond the scope of this text. Emphasis has instead been placed on strategies of diagnosis, therapy, and containment. Where relevant, special considerations such as pregnancy, infection in children, or immunocompromised hosts is included in the discussion of specific pathogens. The potential roles and impacts of these agents in the context of bioterrorism are discussed in detail in Chapter 9. While both this chapter and Chapter 9 focus on those agents of bioterrorism considered most likely, this chapter, in addition, includes brief discussions of several agents, for example *Coxiella burnetii*, the agent of Q fever, which have been identified as agents of concern but for which less is known about the specific scenarios they might cause in a biological attack.

Although therapy is mentioned and, when appropriate, prevention strategies are addressed briefly for each of the organisms and conditions outlined in this chapter, the reader is referred to the appendices found at the end of this book for summaries of pharmacologic and other forms of therapy (including dosing schedules) for all of the infections discussed (see Figure 10.1, Figure 10.2, and Figure 10.3).

SMALLPOX

As indicated in the preceding chapter, smallpox was eradicated through a global campaign conducted during the 1960s and 1970s. Among the major bioterrorism threats, smallpox is the only one that does not currently cause natural infection. As a result, any case of smallpox occurring anywhere in the world would be considered an intentional attack or, at the very least, an indication of accidental release of the virus through improper containment for the purposes of development as an agent of biological warfare or terror.

CAUSATIVE ORGANISM

The etiologic agent of smallpox is the variola virus, a member of the orthopoxvirus group. Clinical and laboratory features of smallpox are as follows.[1,2]

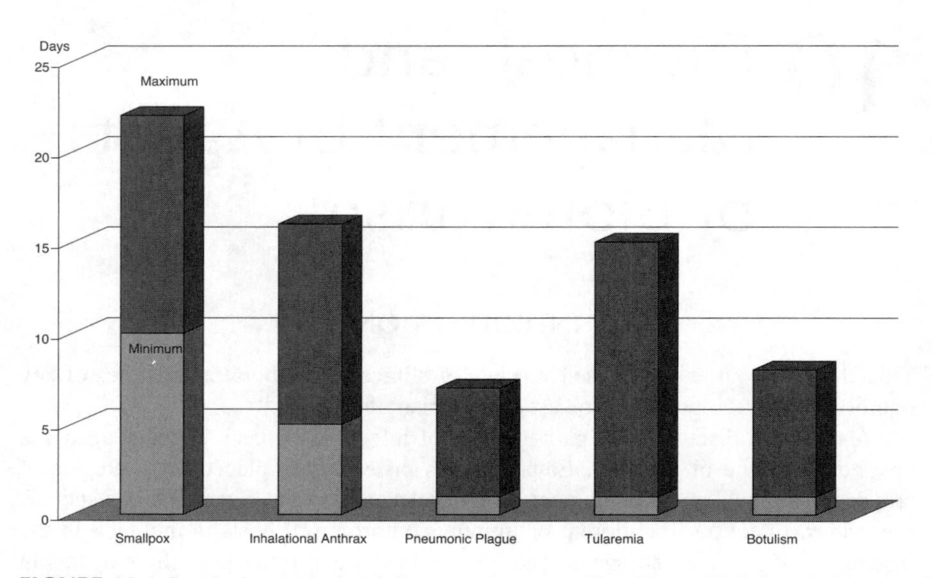

FIGURE 10.1 Incubation periods of Category A agents (See Figure 10.2 for viral hemorrhagic fevers).

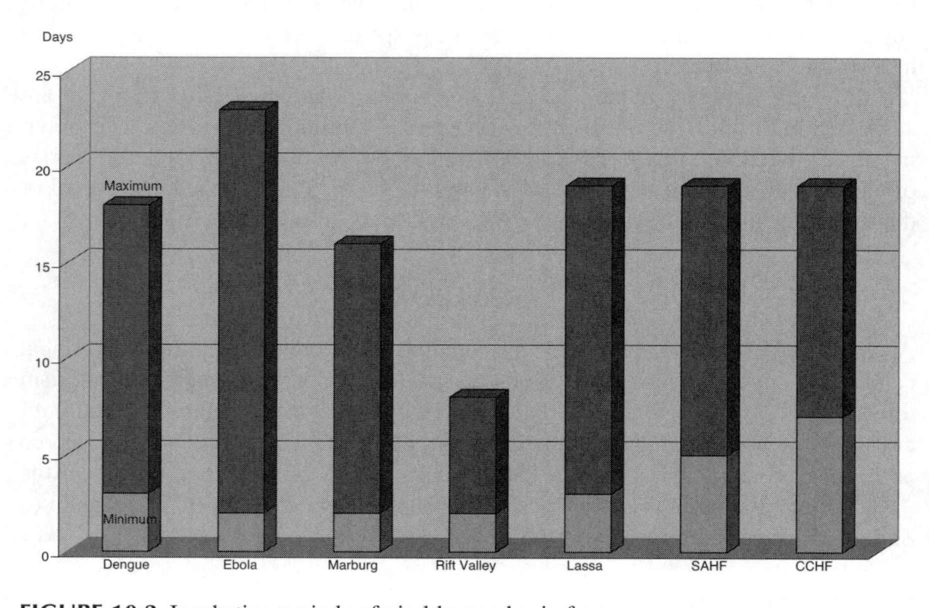

FIGURE 10.2 Incubation periods of viral hemorrhagic fevers.

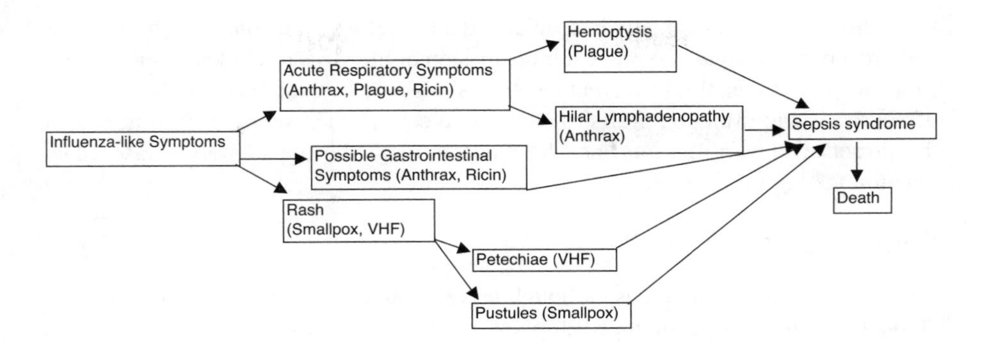

FIGURE 10.3 Progression of symptoms: selected agents. VHF: Viral hemorrhagic fever; Anthrax: inhalational anthrax; Plague: Pneumonic plague.

Route of Transmission

Smallpox may be transmitted in any of three ways. The most frequent route of transmission is by airborne droplets from the nasopharynx of infected individuals. Less frequently, transmission may occur by direct contact with an infected skin lesion or with fomites such as bedding, towels, etc.

Incubation Period

The incubation period averages 10 to 12 days, at which point the prodromal illness begins.[3]

Symptoms

Smallpox typically progresses through several stages. Nonspecific symptoms, including fever, headache, and malaise are followed, after several days, by an erythematous rash appearing first on the face and throat and then spreading to the arms, legs and, finally the torso. Pustules, associated with burning pain, then appear in these same areas. The pustules typically progress to firm nodules that remain painful. In surviving patients, these lesions fall off after several weeks, leaving scars and areas of denuded skin.

Physical and Laboratory Findings

The rash, as described above, is the most characteristic physical finding associated with smallpox. Routine laboratory studies are typically within the normal range. Leukocytosis is rare in the absence of bacterial superinfection.

Laboratory Diagnosis

The techniques required for laboratory confirmation of variola virus infections are not available in routine clinical laboratories. Specimens suspected of containing the virus should be processed only in specialized laboratories with containment facilities and procedures adequate to prevent transmission of the virus to workers (see Chapter 3). In such facilities, fluid from cutaneous lesions may be examined for the presence of characteristic orthopoxviral structures by electron microscopy. Confirmation of the presence of variola virus may be made through the use of polymerase chain reaction testing or viral culture.

Containment Measures

Smallpox is highly contagious, although less so than chickenpox, the most common "lookalike." In an unimmunized population, approximately one third of exposed individuals will develop disease. Because of the long average incubation period (12 days), strict isolation or quarantine for 17 days is recommended for nonimmune individuals who have had direct contact with a proven case. Anyone with a proven or suspected exposure whose immune status is unknown should receive smallpox vaccine as soon after exposure as possible.[4] Vaccination beyond 3 days following exposure is of unproven efficacy. In the hospital setting, the greatest risk of contagion is posed to medical personnel exposed to a smallpox victim before adequate isolation procedures have been put into effect and to laboratory personnel working with contaminated specimens. Clinical and laboratory personnel should wear protective clothing, masks, shoe covers, and goggles.

Contact and airborne precautions are mandatory for the known or suspected victim. The patient should be immediately placed in a negative-pressure isolation room. Optimally, care of the patient should be provided only by recently immunized clinical staff.

Laboratory specimens are best handled in a high-level containment facility (see Chapter 3). For this reason, packaging and transporting of specimens to appropriate public health laboratories will most likely be necessary. The collection and processing of potentially infectious material from a smallpox victim should be handled under the supervision of public health authorities.

Ancillary personnel in virtually any hospital area might be inadvertently exposed to a smallpox victim or infected materials during an attack. Perhaps at greatest risk are housekeepers, mortuary workers, security personnel, and transport workers. Fortunately, effective airborne transmission of the virus appears to require direct face-to-face contact for several hours. For this reason, individuals with only incidental contact with the smallpox victim, such as other patients in a waiting or triage area, are at very little risk of infection. This risk, however, is presumably much greater if the smallpox victim is coughing and thereby aerosolizing infection material over a wider area and in higher concentration.

Decontamination of clothing, bedding, and other materials coming into direct contact with the smallpox victim is recommended to prevent secondary spread. This is best accomplished by placing such items in labeled biohazard bags followed by incineration.

Therapy

The smallpox vaccine, administered within 3 days of contact, can lessen the severity of smallpox or prevent disease completely.[2] No antiviral agent has been demonstrated to be effective in clinical trials in the treatment of smallpox. However, cidofovir, a drug that is currently approved by the U.S. Food and Drug Administration (FDA) for the treatment of other viral infections, has shown promise in animal laboratory studies against the variola virus.[3]

Prevention

As was demonstrated in the campaign to achieve global eradication of smallpox, the vaccine employing a related virus, vaccinia, confers a high level of immunity to smallpox and remains the most effective means of prevention. As noted above, measures to assure the limitation of spread by airborne droplets are recommended to prevent transmission to unvaccinated employees and patients in the hospital setting. These measures include the use of high filtration level respirators (masks) such as N95 or N100 by health care workers who risk potential exposure to an infected patient. In addition, negative-pressure isolation rooms are recommended to prevent airborne spread outside the infected patient's room. Other precautions that are recommended in the hospital setting include use of disposable sheets and food trays and bagging of any clothing or bedding that has come into direct contact with the patient in biohazard bags with subsequent incineration. It is further recommended that bodies of smallpox victims who have died undergo cremation and that tissue and body fluid samples from all infected patients be handled in a manner to prevent contagion among laboratory staff.

Special Considerations

Because few practicing physicians have seen smallpox, the potential for misdiagnosis and confusion with other conditions marked by fever and rash is great. Although many infectious and noninfectious diseases cause generalized rashes, two types of infection that pose a special risk of confusion with smallpox are varicella (either primary or disseminated zoster) and other poxvirus infections.

Differential Diagnosis

Varicella (chickenpox): This can potentially be confused with smallpox, especially during the early phases of illnesses.[2] The primary points of distinction are:

The rash of varicella is typically most dense on the trunk rather than the extremities and often spares the extremities completely, whereas the rash of smallpox is most dense on the extremities.

The progression of the rash of varicella is rapid, passing from erythematous macules to papules to vesicles and to pustules in a matter of several days. The rash of smallpox progresses more slowly, becoming progressively worse over the first 1 to 2 weeks.

The rash of varicella contains lesions at various stages of development (macule, vesicle, pustule) simultaneously, whereas the rash of smallpox more typically progresses synchronously with all lesions at a similar stage of development.

The rash of smallpox is typically associated with burning pain, whereas the rash of varicella is more often pruritic.

Varicella often occurs in an obvious household or schoolwide outbreak. The majority of U.S. adults are immune to varicella, even if they do not recall an episode of chickenpox in childhood.[5] For these reasons, an increase in adult cases with no obvious clustering within households or other closed environments may suggest the early stages of a smallpox attack.

Other poxvirus infections: A variety of poxviruses related to variola that primarily affect nonhuman species may occasionally be seen in human outbreaks. This phenomenon was demonstrated by the limited outbreak of monkeypox attributed to infected prairie dogs in the American Midwestern states in the spring of 2003.[6] The rash of monkeypox, a much less severe disease, can closely resemble that of smallpox.

How the Early Stages of a Smallpox Attack Might Appear

Smallpox is unique among the Category A diseases in that it has been completely eradicated for the past quarter century. For this reason any confirmed case would suggest an intentional release of the virus, that is, a biological attack. Nonetheless, as can be seen from the above discussion, smallpox may pose difficult diagnostic challenges, both for the clinician and the laboratory. Because of inevitable delays in diagnosis compounded by the absence of a rapid diagnostic test, the earliest stages of a smallpox attack would most likely not be detectable before clustering of cases had already occurred. An individual hospital would most likely not be the recipient of the initial case or cluster of cases of smallpox, but would be informed of a suspected or confirmed case in the community, the state, the nation, or internationally by public health authorities. In such an event, all hospitals would immediately be plunged into planning for the careful assessment of all patients with unexplained characteristic clinical syndromes and for rapidly enacting isolation procedures and reinforcing lines of communication with the public health system and other health care facilities in the region.

ANTHRAX

Anthrax is almost unheard of as a naturally occurring infection in the U.S. This fact permitted relatively rapid recognition that the 2001 attacks represented intentional release of the organism. Unlike variola virus, the cause of smallpox, the bacterium that causes anthrax is present in the environment in many areas of the world and access to anthrax spores on the part of potential terrorists is therefore feasible.

CAUSATIVE ORGANISM

The etiologic agent of anthrax is *Bacillus anthracis*, a spore-forming Gram-positive bacillus.

ROUTE OF TRANSMISSION

Anthrax may be transmitted in three ways. Respiratory infection, the most lethal form, is caused by inhalation of spores of the organism. Direct inoculation of spores into cuts or microscopic breaks in the skin can result in cutaneous anthrax. The third means of transmission is by the gastrointestinal route. This is seen almost exclusively in livestock ingesting spores of the organisms contained in soil. Gastrointestinal anthrax is a rapidly fatal illness comparable in mortality to inhalational infection but is almost never seen in humans as a naturally occurring infection. However, because of the potential for easy dissemination through food or water supplies, gastrointestinal anthrax may emerge as a result of a biological attack.

INCUBATION PERIOD

The incubation period of anthrax varies according to the route of transmission. In cases seen during the 2001 attacks, incubation periods of inhalational infection, when they could be accurately estimated, ranged from 5 to 11 days.[7]

SYMPTOMS

Inhalational Anthrax

Inhalational anthrax is a respiratory infection that presents with nonspecific influenza-like symptoms initially. As the organisms transform from the spore to the vegetative form and spread from the lung parenchyma to regional lymph nodes, a variety of toxins are elaborated that result in a syndrome of progressively worsening generalized sepsis characterized by shock, acidosis, and coagulopathy. An analysis of 10 victims of inhalational anthrax during the 2001 attack was indicative of the relatively vague symptoms associated with this illness:[7,8,9]

Fever, chills: 100% of victims
Fatigue, malaise, lethargy: 100%
Cough: 90% (all minimal and nonproductive)
Nausea and/or vomiting: 90%
Shortness of breath: 80%
Sweats: 70%
Chest discomfort: 70%
Myalgias: 60%

No other symptoms were experienced by more than 50% of the victims. Physical findings and laboratory abnormalities were similarly nonspecific. Only the following were manifested by more than 50% of the victims:[7]

Fever > 37.8°C: 70%
Tachycardia: 80%
Neutrophilia: 70%
Transminase elevations: 90%
Hypoxemia: 60%

Roentgenographic features were somewhat more specific, in that all patients had abnormal findings on x-rays, with 70% demonstrating characteristic mediastinal widening on routine chest x-ray, and 88%[7,8] of patients undergoing computed tomography of the chest were found to have mediatinal lymphadenopathy or widening.

It is noteworthy that in some of these patients a brief period of improvement was seen after the onset of symptoms prior to clinical deterioration.

Cutaneous Anthrax

Cutaneous anthrax follows a progression consisting of spread from the site of initial inoculation to produce, over several days, pustular lesions that coalesce to become necrotic with the development of an overlying eschar. Regional lymph nodes may become involved as in inhalational infection. The evolution of cutaneous anthrax typically takes place over a period of 5 to 6 days, after which, in uncomplicated cases, the black eschar is shed and healing takes place. The skin lesion of cutaneous anthrax is typically painless. Systemic symptoms of infection, such as fever and chills, may be minimal or severe. It should be noted that cutaneous anthrax cases seen during the 2001 attacks were, in several instances, misdiagnosed as spider bites.

Gastrointestinal Anthrax

Anthrax involving the gastrointestinal tract begins with a 1- or 2-day period of nausea, vomiting, and fever. This may be complicated by hematemesis and hematochezia. After the initial intestinal phase, this form of anthrax pursues a septicemic course similar to that of inhalational anthrax.

Laboratory Diagnosis

Laboratory confirmation[10,11,12] depends on culture of material from such clinical sources as wound discharge, blood, respiratory secretions, pleural fluid, or cerebrospinal fluid. Nonculture diagnostic techniques including immunohistochemical staining and PCR are available through public health laboratories. Nasal swab cultures, performed in large numbers during the anthrax attacks of 2001, are of little value in excluding the disease, but may be used to prove (if positive) that an individual has been exposed. During influenza season, the use of rapid diagnostic tests for influenza (if negative) may lend support to the diagnosis of inhalational anthrax because the initial symptoms of both infections may be similar.

Containment Measures

Because person-to-person transmission does not occur, standard precautions are sufficient. Although reaerosolization of spores from clothing and other surfaces appears to be unusual, clothing should be placed in biohazard bags and disposed of accordingly. Decontamination with soap and water is adequate for victims. Spores on surfaces can be inactivated with a 10% hypochlorite solution.

Therapy

Prompt antimicrobial therapy is critical to survival. Combination therapy with ciprofloxacin[13] or levofloxacin or doxycycline plus rifampin or clindamycin should be initiated intravenously. Therapy should be continued for 60 days. Oral therapy can be substituted for intravenous therapy when the patient has been stabilized. Supportive care for respiratory infection and sepsis may be required. See Appendix A for specific treatment guidelines.

Prevention

During the anthrax attacks of 2001, a great deal of confusion arose regarding antimicrobial prophylaxis of exposed individuals. Although the appropriate medications (ciprofloxacin or doxycycline) were known to virtually every health care provider and most of the general public within days of the initial attack, challenges were encountered in determining who should receive such prophylaxis. Cultures of nasal swabs were performed on many postal workers and individuals present in the buildings that had received contaminated letters, and those testing positive for anthrax spores were advised to receive prophylaxis. It is possible that this strategy (plus presumed widespread empiric use of prophylactic antibiotics) prevented additional cases. However, infection may occur in the absence of positive nasal cultures, and the technique for obtaining such specimens was not easily standardized. Recommendations for prevention of anthrax are provided in detail in Appendix A of this book.

Anthrax Vaccine

An acellular vaccine against anthrax (AVA) has been used in specific occupational and military settings. This vaccine has been associated with a variety of adverse reactions, including joint pains and hypersensitivity pneumonitis in some studies. However, preliminary data compiled by the CDC on individuals who had received the vaccine after the 2001 anthrax attacks revealed no serious adverse reactions.[14] Concerns about bioterrorism have stimulated research in the development of safer, more effective anthrax vaccines. The current vaccine, if available, should be administered to exposed individuals immediately and followed by subsequent doses at 2 weeks, 4 weeks, and 6 months, 12 months, and 18 months.

It should be noted that the current vaccine has not been shown to be effective in preventing infection by the aerosol route and has not been adequately evaluated. Postexposure antibiotic prophylaxis can be discontinued after the first three doses of vaccine have been administered. It is otherwise continued for 60 days after exposure (see Appendix A for details).

Antibiotic Prophylaxis

Antibiotic prophylaxis should be provided following exposure to airborne spores. A variety of agents, including penicillins, are felt to be effective for preventive therapy, which should be continued for at least 60 days.[15]

Special Considerations

Differential Diagnosis and Look-Alikes

Cutaneous Anthrax

Spider bites: The necrotic lesion of cutaneous anthrax can resemble the bite of the brown recluse spider. Such spider bites are typically quite painful, whereas cutaneous anthrax is typically painless.

Herpesvirus infections: Herpesvirus infections, including those caused by Herpes simplex and Varicella zoster, can produce local areas of painful vesicles that may become necrotic. As in the case of spider bites, these lesions are typically quite painful, whereas anthrax characteristically causes painless lesions.

Necrotizing bacterial infections: Infections caused by other necrotizing bacteria, especially *Streptococcus pyogenes,* can, in rare instances, produce local areas of necrosis that could resemble the lesions of cutaneous anthrax. Such infections typically follow a recognized injury and are accompanied by systemic signs of infection. In some instances, the lesion of cutaneous anthrax is surrounded by an extensive area of soft tissue edema, resembling erysipelas.

Other cutaneous fungal and bacterial infections: Common bacterial soft tissue infections, such as carbuncles and furuncles, differ from cutaneous anthrax in that they are marked by extensive formation of pus, which is not a feature of cutaneous anthrax. Rarely, infection by atypical mycobacteria, *Nocardia* species, or a variety of fungal organisms such as *Sporothrix schenkii* or organisms of the mucor group could produce lesions resembling cutaneous anthrax. Epidemiological and clinical history may be helpful in making distinctions among these entities.

Inhalational anthrax: Because of the rapid progression to sepsis syndrome that characterizes inhalational anthrax, the condition may be confused either with severe respiratory infections or with disseminated bacterial infection from nonrespiratory sources.

Influenza: Because of the nonspecific early symptoms of inhalational anthrax (fever, headache, chills, muscle aches), a mistaken diagnosis of influenza may be initially entertained. During the 2001 attacks, which occurred during influenza season, this potential confusion added to public anxiety and confusion for public health authorities. Because of the limited nature of those attacks and the fact that news organizations and governmental officials seemed to be the primary targets, the distinction from influenza was made somewhat more clear by the nature of the "victim" under evaluation. Much weight was placed on the relative likelihood that an individual patient was a target of the attack. In a more large-scale attack, affecting larger numbers of individuals with no apparent pattern, other means of distinguishing influenza from inhalational anthrax would be necessary. Factors of potential use in making the distinction between influenza and anthrax include leukocytosis (almost never present in influenza but characteristic of inhalational anthrax) and disease progression (improvement typically is seen within 4 to 5 days in influenza, whereas inhalational anthrax, if not specifically treated, would lead to rapid demise within this period).

How the Early Stages of an Anthrax Attack Might Appear

As was seen vividly in the anthrax attacks of 2001, the initial cases of inhalational and cutaneous anthrax might go unrecognized. As the cutaneous version of anthrax is somewhat more distinctive in presentation (a necrotic, spreading ulcerating lesion) than the inhalational form, the early stages of an anthrax attack might manifest in multiple cases of skin infection detected through syndromic surveillance. Because culture results are required to confirm the diagnosis of anthrax (cutaneous or inhalational), a 24- to 48-hour delay in confirmation could be anticipated even after initial suspicious cases were reported by public health authorities. However, as anthrax poses no risk of person-to-person transmission (unlike plague and smallpox), the early stages of an anthrax attack would most likely feature epidemiologic evaluation by public health authorities to identify the source and means of dissemination of anthrax spores and the identification of the population at risk for infection. As in 2001, hospitals close to and remote from the site of the original cases would be confronted with a concerned public and inquisitive press as well as, very likely, demands for preventive antibiotics. Unexplained skin rashes, whether consistent with cutaneous anthrax or not, and severe community-acquired pneumonia cases would require more intense scrutiny at the hospital level.

PLAGUE

Plague, particularly the pneumonic variety, poses a grave potential threat as an agent of biological attack.

Causative Organism

Plague is caused by the Gram-negative bacillus *Yersinia pestis.*

Route of Transmission

Natural transmission of the plague bacillus to humans may occur by either of two routes. Infection may occur through the bite of a flea that has become infected after feeding on infected rodents. Successful transmission by this route results in infection of regional lymph nodes and bacteremia, referred to as bubonic plague. By the hematogenous route, infection can then spread to the lungs, resulting in pneumonic plague. Infection can then be transmitted from person to person by the respiratory route. Plague thus becomes a highly contagious disease — a feature that distinguishes it from anthrax.

If used as a biological weapon, the plague bacilli would most likely be released into the atmosphere and result in the pneumonic form of the infection. Although such a release could also result in infection of the susceptible rodent population and ultimate transmission of bubonic plague to humans, the immediate and devastating impact of widespread pneumonic plague would represent a far greater danger. Unlike anthrax and tularemia, the other respiratory bacterial pathogens considered to be among the most likely agents of bioterrorism, pneumonic plague would also result in human-to-human transmission, thus amplifying greatly the potential impact of such an attack. For these reasons, the following discussion applies to pneumonic plague.

Incubation Period

Symptoms of pneumonic plague would begin within 1 to 6 days after infection occurred, depending on the concentration of aerosolized bacilli. Once lower respiratory tract infection was thus established, death would follow within 1 to 2 days in untreated individuals.[16]

Symptoms

Pneumonic plague would be the most likely form encountered in a biological attack scenario because an aerosol release would be the most likely means of dissemination. Bubonic plague might be seen as a later phenomenon as the rodent population became infected. As noted, pneumonic plague can complicate bubonic plague following hematogenous dissemination of the organism.

Pneumonic Plague

Pneumonic plague is marked by the abrupt and fulminant onset of fever, chills, headache, and myalgias. Respiratory signs and symptoms typically appear within 24 hours and may include cough, hemoptysis, and dyspnea.[16] Cyanosis, respiratory failure, and circulatory collapse follow quickly. Nonspecific abdominal symptoms such as pain, nausea, and vomiting may also be prominent.

Bubonic Plague

The initial manifestations of bubonic plague are high fever, malaise, and tender, enlarged lymph nodes, often in the inguinal area. Hematogenous dissemination of the organism with secondary involvement of the lungs occurs in the majority of cases, although pneumonic plague develops in a minority. A fulminant course similar to that described above then follows rapidly.

Secondary involvement of the central nervous system, plague meningitis, may complicate some cases.

Physical and Laboratory Features

Pneumonic plague, including that resulting from bubonic plague, is a rapidly progressive lower respiratory infection complicated by the sepsis syndrome. Radiographic manifestations are of a progressive, necrotizing pneumonia. Multilobar involvement is common. Laboratory findings are those of severe infection complicated by sepsis and multiorgan failure and typically include leukocytosis, liver function abnormalities, and azotemia.[16] Physical findings are those of a consolidated pneumonia accompanied by typical features of sepsis such as hypotension, bleeding manifestations, and digital cyanosis with necrosis in some cases.

Laboratory Diagnosis

Gram stain of clinical specimens such as sputum or drainage from an involved lymph node may reveal Gram-negative bacilli with a characteristic bipolar staining pattern. Specific fluorescent antibody staining is also available. Culture of blood, sputum, cerebrospinal fluid, or lymph node drainage would be necessary for final identification and antimicrobial susceptibility testing. Laboratory personnel should be alerted when plague is suspected so that specimens can be processed using appropriate containment precautions or can be forwarded to public health laboratories if adequate biological safety level procedures are not in place (see Chapter 3).

Containment Measures

Patients with proven or suspected pneumonic or bubonic plague require droplet isolation until 48 hours of therapy and clinical improvement or, in the case of bubonic plague, until pneumonic infection has been ruled out.[17]

Therapy

Therapy must be initiated within 24 hours of the onset of respiratory symptoms in pneumonic plague. Specific treatment guidelines are provided in Appendix A of this book.

Prevention

Postexposure antibiotic prophylaxis with either doxycycline or ciprofloxacin (see Appendix A) is indicated for close contacts. There is currently no effective vaccine.

Special Considerations

Differential Diagnosis and Look-Alikes

The pneumonic form of plague most closely resembles other rapidly progressive, bacterial respiratory infections complicated by features of sepsis and the multiorgan failure syndrome. Pneumonia caused by *Streptococcus pneumonia, Staphylococcus aureas, Klebsiella pneumoniae,* or *Legionella* species, all far more common than pneumonic plague, would produce similar clinical and laboratory features early in the course of illness.

How the Early Stages of a Plague Attack Might Appear

A sudden surge in fulminant, rapidly fatal pneumonia among previously healthy adults would be expected following an effective aerosol release of plague bacilli. Because culture-confirmation of plague would be required, as in the case of anthrax, a delay of 24 to 48 hours might be anticipated between initial suspicions of a plague attack and confirmation. However, unlike anthrax, pneumonic plague can be transmitted from person to person quite efficiently, and the delay in confirmation of the diagnosis would lead to otherwise avoidable secondary cases. To minimize this risk, suspicion of a terrorist attack employing plague might trigger advisories to hospitals to place all patients presenting with community-acquired pneumonia in respiratory isolation, at least within the geographical region of the suspected cases. In the initial phase of the attack, a point-source outbreak pattern might be discerned, although this might rapidly be obscured by the accumulation of secondary cases of pneumonic plague representing human-to-human transmission. Travel restrictions and quarantine measures might be discussed and imposed early in the event of a suspected plague attack, as the failure to do so, in several large-scale exercises, has been cited as a cause for widespread dissemination of infection (see Chapter 2 and Appendix C).

As there is no effective vaccine against plague, the demand for antibiotics among individuals, symptomatic or not, who feel that they may have been exposed to the infection might intensify rapidly and the "worried well" would be expected to flood hospital emergency rooms. Surge capacity consisting of areas outside of the emergency room and its immediate surroundings might become critically important in such an attack.

TULAREMIA

Tularemia, a rare bacterial infection in the U.S., poses a significant potential threat as an agent of bioterrorism because of its high case-fatality rate and, perhaps, the relatively ready availability of the organisms to potential terrorists.

Causative Organism

Tularemia is caused by the Gram-negative bacillus *Franciscella tularensis.*

Route of Transmission

In the natural setting, spread of tularemia to humans occurs through direct contact with infected animals. The organism can be found in a large variety of animals, as well as in contaminated water and soil throughout various regions of Europe, Asia, and North America. In the U.S., tularemia has been reported from every state except Hawaii, but is most often diagnosed in the Midwestern states. Common animal reservoirs of infection include rabbits, rats, squirrels, and several other small mammals. Transmission to humans may occur through the handling of infected tissues from these animals or by means of the bites of infected mosquitoes, ticks, or flies. Less commonly, ingestion of contaminated water or food or exposure to infectious aerosols is the cause of human infection. The incidence of tularemia in the U.S. has fallen in recent decades from over 1000 cases to fewer than 200 cases annually.[18,19]

Epidemiologic clues to the occurrence of an intentional release of *F. tularensis* would include occurrence in a nonagricultural setting, evidence of a point-source release, and occurrence in a broad age, gender, and socioeconomic spectrum of the population.

Incubation Period

The incubation period and natural history of tularemia vary according to the mode of transmission. Because inhalational tularemia is the likeliest form to be encountered in a terrorist attack, what follows is a description of the features of this entity.[20] The incubation period would be expected to average 3 to 5 days with a range of 1 to 14 days.

Symptoms

Unlike the rapidly progressive and devastating respiratory infection associated with pneumonic plague, inhalational tularemia would typically begin with the onset of relatively mild upper respiratory symptoms with subsequent development of pneumonia in a proportion of victims over the following few days to weeks. The appearance, at that point, of a large number of individuals with a progressive form of pneumonia might be the first indication to public health authorities that an attack was underway. Until the *F. tularensis* was proven to be the cause of these symptoms, severe cases could be easily confused with plague, inhalational anthrax, or severe influenza. Ultimately, severe cases of inhalational tularemia could potentially be distinguished from inhalational anthrax by the absence of mediastinal widening (common in anthrax) and the presence of copious respiratory secretions and pulmonary consolidation (rare in anthrax).

Physical and Laboratory Features

In naturally occurring tularemia, most patients present with the ulceroglandular variety of infection. An obvious skin ulcer, representing the portal of entry of the organism accompanied by regional lymphadenopathy and systemic signs of infection, such as fever and chills, are seen in over 80% of cases, with a smaller number presenting with glandular involvement without skin lesions or a systemic illness referred to as typhoidal tularemia in which the diagnosis may be initially obscure.

However, as noted in the preceding text and chapter, an aerosol release would represent the most likely attack scenario in a bioterrorism event.

Laboratory Diagnosis

F. tularensis is a small, Gram-negative coccobacillary organism that might be recognized on routine microscopic examination of respiratory secretions. Confusion with *Hemophilus* species and anaerobic organisms from the mouth would likely interfere with the diagnosis of inhalational tularemia until the identity of the organism was confirmed by culture and the presence of an intentional release was recognized. Direct fluorescent antibody-staining techniques as well as polymerase chain reaction (PCR) assays are available for rapid identification of *F. tularensis*, but would likely be employed only for rapid screening for the organisms in the setting of a known outbreak of this otherwise-rare infection.

Containment Measures

Because tularemia is not transmitted from human to human, isolation and quarantine are not necessary and standard precautions are recommended. A risk of transmission to technologists in microbiology or other laboratories handling clinical specimens does exist, however, and it is recommended that such specimens be handled in biological safety level 2 (BSL2) conditions (see Chapter 3).[20] If procedures likely to result in aerosolization of organisms (such as centriguation) are to be employed, or if the presence of *F. tularensis* in a clinical specimen has been confirmed, processing should take place only under biological safety level 3 (BSL3) conditions.

Therapy

The aminoglycosides, either streptomycin or gentamicin, represent the therapeutic mainstays. Ciprofloxacin or doxycycline or chloramphenicol may be substituted. See Appendix A for specific treatment regimens.

Prevention

Individuals seen within the maximum incubation period, 14 days, should receive preventive therapy with either ciprofloxacin or doxycycline. After this period, such individuals should initiate therapy only if symptoms develop.[20]

Special Considerations

A great variety of conditions marked by fever and respiratory signs and symptoms as well as conditions featuring lymph node enlargement would mimic tularemia. Among these are typhoid fever, cat scratch disease, brucellosis, and bacterial endocarditis.

How the Early Stages of a Tularemia Attack Might Appear

An intentional aerosol release of *F. tularensis* might be particularly difficult to detect by public health authorities and hospitals because tularemia does not result in rapidly progressive pneumonia such as in pneumonic plague and does not produce characteristic radiographic features such as inhalational anthrax (see the preceding text). Because of the expected delay in diagnosis, a tularemia attack might not be recognized and acknowledged for several days after the initital cases present. A low-level attack, in which a relatively small number of individuals were exposed or exposure occurred over a prolonged period, might further delay the detection of this somewhat insidious infection.

Once an attack was recognized, the hospital would, as in the examples of inhalational anthrax and plague, be obligated to scrutinize community-acquired pneumonia more carefully and devise plans for excluding tularemia efficiently. However, as human-to-human transmission does not occur, issues of travel restriction and quarantine, which would rapidly emerge in smallpox or plague attacks, would be of relatively minor importance. Effective communication with the press and the public regarding the issue of person-to-person transmission would be critically important. A tularemia attack would place relatively little burden on the hospital's isolation and decontamination facilities, but surge capacity to evaluate and educate the "worried well" as in all attacks would be critical.

BOTULISM

As noted in Chapter 9, a biological attack employing botulism would most certainly come as an aerosol release of, or contamination of food or water with, the neurotoxins produced by the organism.

Causative Organism

Botulism is caused by any one of several neurotoxins produced by the Gram-positive anaerobic bacterium *Clostridium botulinum.*

Route of Transmission

In naturally occurring infection, botulism is almost always acquired through the ingestion of preformed toxin in contaminated (frequently home-preserved) foods. In infants, the disease may result from the colonization of the bowel by the organism and subsequent toxin formation. Very rarely, botulism follows contamination of a wound by the organism.

In a biological attack, botulinum toxin would most likely be disseminated through intentional contamination of food or beverages. Contamination of tap water would pose difficult dilutional problems and is considered unlikely. Most concerning of all is the prospect of aerosol dissemination because the toxin may be absorbed through the respiratory tract.

Incubation Period

The incubation period may range from less than 24 hours to several days, depending on the amount of toxin.

Symptoms

Symptoms typically begin with bulbar abnormalities. Patients may present with diplopia, ptosis, dysarthria, or dysphonia. Paralysis progresses in a descending fashion and may result in abrupt respiratory depression. The level of consciousness is preserved. The autonomic nervous system is affected, and symptoms of constipation, urinary retention, and autonomic cardiovascular effects may be prominent.[21]

Physical and Laboratory Features

Fever is absent. Physical findings mirror the symptoms and may include disconjugate gaze, paralysis of extraocular muscles or vocal cords and, subsequently, generalized motor paralysis.

Laboratory Diagnosis

Routine laboratory tests are nondiagnostic. Final confirmation of the diagnosis of botulism requires detection of the toxin in blood, feces, or gastric washings. Electrophysiologic studies typically demonstrate normal nerve conduction. Electromyography may demonstrate characteristic findings.

Containment Measures

Botulism cannot be transmitted from person to person. Standard isolation precautions are sufficient. Decontamination is unnecessary.

Therapy

Gastric lavage and enemas to remove unabsorbed toxin may be beneficial in foodborne dissemination. Antitoxin, which must be obtained from the CDC, must be given prior to the onset of symptoms. Hypersensitivity reactions to antitoxin are common.[21] Antimicrobial therapy is of no benefit. Supportive care, including ventilatory support, represents the mainstay of therapy. Although complete recovery is common, patients with respiratory paralysis typically remain ventilator-dependent for several weeks and, occasionally, for months.

Prevention

Individuals known to have been exposed to botulinum toxin should receive antitoxin under the direction of public health authorities.

Special Considerations

Differential Diagnosis and Look-Alikes

Several conditions associated with generalized paralysis may mimic some of the findings of botulism. Among these are hypokalemic periodic paralysis, Guillain–Barre syndrome, tick paralysis, poliomyelitis, and myasthenia gravis.

How the Early Stages of a Botulism Attack Might Appear

Detection of an intentional release of botulinum toxin would pose special and unique challenges to hospitals and the public health system. Because botulism causes symptoms of weakness, progressing to paralysis, the opportunities for a delay in diagnosis of this otherwise-rare condition would be great. Illnesses such as the Guillain–Barre syndrome, hypokalemic paralysis, polio-like illness following enteroviral infection, and other neurological conditions, both infectious and noninfectious, would be included in the differential diagnosis of an individual patient with botulism. Furthermore, because botulism does occasionally occur in individuals and in outbreaks within narrow geographical areas (resulting, for example, from distribution of unintentionally contaminated food), the recognition that a terrorist attack employing botulinum toxin was underway might not be apparent for days to weeks.

The demands that an outbreak of botulism (either intentional or unintentional) would place on the hospital and public health systems would also be quite different from those of other agents of bioterrorism. Human-to-human transmission does not occur. As a result, there would be no need for isolation facilities. Decontamination of victims is unnecessary. Several daunting challenges would remain, however. For actual victims of botulism, paralysis of respiratory muscles necessitating mechanical ventilation might occur rapidly. This would require pre-event planning for the equipment needs and intensive care monitoring that it would necessitate. For victims who do not suffer respiratory paralysis, hospitalization for evaluation, observation, and rehabilitation would be necessary. Public concerns about the safety of the food and water supplies might dominate the situation, and hospitals might be seen as sources of reassurance and, misguidedly, a means to have food or water tested for the toxin.

VIRAL HEMORRHAGIC FEVERS

Causative Organisms

Several unrelated viruses are capable of producing viral hemorrhagic fever (VHF) and are felt to represent potential agents of biological terrorism or warfare. Viruses in this category include:

Dengue hemorrhagic fever (DHF) virus
Ebola virus
Marburg virus
Rift Valley fever (RVF) virus
Lassa fever virus
South American hemorrhagic fever (SAHF) virus
Crimean-Congo hemorrhagic fever (CCHF) virus

Ebola and Marburg viruses are members of the Filoviridae family. They are among the most pathogenic viruses known, with some strains causing mortality rates as high as 90%.[22] The agents of Lassa fever and SAHF are members of the Arenavirus family and are associated with lower mortality rates, ranging from 15 to 30%. RVF and Crimean-Congo hemorrhagic fever are caused by viruses in Bunyaviridae group. Naturally occurring RVF is associated with much lower mortality rates than other hemorrhagic fevers (approximately 1%) in naturally occurring infections; CCHF is associated with 20 to 50% mortality rates. DHF, caused by a member of the Flavivirus group, is associated with a mortality of approximately 1%.[23]

Clinical Features

Although genetically distinct, the agents of VHF listed in the preceding text share several features:

- Each requires an animal or insect vector for natural transmission.
- Each is geographically restricted in its distribution in nature.
- All are RNA viruses.
- With the exception of DHF, none is a common cause of human infection.
- None has been employed in biological warfare or terrorism.
- All produce thrombocytopenia and clinical bleeding in human cases.
- No vaccine has been developed or licensed for any of these agents.

Route of Transmission

Person-to-person transmission has not been documented for DHF, Crimean-Congo HF, or RVF. Such transmission has been documented for the other hemorrhagic fevers.

Incubation

In naturally occurring infections, the following incubation periods have been observed:

DHF: 3 to 15 days
Ebola: 2 to 21 days
Marburg: 2 to 14 days
RVF: 2 to 6 days
Lassa fever: 3 to 16 days
SAHF: 5 to 14 days
Crimean-Congo HF: 7 to 12 days

Intentional release of the agents of any of these infections, possibly by aerosol, might result in shorter incubation periods.

Symptoms

All are associated with fever and bleeding diathesis related to thrombocytopenia with or without disseminated intravascular coagulation. DHF, Ebola, Marburg, CCHF, and RVF may progress rapidly to hypotension and multiorgan failure. Lassa fever and SAHF may progress more gradually.

Physical and Laboratory Features

Abnormalities to be expected on physical examination and in laboratory studies vary with the specific agent and are indicated in the above discussion.

Laboratory Diagnosis

Hospital clinical laboratories do not provide the diagnostic studies necessary to distinguish among the many viral pathogens that cause VHF. Antibody tests, employing a variety of techniques, are available through the CDC. Any suspected case should warrant immediate involvement of public health authorities to, among other things, facilitate confirmation of the diagnosis.

Containment Measures

Various degrees of isolation procedures are recommended, reflecting the relative contagiousness and routes of transmission of these pathogens:[24]

Lassa and South American VHF: airborne and contact precautions
Dengue: standard precautions
Ebola and Marburg: airborne precautions
Rift Valley fever: droplet and contact precautions
Crimean-Congo HF: contact precautions

Therapy

Supportive care, including efforts to improve coagulation parameters through the infusion of platelets or clotting factors, is the mainstay of therapy of all the hemorrhagic fevers. The antiviral agent ribavirin is indicated in Lassa fever and SAHF.

Prevention

Prevention efforts must focus on containment strategies as effective vaccines are currently unavailable.

How the Early Stages of a Hemorrhagic Fever Virus Attack Might Appear

Initial cases presenting with fever and rash with hemorrhagic features would likely be misdiagnosed until a clear-cut attack was identified. Hematological disorders such as autoimmune thrombocytopenic purpura (ITP) or vasculitic syndromes, either idiopathic or related to more common systemic infections such as endocarditis, meningococcemia, hepatitic B or C, or a host of other possibilities would likely be entertained before VHF unless travel to an endemic region for one of these syndromes was identified.

FOODBORNE BACTERIAL INFECTIONS

Biological attack employing foodborne bacterial pathogens such as brucella, salmonella, shigella, and *E. coli* represents a potentially feasible and relatively "low-tech" means of terrorism. Although not considered Category A agents, these and related organisms could be easily obtained and disseminated through contamination of food and water supplies. Rarely fatal, the infections resulting from such an intentional release could potentially produce substantial morbidity and create legitimate fears concerning the safety of the food supply that could result in panic, hoarding, and a dramatically negative impact on the food supply chain and related industries.

SALMONELLOSIS

A variety of *Salmonella* species are capable of causing human disease, ranging from self-limited gastroenteritis to fatal typhoid fever or extraintestinal infection. Unlike most enteric pathogens, many salmonella strains are also associated with long-term asymptomatic carrier states.

Clinical Features

Given the diversity of syndromes produced by these organisms, the clinical features of disease may vary widely. Foodborne spread of *Salmonella* species, as might be expected in a bioterrorist attack, would most likely be recognized as an outbreak of diarrheal illness.

Route of Transmission

Salmonella infection is typically transmitted by the gastrointestinal route. Depending on the species of the bacterium, naturally occurring infection may occur after exposure to contaminated food or water or through close, including sexual, contact with an infected individual.

Incubation Period

Depending on the strain of the organism employed and the amount ingested, the incubation period of salmonellosis varies from days (gastroenteritis) to weeks (typhoid fever).

Symptoms

The symptoms of salmonellosis also vary with the species of salmonella and with the size of the innoculum. When symptomatic, infection may present with mild upper (nausea, vomiting) and or lower (diarrhea, cramping) intestinal complaints. In severe cases, frank dysentery (bloody diarrhea), extraintestinal spread with bacteremia, or bowel perforation may occur.

Physical and Laboratory Features

The physical findings associated with salmonellosis also vary with inoculum size and with the *Salmonella* species. Although fever and diffuse abdominal tenderness are commonly seen, both may be absent. Obviously, in severe cases, complicated by extraintestinal spread of the infection, signs of advanced infection, including fever, chills, shock, diminished bowel sounds, and abdominal rigidity may be present in any combination. Laboratory features of severe salmonellosis may be confusing, as the organism may spread via the hematogenous route to various visceral sites, including the liver, lungs, and central nervous system. Evidence of infection in any of these sites may dominate the clinical picture in individual cases. Leukocytosis may be pronounced or absent. Examination of the stool for occult blood and for leukocytes may be positive or negative.

Laboratory Diagnosis

The diagnosis of salmonellosis can only be confirmed by isolation of the organism through culture of appropriate body fluids (stool, blood, urine).

Containment Measures

Person-to-person spread of salmonella infection may occur through fecal contamination of water, food, eating utensils, and through anal–oral contact during sexual intercourse. Individuals with known or suspected salmonellosis should observe precautions to avoid such routes of transmission to others until repeated cultures of stool are negative for the organism. Salmonella infection cannot be transmitted through the respiratory tract, and for this reason, standard precautions are acceptable for hospitalized patients.

Therapy

Supportive therapy with intravenous fluids may be necessary in patients with severe vomiting and/or diarrhea. Antibiotic therapy is necessary and may be lifesaving in cases of *Salmonella typhi* or *Salmonella paratyphi* infection (typhoid fever or paratyphoid fever) or in any case of salmonellosis complicated by bacteremia or other clear evidence of extraintestinal infection. In some categories of patients (e.g., neonates, individuals with sickle cell disease or other hemoglobinopathies, aortic aneurysm, or prosthetic cardiac or orthopedic devices) antibiotic therapy may prevent extraintestinal complications for which such individuals are at higher risk. In otherwise uncomplicated salmonella gastroenteritis, antibiotic therapy is usually unnecessary, as the illness is self-limited. Obviously, in the rare eventuality of bowel perforation, urgent surgery is required. Patients infected with *S. typhi* may become chronic carriers of the organism and thus represent an ongoing source of infection within a population. Prolonged antibiotic therapy is recommended for such individuals. Although the choice of antibiotic therapy of specific individuals with salmonella infection should be guided by susceptibility of the specific isolate cultured, a variety of agents are often effective. These include third-generation cephalosporins (e.g., ceftriaxone), quinolones (e.g., ciprofloxacin), sulfonamides (e.g., trimethoprim-sulfamethoxazole), and ampicillin or amoxicillin.

Prevention

Although a vaccine exists to prevent typhoid in travelers, no vaccine is available to prevent other forms of salmonellosis. Prevention efforts focus on identification of contaminated food and asymptomatic carriers.

Shigellosis

Infections caused by four species of the genus Shigella (*Shigella sonnei, Shigella flexneri, Shigella boydii*, and *Shigella dysenteriae*) are common worldwide. In recent years, it is estimated that approximately 163 million cases occur in developing countries and 1.5 million cases in developed countries annually.[25] In the U.S., approximately 14,000 confirmed and 450,000 suspected cases of shigellosis occur each year. Shigellae are Gram-negative bacteria that can readily be identified in clinical laboratories.

Route of Transmission

Shigella infection is typically transmitted from person to person through close physical contact or shared eating utensils. Less commonly, food or water can serve as the vehicle for transmission. Because the gastrointestinal tract is the only known portal of entry for infection with these organisms, a biological attack would presumably be carried out by contamination of food or water supplies.

Incubation Period

Symptoms typically follow within 24 to 48 hours of ingestion of a sufficient quantity of the organism.

Symptoms

Intestinal: All strains of the organism are capable of producing a diarrheal illness, sometimes following a brief period of nausea, vomiting, and abdominal pain. Diarrhea may be watery or bloody. Although fever is common, systemic spread of the organism to extraintestinal sites is unusual.

Extraintestinal: Shigellosis, by virtue of toxins manufactured by the organism, can nonetheless produce extraintestinal signs and symptoms in some individuals. Among these are the hemolytic–uremic syndrome (associated with *S. dysenteriae* infection) and Reiter's syndrome (*S. flexneri*). These extraintestinal manifestations are felt to represent autoimmune phenomena.

Physical and Laboratory Features

In the absence of extraintestinal complications as noted in the preceding text, physical findings and laboratory features are similar to those seen with other infections caused by invasive intestinal pathogens. Fever, tachycardia, and nonspecific abdominal pain are common. Laboratory evidence of dehydration as well as blood loss may be present.

Laboratory Diagnosis

Laboratory confirmation of the diagnosis of shigellosis requires isolation of the organism from clinical specimens, usually stool.

Containment Measures

Because shigella infection can be transmitted from person to person by the fecal–oral route, effective containment requires meticulous handwashing on the part of victims, contacts, and health care workers, as well as careful disposal of feces from infected patients. Airborne and droplet precautions are unnecessary. Transmission to laboratory workers is unusual and can be prevented by standard precautions taken in clinical laboratories in the handling of patient specimens.

Therapy

Antibiotic therapy is indicated in proven cases to reduce the likelihood of transmission and to shorten the course of the illness. A variety of antibiotics are effective, although increasing resistance to ampicillin and trimethoprim-sulfamethoxazole represents a challenge. Ciprofloxacin, azithromycin, and ceftriaxone remain as viable alternatives.

Prevention

No vaccine exists, and preventive antibiotics are of no proven effectiveness. Prevention measures should focus on the containment strategies mentioned above and screening of household contacts.

ESCHERICHIA COLI

Escherichia coli may represent a special threat in foodborne bioterrorism. Large-scale unintentional outbreaks have occurred on several occasions in the U.S. in recent years. A specific strain of the organism, type O157:H7, so-called enterohemorrhagic *E. coli* (EHEC) is notoriously associated with severe illness. Over 70,000 cases of infection with this strain, resulting in approximately 60 deaths, are seen annually in the U.S. Multiple recent outbreaks have been traced to undercooked ground beef. Because of such unintentional outbreaks and because EHEC cannot be distinguished from less pathogenic strains of *E. coli* that are ubiquitous in the normal human gastrointestinal tract, an insidious attack with this organism might go undetected.

Clinical Features

Although strains of the organism produce diarrheal toxins, the focus of this discussion will be on EHEC because of its high degree of pathogenicity. Diarrhea, which may range from mild and watery to severe and bloody, is typically seen. The hemolytic–uremic syndrome complicates some infections and has accounted for a disproportionate number of fatal cases. Although fever is usually absent, the severity of diarrhea and other features of the syndrome caused by EHEC may result in profound dehydration and significant blood loss with the associated findings of hypotension and tachycardia.

Route of Transmission

Infection is typically transmitted by contaminated food, although person-to-person transmission has also been documented.

Incubation Period

The incubation period is variable, averaging 4 to 5 days.

Symptoms

Cramping abdominal pain and severe diarrhea, often with bloody stools, mark the syndrome.

Physical and Laboratory Features

Physical and laboratory features are nonspecific and comparable to those seen in other severe diarrhea illness. The hemolytic–uremic syndrome is marked by acute renal failure and intravascular hemolysis. Renal abnormalities persist beyond the acute stage of infection in approximately one third of victims.

Laboratory Diagnosis

Routine stool culture techniques cannot distinguish pathogenic from nonpathogenic strains of *E. coli*. Although serotyping can confirm the presence of the O157:H7 strain, clinical laboratories do not routinely perform this test.

Containment Measures

Because person-to-person transmission has been documented, standard precautions regarding handling of stool specimens and handwashing are the most important containment measures.

Therapy

Antibiotic therapy has been shown to dramatically increase the risk of development of the hemolytic–uremic syndrome.[26] For this reason, antibiotics are relatively contraindicated. Therapy is supportive.

Prevention

There is no vaccine available, and preventive antibiotic therapy plays no role. Containment measures as noted in the preceding text are the most effective means of prevention of transmission.

BRUCELLOSIS

Brucellosis has been cited by several authors as an infection that could potentially be intentionally caused by bioterrorists.[27,28]

Causative Organisms

Brucellosis may be caused by any of several species of the genus Brucella, including *Brucella abortus, Brucella melitensis, Brucella suis, and Brucella canis.* Brucellosis is a naturally occurring infection that exists in endemic zones throughout the world. In the U.S., natural infection is most often caused by *B. abortus*, resulting from occupational exposure to cattle, or by *B. melitensis*, resulting from exposure to cattle or goats or through ingestion of unpasteurized milk.

Clinical Features

Brucellosis occurs in both acute and chronic forms, and the clinical manifestations differ somewhat among the species of brucella involved. Acute infection is usually a dramatic illness manifested as high fever, malaise, arthralgias, and headache. Involvement of the skeleton, including the joints and the spine, may be seen as manifestations of acute infection, and other end-organ involvement including that of the central nervous system, the liver (in the form of granulomatous hepatitis), or the heart may also be seen. Infection with *B. melitensis* is particularly associated with chronic brucellosis, an insidious illness, often characterized by repeated episodes of undifferentiated fever and chronic end-organ damage, particularly vertebral osteomyelitis.

Route of Transmission

Naturally occurring brucellosis is transmitted through the ingestion of contaminated dairy products or by contact with tissues or body fluids of infected animals through microscopic breaks in the skin. In a biological attack, brucellosis would most likely be released through contamination of food or beverages and enter the body through the gastrointestinal tract.

Incubation Period

The incubation period of brucellosis is quite variable, ranging from 5 to 60 days in most cases, but occasionally several months.

Symptoms

The symptoms of brucellosis vary greatly among patients. Acute brucellosis is most often experienced as an undifferentiated febrile illness, often with pronounced bone and joint pain. Specific end-organ localization (see the preceding text) may produce complaints referable to the spine, the central nervous system, or the liver as dominant features in some cases.

Physical and Laboratory Features

Physical findings of brucellosis are typically nonspecific. Often fever occurs in the absence of other specific abnormalities. When spinal involvement is present, point tenderness over the lumbar area may be present. Leukocytosis may or may not be present.

Laboratory Diagnosis

The laboratory diagnosis of brucellosis is typically made by means of agglutination tests on serum that detect antibodies to the organism. Cultures of blood or bone marrow may be positive, but require prolonged incubation.

Containment Measures

No isolation is necessary for patients with brucellosis unless there is uncontrolled drainage of potentially infectious material, such as pus. No immunization or preventive antibiotic therapy of contacts is required.

Therapy

Effective therapy of brucellosis requires prolonged courses (45 days or more) of combinations of antibiotics. Doxycycline, combined with either streptomycin or gentamicin, or with rifampin are recommended regimens (see Appendix A).

Prevention

Postexposure preventive therapy with either doxycycline or doxycycline plus rifampin continued for 3 to 6 weeks is recommended (see Appendix A). There is currently no vaccine available to prevent human brucellosis.[29] Animal vaccines against brucellosis are available, and substantial research has been conducted in preventing brucellosis in livestock. Adverse reactions, including brucellosis itself, in humans have resulted from inadvertent exposure to the veterinary vaccines.[30]

Special Considerations

The vague nature of the clinical manifestations of brucellosis make misdiagnosis likely. Other conditions associated with undifferentiated fever (such as tuberculosis, typhoid fever, osteomyelitis, or endocarditis) may be considered first before a diagnosis of brucellosis is entertained, particularly in urban or other nonendemic settings.

SELECTED OTHER PATHOGENS OF CONCERN

Melioidosis and Glanders

Causative Organisms

The etiologic agents of melioidosis and of glanders are the Gram-negative bacteria *Burkholderia pseudomallei* and *Burkholderia mallei*, respectively. Naturally occurring glanders is an extremely rare infection of humans. It can, also rarely, cause a rapidly spreading infection among horses, donkeys, and mules. Melioidosis, although also uncommon, is a more frequent cause of human infection that is endemic in scattered areas of Asia, the middle East, and Latin America. Although a variety of mammals and birds can become infected with *P. pseudomallei*, there is no defined animal reservoir of melioidosis. It can, however, be found in the soil and water of endemic areas. Of these two unusual infections, more is known regarding the human infection caused by *P. pseudomallei* (melioidosis) than about human glanders. For this reason, the following discussion applies, unless otherwise indicated, to melioidosis. As noted, however, both organisms have been suggested as potential agents of biological attack.

Route of Transmission

Naturally occurring melioidosis is thought to be acquired in several ways, including through direct contact with contaminated soil or water through microscopic breaks in the skin as well as through ingestion or inhalation of contaminated environmental materials.[5] As a putative agent of bioterrorism, *P. pseudomallei* could therefore be released by means of an aerosol or through the food and water supply.

Incubation Period

Serologic studies suggest that the majority of individuals infected with *P. pseudomallei* never develop symptoms of melioidosis.[5] For this reason, the incubation period after various routes of exposure is largely unknown. Rapidly progressive pulmonary infection can apparently occur within 2 days of exposure in rare instances.

Symptoms

As noted, the majority of cases of melioidosis appear to be asymptomatic. When symptoms are related to the infection, they typically involve the respiratory tract. Acute or subacute infection may follow significant exposure with the development of signs and symptoms of necrotizing pneumonia (cough, hemoptysis) or with insidious symptoms such as weight loss and obscure fever. This range of respiratory symptoms and the frequency of asymptomatic infection is somewhat reminiscent of tuberculosis. Extrapulmonary sites of involvement, particularly osteomyelitis, may also be seen in melioidosis with the expected symptoms of fever and bone or joint pain.

Physical and Laboratory Features

As noted, melioidosis varies greatly in severity and rapidity of progression. In severe respiratory infection, the typical findings of fulminant pneumonia with septicemia (high fever, pulmonary consolidation, and hypotension) would be expected. Milder or more chronic cases may present with intermittent fever and progressive cachexia.

Laboratory Diagnosis

Confirmation of infection requires isolation of the organism from respiratory secretions or other sites of involvement.

Containment Measures

Person-to-person transmission of melioidosis appears not to occur. Nonetheless, because of uncertainty in this area, respiratory precautions are recommended for proven or suspected cases.[5]

Therapy

Trimethoprim-sulfamethoxazole, ceftazidime, doxycycline, chloramphenicol, and ampicillin-sulbactam represent effective therapeutic options. Specific treatment regimens may be found in Appendix A.

Prevention

There is currently no means of immunization against melioidosis available, and the role of postexposure antibiotic therapy is undefined. Respiratory precautions would most likely be adequate to prevent transmission to first responders and health care workers, but the ramifications of a massive exposure to airborne organisms, as might occur in an attack, are unknown.

Special Considerations

Because of its rarity, melioidosis is unlikely to be diagnosed prior to culture confirmation of infection with *P. pseudomallei*. The range of acute and chronic respiratory syndromes it may cause would predictably result in its confusion with more common causes of acute and subacute community-acquired pneumonia. The sudden appearance of multiple cases in regions where the infection is not endemic would likely be required before a biological attack with this organism would be recognized.

Q Fever

Causative Organism

The etiologic agent of Q fever is the obligate intracellular bacterium *Coxiella burnetii.*

Route of Transmission

In naturally occurring infections, *Coxiella burnetii* typically enters the body through the respiratory route following exposure to infected aerosols from the milk, cheese, or products of conception of infected animals, usually sheep, rabbits, or cats.[17] Aerosolization of the organism would be the likely route of transmission in a biological attack.

Incubation Period

In naturally occurring infection, Q fever has a prolonged incubation period, averaging 3 to 4 weeks.

Symptoms

Q fever may occur in both acute and chronic forms. Acute Q fever is a respiratory infection indistinguishable from other causes of community-acquired pneumonia, presenting with fever, myalgias, and cough that is typically nonproductive. The liver may be secondarily involved, and right upper quadrant pain and tenderness, sometimes accompanied by hepatomegaly with or without splenomegaly, may be present. Chronic Q fever may manifest as endocarditis with typical associated signs and symptoms or may present as a persistent pulmonary infiltrate or pseudotumor or simply as a "fever of unknown origin."

Physical and Laboratory Features

Although fever and respiratory symptoms are common in acute Q fever, physical findings of lung consolidation may be absent. A so-called pulse–temperature deficit, in which high fever may occur in the absence of tachycardia, may be seen in Q fever. As noted, hepatosplenomegaly may be found. Liver function abnormalities may be detected in acute or chronic cases as a manifestation of granulomatous hepatitis.

Laboratory Diagnosis

Although *C. burnetii* may be recovered from blood using specialized culture media, it poses a hazard to laboratory workers. Serologic studies represent the mainstay of diagnosis of Q fever. A variety of techniques for detecting antibody to various stages of the organism is available.

Containment Measures

Person-to-person transmission of *C. burnetii* appears to occur rarely, if at all. Standard precautions are sufficient. Contaminated clothing, however, may represent a source of infection.

Therapy

Q fever may be treated with tetracyclines or ciprofloxacin. Therapy of Q fever endocarditis must be continued for several years. See Appendix A of this book for detailed treatment protocols.

Prevention

No vaccine is currently commercially available in the U.S. However, an investigational vaccine is used to protect workers in high-risk occupations.[5]

RICIN POISONING

Clinical Features

The clinical features of ricin intoxication are somewhat unpredictable because of the limited nature of human and animal data available. What follows is a discussion, somewhat speculative, of the clinical scenarios to be anticipated.

Route of Transmission

Poisoning with ricin, a naturally occurring substance derived from castor plants and beans, may occur by the gastrointestinal, inhalational, or parenteral route. The toxin accumulates naturally as a by-product of the production of castor oil and is also present in sufficient quantities in castor beans to cause poisoning, which may be fatal. It is assumed, however, that a biological attack would come by aerosolization of powdered ricin toxin distributed through the mail or air-handling systems.

Incubation Period

Inhalational ricin poisoning has not been described either as naturally occurring or as intentional occurrence at the time of this writing. For this reason, details such as the required innoculum size and the incubation period of intoxication represent extrapolations from animal data. It appears from such data that the incubation period may be as short as several hours and the innoculum required to produce disease may be as little as 500 micrograms, making ricin toxin one of the most poisonous compounds known.

Symptoms

Because ricin intoxication has rarely been described in humans, the symptoms to be expected in victims of a ricin attack are not completely known. However, data from animal experiments and limited information for both gastrointestinal and inhalational exposure to the toxin provide some insights. If ingested, ricin toxin would be expected to produce nausea, vomiting, and diarrhea with or without abdominal pain and cramping. In severe poisoning by this route, hepatic and renal failure would be anticipated within 2 to 3 days. Animal studies of gastrointestinal ricin poisoning have demonstrated diffuse ulcerations within the gastrointestinal tract with hemorrhage and necrosis of mesenteric lymph nodes.

Inhalational ricin intoxication would be expected to result in the rapid onset (within 4 to 6 hours) of nonspecific complaints including dyspnea, chest tightness, and fever. In animal studies, pulmonary edema and hemorrhage, hypotension, and death occurred within 2 to 3 days.[31]

Physical and Laboratory Features

The physical findings associated with ricin intoxication reflect the level and route of exposure. In extreme cases, hypotension would be anticipated and inhalational exposure would result in a pattern of noncardiogenic pulmonary edema, whereas massive ingestion would produce a picture suggestive of severe enterocolitis. Systemic signs of infection, including fever and leukocytosis, may or may not be present. The results of other routine laboratory and radiographic studies would reflect the end-organ involvement (e.g., respiratory, hepatic, renal, gastrointestinal tract) and severity of individual cases.

Laboratory Diagnosis

Laboratory confirmation of ricin intoxication would require identification of the agent in environmental sources to which the victim was exposed. No reliable tests for ricin in body fluids are available at the time of this writing.

Containment Measures

Containment procedures to be observed during a ricin attack are largely speculative. Aerosol exposure to ricin, in which contamination of skin and clothing should be anticipated, necessitates gross decontamination (removal of exposed clothing and jewelry and washing of exposed areas of skin), which should be carried out prior to arrival at the hospital, if feasible.[31] Such field decontamination is unnecessary for victims exposed through ingestion. Environmental surfaces and nondisposable personal protective gear should be washed with water and soap or 0.1% sodium hypochlorite solution. Personal protective equipment for first responders and for hospital personnel involved in gross decontamination should include a full chemical-resistant suit with gloves, surgical mask, and protective eyewear. Such personnel should shower after completing decontamination procedures.

Therapy

Therapy of victims of ricin intoxication is largely supportive. Ricin cannot be removed by dialysis. Gastric lavage and activated charcoal may be appropriate in management of ricin ingestion.

Prevention

There is no means of preventing ricin intoxication after significant exposure other than removal of unabsorbed toxin from the intestinal tract. As noted above, the likelihood of inhalational poisoning may be reduced through the use of appropriate personal protective equipment.

Special Considerations

Given the nonspecific and dose-related nature of the clinical syndrome produced by ricin intoxication, the differential diagnosis of victims of a ricin attack by aerosol would be lengthy and would include, among other entities, the following:[31]

1. Staphylococcal enterotoxin syndromes, including gastroenteritis and toxic-shock syndrome
2. Exposure to by-products of organofluorines-pyrolysis (Teflon, Kevlar)
3. Nitrogen oxide intoxication
4. Phosgene exposure
5. Influenza
6. Anthrax
7. Q fever
8. Pneumonic plague

Gastrointestinal ricin intoxication might mimic, among other entities:

1. Salmonellosis, shigellosis, or other infection with enteric pathogens
2. Mushroom poisoning
3. Caustic ingestions
4. Poisoning with iron or arsenic
5. Colchicine overdose

References

1. Henderson, D.A. et al., Smallpox as a biological weapon: medical and public health management, *JAMA*, 281, 2127, 1999.
2. Breman, J.G. and Henderson, D.A., Diagnosis and management of smallpox, *N Engl J Med*, 46, 130, 2002.
3. Artenstein, A.W., Bioterrorism and biodefense, in Cohen, J. and Powderly, W.G. (Eds.), *Infectious Diseases*, Mosby, New York, 2004.
4. Dixon, C.W., *Smallpox*, Long, England: J. & A. Churchill, 1962:1460.
5. Chin, J. (Ed.), *Control of Communicable Diseases Manual: An Official Report of the American Public Health Association*, American Public Health Association, Washington, D.C., 2000.
6. Centers for Disease Control and Prevention, Multistate outbreak of monkeypox — Illinois, Indiana, and Wisconsin, 2003, *Morbid Mortal Weekly Rep* 13, 537, 2003.
7. Jernigan, J.A. et al., Bioterrorism-related inhalational anthrax: the first 10 cases reported in the United States, *Emerg Infect Dis*, 7, 933, 2001.

8. Mayer, T.A. et al., Clinical presentation of inhalational anthrax following bioterrorism exposure: report of 2 surviving patients, *JAMA*, 286, 2549, 2001.
9. Borio, L. et al., Death due to bioterrorism-related inhalational anthrax: report of 2 patients, *JAMA*, 286, 2554, 2001.
10. Dixon, T.C. et al., Anthrax, *N Engl J Med.*, 341, 815, 1999.
11. Inglesby, T.V. et al., Anthrax as a biological weapon 2002: updated recommendations for management, *JAMA*, 287, 2236–2652, 2002.
12. Centers for Disease Control and Prevention, Update: Investigation of bioterrorism-related anthrax and interim guidelines for clinical evaluation of persons with possible anthrax. *Morbid Mortal Weekly Rep*, 50, 941, 2001.
13. Franz, D.R. et al., Clinical recognition and management of patients exposed to biological warfare agents, *JAMA*, 278, 399, 1997.
14. Tierney, B.C. et al., Serious adverse events among participants in the Centers for Disease Control and Prevention's anthrax vaccine and antimicrobial availability program for persons at risk for bioterrorism-related inhalational anthrax, *Clin Infect Dis*, 37, 905, 2003.
15. Centers for Disease Control and Prevention, Suspected brucellosis case prompts investigation of possible bioterrorism-related activity — New Hampshire and Massachusetts, 1999, *Morbid Mortal Weekly Rep*, 49(23), 509, 2000.
16. Inglesby, T.V. et al., Plague as a biological weapon: medical and public health management, *JAMA*, 283(17), 2281, 2000.
17. Betts R.F., Chapman, S.W., Penn, R.L. (Eds.) Lower respiratory tract infections, in Reese and Betts' *A Practical Approach to Infectious Diseases*, Lippincott Williams & Wilkins, Philadelphia, p. 334, 2003.
18. Centers for Disease Control and Prevention, Summary of notifiable diseases: United States, 1997, *Morbid Mortal Weekly Rep*, 46, 71, 1998.
19. Boyce, J.M., Recent trends in the epidemiology of tularemia in the United States, *J Infect Dis*, 131, 197, 1975.
20. Dennis, D.T. et al., Tularemia as a biological weapon: medical and public health management, *JAMA*, 285(21), 2763, 2001.
21. Wood, M.J., Toxin-mediated disorders: tetanus, botulism, and diphtheria, in Cohen, J. and Powderly, W.G. (Eds.), *Infectious Diseases*, 2nd edition, Mosby, New York, 2004.
22. Bronze, M.S. et al., Viral agents as biological weapons and agents of bioterrorism, *Am J Med Sci*, 323(6), 316, 2002.
23. Borio, L. et al., Hemorrhagic fever viruses as biological weapons: medical and public health management, *JAMA*, 297(18), 2391, 2002.
24. Weinstein, R.S. and Alibek, K., *Biological and Chemical Terrorism: A Guide for Healthcare Providers and First Responders*. Thieme, New York, 2003.
25. Kotloff, K.L. et al., Global burden of Shigella infections: implications of vaccine development and implementation of control strategies, *Bull World Health Organ*, 77, 651, 1999.
26. Conlon, C.P., Food-borne and water-borne infections, in Cohen, J. and Powderly, W.G. (Eds.), *Infectious Diseases*, 2nd edition, Mosby, New York, 2004.
27. Voskuhl, G.W. and Greenfield, R.A., Other bacterial diseases as a potential consequence of bioterrorism: Q fever, brucellosis, glanders, and melioidosis, *J Okla State Med Assoc*, 96(5), 214, 2003.
28. Chang, M.H., Glynn, M.K., and Groseclose, S.L., Endemic, notifiable bioterrorism-related diseases: United States, 1992–1999, *Emerg Infect Dis*, 9(5), 556, 2003.

29. Ko, J. and Splitter, G.A., Molecular host-pathogen interaction in brucellosis: current understanding and future approaches to vaccine development of mice and humans, *Clin Microbiol Rev*, 16(1), 65, 2003.
30. Berkelman, R.L., Human illness associated with use of veterinary vaccines, *Clin Infect Dis*, 37, 407, 2003.
31. Daniels, K., Recognition, management and surveillance of ricin-associated illness, www.phppo.cdc.gov/phtn/webcast/ricin/tp_ricin_final_12-17-03, 2003.

11 Meeting the Needs of Children

INTRODUCTION

Biological weapons development has its roots in military planning, so it is not surprising that planning for treatment of potential victims has tended to focus on healthy young adults — namely, soldiers.

Many references and training materials in the field, such as the handbook *Medical Management of Biological Casualties*, have been produced by the U.S. Army Medical Research Institute of Infectious Diseases. Even as the literature on bioterrorism expanded in recent years, the needs of children and the planning requirements of pediatrics services within hospitals received relatively little attention. Analyses of large-scale exercises and drills have provided little insight into issues specific to children. Research into how children react to disasters, both natural and man-made, is limited.[1] As recently as 1997, no state disaster plans specifically addressed pediatric issues.[2]

Nonetheless, obvious questions emerge when one examines what a bioterrorist attack — or any attack with a weapon of mass destruction — might mean for children and the hospitals that care for them. These issues need to be addressed in planning by all medical providers, whether or not they normally care for pediatric patients.

In emergency conditions, victims and potential victims often appear at hospitals without regard to niceties of specialization or census. This can occur even when all victims are transported by emergency services workers, as with the 1990 Avianca plane crash on Long Island, where severely injured pediatric survivors were not taken to the most appropriate facilities available.[3] However, it is especially likely when victims come in without EMS transport, usually choosing the geographically closest hospitals.[4,5] Such self-referral is particularly likely after a biological attack, which can be expected to occur in stealth and come to attention over time as ill people seek treatment. Pediatric cases are likely to begin as a trickle of ill children brought in by their parents, and then become a torrent of the ill and the well, as knowledge of the attack spreads.

In a widespread biological attack, most pediatric patients are likely to be seen at hospitals without specialized pediatric facilities. Of the approximately 5300 U.S. hospitals that have emergency departments, it is estimated that only one third have separate pediatric departments or wards and only 23% have pediatric emergency physicians in house or on call 24 hours a day.[6] It would be wise to assume that in a large-scale attack, many children would be cared for by providers without pediatric training or experience.

The dosages and safety profiles of medications, as well as recommendations for vaccination, may differ for children of various ages and body weights. In this book, medication and vaccine-related issues pertaining to children are addressed along with those of adults in Appendix A. Other important issues concerning children are discussed in this chapter.

CHILDREN'S SUSCEPTIBILITY TO BIOLOGICAL AGENTS

For a variety of reasons, children can be expected to have special vulnerabilities to biological agents. It has been suggested that these differences could lead to a disproportionate number of pediatric casualties in a mass casualty event.[7,8] In the 1995 bombing of the Alfred P. Murrah Federal Building, which contained a day-care center, 31% of the pediatric casualties died, compared to 21% of the adult casualties.[9]

PHYSIOLOGICAL VULNERABILITY

Children's greater rate of respiration and closeness to the ground may expose them to relatively higher doses of agents that are aerosolized, such as the anthrax used in the 2001 attacks.[10]

Because their skin is thinner and less well keratinized, and their surface to mass ratio is higher, children may be more susceptible than adults to agents that are absorbed through the skin.[10–12]

Children's relatively greater surface area also increases their heat loss, and several experts have counseled that use of heat lamps, blankets, and other heat-maintenance measures may be needed to prevent hypothermia after decontamination showering.[10,13,14]

Both transdermal absorption and decontamination hypothermia would be more likely to pose problems in a chemical rather than a biological attack. Relatively few biological agents thought likely to be used as weapons are absorbed through intact skin, and biological weapons are less likely than chemical ones to require decontamination.[10,12,13]

In biological attacks, as in naturally occurring outbreaks, young children's developmental and cognitive characteristics could make them more likely than adults to become infected with pathogens that can be transmitted orally. More generally, young children's limited ability to comprehend risk, follow instructions, and take steps to protect themselves, especially in the absence of their parents, could leave them more prone to infection.

If infected with an agent that causes vomiting and diarrhea, young children, with their smaller reserves of fluid, are more likely than adults to suffer rapid and dangerous dehydration.

In the event of an attack with smallpox, children might be expected to have higher rates of mortality than adults because they lack any residual protection from old vaccinations. Although routine smallpox vaccination ended in the U.S. in 1972, some experts think that vaccinations given before that date might lessen the severity of smallpox in some adults.[12] In the 2003 smallpox vaccination campaign, which focused on military service members and health care workers, children were not vaccinated. CDC guidelines recommend against vaccinating children under age 1 in the current low-risk environment.

Despite their potential vulnerabilities, in a study of U.S. cases of illness involving seven pathogens often mentioned as potential weapons, most occurred in adults at least 25 years old. The exceptions were the two most common agents: Tularemia, which caused an average 111 cases a year, was most common in children 1 to 14 years of age; foodborne botulism, which averaged 102 cases a year, was most common in infants under 1 year. The data came from 1992 through 1997; the other illnesses reviewed were anthrax, brucellosis, cholera, plague, and viral encephalitides.[15]

DIFFERENCES IN THE CLINICAL COURSE OF DISEASES

The clinical presentations in children of the most likely agents of biological attack are generally comparable to those seen in adults, but potential differences do exist. In addition, diagnosis of young children may be complicated by their inability to recount their recent activities and contacts or to describe how they are feeling.

ANTHRAX

It has been suggested that children may be more resistant than adults to anthrax; evidence cited includes the absence of child victims in 1979, when anthrax was inadvertently released from a Soviet bioweapons factory in Sverdlovsk, killing more than 60 people.[12,16] In the U.S., where anthrax is rare at any age, it is vanishingly rare among children. Of 224 cases of cutaneous anthrax reported in the U.S. from 1944 to 2000, none occurred in children.[17] But in other countries, children have been well represented in case series. In a Centers for Disease Control (CDC) review of 366 cutaneous anthrax cases in Haiti in 1973 to 1974, the age distribution of cases generally paralleled that of the population, although the proportion of cases in the 15- to 44-year age group was lower than the proportion of people in that age group.[18] Of 23 cutaneous anthrax cases admitted to an Indian hospital in 1998 to 2001, most were children.[19]

When infection occurs in children, its clinical course has been described as being similar to that in adults, with cutaneous anthrax presenting as primarily a local infection; if systemic disease develops, it generally responds well to antibiotics.[17] But among the U.S. cases in 2001, when anthrax spores were sent through the mail, one child, a previously healthy 7-month-old boy, contracted cutaneous anthrax and quickly developed severe systemic illness, with hemolytic anemia, coagulopathy and hyponatremia.[17]

The infant, the only child among the 22 people infected in the outbreaks, apparently contracted anthrax during an hour he spent in his mother's office, which was later found to be contaminated with anthrax spores. His illness was initially thought to have been caused by the bite of a brown recluse spider, *Loxosceles recluse*;

anthrax was not diagnosed until day 12 of his 17-day hospitalization. Several of his signs and symptoms were more commonly associated with venomous bites than with cutaneous anthrax, according to the physicians who treated him.[17]

Because of the speed with which severe illness developed in this case, the physicians who treated the infant urged that if anthrax is suspected, a child should be quickly hospitalized and started on intravenous antibiotics, with close monitoring of electrolyte and hematological status.[17]

VENEZUELAN EQUINE ENCEPHALITIS

Children, like the elderly, are more likely than most adults to suffer life-threatening encephalitis after infection with Venezuelan equine encephalitis, usually a self-limited disease in adults. In natural epidemics, such encephalitis has been seen in about 4% of cases.[20]

MELIOIDOSIS (*BURKHOLDERIA PSEUDOMALLEI*)

Melioidosis, which is endemic in many parts of Asia and Africa, is caused by *Burkholderia* (formerly *Pseudomonas*) *pseudomallei*, a bacterium that was studied as a potential biological agent by the Soviet Union.[21] Infected children commonly have suppurative parotitis, a manifestation rarely seen in adult patients.[22] In a series of 55 infected children in Thailand, 35 had localized infections; of these, 40% had suppurative parotitis, which was the most common manifestation of disease in these patients. While the localized disease caused no deaths, 20 of the 55 children had septicemia; the fatality rate in this group was 60%.[23]

CHILDREN'S PSYCHOLOGICAL NEEDS

Children, like adults, are likely to have painful psychological and emotional responses to terrorism that in most cases will resolve with time and normal social supports. There is some evidence that children may be especially vulnerable to psychological distress.[24] Children of all ages may show signs of anxiety or posttraumatic stress disorder (PTSD), such as traumatic dreams, sleep problems, irritability, intense distress at reminders of the trauma, and feelings that they are reexperiencing the event.[25]

Emotional and psychological responses occur even in children who have witnessed terrorism only indirectly, such as through the media. Six months after the September 11, 2001, terrorist attacks on the World Trade Center and the Pentagon, a survey of more than 8000 children in grades 4 to 12 in New York City found 10.5% reported symptoms of PTSD. Researchers estimated the rate of such symptoms before 9/11 would have been 2%, based on data from other cities; no comparable data for New York City existed.[26]

Two years after the Oklahoma bombing, 16% of children who lived approximately 100 miles away reported significant PTSD symptoms related to the event.[27] These children were not directly exposed to the trauma and did not lose relatives in the attack.

TABLE 11.1
Psychic Impact on Children of Terrorism

Study	Subjects	Postevent	Event-Related Effects
After Oklahoma City Bombing			
Pfefferbaum, 2000	88 sixth-graders, living 100 miles away	2 years	16% had significant PTSD symptoms
After September 11, 2001 Attacks			
Fairbrother, 2003	NYC parents	4 months	18% of children had severe or very severe posttraumatic stress reaction (PTSR) 66% had moderate PTSR
Applied Research and Consulting, 2002	8266 NYC children (grades 4–8)	6 months	10.5% had symptoms of PTSD
Redlener, 2002	400 NYC parents with children ages 4–18	6 months	19% (of children) had new somatic complaints

Sources: Pfefferbaum et al., Posttraumatic stress two years after the Oklahoma City bombing in youths geographically distant from the explosion, *Psychiatry*, 63, 358, 2000. Fairbrother, G. et al., Posttraumatic stress reactions in New York City children after the December 11, 2001, terrorist attacks, *Ambul Pediatr*, 3, 304, 2003. Applied Research and Consulting LLC, Columbia University Mailman School of Public Health and New York State Psychiatric Institute, Effects of the World Trade Center Attack on NYC Public School Students: Initial Report to the New York City Board of Education, 2002. Redlener, I. and Grant, R., The 9/11 terror attacks: Emotional consequences persist for children and their families, *Contemp Pediatr*, September 2002.

Children may also develop minor somatic complaints after terrorism, such as stomachache and headache. A survey of 400 New York City parents with children between ages 4 and 18, conducted in 2002, suggests that nearly one in five children developed new somatic complaints after September 11, 2001.[28]

In addition, as shown in the accompanying chart, there is ample evidence that children can suffer stress after hospitalization for serious illness, as might occur in a biological attack. For the parents of critically ill children, stress levels can approach panic levels initially upon emergency admission. As a result, parents may have difficulty remembering or asking questions.[29] In a biological attack, the usual stress from illness could be expected to be amplified if the treatment and transmission routes of the pathogen are not clear (see Table 11.1 and Table 11.2).

Factors Affecting Children's Responses

Several factors have been identified as affecting children's responses, including:

- Children's cognitive, emotional, and social developmental level: Toddlers may regress and grow clingy. School-age children may regress, show hostility, reenact the trauma, and shun activities they once enjoyed.

TABLE 11.2
Psychic Impact of Illness on Children

Study	Subjects	Postevent	Event-Related Effects
Connolly, 2004	43 pediatric (age 5–12) cardiac surgery survivors	Post-op	12% had PTSD
Judge, 2002	29 PICU survivors (age 2–15) with meningococcal disease; patients' mothers	3–12 months	10% of children probable PTSD; 62% had symptoms 48% of mothers had significant PTSD symptoms
Rees, 2004	19 PICU survivors (age 5–18); 33 of patients' parents	6–12 months	21% of children had PTSD 27% of parents screened positive for PTSD

Source: *Connolly, D. et al., Posttraumatic stress disorder in children after cardiac surgery, J Pediatr*, 144, 480, 2004. Judge D. et al., Psychiatric adjustment following meningococcal disease treated on a PICU, *Intensive Care Med*, 28, 648, 2002. Rees, G. et al., Psychiatric outcome following paediatric intensive care unit (PICU) admission: a cohort story, *Intensive Care Med*, epub, 2004.

Adolescents may also shun previously favored activities and may use illicit substances.[30–33]

- The degree of disruption of daily life, including injury of self, relatives, or friends, and bereavement:[32–34] In the study of New York schoolchildren 6 months after 9/11, children who had to leave their homes or who had a relative who experienced the attack were twice as likely to report symptoms of PTSD as other children. Children who lost a family member were three to four times as likely to report symptoms.[26] Experts counsel that, to the extent possible, it is helpful to maintain daily routines for children after a traumatic event.[32,33]
- Children's prior experiences with trauma: For children, as for adults, those with a history of trauma are more likely to develop symptoms of PTSD.[26,30] In the study of New York schoolchildren 6 months after 9/11, factors linked to PTSD symptoms included younger age (grades 4–5); female gender; previous traumatic experience; and, to a lesser extent, Hispanic ethnicity.[26] It can be sobering to contemplate how common traumatic experience may be in children's lives, especially in a lower-income urban environment. In the New York City study, 64% of students reported having been exposed to one or more traumatic events before 9/11; 39% said they had seen someone get killed or seriously injured.[26] Young immigrants also may have experienced high levels of stress in the past. A 2002 study of 1004 recent immigrant schoolchildren in Los Angeles found that 32% reported PTSD symptoms in the clinical range, and 16% reported depressive symptoms in the clinical range. Participants were aged 8 to 15 years and spoke Spanish, Korean, Russian, and Western Armenian.[35]

- The emotional and psychological state of parents and other important adults. Children can cope better with disaster if their parents or other caretakers are functioning well. Helping parents cope well is an important way to help children. School, faith-based and other voluntary organizations can help bolster parents' resilience, in part by offering practical support.[30,31]
- The level of support available within the family and community:[30,31]
- Extensive exposure to media reports about the traumatic event: Pediatric experts commonly counsel caretakers not to allow young children to watch repeated television reports about a disaster or, at the least, to make sure a responsible adult watches with the child to provide reassurance and explanation.[30] Most discussions of media impact have focused on television, the primary media of young children. But a study of children living 100 miles from Oklahoma City 2 years after the bombing of that city's federal building found that reading print coverage of the event was more strongly associated with enduring PTSD symptoms than was watching television. One possible explanation is that, while many children are passively exposed to television reports without seeking exposure, children who had more intense reactions to the bombing may have sought out print stories about it.[34]

Lack of Child-Oriented Resources

Pediatric inpatient units, including intensive care and isolation areas, typically have smaller capacity than adult units and, therefore, less flexibility in accommodating significant surges in numbers of patients. In addition, some institutions that might be enlisted to help provide surge capacity in an emergency, such as the Veterans Administration hospitals, lack pediatric beds and personnel trained in pediatrics.

Rescue units and emergency departments may also have only limited amounts of pediatric resuscitative and other equipment. Decontamination units, personal protective equipment, and isolation facilities for adults may not be appropriate for young children.

Some of the drugs, such as quinolones and tetracyclines, which are recommended for treatment and prophylaxis of many potential biological agents, are not widely used in children. As a result, pharmacies are unlikely to stock large amounts in liquid formulations, and pediatricians may have little experience with them.[12]

In the event of a widespread biological attack, the need to care for infants and children would be likely to present problems that go far beyond strictly medical matters. Young patients might present to hospitals without a responsible adult to provide emotional support, legal consent, or medical histories. Such children might be expected to arrive at the hospital terrified, and some could be expected to panic when strange adults in scary-looking protective suits and masks try to examine or treat them.

In such a crisis, hospitals might need to play an unaccustomed role in reuniting families; in sheltering children whose guardians are ill or otherwise unavailable; in meeting the daily needs of feeding, changing, and nurturing a large number of babies and toddlers; and in providing psychological and social supports for children who may have lost their families, temporarily or permanently.

In planning for surge capacity, practitioners need to try to address such needs, perhaps by forming liaisons with voluntary or religious organizations that could provide volunteers to care for children. Planners may also want to consider ways of keeping parents and children, or sibling groups, together where possible, even if they would normally be separated by age. Not only could that help patients emotionally, but it could allow older relatives to perform some of the daily care functions and monitoring of health status for younger children. Keeping infants and mothers together is obviously of special importance both medically and emotionally.

Triage of Children in a Mass Casualty Situation

Need for a Triage System

In normal conditions, hospital emergency medical staff try to save every patient's life, and typically make especially heroic efforts to save children. In an extreme mass casualty situation, however, as in military combat, victims unlikely to be saved might have to be left untreated, and some would be classified as deceased at a time when resuscitation normally would be attempted. It is possible that such emotionally wrenching decisions would have to be made about children by medical professionals who have relatively little experience treating critically ill children.

To minimize triage errors in this difficult setting, and to buffer practitioners from bearing the full weight of these decisions, experts at a consensus conference, convened in 2003 by the Columbia University Mailman School of Public Health's National Center for Disaster Preparedness, advocated that first responders and hospitals incorporate use of a pediatric-specific triage system that provides objective standards for decision making.[2]

JumpSTART

As of 2003, the only such system was the JumpSTART Pediatric Multiple Casualty Incident Triage system, developed in 1995 by Dr. Lou E. Romig, a pediatric emergency specialist at Miami Children's Hospital in Miami, FL.[2] Her triage algorithm for pediatric mass casualties, which was updated in 2001, is based on the widely used START (Simple Triage and Rapid Treatment) system developed by the Newport Beach Fire Department and Hoag Memorial Presbyterian Hospital in California.[36] START aims to assess respiration, perfusion, and mental status and reach a primary triage decision in less than a minute. It sorts patients into four categories, represented by colored tags: red (critical; needs immediate treatment), yellow (needs treatment, but it can be delayed), green (ambulatory; minor symptoms), and black (unsalvageable; deceased or "expectant").

In the adult START system, if a patient is not breathing once an airway is cleared, he is deemed unsalvageable. In the pediatric JumpSTART system, an apneic patient is given a pulse check. If a pulse is found, the patient receives a five-breath ventilatory trial with a mouth-to-mask apparatus, the "jumpstart" in the system. If apnea persists, the patient gets a black tag; if breathing starts, the patient is classified as critical (red tag). This difference reflects the fact that children are more likely than adults to present with apnea when their cardiovascular system is still functioning. If a pulse check cannot be performed or the practitioner doubts his ability to find a pulse, the five-breath trial is given without the check. JumpSTART's other features parallel those in START, with assessment standards modified to reflect pediatric physiology.[37]

The JumpSTART algorithm and supporting materials may be found at Romig's website (www.jumpstarttriage.com).

Triage Training

There is reason to believe that training can improve practitioners' somewhat shaky abilities to perform triage in mass casualty scenarios. In a study of triage accuracy in 109 practitioners, including emergency medical technicians, paramedics, and registered nurses, the mean score rose from 55% correct to 75% correct after a 2-hour slide and video presentation on use of START; the improvement persisted 1 month later.[38] A similar test of 30 practitioners, including four physicians, found mean scores rose from 55.8% correct to 87.8% correct after a 1-hour lecture on START.[39] Although these studies dealt with adult triage, it seems likely that practitioners unfamiliar with treating children will have even more room for improvement in performing pediatric triage. Emergency medical services experts also recommend using tabletop exercises and repeated, realistic simulations involving rescue workers and local hospitals.[40]

Other Special Provisions for Children

For secondary triage of unaccompanied children with minor injuries, experts recommend a separate holding area.[7,8] It might be wise to have toys, videos, and books on hand. Accurate tracking of unaccompanied children is obviously of high importance.

If decontamination is necessary, plain water or soap and water are preferable to bleach because the thinner skin of children makes them particularly prone to irritation.[8] As mentioned earlier, care needs to be taken to prevent hypothermia in children.

Recent Recommendations of Expert Panels

Consensus Conference (2003)

The Columbia University Mailman School of Public Health's National Center for Disaster Preparedness consensus conference, held in February 2003, was intended to make specific recommendations about emergency preparedness from the pediatric perspective that could be incorporated into state and local planning efforts.[2]

The group developed recommendations involving emergency and prehospital care, hospital care, emergency preparedness, terrorism preparedness and response, mental health needs, school preparedness and response, training and drills, and future research needs and funding.

Among other recommendations specifically relevant to bioterrorism planning were the following:

- First responders should be provided with equipment and medications appropriate for children.

- Hospitals should maintain a 48-hour supply of relevant medications and equipment to treat children for the typical hospital pediatric census plus 100 additional pediatric patients.
- All hospital preparedness plans should include specific provisions for the care of children.
- Pediatric health care providers should be trained in disaster response.
- Children's hospitals should be employed as centers of learning and education of professionals and the public. They should help direct the care of children in general hospitals if it is impossible to bring the patients to children's hospitals.
- Pediatric specialists should be involved in local and regional planning activities, including volunteer programs that would provide pediatric specialists to other health care facilities that need them during a crisis.
- Every state and regional disaster plan should designate a pediatric specialty resource center to provide critical, burn, and trauma care.
- Plans should be developed in conjunction with school districts and child care facilities for reuniting families, as well as plans for temporary shelter and guardianship of children when necessary.
- Evacuation plans should be developed that allow for reuniting children with their families.
- Decontamination units should be designed so that they may be adapted for use with children of all ages.
- Pediatric disaster drills should be conducted annually in every school in collaboration with local response agencies and governmental officials.

An executive summary of the group's recommendations, "Pediatric Preparedness for Disasters and Terrorism: A National Consensus Conference," is available at www.ncdp.mailman.columbia.edu.

National Advisory Committee on Children and Terrorism (2003)

The National Advisory Committee on Children and Terrorism was created in 2002 to make recommendations to the U.S. Secretary of Health and Human Services about changes that would allow the health care and emergency services systems to better meet the needs of children in the event of terrorism.[31] Many of its recommendations are for actions on the national level by the Department of Health and Human Services, such as reviewing hospital preparedness plans to make sure they specifically include care of children.

Among its recommendations with more local applications are the following:

- A system should be established to designate a temporary responsible adult to accompany each child through the system in case parents are not present during the initial hours of triage and stabilization. These could be community volunteers.
- Communications must be improved within and between hospitals and between the field and hospitals.

- Information systems must be developed to ensure communication between hospitals, schools, child-care facilities, faith-based community resources, primary care pediatric providers, public health departments, local officials, and the media.
- A Children's Disaster Network should be established to help facilitate surge capacity by identifying available beds, clinicians with expertise, and equipment and sources of transportation. Although the recommendation appears to be a national one, this could be done regionally or locally as well.
- Drills should be conducted in which all or most victims are children, and some are children with special needs, with scenarios occurring in schools, day care, school buses, and the like.
- Responders with pediatric experience should be part of response teams in all disaster drills.

REFERENCES

1. Schonfeld, D.J., Supporting children after terrorist events: potential roles for pediatricians, *Ped Ann*, 32, 182, 2003.
2. Markenson, D. and Redlener, I., Pediatric Preparedness for Disasters and Terrorism: A National Consensus Conference, executive summary of Mailman School of Public Health's National Center for Disaster Preparedness consensus conference, 2003.
3. van Amerongen, R.H. et al., The Avianca plane crash: an emergency medical system's response to pediatric survivors of the disaster, *Pediatrics*, 92, 105, 1993.
4. Hogan, D.E. et al., Emergency department impact of the Oklahoma City terrorist bombing, *Ann Emerg Med*, 34, 160, 1999.
5. Waeckerle, J.F., Disaster planning and response, *N Engl J Med*, 324, 815, 1991.
6. Athey, J. et al., Ability of hospitals to care for pediatric emergency patients, *Ped Emerg Care*, 17, 170, 2001.
7. Wheeler, D.S. and Poss, W.B., Mass casualty management in a changing world, *Ped Ann*, 32, 98, 2003.
8. Rotenberg, J.S., Burklow, T.R., and Selaniko, J.S., Weapons of mass destruction: the decontamination of children, *Ped Ann*, 32, 261, 2003.
9. Mallonee S. et al., Physical injuries and fatalities resulting from the Oklahoma City bombing, *JAMA*, 276, 382, 1996; cited in Rotenberg, Burklow, and Selaniko.
10. American Academy of Pediatrics, Committee on Environmental Health and Committee on Infectious Diseases, Chemical-biological terrorism and its impact on children: a subject review, *Pediatrics*, 105, 662, 2000.
11. Bearer, C.F., How are children different from adults? *Environ Health Perspect*, 103, 7, 1995.
12. Cieslak, T.K. and Henretig, F.M., Ring-a-ring-a-roses: bioterrorism and its peculiar relevance to pediatrics, *Current Opinion in Pediatrics*, 15, 107, 2003.
13. Wheeler, D.S. and Poss, W.B., Mass casualty management in a changing world, *Ped Ann*, 32, 98, 2003.
14. Hogan, D.E. and Burstein, J.L., Eds., *Disaster Medicine*, Lippincott, Williams & Wilkins, Philadelphia, 2002, 17.
15. Chang, M., Glynn, M.K., and Groseclose, S.L., Endemic, notifiable bioterrorism-related diseases, United States, 1992–1999, *Emerg Infect Dis*, 9, 556, 2003.

16. Meselson, M. et al., The Sverdlovsk anthrax outbreak of 1979, *Science*, 266, 1202, 1994.
17. Freedman, A. et al., Cutaneous anthrax associated with microangiopathic hemolytic anemia and coagulopathy in a 7-month-old infant, *JAMA*, 287, 869, 2002.
18. Kaufmann, A.F. and Dannenberg, A.L., Age as a risk factor for cutaneous human anthrax: evidence from Haiti, 1973–1974, *Emerg Infect Dis*, 8, 874, 2002.
19. Vijaikumar, M., Thappa, D.M., and Karthikeyan, K., Cutaneous anthrax: an epidemic outbreak in south India, *J Trop Pediatr*, 48, 225, 2002.
20. Daza, E. et al., Venezuelan equine encephalitis — Colombia, 1995, *MMWR*, 44, 721, 1995.
21. Alibek, K. with Handelman, S., *Biohazard*, Random House, New York, 1999, chaps. 2, 3, 12.
22. Dance, D.A. et al., Acute suppurative parotitis caused by *Pseudomonas pseudomallei* in children, *Infect Dis*, 159, 654, 1989.
23. Lumbiganon, P. and Viengnondha, S., Clinical manifestations of melioidosis in children, *Pediatr Infect Dis J*, 14, 136, 1995.
24. Committee on Responding to the Psychological Consequences of Terrorism, Institute of Medicine, Butler, A.S., Panzer, A.M., and Goldfrank, L.R., Eds., *Responding to the Psychological Consequences of Terrorism: A Public Health Strategy*, National Academies Press, Washington, D.C., 2003.
25. American Academy of Pediatrics policy statement, How pediatricians can respond to the psychosocial implications of disasters, *Pediatrics*, 103, 521, 1999.
26. Applied Research and Consulting LLC, Columbia University Mailman School of Public Health and New York State Psychiatric Institute, Effects of the World Trade Center Attack on NYC Public School Students: Initial Report to the New York City Board of Education, 2002.
27. Pfefferbaum et al., Posttraumatic stress two years after the Oklahoma City bombing in youths geographically distant from the explosion, *Psychiatry*, 63, 358, 2000.
28. Redlener, I. and Grant, R., The 9/11 terror attacks: emotional consequences persist for children and their families, *Contemporary Pediatr*, September 2002.
29. Huckabay, L.M. and Tilem-Kessler, D., Patterns of parental stress in PICU emergency admission, *Dimens Crit Care Nurs*, 18, 36, 1999.
30. Schonfeld, D.J., Potential roles for pediatricians, *Ped Ann*, 32, 182, 2003.
31. National Advisory Committee on Children and Terrorism, Recommendations to the Secretary, 2003.
32. American Academy of Pediatrics, Work Group on Disasters, Psychosocial Issues for Children and Families in Disasters: A Guide for the Primary Care Physician, 1995.
33. American Academy of Pediatrics, Committee on Psychosocial Aspects of Child and Family Health, *Pediatrics*, 103, 521, 1999.
34. Pfefferbaum, B. et al., Children's response to terrorism: a critical review of the literature, *Curr Psychiatry Rep*, 5, 95, 2003.
35. Jaycox, L.H. et al., Violence exposure, posttraumatic stress disorder, and depressive symptoms among recent immigrant schoolchildren, *J Am Acad Child Adolesc Psychiatry*, 41, 1104, 2002.
36. Statement on JumpSTART website, www. jumpstarttriage.com.
37. Romig, L., The "JumpSTART" Rapid Pediatric Triage System, lecture handout, 2002, on website www.jumpstart triage.com.
38. Risavi, B.L. et al., A two-hour intervention using START improves prehospital triage of mass casualty incidents, *Prehosp Emerg Care*, 5, 197, 2001.

39. Chen K.C., Chen, C.C., and Wang, T.L., The role [of] tabletop exercise using START in improving triage ability in Disaster Medical Assistance Team, *Ann Disaster Med*, 1, 78, 2003.
40. Streger, M.R., Prehospital triage, *Emerg Med Serv*, June 1998, 21.

12 The Role of Clinicians in Private Practice or Clinic Settings in Responding to a Biological Attack

INTRODUCTION

The roles and the resource needs of a variety of professionals in the event of a biological attack are clear and discussed elsewhere in this book. Much less well-defined is the place of the family physician or other primary care provider (whether in a private practice setting or hospital-based) in a coordinated response to the challenge of bioterrorism. Of the common points of entry into the health care system — emergency departments, emergency medical services, diagnostic and walk-in clinics, public health clinics — the private physician's office has, perhaps, received the least attention in planning discussions. Nonetheless, it can be assumed that many individuals will turn to their private physicians for advice in the event of a biological attack, and some victims of such an attack might present first to their own physicians rather than to emergency rooms.

Little information has been reported regarding the knowledge level of community physicians in areas relevant to bioterrorism. The only large-scale published survey yielded discouraging but not surprising results.[1] In this study, conducted in the autumn of 2001, 614 of 976 physician members of the American Academy of Family Physicians responded to a questionnaire regarding bioterrorism. Nearly 95% indicated that they believed that a bioterrorist attack was a genuine threat, but only 26% believed strongly that they knew what to do in the event of an attack, whereas 49% felt strongly that they did not know what to do. Although more than half (57%) believed that they would know how to report a suspected attack, only 24% felt that they knew how to recognize the signs and symptoms of a bioterrorism-related infection. Finally, although 18% had received prior training in bioterrorism preparedness, only 5% characterized their current knowledge of the management of bioterrorist-related illness as excellent or very good (see Figure 12.1).

Nonetheless, an analysis of the public impact of the anthrax attacks in the cities involved in the 2001 attacks indicated that Americans would rely extensively on the advice of their own physicians.[2] Utilization of private physicians was underscored by a dramatic upsurge in prescriptions for ciprofloxacin and other antibiotics recommended for treatment or prevention of anthrax in the weeks after the attacks, even in areas not reporting any anthrax cases.[3,4,5]

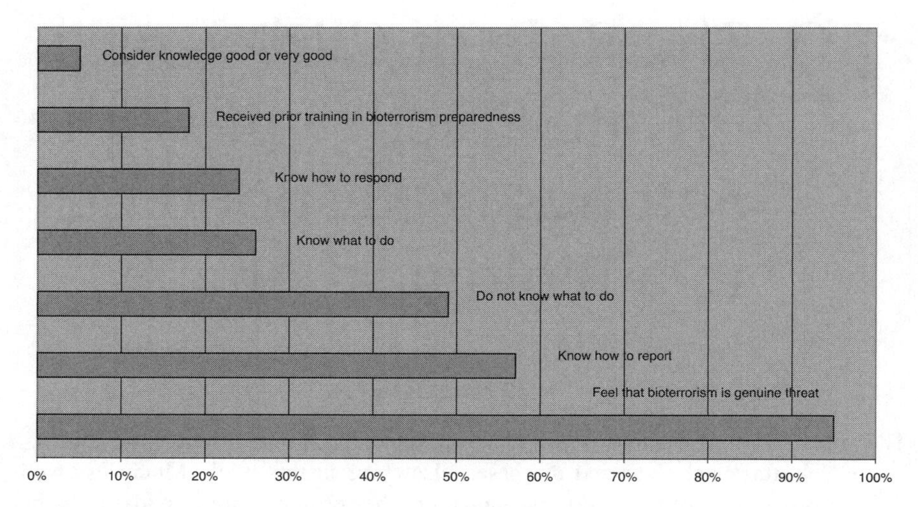

FIGURE 12.1 Self-described preparedness: family physicians. (From Chen, F.M. et al., On the front lines: Family physicians' preparedness for bioterrorism. *J Fam Pract*, 51, 745, 2002.)

Although general guidelines in the recognition of symptoms of biological attack have been published in general medical journals,[6] it would seem unlikely that busy office practitioners would place a high priority on maintaining their level of expertise in this area. More likely, they would rely, along with the general public, on the recommendations of public health authorities after an attack has already been detected.

How best then to address the likely central role, as a source of information and an initial point of triage, that the private practitioner's office or clinic would likely represent in the event of an attack? Other sections of this book, particularly Chapter 8 (Frequently Asked Questions) and Chapter 13 (Internet Sources of Information), would best serve this purpose. In this chapter, we briefly review what would appear to be the key issues at stake for the practicing provider.

THE ROLE OF CLINICIANS IN RECOGNIZING A BIOTERRORIST ATTACK

The anthrax attacks of 2001 dramatically demonstrated the importance of individual medical providers in detecting the early stages of a biological attack and alerting public health authorities. Regardless of the specific agent suspected or directions provided to the public as to how and where to seek care and evaluation, private providers will inevitably play a role in the recognition and triage of suspected victims. A mechanism for rapid referral to local hospitals would be a minimum standard. Dermatologists, pediatricians, infectious disease experts, neurologists, and other specialists, depending on the biological agent used, might come to play a special role by effectively triaging potential victims who come to their offices and reducing the burden on hospital emergency rooms.

WHEN TO SUSPECT AN INFECTION RELATED TO BIOTERRORISM

A great variety of clinical scenarios may represent the earliest stages of a biological attack. The signs and symptoms as well as the clinical scenarios likely to prevail of an attack employing one of the predicted agents of bioterrorism are discussed in Chapter 5. Confounding the rapid recognition of biological attack by an isolated clinician is the fact that far more common illnesses cause the "typical" signs and symptoms of infections such as anthrax, plague, tularemia, and botulism. Even such unusual entities as smallpox and viral hemorrhagic fever may, in their earliest stages, present as undifferentiated, innocent-appearing febrile illnesses before characteristic clinical features appear. As was seen in the monkeypox cases diagnosed in 2003 in several Midwestern states, even highly suspicious illnesses may go unreported for prolonged periods[7] unless the expectation of biological attack is present in advance.

The troubling reality is that an individual provider, even one with special expertise in infectious diseases, may well fail to consider the possibility of bioterrorism when seeing the first victim. Once an attack is underway and recognized, such that clinical signs and symptoms of the specific agent involved are publicized, the likelihood of early diagnosis (as seen in the anthrax attacks) increases. With this enhanced recognition of an attack, of course, comes the increasing likelihood of overreporting, as was also seen in the anthrax attacks.

HOW TO REPORT SUSPICIONS

Hospital-based providers should report suspicions of illness potentially related to bioterrorism promptly to institutional safety officers, infection control officers, and senior medical and administrative leadership staff. Reporting to public health authorities should then be carried out by one or more of these individuals. Clinicians working in a private office face greater logistical challenges and should rapidly report any such suspicions directly to local public health authorities. Such authorities are in the best position to place individual reports into the context of other data from providers, syndromic surveillance, and law enforcement and emergency management agencies.

Despite the many difficulties that staff working in the private provider's office would confront, it is imperative that a reliable means of communicating with local hospitals and public health authorities be maintained. Where hospitals may require dedicated radio frequencies and secure Internet connections for the office practice, this may simply consist of up-to-date telephone numbers, e-mail addresses, and other contact information.

OTHER STEPS TO BE TAKEN

Pending instructions from governmental authorities, it may be sensible to ask patients to remain until they can be examined or interviewed further. If a highly contagious disease (such as smallpox or plague) is suspected, protection of other patients and office staff must, of course, take priority, and appropriate personal protective equipment for the specific agent suspected (see Chapter 3, Chapter 9, and Chapter 10) and transport to a local hospital should be arranged for the patient. Emergency medical services and any potentially receiving hospital should be informed about the likelihood that a patient with a highly contagious disease has been seen.

If a suspected victim of biological attack refuses to remain until authorities arrive, contact information should be obtained and public health and law enforcement officials should be informed immediately.

HOW TO EDUCATE PARAPROFESSIONAL STAFF ABOUT BIOTERRORISM

Staff education regarding bioterrorism within a clinic or private office environment will likely assume a low priority unless an attack is recognized as already in progress. Nonetheless, it was learned during the World Trade Center and anthrax attacks of 2001 that victims seek care in a variety of locations and advice from any medical professional to whom they have access. The anthrax attacks, in particular, placed stress on medical personnel working in private as well as hospital-based setting as questions regarding antibiotic prophylaxis for individuals who felt that they might have been at risk mounted.

For these reasons, the clinical staffs working in private physicians' offices and freestanding clinics do require a basic familiarity with issues regarding bioterrorism. The challenge is to provide convenient but meaningful education that is relevant to their specific duties.

As hospitals and local public health departments continue to develop curricula in this area of knowledge, it should become easier to find educational activities to which office staff can be referred. In addition, the many online guidelines and algorithms available for identifying and responding to terrorist attacks can be made easily accessible (see Chapter 13). As is discussed in Chapter 4 of this book, the need for information varies with specific job categories and that chapter can be used as a guide for education of office and clinic staff as well as hospital and emergency staff.

HOW TO PROTECT OFFICE STAFF IN THE EVENT OF AN ATTACK

Information regarding the use of personal protective equipment as well as isolation procedures recommended for the various agents of biological attack is provided in Chapter 3. Office staff should be familiar with the use of surgical masks and, ideally, more high-efficiency respirators (e.g., N95 — see Chapter 3). This familiarity with the proper use of such equipment would at least permit staff to follow recommendations of public health authorities in the event of an attack.

LIKELY OBSTACLES TO BE CONFRONTED BY NON-HOSPITAL-BASED PROVIDERS IN THE EVENT OF AN ACTUAL ATTACK

Several types of response would appear to be impractical for the office practice or freestanding clinic. Among these are:

- Holding patients against their will for purposes of quarantine or for questioning by law enforcement authorities
- Providing safe and effective decontamination of victims and disposal of contaminated clothing, when required
- Providing isolation facilities to prevent spread of airborne pathogens such as variola virus
- Serving as a dispensary for antibiotics or other key pharmaceuticals or vaccines

The task of providing up-to-date information and advice to the public or accurate information to the press may also be beyond the abilities of independent providers under the confusing conditions of an actual attack.

For this reason, this book places the emphasis of the health care community on hospital preparations both in acknowledgment of these obstacles and in recognition that victims or their contacts would likely be rapidly referred to either hospitals or public health departments.

REFERENCES

1. Chen, F.M. et al., On the front lines: family physicians' preparedness for bioterrorism. *J Fam Pract*, 51, 745, 2002.
2. Blendon, R.J., et al., The impact of anthrax attacks on the American public. *Med Gen Med*, 4, 1, 2002.
3. Jones, J.W. and Kiefe, C.I., Anthrax attacks and practice patterns: a learning opportunity for health care systems. *Qual Manage Health Care*, 10, 31, 2002.
4. Shaffer, D. et al., Increased U.S. prescription trends associated with the CDC *Bacillus anthraxis* antimicrobial postexposure prophylaxis campaign. *Pharmacoepidemiol Drug Saf*, 12, 177, 2003.
5. Goldenberg, A. et al., Early statistical detection of anthrax outbreaks by tracking over-the-counter medication sales, *Proc Natl Acad Sci USA*, 99, 5237, 2002.
6. O'Brien, K.K., Higdon, M.L., and Halverson, J.J., Recognition and management of bioterrorism infections. *Am Fam Physician*, 67, 1887, 2003.
7. Centers for Disease Control and Prevention, Multistate outbreak of monkeypox — Illinois, Indiana, and Wisconsin, 2003, *MMWR*, 52, 537, 2003.

13 Internet Sources of Information

INTRODUCTION

The Internet has been increasingly used by public agencies and professional groups as a primary means of communicating information, both to colleagues and to the public.[1] Its strengths — capacious, searchable archives coupled with ease of updating — seem particularly well suited to a field like bioterrorism, where health care providers may need simultaneous access to bodies of medical knowledge, clinical images, fast-changing news and public health advisories.

It's not surprising, then, that the Internet is full of information that may be of interest to hospitals and clinicians readying themselves to respond to a biological attack. A 2002 book, *Bioterrorism and Public Health: An Internet Resource Guide*, devotes more than 300 pages to describing and ranking websites that relate, if only marginally in some cases, to the topic.[2]

Amid thickets of sites and documents, however, it is easy to spend hours wandering the Web and come away with only a modest handful of useful information. Many promising sites consist largely of links to other sites, and the intrepid explorer can feel lost in an endless loop of cross references. In others, useful documents are present, but nearly impossible to find unless the searcher knows exactly where they are. Others present unattributed or undated documents and obsolete links. Partial maps to this wilderness are being drawn. Ferguson et al., for instance, classified the content of 43 bioterrorism sites, out of more than 100 identified considered, into categories useful for infectious disease and epidemiology professionals.[1]

This chapter is intended as another of these partial maps, a selective guide to online bioterrorism resources. It aims to be targeted, not comprehensive, focusing on information most likely to be of direct use to health care preparedness planners. Categories include:

- Templates and models for hospital preparedness plans
- Interhospital compacts
- Clinical information about diagnosis, treatment, prevention, and infection control
- Public health notification information
- E-mail networks
- Information for patients and the public
- Information on biological weapons control and policy issues

The first section of this chapter lists documents and a handful of websites by topic, grouped into the categories mentioned in the preceding text. The second section lists 38 websites alphabetically, describing the kind of information they offer on bioterrorism. Although this structure requires the repetition of some information, it was chosen in hopes of making the chapter as useful as possible.

For ease of use, we have also listed, in most cases, specific page addresses of documents as well as the home-page addresses of the sites that offer them. On some sites, however, organization was so transparent that document addresses seemed unnecessary; on others, they seemed too unstable to list.

Besides the sites listed here, which are open to all, there exist Internet-based bioterrorism communications systems reserved for approved persons. These include the Health Alert Network or HAN (www.phppo.cdc.gov/HAN), a nationwide system linking the CDC with state and local health departments through the Internet, and Epi-X (www.cdc.gov/epix), a secure Internet-based communication system for sharing of information by public health officials across jurisdictions. More recently created is LLIS.gov (www.llis.dhs.gov), a restricted-access site to allow emergency response personnel and homeland security officials to share an archive of "Lessons Learned and Best Practices" information.

The information here was current as of March 2004. Although websites and addresses change, we have tried to use sources that are likely to offer authoritative and useful information in future years, even if it is not necessarily the same information as when we last surveyed them.

INTERNET RESOURCES BY TOPIC

HOSPITAL PREPAREDNESS PLANNING

Templates and Models for Hospital Plans

For the most part, links to these documents can be found on numerous websites. Most are available through the Disaster Readiness page of the American Hospital Association (AHA) — www.hospitalconnect.com/aha/key_issues/ disaster_ readiness/index.html — or the Bioterrorism Resources page of the Association for Professionals in Infection Control and Epidemiology (APIC) — www.apic.org/bioterror.

Bioterrorism Readiness Plan: A Template for Health Care Facilities

www.hospitalconnect.com/aha/key-_issues/diasaster_readiness/content/APICReadinessNewFormat.doc

A zipped version can be downloaded from: www.apic.org/bioterror.

This 43-page document, issued in 1999, was a joint production of the Association for Professionals in Infection Control and Epidemiology (APIC) and the Centers for Disease Control and Prevention (CDC). According to its authors, it was "intended to serve as a tool for infection control (IC) professionals and health care epidemiologists to guide the development of practical and realistic response plans for their institutions in preparation for a real or suspected bioterrorism attack."

Some of the specific clinical information about prophylaxis or treatment included may need updating; the document itself notes: "Up-to-date recommendations should be obtained in consultation with local and state health departments and CDC." But it remains useful as a template.

California Hospital Bioterrorism Response Planning Guide (2002)

www.dhs.ca.gov/ps/ddwem/environmental/epo/PDF/ca_hosp_guide.pdf

Available through the website of the California Department of Health Services.

This 134-page document from the California Department of Health Services (www.dhs.ca.gov) includes a general section about hospital response and the roles of various government agencies, followed by specific information on anthrax, brucellosis, botulism, Q fever, tularemia, plague, smallpox, and viral hemorrhagic fevers. The initial overview was written before the creation of the Department of Homeland Security, and is specific to California in some regards. But the agent-specific sections are unusually practical. For each agent, the guide provides an overview, a quick reference sheet for medical professionals, a set of FAQs (frequently asked questions) for the public, home-care instructions for patients and families, and a screening form.

Disaster Preparedness and Response in Texas Hospitals

www.healthpolicyinstitute.org/projects/disaster_response/guidance_document.pdf

This 159-page manual, dated 2003, was produced by the Texas Department of Health and the Texas Institute for Health Policy Research to help hospitals develop regional response plans to bioterrorism.

Hospital Emergency Incident Command System (HEICS) Manual

www.emsa.cahwnet.gov./dms2/heics3.htm

HEICS is the hospital version of a widely used emergency management system called the Incident Command System. Its centerpiece is an organizational chart of positions, each with a prioritized list of duties, which is activated when an emergency is declared. Its strengths are said to be defined responsibilities, clear reporting channels, and better documentation of actions and common nomenclature, which makes it easier for agencies to communicate with each other. A version of this system, called the National Incident Command System, was adopted by the U.S. Department of Homeland Security in 2004 to be used by local, state, and federal government agencies in the event of an emergency. Many hospitals have adopted HEICS in recent years in hopes of improving coordination with each other and with emergency response personnel during a crisis. HEICS is designed to serve as the "response" portion of a hospital's overall emergency preparedness plan, which by JCAHO requirements must also include mitigation, preparedness, and recovery activities.

The HEICS manual, in its third edition as of 1998, comes with templates and lesson plans. It is the joint property of the State of California Emergency Medical

Services Authority and the San Mateo County Emergency Medical Services Agency, which offer it free to health facilities.

Hospital Planning Documents from Stanford University Medical Center

Bioterrorism and Emergency Preparedness page: www.stanfordhospital.com/forPhysiciansOthers/bioterrorism/bioterrorism.html

This site offers an array of documents designed for use by the medical center's staff and patients; many of them may serve as useful models for other hospitals. The documents include a bioterrorism preparedness plan for the hospital; rules for calling a "Code Zebra," the hospital's code for a bioterrorism event; a bioterrorism exposure tracking form, to be filled out by patients; a chart of infection control procedures for various agents; clinical pathways for anthrax and smallpox; triage plans for the hospital and clinics; and information sheets to be distributed to patients. These materials were produced by the Bioterrorism and Emergency Preparedness Task Force of Stanford Hospital & Clinics, Lucile Salter Packard Children's Hospital, and Stanford University's School of Medicine.

Hospital Preparedness Checklists

These two checklists, intended to help hospitals assess and improve their state of readiness, are complementary. The first, a 17-page document by APIC, is generally more detailed, asking specific questions about how goals would be carried out. For instance, its section on "reception of casualties and victims" has 11 questions, including several multipart items. The second, the AHA's 8-page checklist, has more items dealing with formulary and supply questions, and with contact between the hospital and public agencies.

Mass Casualty Disaster Plan Checklist: A Template for Health Care Facilities
www.apic.org/bioterror/checklist.doc

American Hospital Association Chemical and Bioterrorism Preparedness Checklist
Available at many sites, including:
www.mtha.org/prepare/pdf/AHAChecklist.pdf
www.hospitalconnect.com/aha/key_issues/disaster_readiness/content/MaAtChecklistB1003.doc

Hospital Preparedness for Mass Casualties

www.hospitalconnect.com/ahapolicyforum/resources/disaster.html

This is the final report of the "Invitational Forum on Hospital Preparedness for Mass Casualties" held by AHA in 2000. It contains recommendations on communitywide preparedness, staffing, staff training, and support, and internal and external communications.

Rural Hospital Disaster Readiness

www.hospitalconnect.com/aha/member_relations/small_rural_hospitals/disaster.htl

This article, from November 2001, constituted a special issue of *Update*, the newsletter of the American Hospital Association's Section for Small or Rural Hospitals.

Sentinel (Level A) Laboratory Guideline for a Clinical Laboratory Bioterrorism Readiness Plan

www.asm.org/Policy/index.asp?bid=6342

This document, issued by the American Society of Microbiology in 2003, is a template for laboratory readiness planning. (For more on laboratory issues, see listings later in the chapter for American Society of Microbiology and Food and Drug Administration.)

Weill/Cornell Computer Staffing Model for Bioterrorism Response

www.ahrq.gov/research/biomodel.htm

This model, funded by the Agency for Health Research and Quality (AHRQ), is designed to help plan large-scale antibiotic dispensing and vaccination campaigns. It can be downloaded as a spreadsheet or used in a Web-based version.

Wisconsin Hospital Disaster Plan

www.dhfs.state.wi.us/rl_dsl/hospital/hospitaldisastrplng.htm

This plan, by the Wisconsin Department of Health and Family Services, identifies responsibilities of individuals and departments and suggests guidelines for emergency responses.

Hospital Compacts for Mutual Aid

District of Columbia Hospital Association Mutual Aid Memo of Understanding

www.dcha.org/EP/EmergencyPrep.htm

This agreement was adopted by the DCHA about 2 weeks after September 11, 2001.

AHA Model Hospital Mutual Aid Memo of Understanding

www.hospitalconnect.com/aha/key_issues/disaster_readiness/resources/content/ModelHospitalMou.doc

This American Hospital Association memo of understanding is based on the DCHA agreement.

Metropolitan Area Hospital Compact

www.hospitalconnect.com/aha/key_issues/disaster_readiness/resources/content/TwinCitiesMetroCompact.doc

This agreement was signed by 22 hospitals in the Minneapolis–St. Paul metropolitan area in 2002.

Preparedness Overviews

Disaster Response: Principles of Preparation and Coordination

http://orgmail2.coe-dmha.org/dr/static.htm

This widely cited textbook by Erik Auf der Heide (Mosby, St. Louis, 1989), is out of print but is available in its entirety online through the Center of Excellence in Disaster Management and Humanitarian Assistance. As its title suggests, the book presents principles and context for preparedness planning rather than stipulating step-by-step instructions. Its approach is concrete and practical, with generous use of examples drawn from past disasters. It is not specifically oriented toward hospitals or bioterrorism, and its examples tend to feature natural or wartime disasters. But it provides valuable background for thinking about human and institutional behavior in an emergency.

Guide to Emergency Management Planning in Health Care

This valuable book, published in 2002 by Joint Commission Resources, the publishing arm of the Joint Commission on the Accreditation of Healthcare Organizations (JCAHO), provides guidance on improving existing emergency plans; establishing cooperative relationships with other health care facilities and with community agencies; improving internal and external communications; and training staff. It draws on the experience of hospital staff in New York City during the September 11th attack and the anthrax attack of 2001. It can be purchased through www.jcrinc.com.

Recurring Pitfalls in Hospital Preparedness and Response

www.homelandsecurity.org/journal/articles/rubin.html

This article by Jeffrey N. Rubin, in the *Journal of Homeland Security*, January, 2004, presents an overview of the issues and the problems hospitals have encountered. It could serve as useful background for hospital personnel who are new to preparedness planning.

Building Protection and Maintenance

These documents are not specifically aimed at hospitals, but offer general guidance for protecting buildings from airborne biological pathogens and other airborne contaminants. The first two are from the National Institute of Occupational Safety and Health (NIOSH). The third is from the Army Corps of Engineers.

Guidance for Protecting Building Environments from Airborne Chemical, Biological, or Radiological Attacks
www.cdc.gov/niosh/bldvent/pdfs/2002-139.pdf
Guidance for Filtration and Air-Cleaning Systems to Protect Building Environments from Airborne Chemical, Biological, or Radiological Attacks, April 2003
www.cdc.gov/niosh/docs/2003-136/2003-136.html
Protecting Buildings and Their Occupants from Airborne Hazards, 2001
http://buildingprotection.sbccom.army.mil/basic/airborne_hazards_report_download.htm

CLINICAL INFORMATION ON POTENTIAL BIOLOGICAL AGENTS

Websites with Clinical Information

American College of Physicians–American Society of Internal Medicine (ACP–ASIM)

Bioterrorism Resources page: www.acponline.org/bioterro/index.html?idxt

Information on major biological agents includes interactive algorithms, listed here as "decision support tools," with detailed clinical information on diagnosis and treatment of anthrax and smallpox. This site also offers 12 pages of self-assessment questions (www.acponline.org/bioterro/self_assessment.htm) as well as a useful set of links.

Bioterrorism Information Centers

These university-based bioterrorism centers, with their partners, are good sources of clinical information on the major biological agents:

- The Center for Infectious Disease Research and Policy (CIDRAP) at the University of Minnesota offers well-organized and detailed clinical information on identifying and treating illnesses caused by major biological agents, with documents prepared in collaboration with the Infectious Diseases Society of America, as well as up-to-date news listings and other resources.
  - www.cidrap.umn.edu
- Much of the same clinical information is available at the IDSA website's Bioterrorism Information and Resources page.
  - www.idsociety.org/Template.cfm?Section=Bioterrorism
- The Center for the Study of Bioterrorism and Emerging Infections at the Saint Louis University School of Public Health also offers a broad range of content, with fact sheets and images on the Category A biological agents.
  - www.bioterrorism.slu.edu
- The federal Agency for Health Research and Quality (AHRQ), with the University of Alabama at Birmingham's Center for Emergency Care and Disaster Preparedness, offers a Bioterrorism and Emerging Infections

page with in-depth fact sheets on Category A biological agents, as well as differential diagnosis information and interactive continuing-education modules for different medical specialties.
– www.bioterrorism.uab.edu/index.htm

Centers for Disease Control and Prevention

Public Health Emergency Preparedness and Response: www.bt.cdc.gov

The Centers for Disease Control and Prevention, part of the Department of Health and Human Services, is the most authoritative single source for bioterrorism preparedness and response. During an emergency, it could be expected to be a key national source of medical news and clinical recommendations.

The CDC's Public Health Emergency Preparedness and Response page lists many of its bioterrorism resources, cross-referenced by agent and by topic. With more than 30 agents listed, the amount and depth of information for each varies. Many of the agent entries offer overall fact sheets and Q&As for the public and for health professionals, along with in-depth information on diagnosis, infection control, surveillance, treatment, vaccination, and worker safety. The site also offers photographs as well as many downloadable journal articles and reports.

Consensus Statements on Category A Biological Agents

Available at many sites, including:

The National Library of Medicine's PubMed service at www.ncbi.nlm.nih.gov/PubMed
JAMA's bioterrorism archives at http://jama.ama-assn.org/cgi/collection/bioterrorism?notjournal=amajnls&page=2
APIC's Bioterrorism Resources page at www.apic.org/bioterror
The Working Group on Civilian Biodefense published consensus statements on anthrax, smallpox, plague, tularemia, botulinum toxin, and hemorrhagic fever viruses in the *Journal of the American Medical Association* (JAMA) in 1999–2002. Each contains recommendations for measures to be taken by medical and public health professionals if the agent in question is used as a biological weapon against a civilian population.

The statements are:

Henderson, D.A. et al., Smallpox as a biological weapon: medical and public health management, *JAMA*, 281, 2127, 1999.
Inglesby, T.V. et al., Plague as a biological weapon: medical and public health management, *JAMA*, 283, 2281, 2000.
Arnon, S.S. et al., Botulinum toxin as a biological weapon: medical and public health management, *JAMA*, 285, 1059, 2001.
Dennis, D.T. et al., Tularemia as a biological weapon: medical and public health management, *JAMA*, 285, 2763, 2001.

Inglesby, T.V. et al., Anthrax as a biological weapon, 2002: updated recommendations for management, *JAMA*, 287, 2236, 2002.
Borio, L. et al., Hemorrhagic fever viruses as biological weapons: medical and public health management, *JAMA*, 287, 2391, 2002.

Online Books and Manuals

Medical Aspects of Chemical and Biological Warfare

Available at several sites, including:

www.bordeninstitute.army.mil/cwbw/default_index.htm (BordenInstitute)
www.vnh.org/MedAspChemBioWar/ (Virtual Naval Hospital)

This 721-page medical textbook on the pathophysiology, diagnosis, and management of biological and chemical weapons injuries was published in 1997 by the Office of the Surgeon General, Department of the Army, Borden Institute, Walter Reed Army Medical Center.

Medical Management of Biological Casualties Handbook

www.usamriid.army.mil/education/bluebook.html

This handbook, also called the Blue Book, is issued by USAMRIID (the U.S. Army Medical Research Institute of Infectious Diseases). The introduction states, "The purpose for this handbook is to serve as a concise pocket-sized manual that will guide medical personnel in the prophylaxis and management of biological casualties. It is designed as a quick reference and overview, and is not intended as a definitive text on the medical management of biological casualties.

"It covers anthrax, brucellosis, glanders and melioidosis (*Burkholderia mallei* and *B. pseudomallei*), plague, Q fever (*Coxiella burnetii*), tularemia, smallpox, Venezuelan equine encephalitis complex viruses, viral hemorrhagic fever, botulinum, ricin, staphylococcal enterotoxin B, and T-2 mycotoxins. The fourth edition, issued in 2001, can be downloaded by chapter in several formats, including Word, PDF, or Palm OS."

NATO Handbook on the Medical Aspects of NBC Defensive Operations

Available at several sites, including:

www.fas.org/nuke/guide/usa/doctrine/dod/fm8-9/2toc.htm (Federation of American Scientists)
www.vnh.org/MedAspNBCDef/toc.htm (Virtual Naval Hospital)

This 1996 handbook is intended as a reference source of information for training. It deals with nuclear, biological, and chemical as well as conventional battle casualties suffered in an NBC environment.

Big Bad Bug Book (Foodborne Pathogenic Microorganisms and Natural Toxins)

www.cfsan.fda.gov/~mow/intro.html

This handbook, from the Food and Drug Administration's Center for Food Safety and Nutrition, devotes a chapter to each of more than 40 foodborne pathogenic microorganisms or natural toxins. The book does not deal with treatment or medical prevention. It is not intended to serve as a comprehensive reference source, according to its preface, but provides basic facts about the pathogens' characteristics, source, associated foods, infective dose, disease symptoms, recent outbreaks, and susceptible populations. The book was issued in 1992, but has been updated online with links to relevant MMWR articles, CDC documents, and other information.

Anthrax and Smallpox chapters, from Control of Communicable Diseases Manual

The American Public Health Association offers online access to the chapters on anthrax and smallpox from its *Control of Communicable Diseases Manual*, 17th Edition, Ed. James Chin, MD, MPH, 2000.

Anthrax chapter: www.apha.org/media/anthrax.htm
Smallpox chapter: www.apha.org/media/smallpox.htm

Public Health Notification

These sites offer information on notifying health and law enforcement authorities if bioterrorism is suspected.

Information Networks and Other Information Sources

www.cdc.gov/other.htm#states

This CDC page contains links to many federal and international public health agencies and organizations, as well as state and some county health departments.

Protocols: Interim Recommended Notification Procedures for Local and State Public Health Department Leaders in the Event of a Bioterrorist Incident

www.bt.cdc.gov/EmContact/Protocols.asp

This CDC page contains a flowchart of steps in notifying health and law enforcement agencies if bioterrorism is suspected.

Public Health Resources: State Health Departments

www.cdc.gov/mmwr/international/relres.html

This *MMWR* page not only can take readers to the state health department of their choice, but can also allow readers to search multiple state health departments simultaneously.

State Public Health

www.statepublichealth.org/index.php

This page from the Association of State and Territorial Health Officials (ASTHO) provides indexes to current and past state health officials, as well as to state health agencies and public hotlines.

FBI Field Divisions

www.fbi.gov/contact/fo/fo.htm

This FBI page lists agency field offices by city and by areas covered within states.

Emergencies and Disasters, Planning and Prevention, State Homeland Security

www.dhs.gov/dhspublic/display?theme=14&content=3283

This page, from the Department of Homeland Security, lists homeland security and emergency preparedness agencies for each state.

E-mail Networks

Real-Time Alert Services

CDC Clinicians' Registry

www.bt.CDC.gov/clinregistry/index.asp

Clinicians can register at this page to receive e-mail updates on terrorism issues and training. The site says it aims to provide clinicians with "real-time information to help prepare for (and possibly respond to) terrorism and other emergency events."

ProMED-mail

www.promedmail.org

ProMED-mail, the Program for Monitoring Infectious Diseases, uses a website and e-mail subscription service to disseminate information about infectious disease outbreaks around the world. A project of the International Society for Infectious Diseases, it features screened information drawn from media, official notices and individuals' reports, and electronic communications to provide up-to-date and reliable news on disease outbreaks. It is also available in Spanish and Portuguese.

Medline Alert Services

Several free Medline alert services will automatically search PubMed at regular intervals — generally daily, weekly, or biweekly — and then e-mail each subscriber with notice of new articles that fit the terms he or she has specified. Most allow multiple searches; some offer additional archiving features or allow retrieval of results from a website. Medline alert services can make it easier to keep up with developments in vaccine development, readiness assessments, or any other medical or public health topic relating to bioterrorism.

BioMail is hosted by the Medical Informatics Department of the State University of New York at Stony Brook's University Hospital and Medical Center — http://biomail.sourceforge.net/biomail.

Pubcrawler is hosted by the Department of Genetics, Trinity College, Dublin, Ireland — www.pubcrawler.ie.

JADE (Journal Abstracts Delivered Electronically) is issued by the National Center for Emergency Medicine Informatics — www.biodigital.org/jade.

Other Federal Update Services

National Guidelines Clearinghouse Update Service

www.guideline.gov/whatsnew/subscription.aspx

The clearinghouse, run by the Agency for Healthcare Research and Quality, offers a weekly e-mail service telling subscribers of new content on the site.

GAO Subscription List

The GAO website also offers an e-mail subscription service (listed under the heading "For the Press"). Users can sign up to get daily, weekly, or monthly alerts on GAO releases, or can request notification when new reports are issued in selected topic areas, such as health or homeland security.

Sites for Patients and the Public

These sites, described in greater detail in the alphabetical listings later in this chapter, offer information for the public.

American Academy of Pediatrics

www.aap.org

Children, Terrorism, and Disasters page: www.aap.org/terrorism/index.html

The site offers materials for patients, including "Family Readiness Kit: Preparing to Handle Disasters," at www.aap.org/family/frk/frkit.htm

American Red Cross

www.redcross.org

The disaster relief agency offers basic disaster preparedness information.

Centers for Disease Control and Prevention (CDC)

www.cdc.gov

Public Health Emergency Preparedness and Response page: www.bt.cdc.gov

The CDC offers fact sheets and Q&As on biological agents for the public, as well as for medical professionals.

Department of Homeland Security Public Readiness Site

www.ready.gov

This site offers basic disaster readiness information, on topics such as emergency supplies, sheltering in place, and preparing a family plan.

Kidshealth.org

www.kidshealth.org

This nonprofit site offers simple, upbeat articles for parents and children on anthrax, smallpox, and coping psychologically with terrorism.

Medline Plus

www.nkm.nih.gov/medlineplus

Biodefense and Bioterrorism page: www.nlm.nih.gov/medlineplus/biodefenseand-bioterrorism.html

Medline Plus, a federal information service, offers a selection of information for the public, most of it drawn from federal agencies or the Mayo Clinic's website, as well as news stories from Reuters Health.

The RAND Corporation

www.rand.org

RAND, a nonprofit think tank, offers a 26-page manual, *Individual Preparedness and Response to Chemical, Radiological, Nuclear, and Biological Terrorist Attacks: A Quick Guide.*

www.rand.org/publications/MR/MR1731

Biological Weapons and Terrorism Policy Issues

These websites, described in greater detail in the alphabetical listing in Section III, offer a wide range of news, research reports, documents, and analysis on issues of biological weapons control, nonproliferation, and terrorism.

Federation of American Scientists

www.fas.org

Center for Nonproliferation Studies of the Monterey Institute of International Studies

http://cns.miis.edu

Henry L. Stimson Center

Chemical and Biological Weapons Nonproliferation Project: www.stimson.org/cbw

Carnegie Endowment for International Peace

www.ceip.org

Chemical and Biological Arms Control Institute

www.cbaci.org

National Memorial Institute for the Prevention of Terrorism (MIPT)

www.mipt.org

ALPHABETICAL LISTING OF WEBSITES

Agency for Health Research and Quality (AHRQ)

Bioterrorism and Emerging Infections site: www.bioterrorism.uab.edu/index.htm

This site, produced by the federal Agency for Health Research and Quality, with the University of Alabama at Birmingham's Center for Emergency Care and Disaster Preparedness, offers in-depth fact sheets on Category A biological agents, as well as differential diagnosis information and interactive continuing-education modules for different medical specialties.

American Association of Blood Banks

www.aabb.org

Disaster Response page: www.aabb.org/About_the_AABB/Disaster_Response/disastercontact.htm

The page offers the organization's *Disaster Operations Handbook*, subtitled *Coordinating the Nation's Blood Supply during Disaster and Biological Events*. The handbook is intended for blood centers and hospitals that collect allogenic blood. It includes a "Hospital Supplement" for hospitals that collect only autologous blood; the supplement is also available separately from the same web page. The handbook says it is intended to improve coordination between facilities and to help them determine and meet the need for blood in an emergency.

American Academy of Pediatrics (AAP)

www.aap.org

Children, Terrorism, and Disasters page: www.aap.org/terrorism/index.html

The site offers a set of links to the CDC, FDA, and other standard sources, as well as materials for patients, including "Family Readiness Kit: Preparing to Handle Disasters," at www.aap.org/family/frk/frkit.htm.

Emergency Preparedness for Children with Special Health Needs:
www.aap.org/advocacy/emergprep.htm

This page offers information forms to be filled out by parents to facilitate proper care in the event of an emergency.

Several AAP policy statements or clinical reports relevant to hospital planning are available through the site's search engine. Originally published in *Pediatrics*, they are accessible though Medline searches as well. These include:

- Care of Children in the Emergency Department: Guidelines for Preparedness, *Pediatrics*, 107, 777, 2001.
- Emergency Preparedness for Children with Special Health Care Needs, *Pediatrics*, 104, 1999, e53 [sic].

American College of Emergency Physicians (ACEP)

www.acep.org

Bioterrorism Resources page: www.acep.org/1,4634,0.html

This site offers a standard set of links, as well as some information generated by the ACEP, including the February 2003 issue of *Critical Decisions in Emergency Medicine*, which has articles on diagnosing and handling dermatology-related symptoms of chemical and biological attacks, and on handling mass casualties in the emergency department.

American College of Physicians–American Society of Internal Medicine (ACP–ASIM)

Bioterrorism Resources page: www.acponline.org/bioterro/index.html?idxt

Information on major biological agents includes interactive algorithms, listed here as "decision support tools," with detailed clinical information on diagnosis and treatment of anthrax and smallpox. This site also offers 12 pages of self-assessment questions (at www.acponline.org/bioterro/self_assessment.htm) as well as a useful set of links.

American Hospital Association (AHA)

www.hospitalconnect.com

Disaster Readiness: www.hospitalconnect.com/aha/key_issues/disaster_readiness/index.html

The American Health Association's Disaster Readiness pages offer a good selection of useful information from others, including the CDC, JCAHCO, and the California Department of Health Services, as well as its own documents. Many of these are listed and described earlier in this chapter, in the section "Hospital Preparedness Planning." When the site was checked in March 2004, some of the links were no longer working.

Some of the documents posted here include:

- Bioterrorism Readiness Planning: A Template for Healthcare Facilities
  - www.hospitalconnect.com/aha/key_issues/disaster_readiness/content/APICReadinessNewformat.doc
- Hospital Preparedness for Mass Casualties
  - www.hospitalconnect.com/ahapolicyforum/resources/disaster.html
- Mass Casualty Disaster Plan Checklist
  - www.apic.org/bioterror/checklist.doc
- Weill/Cornell Computer Staffing Model for Bioterrorism Response
  - www.ahrq,gov/research/biomodel.htm
  - Designed to help plan large-scale antibiotic dispensing and vaccination campaigns
- AHA Model Hospital Mutual Aid Memo
  - www.hospitalconnect.com/aha/key_issues/disaster_readiness/resources/ content/ModelHospitalMou.doc
- Metropolitan Area Hospital Compact
  - www.hospitalconnect.com/aha/key_issues/disaste_readiness/resources/content/TwinCitiesMetroCompact.doc
- Hospital Disaster Plan, Wisconsin Department of Health and Family Services
  - www.dhfs.state.wi.us/rl_dsl/hospital/hospitaldisastrplng.htm
- Guidance for Protecting Building Environments from Airborne Chemical, Biological, or Radiological Attacks
  - www.cdc.gov/niosh/bldvent/pdfs/2002-139.pdf

American Medical Association (AMA)

Center for Disaster Preparedness and Emergency Response

www.ama-assn.org/ama/pub/category/6206.html

The site offers a modest collection of terrorism resources for physicians and patients, including FAQs on anthrax and smallpox for the public.

JAMA Bioterrorism page: http://jama.ama-assn.org/cgi/collection/bioterrorism?not-journal=amajnls

This site links to full-text articles about bioterrorism from *JAMA* and the Archives journals.

The AMA also offers for download "Diagnosis and Management of Foodborne Illness: A Primer for Physicians and Other Health Care Professionals," at www.ama-assn.org/ama/pub/category/3629.html#contents.

This paper contains guidelines for diagnosis, treatment, reporting, and prevention of foodborne illness; scenarios and clinical vignettes with which health professionals can test their knowledge and judgment; reading lists; summaries of basic information in chart form, and patient education material. Originally published in 2001, it was expanded and updated in 2004 to reflect the "post 9/11 environment," according to a press release by the groups that produced it: the AMA, the American Nurses

Association, the CDC, the FDA's Center for Food Safety and Applied Nutrition, and the U.S. Department of Agriculture's Food Safety and Inspection Service.

American Psychiatric Association

www.psych.org

Disaster Psychiatry page: www.psych.org/disasterpsych

The association offers materials for psychiatrists including this handbook: *Disaster Psychiatry Handbook,* Hall, R.C.W. and Norwood, A.E., Eds., American Psychiatric Association Committee on Psychiatric Dimensions of Disaster.

American Psychological Association

www.apa.org

APA Task Force on Promoting Resilience in Response to Terrorism: www.apa.org/psychologists/resilience.html

The APA offers nine fact sheets to help mental health workers seeking to foster resilience in various populations, including children, older adults, people of color, primary care providers, first responders, and mental health workers. It offers information on resilience aimed at the lay public at its Help Center, http://helping.apa.org (no www).

American Public Health Association

The APHA offers online access to the chapters on anthrax and smallpox from its *Control of Communicable Diseases Manual*, 17th Edition, Ed. James Chin, MD, MPH, which it published in 2000.

Anthrax chapter: www.apha.org/media/anthrax.htm
Smallpox chapter: www.apha.org/media/smallpox.htm

American Red Cross

www.redcross.org

Disaster Services page: www.redcross.org/services/disaster/0,1082,0_500_,00.html

The American Red Cross offers basic information for individuals, families, children, and disabled people on planning for disaster and assembling disaster supplies.

American Society of Microbiology

www.asm.org

Biological Weapons Resource Center: www.asm.org/Policy/index.asp?bid=520

ASM offers several documents to help laboratories plan their responses to possible bioterrorism and to guide them in ruling out or referring possible bioterrorism agents:

- The Sentinel (Level A) Laboratory Guideline for a Clinical Laboratory Bioterrorism Readiness Plan, issued in 2003, a template for laboratory readiness planning
- Laboratory guidelines, issued in 2003, for packing and shipping infectious substances and diagnostic specimens
- Laboratory protocols for anthrax, botulinum toxin, brucella, plague, tularemia, *Coxiella Burnetii*, *Burkholderia mallei*, and *B. pseudomallei*, staphylococcal enterotoxin B, and unknown viruses

Armed Forces Institute of Pathology

www.afip.org

Modules called "Hot Topics" include diagnostic images and explanations of pathogenesis concerning selected diseases of current interest. In early 2004, these included inhalational anthrax, mad cow disease, buruli ulcer, monkeypox, cutaneous leishmaniasis, and SARS. Its Department of Infectious and Parasitic Diseases also offers a review article about smallpox: www.afip.org/Departments/infectious/index.html.

Association for Professionals in Infection Control (APIC)

www.apic.org

Bioterrorism Resources page: www.apic.org/bioterror

APIC's Bioterrorism Resources offers conveniently organized links to many of the most useful references in the field, including the Working Group on Civilian Biodefense's consensus statements on the major biological agents, originally published in *JAMA*; *The Big Bad Bug Book*, the Food and Drug Administration's guide to foodborne pathogens; U.S. Army and NATO manuals on recognizing and managing biological attacks; published hypothetical scenarios for anthrax and smallpox attacks; and other information. When last checked, in March 2004, not all APIC's listings were up to date.

Other offerings include:

- Bioterrorism Readiness Planning: A Template for Healthcare Facilities
  - www.hospitalconnect.com/aha/key_issues/disaster_readiness/content/APICReadinessNewformat.doc
- Mass Casualty Disaster Plan Checklist
  - www.apic.org/bioterror/checklist.doc
- Assessing Facility Bioterrorism Preparedness: A Guide for Infection Control Professionals, an online course
  - www.apicelearn.org/home

- Anthrax: Protecting and Preparing Your Family, an online course for the public
  - www.apicelearn.org/home
- Anthrax: Critical Information for Nurses, an online course for nurses
  - www.resourcenurse.com/RN/CE/course_intro?course_id=22

APIC also sells a Disaster and Pandemic Toolkit, described as containing "all the tools and materials necessary for surveillance, education, communications, laboratory, and management of personnel and patients are included. Handy forms, references, fact sheets, flowcharts, checklists, and samples provide the framework to interface with healthcare facilities and local public health preparedness plans."

Center for Biosecurity of the University of Pittsburgh Medical Center

www.upmc-biosecurity.org/index.html

The Center for Biosecurity of the University of Pittsburgh Medical Center is a nonprofit organization whose analysts and researchers work on issues related to preventing and defending against use of biological weapons. Until 2003, the program was well known as the Johns Hopkins Center for Civilian Biodefense. It publishes a journal called *Biosecurity and Bioterrorism*, available online at www.biosecurity-journal.com, and a quarterly, *Biosecurity Bulletin*, which can be accessed through the homepage listed above.

Biosecurity and Bioterrorism articles available on the website include some of direct relevance to hospitals, including:

- Grow, R.W. and Rubinson, L., The challenge of hospital infection control during a response to bioterrorist attack, *Biosecur Bioterror*, 1, 215, 2003.
- Gursky, E., Inglesby, T.V., and O'Toole, T., Anthrax 2001: observations of the medical and public health response, *Biosecur Bioterror*, 1, 87, 2003.

The center's website includes fact sheets and links to other information on Category A biological agents, including the consensus statements on each agent as a biological weapon published in *JAMA*. A good list of websites is found at www.upmc-biosecurity.org/pages/resources/internet.html.

Center for Infectious Disease Research and Policy (CIDRAP) at the University of Minnesota

www.cidrap.umn.edu

Extraordinarily informative and well organized, this is a model website. When last checked, in March 2004, it was up to date and clearly tended with care. Entries bore dates and were clearly attributed, including bylines for items created by the center's staff.

The site features sections on bioterrorism in general and, individually, on anthrax, botulism, plague, smallpox, tularemia, and viral hemorrhagic fevers, all reachable from the home page.

Each of those sections includes:

- Up-to-date news postings, drawn from the press, official announcements, and the center's staff. Archived back to September 11, 2001, these form a helpful and otherwise hard-to-find chronology, labeled "Bioterrorism Watch." The items cover developments concerning these pathogens whether or not they directly concern bioterrorism.
- Links to recent relevant journal articles, each accompanied by a reading list.
- A detailed overview. For the pathogens, this consists of clinical information prepared by the center in collaboration with the Infectious Diseases Society of America.
- Clinical pathways.
- Published guidelines.
- Resource lists and links.

A similar array of information is offered on SARS, West Nile fever, influenza, and monkeypox. Ricin is covered under the heading "Chemical Terrorism."

Center for Nonproliferation Studies of the Monterey Institute of International Studies

http://cns.miis.edu

The Center for Nonproliferation Studies' mission is to combat the spread of weapons of mass destruction. Its resources on chemical and biological weapons are housed at http://cns.miis.edu/research/cbw/index.htm.

The center's work focuses on nonproliferation and largely concerns national and international policy. It publishes the *Non-Proliferation Review* three times a year, as well as a series of occasional papers.

Its WMD Terrorism Database, which goes back to 1900, contains incidents reported in open sources that involve groups or individuals trying to acquire, use, or threaten to use chemical, biological, radiological, or nuclear materials. It is available by subscription, but yearly chronologies of the same information from recent years are offered on the website.

Center for the Study of Bioterrorism and Emerging Infections, Saint Louis University School of Public Health

www.csbei.slu.edu

Bioterrorism site: www.bioterrorism.slu.edu

This site has a broad range of content, generally in well-organized form. It has sections for each Category A biological agent, as well as for ricin, bioterrorism in general, and chemical, radiological, and nuclear terrorism. For each agent it offers:

- Quick references, including clinical fact sheets and images.
- Links to news and journal articles.
- Education and training tools, including several online training opportunities, done in cooperation with APIC. These include "Bioterrorism — Primary Care Preparedness" and "Assessing Facility Bioterrorism Preparedness: A Guide for Infection Control Professionals."
- Key documents from government, professional, and academic sources. Its own products, listed in the academic section, include a chart of isolation guidelines for biological agents; www.bioterrorism.slu.edu/bt/key_ref/Isolation.pdf.
- Official statements.
- Internet resources.
- Products.

Centers for Disease Control and Prevention (CDC)

www.cdc.gov

Public Health Emergency Preparedness and Response page: www.bt.cdc.gov

This federal agency, part of the Department of Health and Human Services, is the most authoritative single source on bioterrorism preparedness and response. Its Public Health Emergency Preparedness and Response page lists a wide range of clinical resources, cross-referenced by agent and by topic. With more than 30 agents listed, the depth of information varies. Many of the entries offer overall fact sheets and Q&As for the public and for health professionals, along with in-depth information on diagnosis, infection control, surveillance, treatment, vaccination, and worker safety.

The topic listings include laboratory information, training, preparation and planning, surveillance, mass trauma, preparedness and children, and news, which holds an archive of press releases and briefing transcripts. The site also offers photographs, as well as many downloadable journal articles and reports. (Two CDC journals — *Emerging Infectious Diseases* and *Morbidity and Mortality Weekly Report* — are listed separately in the following text.)

Clinicians' registry: www.bt.CDC.gov/clinregistry/index.asp

Clinicians can register at this page to receive e-mail updates on terrorism issues and training. The registry aims to provide clinicians with "real-time information to help prepare for (and possibly respond to) terrorism and other emergency events."

Emergency and Risk Communication, ERC training: www.cdc.gov/communication/emergency/erc_training.htm

This page offers information about training sessions provided by the CDC to help medical and health professionals deal more effectively with the media in the event of an emergency. The page contains links to a 13-part CDC primer on emergency risk communication.

The CDC's page on Information Networks and Other Information Sources, at www.cdc.gov/other.htm#states, contains links to many federal and international public health agencies and organizations, as well as state and some county health departments.

Media relations: www.cdc.gov/od/oc/media

This site has briefing transcripts and CDC guidelines and other documents for newsworthy topics; in early 2004, these included SARS, flu, and smallpox vaccination. For anthrax the materials date back to October 18, 2001, about 2 weeks after the first case. The site includes an archive of press releases going back to 1995 and summaries of the MMWR back to 1999. While intended for the media, it could be useful for health professionals.

Department of Homeland Security (DHS)

www.dhs.gov/dhspublic/index.jsp

DHS began operating in 2003 as the lead agency for federal preparedness and response to terrorism. In 2004 it adopted a National Incident Management System to provide a unified structure for local, state, and federal government responses to terrorist incidents. The plan can be read at www.dhs.gov/interweb/assetlibrary/NIMS-90-web.pdf.

DHA includes the Federal Emergency Management Agency (FEMA), which oversees the National Disaster Medical System that mobilizes medical response teams to augment local medical staff in an emergency. The program includes medical, pharmaceutical, nursing, mortuary, and veterinary teams. The website includes information for those interested in joining or sponsoring a team, but is largely aimed at team members: http://ndms.dhhs.gov.

DHS public readiness site: www.ready.gov

This site offers clear and simple advice for individuals and families on preparing for terrorism. Its fact sheets cover emergency supplies, sheltering in place, and other matters, with links to similar American Red Cross information.

Emerging Infectious Diseases

www.cdc.gov/ncidad/EID/index.htm

This peer-reviewed CDC monthly journal is available online, with some articles available online before publication. Although its focus is not specifically on bioterrorism, many of its articles, on topics like surveillance or on specific organisms, are relevant. Two special issues, which reside in the site's archives, are of particular interest:

- Vol. 8, No. 10 from October 2002 was devoted to bioterrorism-related anthrax, mainly the 2001 attacks. It is available at www.cdc.gov/nicdad/EID/vol8no10/contents_v8n10.htm.
- Vol. 5, No. 4 from July–August, 1999, consists of presentations from a National Symposium on Medical and Public Health Responses to Bioterrorism, sponsored by the Johns Hopkins Center for Civilian Biodefense in 1999. Among articles dealing with trends in terrorism and policy considerations are those concerned with the clinical features and epidemiology of smallpox and anthrax, as well as hypothetical attack scenarios for these two diseases. It is available at www.cdc.gov/ncidod/eid/vol5no4/contents.htm.

Food and Drug Administration (FDA)

www.fda.gov

Center for Drug Evaluation and Research
Drug Preparedness and Response to Bioterrorism page
www.fda.gov/cder/drugprepare/default.htm

This page contains information on drugs and vaccines for dealing with biological agents, as well as chemical and radiological weapons.

Center for Food Safety and Applied Nutrition
www.cfsan.fda.gov/list.html (Home Page)
www.cfsan.fda.gov/~dms/hpro-toc.html (Information for Health Professionals)

Information links on these pages include:

- The *Big Bad Bug Book (Foodborne Pathogenic Microorganisms and Natural Toxins)*, a manual describing more than 40 foodborne pathogenic microorganisms or natural toxins.
- The FDA's *Bacteriological Analytical Manual (BAM)* presents the agency's preferred laboratory procedures for microbiological analyses of foods and cosmetics. Along with other microbiological resources and links, it can also be found at www.cfsan.fda.gov/~comm/microbio.html.

General Accounting Office (GAO)

www.gao.gov

The General Accounting Office, the U.S. Congress' audit and investigatory agency, examines and evaluates a wide range of federal programs and activities. Since September 11, 2001, it has issued reports on many topics related to bioterrorism, including the handling of the anthrax attacks, the conduct of smallpox vaccination programs, security at federal research institutions, the use of federal preparedness money, and the state of readiness of public health agencies around the country. These can be accessed either through the website's search engine or through its "special collections" on homeland security and terrorism. GAO reports usually have a succinct background section that can serve as a quick introduction to a given topic.

The GAO website also offers an e-mail subscription service (listed under the heading "For the Press"). Users can sign up to get daily, weekly, or monthly alerts on GAO releases, or can request notification when new reports are issued in selected topic areas, such as health or homeland security.

Health Resources and Services Administration (HRSA)

Bioterrorism and Emergency Preparedness: www.hrsa.gov/bioterrorism.htm-#Introduction

HRSA, an agency within the Department of Health and Human Services, offers information about grants and other funding possibilities.

The Infectious Diseases Society of America (IDSA)

www.idsociety.org

Bioterrorism Information and Resources: www.idsociety.org/Template.cfm=?Sec-tion =Bioterrorism

This website offers a wealth of detailed, well-organized, and updated information for the clinician faced with identifying and treating illnesses caused by any of the six Category A biological agents. For each agent, the site offers an in-depth medical summary that includes not only diagnosis and treatment recommendations but pathogenesis, pediatric considerations, environmental testing, public health reporting, and other aspects. Each agent's entry includes a list of references and web resources and a clinical pathways chart. The material is produced and updated by the Center for Infectious Disease Research and Policy at the University of Minnesota.

The site also contains links to CDC notification procedures, laboratory protocols from the American Society of Microbiology, slide sets, pictures, and teaching modules.

Joint Commission on the Accreditation of Healthcare Facilities (JCAHO)

www.jcaho.org

The Joint Commission (JCAHO), the independent body that accredits hospitals and other health care facilities in the U.S. through on-site examinations, incorporates emergency planning in its detailed standards. These are published in manuals sold by JCAHO.

JCAHO's Emergency Management Standards — EC.1.4 and EC.2.9.1 — for hospitals are available at www.jcrinc.com/subscribers/perspectives.asp?durki=2914 &site=10&return=2897.

In summary, they say a hospital must have an emergency management plan that comprehensively addresses mitigation, preparedness, response, and recovery for emergencies and must test or use it twice a year. They do not deal specifically with bioterrorism.

Its standards aside, the Joint Commission has produced several helpful documents on emergency planning for health care facilities. These include:

- *Emergency Management in the New Millennium*
  - www.jcrinc.com/subscribers/perspectives.asp?durki=1122
  - This special edition of the Joint Commission's journal *Perspectives*, published after September 11, 2001, relates JCAHO standards to hospital responses in New York City and focuses on key issues that arose as New York hospitals coped with the terrorist attack. The issue is still relevant today, with articles on using JCAHO standards as a basis of emergency planning, maintaining communications and transportation, using medical and lay volunteers, and other subjects. The articles include many small, practical points based on the experience of hospital staff in New York.
- *Guide to Emergency Management Planning in Health Care*
  - This book, published by Joint Commission Resources, is a much expanded version of *Emergency Management in the New Millennium.* As of March 2004, it was not available online but could be purchased through www.jcrinc.com. It is well worth reading. It focuses on improving existing emergency plans for mitigation, preparedness, response, and recovery; establishing cooperative relationships with other health care facilities and with community agencies; improving internal and external communications; and training staff.
- *Health Care at the Crossroads: Strategies for Creating and Sustaining Communitywide Emergency Preparedness Systems*
  - www.jcaho.org/news±room/press±kits/em_ppi.htm
  - This 50-page paper, published in 2003, thoughtfully raises some key issues that health care facilities encounter in preparing for emergencies. These include trying to provide surge capacity; protecting and supporting hospital personnel; and making provision for "normal" medical care during a time of crisis by allowing so-called graceful degradation of standards of care.

KIDSHEALTH.ORG

www.kidshealth.org

This site, created by The Nemours Foundation's Center for Children's Health Media, offers separate articles aimed at parents, teenagers, and children on a wide range of health topics. These include basic information on anthrax and smallpox, as well as articles on coping with the psychological impact of terrorism. The articles tend to be simple in language and reassuring in tone.

MEDLINE PLUS

Biodefense and Bioterrorism page: www.nlm.nih.gov/medlineplus/biodefenseand-bioterrorism.html

Medline Plus, a service of the National Library of Medicine and the National Institutes of Health, offers a selection of information for the public, most of it drawn from federal agencies or the Mayo Clinic's website, as well as news stories from Reuters Health.

Morbidity and Mortality Weekly Report (MMWR)

www.cdc.gov/mmwr

This CDC weekly journal is fully available online and through e-mail subscriptions, as well as on paper. It publishes information about investigations of disease outbreaks, surveillance of illness and of health-related behaviors, epidemiology, and related topics. Many of its articles are based on information from state health departments. Although its focus is not specifically bioterrorism, many of its articles are relevant.

Its Terrorism Preparedness Compendium, a listing of relevant articles from its pages, is at www.cdc.gov/mmwr/indexbt.html.

The MMWR's page on Public Health Resources: State Health Departments, at www.cdc.gov/mmwr/international/relres.html, not only takes readers to the state health department of their choice, but also allows readers to search multiple state health departments simultaneously.

National Bioterrorism Civilian Medical Response Center (CiMeRC)

www.cimerc.org

The National Bioterrorism Civilian Medical Response Center (CiMeRC) is a project of Drexel University in partnership with the Center of Excellence for Remote and Medically Under-Served Areas (CERMUSA) at Saint Francis University. Its mission is "to promote the development of an effective response by the civilian medical community to biological terrorist attacks through the use of advanced Command and Control technologies that effectively coordinate efforts between civilian medical responders and local, State, and Federal government agencies." It offers training materials including:

Strategies for Incident Preparedness: A National Model
www.cimerc.org/content/projects/strategies_for_incident_preparedness/sip.pdf

This 105-page document consists of some 20 disaster scenarios, from fire to plague, to anthrax to nuclear attack, followed by a series of questions designed to aid hospitals and other health care organizations in planning and exercising for mass casualty emergencies. The document was sponsored by Mercy Health System of Pennsylvania and CiMeRC.

Under the heading "Problem Simulations," site users can submit their answers on individual scenarios and get back comments on their responses. The site also offers a 14-question "Hospital Self Assessment" that can be taken online.

The National Center for PTSD (Posttraumatic Stress Disorder)

www.ncptsd.org/index.html

The center, which is part of the Department of Veterans Affairs, offers a wealth of information online concerning the psychological effects and treatment of trauma and disaster in many different settings and population groups. Offerings include fact sheets, book excerpts, and this guidebook: Young, B.H. et al., *Disaster Mental Health Services:A Guidebook for Clinicians and Administrators*, National Center for PTSD, Washington, D.C., 2002, published online at www.ncptsd.org//publications/disaster/index.html.

National Guideline Clearinghouse

www.guideline.gov

Bioterrorism Guidelines: www.guideline.gov/resources/bioterrorism.aspx

The National Guideline Clearinghouse is intended to be a repository of evidence-based clinical practice guidelines. It is sponsored by the Agency for Healthcare Research and Quality (AHRQ), in collaboration with the American Medical Association and the American Association of Health Plans–Health Insurance Association of America.

In March 2004 its bioterrorism page listed 11 items, all either recommendations from the CDC or consensus statements of the Working Group on Bioterrorism. Users can sign up for a weekly e-mail service telling them of new content on the site: www.guideline.gov/whatsnew/subscription.aspx.

National Memorial Institute for the Prevention of Terrorism (MIPT)

www.mipt.org

The institute was established in 1999 in response to the terrorist bombing of the Murrah Federal Building in Oklahoma City in 1995. It maintains a large, web-accessible library of information about various aspects of terrorism, including biological weapons, biodefense, and agricultural terrorism. It is unusual in that it includes a strong emphasis on meeting the needs of first responders for protection, training and support, as well as being a major repository of information on international terrorism. On its website it offers a collection of "Lessons Learned" reports; a "Responder Knowledge Base" of information about specific pieces of equipment; bibliographies; and a database of training sessions, searchable by state, subject matter, or target audience.

Its Terrorism Databases, available at http://db.mipt.org/index.cfm, include the RAND Terrorism Chronology Database (international terrorist incidents between 1968 and 1997), RAND–MIPT Terrorism Incident Database (domestic and international terrorist incidents from 1998 to the present), and the MIPT Indictment Database (U.S. court cases since 1978). The University of Oklahoma and the University of Alabama have contributed to the construction of these databases, according to the site's self-description.

National Institute for Occupational Safety and Health (NIOSH)

Emergency Response Resources: www.cdc.gov/niosh/topics/emres/default.html

This agency, which is part of the CDC, provides information on protecting workers and workplaces from biological agents. Documents available here include:

- Guidance for Protecting Building Environments from Airborne Chemical, Biological, or Radiological Attacks
  - www.cdc.gov/niosh/bldvent/pdfs/2002-139.pdf
- Guidance for Filtration and Air-Cleaning Systems to Protect Building Environments from Airborne Chemical, Biological, or Radiological Attacks, April 2003
  - www.cdc.gov/niosh/docs/2003-136/2003-136.html

It also provides information on personal protective devices, including a detailed Respirator Fact Sheet, headlined, "What you should know in deciding whether to buy escape hoods, gas masks, or other respirators for preparedness at home and work," at www.cdc.gov/niosh/npptl/npptlrespfact.html.

The National Mental Health Information Center

www.mentalhealth.samhsa.gov

This service of HHS' Substance Abuse and Mental Health Services Administration (SAMHSA) offers many fact sheets on stress and trauma for both lay readers and professionals. Among its online disaster/trauma publications is a useful book: DeWolfe, D.J., *Training Manual for Mental Health and Human Service Workers in Major Disasters,* 2nd edition, Department of Health and Human Services, Washington, D.C., 2000.

Premier Safety Institute

www.premierinc.com

Disaster Readiness page: www.premierinc.com/frames/index.jsp?pagelocation=/safety

The Premier Safety Institute is part of Premier Inc., a national alliance of nonprofit hospitals that attempts to improve hospital efficiency and effectiveness through such measures as group purchasing and sharing of information.

Its Disaster Readiness site provides a good overview of the major issues for health care facilities and has a useful collection of links and documents on clinical and planning topics. It is especially strong on building protection and maintenance, and equipment supply and formulary issues.

The RAND Corporation

www.rand.org

RAND (as in Research and Development) is a large nonprofit think-tank that does research on behalf of public and private clients, as well as independent inquiries of its own, in about a dozen areas, including terrorism and homeland security. Its homepage offers a search engine for its voluminous archives; many of its reports, including book-length works, are fully available online.

Its terrorism reports usually concern national strategy, policy issues, and analysis of terrorist groups and trends. But some bear on preparedness, including these:

Individual Preparedness and Response to Chemical, Radiological, Nuclear, and Biological Terrorist Attacks
www.rand.org/publications/MR/MR1731
Are Local Health Responders Ready for Biological and Chemical Terrorism?
www.rand.org/publications/IP/IP221/IP221/index.html

Stanford University Medical Center

Bioterrorism and Emergency Preparedness: www.stanfordhospital.com/forPhysiciansOthers/bioterrorism/bioterrorism.html

This site offers an array of documents designed for use by the medical center's staff and patients; many of them may serve as useful models for other hospitals. The documents include a bioterrorism preparedness plan for the hospital; rules for calling a "Code Zebra," the hospital's code for a bioterrorism event; a bioterrorism exposure tracking form, to be filled out by patients; a chart of infection control procedures for various agents; clinical pathways for anthrax and smallpox; triage plans for the hospital and clinics; and information sheets to be distributed to patients. These materials were produced by the Bioterrorism and Emergency Preparedness Task Force of Stanford Hospital & Clinics, Lucile Salter Packard Children's Hospital, and Stanford University's School of Medicine.

In addition, the site has links to documents that are of clinical utility, such as "Sentinel Laboratory Guidelines, Clinical Laboratory Bioterrorism Readiness Plan," a 2003 template for laboratory planning, issued by the American Society of Microbiology in 2003.

USAMRIID (The U.S. Army Medical Research Institute of Infectious Diseases)

www.usamriid.army.mil

USAMRIID, based at Ft. Detrick, Maryland, works toward developing vaccines, drugs, and diagnostic techniques for biological agents, as well as developing plans and running training programs for medical defense against biological weapons. A 6-day, on-site training program for medical personnel is conducted several times a year, and is open to civilians. USAMRIID is also involved in investigation of natural outbreaks of disease and maintains a major reference laboratory for identification of agents.

Its so-called Blue Book, *Medical Management of Biological Casualties Handbook*, can be downloaded by chapter in several formats, including Word, PDF, and Palm OS, at www.usamriid.army.mil/education/bluebook.html.

USAMRIID offers several other training resources, including:

- "Advanced Topics on Medical Defense Against Biological and Chemical Agents," a series of six 2-hour lectures that are available as a webcast, VHS tape, or DVD set. These programs focus on recognition and management of biological and chemical casualties.
- "Medical Aspects of Chemical and Biological Warfare" from the *Textbook of Military Medicine.*
- Defense Against Toxin Weapons Manual.

All can be ordered or downloaded from www.usamriid.army.mil/education/instruct.html.

REFERENCES

1. Ferguson et al., Bioterrorism web site resource for infectious disease clinicians and epidemiologists, *Clin Infect Dis*, 36, 1458, 2003.
2. Bartlett, J.G. et al., Eds., *Bioterrorism and Public Health: An Internet Resource Guide*, Thomson PDR, Montvale, NJ, 2002.

Section IV

Tabletop Exercises

Tabletop Exercises

EDUCATING HOSPITAL STAFF AND MAINTAINING PREPAREDNESS FOR BIOTERRORISM

Perhaps the greatest obstacle to effective planning for the hospital's response to bioterrorism is educating and maintaining preparedness among its own staff. Hospitals typically provide required in-service training in diverse areas such as safety, infection control, patient rights, etc. These areas are emphasized because hospital workers at all levels are often faced with situations requiring specific knowledge of policy and procedures. The challenge in planning for events that the health care worker may never encounter, such as bioterrorism, comes in reinforcing knowledge and behaviors that may never be needed. Printed educational material may be lost, never read, or unavailable for review when needed. Standard educational formats such as lectures and conferences (whether live or taped) must be repeated frequently to diverse groups of workers and may consume large amounts of time and resources in their preparation. Any educational strategy must take into account that hospital staff may turn over at a rapid rate and that employees may work at more than one hospital or health care facility and thus be exposed to differing messages and divergent policies.

These obstacles to effectively educating the entire hospital staff may prove insurmountable for many facilities. Various strategies to attempt to overcome them may include:

- Concentrating educational efforts on senior leadership, both clinical and nonclinical
- Providing short lists of steps to be taken in a bioterrorism event that are job-title specific and easily kept available for quick referral (e.g., laminated cards)
- Posting key elements of procedures to be followed in permanent signs in employee-only lounges, locker rooms, cafeterias, etc.

However, effectiveness of strategies such as these has not been established, and hospitals must choose among such unproven strategies simply to come into compliance with required standards.

Individuals not in the health care system may also benefit from such mock exercises. In a simulated outbreak of the viral infection Rift Valley fever, DiGiovanni and colleagues[1] surveyed journalists and spouses or partners of first responders as well as first responders themselves. In this study, journalists demonstrated a high level of fear and confusion. This fact, coupled with the finding in the same study that all groups indicated that they would have the greatest confidence in local sources of information, suggests that preparation of journalists for the likely circumstances to be encountered in a biological attack might also be worthwhile.

TABLETOP EXERCISES

An educational strategy that has come into increasingly widespread use is the so-called tabletop exercise. As distinct from a drill in which participants carry out the actual functions that would be required of them in the event of an emergency (e.g., transport mock patients, don personal protective equipment, activate decontamination showers, etc.), tabletop exercises emphasize the cognitive aspects of preparedness. The format typically involves a limited number of participants who, led by a moderator or facilitator, confront mock scenarios and individually and collectively respond to questions and develop strategies by which they would react. Tabletop exercises are particularly relevant to bioterrorism planning because many of the most feared agents do not require decontamination, and the need for proper use of equipment (except for personal protective equipment by first responders) often takes a backseat to such issues as defining personnel needs, isolation capacity, surge capacity, communication with the press and the public, and interagency cooperation.

The value of such exercises was demonstrated in a recent study by Henning and colleagues[2] involving various categories of health care workers from 16 hospital departments. In this study 94% and 95% of physicians and nurses, respectively, considered the exercise (which cost $225 to conduct) valuable.

The realities of daily life in busy hospitals make it imperative that emergency preparedness planning activities be easily accessible and educationally valid and worthwhile. It is hoped that the exercises presented in this chapter can be used by hospitals to form the framework of an ongoing curriculum in preparation for bioterrorism.

In this chapter we present a series of tabletop exercises addressing the Category A agents of possible use in a bioterrorism attack. These exercises are intended to be used in the following manner:

A small group (10 to 12) of selected individuals representing key areas of the hospital that would be involved in a bioterrorism incident is brought together.

- A mediator presents a scenario likely to be encountered in a bioterrorism event.
- The scenario is presented as an unfolding, often confusing, picture.
- Following each phase of the scenario is a series of questions to be directed to specific members of the group or to the group as a whole.
- Following the questions for each scenario are the suggested correct responses.
- Because any biological attack would pose multifaceted challenges to a hospital and its staff, which, perhaps, no single exercise can fully address, the emphasis varies among the exercises in this chapter. Although all place emphasis on emergency department procedures, isolation, and decontam-

ination when necessary, some explore such issues as media relations, legal issues, and a variety of other key areas covered elsewhere in this book.
- Chapter references and a suggested audience for each exercise are provided.

For ease of use and presentation, these exercises are separated into sections for sequential presentation and discussion.

REFERENCES

1. DiGiovanni, C. et al., Community reaction to bioterrorism: prospective study of simulated outbreak, *Emerg Infect Dis*, 9, 708, 2003.
2. Henning, K.J. et al., Health system preparedness for bioterrorism: bringing the tabletop to the hospital, *Infect Control Hosp Epidemiol*, 25, 146, 2002.

Tabletop Exercise: Plague

Suggested participants:

Director of Emergency Department
Emergency Department Physicians
Emergency Department Nurses
Microbiology Laboratory Supervisor
Infection Control Officer
Director of Pharmacy
Chief Operating Officer
Safety Officer

SCENARIO: PART I

The director of your hospital's emergency department receives an e-mail and fax from the local health department indicating a surge in cases of hemorrhagic pneumonia in a county neighboring yours. The etiology of the pneumonia cases and their relationship, if any, to each other are unknown. Because of the abrupt nature of the surge, a biological attack or natural outbreak is suspected.

QUESTIONS: PART I

1. Among the Category A agents, which might present in this fashion?
2. What additional information about the patients would be useful in making a preliminary diagnosis?
3. What are your immediate concerns regarding:
   - Equipment
   - Staff safety
   - Staffing needs
   - Pharmaceutical and vaccine supplies

ANSWERS: PART I

1. Of the Category A agents (smallpox, anthrax, plague, botulism, tularemia, and hemorrhagic fever viruses), only plague, anthrax, and tularemia would be likely to present in this fashion.
2. An abrupt onset of illness would favor plague or anthrax.
   - Central nervous system involvement would favor anthrax more than plague.

- If the cases seen in the neighboring county represented an obvious cluster of individuals who had had prior contact with each other, plague would be likely.

3. Equipment Concerns
   - The adequacy of facilities for respiratory isolation (negative pressure rooms, high-efficiency respirator masks) should be quickly assessed for a presumed, though unproven, highly contagious agent.
   - Communication lines with public health and other civil authorities should be tested.
   - Decontamination procedures should be reviewed with appropriate staff until the nature of the possible attack is better understood.
   - Signs should be placed in waiting areas advising individuals with respiratory complaints to report to the triage area.
   - Areas for potential surge capacity, addressing the worried well as well as possible victims, should be identified.
4. Staff Safety
   - Triage staff are at greatest risk. They should be instructed to place a surgical mask on any individual with fever or respiratory symptoms.
   - Patients with cough should be rapidly escorted to isolation rooms or, if this proves unfeasible, placed in a different room, away from other individuals in the waiting area.
   - Patients coughing bloody sputum should immediately be placed in respiratory isolation.
   - Services likely to be involved in the transport of infected patients or their body fluids should be informed of the situation. These include transport, messenger, laboratory accessioning, laboratory technologists, radiology, and mortuary staff.
5. Staffing Needs
   - Consideration should be given to instituting the hospital's incident command system and establishing a command post to coordinate staffing of the emergency room, intensive care units, and appropriate laboratory and diagnostic areas of the hospital.
   - Infection control, infectious diseases, pulmonary, and critical care staff should be specifically informed of the situation.
   - Public affairs officers should be prepared to answer questions.

SCENARIO: PART II

After rapid screening of individuals in the waiting area, you find none with cough productive of bloody sputum. However, a patient who had been placed in an examination room earlier is complaining of shortness of breath, cough productive of bloody sputum, and has a fever of 104ºF. An official from the health department calls the hospital infection control officer and the emergency room director to inform them that sputum from three of the patients in the neighboring county has been found to contain numerous Gram-negative rods. One of the patients has died of septic shock and respiratory failure.

QUESTIONS: PART II

1. Based on the information from the department of health, which Category A organism would be most likely?
2. How should the patient in your emergency department be isolated?
3. How should his or her respiratory secretions be processed?
4. Should decontamination procedures be initiated?
5. What further information would you need from your patient?

ANSWERS: PART II

1. The presence of Gram-negative bacilli in the respiratory secretions of the three of the patients suggests the possibility of plague or tularemia (among the Category A agents). The speed of progression indicated by the rapid death of one of the reported patients and the presence of blood in the sputum would favor plague.
2. Your patient should be placed in respiratory isolation on the assumption that he or she has pneumonic plague. Although tularemia remains a possibility, person-to-person spread of tularemia is extremely unlikely. Pneumonic plague is, however, highly contagious.
3. Under the circumstances described, in which pneumonic plague is a strong consideration, it may be appropriate to avoid processing of respiratory secretions by the hospital laboratory. They may be collected and placed in sealed containers by staff wearing appropriate respirators (N95 or N100) and stored for processing in appropriate public health laboratories.
4. Secondary infection with plague bacillus from contaminated environmental sources is thought to be unlikely because the plague bacillus does not survive for long outside the body. For this reason, decontamination of the individual, clothing, or other objects with which he or she has come into contact probably offers no benefit. Although the tularemia bacillus may persist on environmental surfaces for prolonged periods, it is thought that decontamination other than hand washing is not necessary.
5. Additional information should be sought from the patient regarding the following:
   - Potential or known contact with the patients being seen at the other hospital
   - Recent travel
   - The names and locations of household or other close personal contacts

SCENARIO: PART III

The health department issues a confidential advisory indicating that the organism in the sputum of the three patients at the other hospital has been preliminarily identified as *Yersinia pestis* and that all five pneumonia patients had attended the same church service 3 days prior to the onset of their symptoms.

QUESTIONS: PART III

1. What are the implications of this information?
2. What additional specific information would you request of your patient?
3. What would cause you to report your case to the department of health as suspicious of plague?
4. Should therapy for plague be initiated?
5. What is the appropriate therapy?

ANSWERS: PART III

1. The information from the health department implies that:
   - An intentional release of plague bacillus has occurred. This can be concluded both by the large number of simultaneous cases of this rare disease and the fact that the infection appears to have been contracted at an indoor location.
   - A likely point/source of release existed either at the church or an adjacent structure or vehicle.
   - There is a high likelihood that additional cases will be seen related both to the initial release and to subsequent person-to-person spread.
2. Your patient should be asked:
   - Whether he attended the church identified as the potential point of release? If so, when?
   - Can he trace his activities since last attending the church?
   - With whom has he come into close contact since the onset of his symptoms? Is he aware of symptoms in any of his close contacts?
3. Your patient should be reported to the health department as a potential case of pneumonic plague, regardless of his answers to these questions. His contact information should be given to the health department.
4. Therapy for pneumonic plague as well as for community-acquired bacterial pneumonia should be instituted immediately.
5. Recommended regimens for plague include:
   - Streptomycin 1 g intramuscularly twice daily *or*
   - Gentamicin 5 mg/kg intramuscularly or intravenously once daily or 2 mg/kg loading dose followed by 1.7 mg/kg intramuscularly or intravenously daily *or*
   - Doxycycline 100 mg intravenously twice daily *or*
   - Ciprofloxacin 400 mg intravenously twice daily

Public health authorities may recommend specific treatment regimens based on availability of various antibiotics and specific susceptibility patterns of the organisms isolated. Streptomycin is currently in short supply.

Questions to be addressed by Public Health Authorities:

- What other agencies should be notified of the apparent attack?
- What potential jurisdictional issues might arise?
- What level of contact tracing would be appropriate?
- Should travel restrictions be imposed?
- Should quarantine be imposed? How?

LESSONS OF THE EXERCISE

Hemorrhagic pneumonia occurring in clusters should suggest pneumonic plague.

Prompt triage, assessment, and therapy of potential victims of plague is imperative.

Hospitals may have to impose containment strategies when confronted by potential biological attack prior to confirmation.

Chapter references: 2, 3, 9, 10, and Appendix A.

Tabletop Exercise: Smallpox

Suggested participants:

Director of Emergency Department
Emergency Department Physicians
Emergency Department Nurses
Microbiology Laboratory Supervisor
Infection Control; Infectious Disease Clinician
Director of Pharmacy
Chief Operating Officer
Safety Supervisor
Housekeeping Supervisor
Mortuary Supervisor

SCENARIO: PART I

On Tuesday morning at 9 A.M., the administrator on duty in the emergency department is notified by the health department that a suspected case of smallpox has been reported from a hospital 5 miles from yours. Public health physicians have examined the patient and consider smallpox to be highly likely.

QUESTIONS: PART I

1. What are the implications of the reported case?
2. How should you assess the likelihood of a smallpox victim arriving at your hospital?
3. What steps should be taken by the emergency department?

ANSWERS: PART I

1. A case of smallpox anywhere in the world should be regarded as the beginning of a global pandemic until proven otherwise.
2. Contacting the health department to determine such specifics about the reported case as the patient's place of residence, employment, and household contacts might provide insight into the likelihood that a patient with smallpox will be seen at your hospital.
3. Steps to be taken include the following:
   - Reinforce triage procedures so that patients with known contact with the index case or with fever and rash are isolated promptly.
   - Contact infection control staff, infectious disease consultant, and hospital administration.

- Consider activation of the incident command system.
- Individuals in the waiting room should be rapidly screened for known contact with the index case as well as for symptoms of fever and rash.
- If negative-pressure isolation rooms are available, they should be evaluated by engineering or infection control staff.
- The supply of particulate respirators should be inventoried and emergency department staff should be alerted to the possible arrival of a patient with smallpox and reminded of proper isolation procedures.

SCENARIO: PART II

You learn that the patient at the other hospital is a 36-year-old woman from Ecuador. She works as a housekeeper in an apartment building several blocks from your hospital.

At noon, a 30-year-old man with high fever is seen in your triage area. He arrived at the emergency department by taxi.

QUESTIONS: PART II

1. What information should be elicited from the patient in triage?
2. What procedures should the triage nurse follow?
3. What procedures should the examining physician follow?
4. Should anyone else be notified?

ANSWERS: PART II

1. His exact place of residence should be determined and he should be questioned about possible exposure to the index case.
2. The patient in triage should be provided with a surgical mask.
3. The patient should be placed in isolation and airborne precautions maintained.
4. Infection control staff and infectious diseases consultant should be notified.

SCENARIO: PART III

The patient reports that he lives at the address, but not in the apartment, where the index case is employed.

QUESTIONS: PART III

1. What is your level of suspicion that the patient has smallpox?
2. What information should be sought about the apartment building?
3. Who else should be contacted internally and externally?

ANSWERS: PART III

1. Your level of suspicion should be very high.
2. The patient should be questioned about the health status of household contacts and other contacts within the apartment building.
3. You should report your patient to the health department as a suspected case of smallpox.

SCENARIO: PART IV

At 2 P.M. the hospital administration notifies the emergency department that the health department has confirmed that the index case at the other hospital is, in fact, smallpox. In addition, through syndromic surveillance, an increase in emergency department visits by individuals complaining of fever and rash has been detected throughout the county.

QUESTIONS: PART IV

1. How do you recognize smallpox?
2. What procedures should be followed in the emergency department for triaging and isolating possible cases?
3. What steps should be taken to evaluate patients and visitors in the waiting area?
4. What should be done if no isolation rooms are available?

ANSWERS: PART IV

1. **Typical clinical features of smallpox:**
   - Average incubation period: 12 days
   - Stages:
     - Fever, headache, and malaise.
     - Erythematous rash appearing first on the face and throat, then spreading to the arms, legs, and torso.
     - Pustules associated with burning pain develop in the same distribution.
   - Facilities to confirm the diagnosis of smallpox are not available in hospital clinical laboratories.
2. **Triage and Isolation in the Emergency Department:**
   - The patient should be instructed to put on a mask immediately and placed in a negative-pressure isolation room with HEPA filtration of vented air.
   - Airborne precautions, including the use by staff of fit-tested N95 or N100 particulate respirators, should be maintained.

- All laundry and waste should be placed in biohazard bags and left in the room with the patient.
- In collaboration with public health officials, all potential victims and health care workers caring for them should receive smallpox vaccination as early as possible. Vaccinia immune globulin is recommended for individuals exposed more than 72 hours previously.
- Hospital administration and infection control staffs should develop lists of other hospital workers who should be vaccinated. It should be noted that smallpox outbreaks among laundry workers and mortuary workers, among others, have been reported.

3. **The Waiting Area:**
   - The risk of contagion of smallpox in the waiting area should be considered low unless the patient was coughing and present in the waiting area for several hours.
   - Individuals in the waiting area should be rapidly assessed for symptoms of smallpox, as multiple cases would be expected in an attack.
   - Contact information should be obtained from all individuals potentially exposed to the suspected case while in the waiting area and, if feasible, they should be moved to a separate area of the hospital where they can later be interviewed by public health officials.
   - If the patient suspected of having smallpox was coughing, the waiting area should be temporarily closed and subjected to surface decontamination.
4. **Isolation Rooms:**
   - No patient suspected of having smallpox should be transferred out of his or her isolation room under any circumstances.
   - If all available isolation rooms have been filled, steps must be taken to redirect ambulance cases to other hospitals in accordance with directions from public health authorities.
   - Patients should wear particulate respirator masks if they are transported out of isolation rooms.
   - Cohorting of suspected cases together in isolation rooms may be necessary if capacity is exceeded.
   - If the emergency department is overwhelmed with suspected cases requiring isolation, infection control staff in conjunction with public health authorities should direct the isolation of patients in negative-pressure rooms outside the emergency department or transfer them, with proper precautions, to other facilities.

SCENARIO: PART V

It is 36 hours after the original case was reported; two patients have died in your emergency department of probable smallpox.

QUESTIONS: PART V

1. What should be done with the bodies of the victims?
2. How should the bedding and other materials from the victims be handled?
3. Should the room be decontaminated?

ANSWERS: PART V

1. Mortuary workers should observe standard precautions and wear fit-tested N95 or N100 particulate respirators.
   The bodies should be completely wrapped for transport.
   Cremation is recommended.
2. The bedding and other disposable items should be placed in biohazard bags and autoclaved prior to laundering or, when possible, incinerated. Clinical specimens can be processed only in a high biological-safety-level public health laboratory.
3. Standard hospital disinfectants including those containing sodium hypochlorite or quaternary ammonia are effective at inactivating variola virus. The virus can remain aerosolized for 24 hours and remain viable on fomites for several days. Therefore surface decontamination is indicated.

LESSONS OF THIS EXERCISE

Any case of smallpox reported anywhere in the world should be regarded as evidence of an intentional release of the virus.

Emergency departments should prepare for the arrival of victims of smallpox after any reported case and be prepared to identify and isolate potential victims at the earliest stages of infection.

The presence of a smallpox victim represents a potential threat to other patients, staff, and visitors.

Because of the relatively long incubation period of smallpox (average 12 days), subsequent waves of infected patients should be anticipated over the weeks following an initial case.

Chapter references: 2, 3, 9, 10, 11, and Appendix B.

Tabletop Exercise: Anthrax

Suggested participants:

Director of Emergency Department
Emergency Department, Critical Care Physicians
Emergency Department Nurses
Microbiology Laboratory Supervisor
Infection Control; Infectious Disease Clinician
Director of Pharmacy
Chief Operating Officer
Safety Supervisor
Housekeeping Supervisor
Mortuary Supervisor

SCENARIO: PART I

A 41-year-old female presents to your hospital's diagnostic clinic complaining of a nonhealing ulcer on her left forearm. She first noted the lesion 2 days earlier and has sought medical attention because it has doubled in size since that time. She denies trauma, including insect bites, and has no significant chronic illnesses.

QUESTIONS: PART I

1. What is your differential diagnosis?
2. What additional history would you like?
3. Should the patient be placed in isolation?
4. Should the patient undergo decontamination?
5. How should diagnostic specimens be obtained and processed?
6. Should you notify anyone else?

ANSWERS: PART I

1. **Differential Diagnosis**
   - Cutaneous anthrax
   - Spider bite
   - Staphylococcal abscess
   - Basal cell carcinoma
   - Mycobacterial infection
   - Fungal infection

- Cutaneous leishmaniasis
- Necrotic herpes simplex lesion
- Ulceroglandular tularemia
- Ecthyma gangrenosum

2. **Additional information desired**
   - **Medical history:** The patient should be questioned about fever, chills, pain, respiratory symptoms, and lymphadenopathy.
   - **Travel history:** In order to better prioritize the differential diagnosis given in the preceding text, the patient should be thoroughly questioned about significant travel within the past several months, particularly to tropical or subtropical areas.
   - **Occupational history:** The exact nature of the patient's current occupation should be ascertained.
   - As was learned in the 2001 anthrax attacks, exposure in mail-sorting facilities or simply to mail delivered to an office building represented risk factors for cutaneous and inhalational anthrax. Occupational association with political figures or news outlets was also common among the victims in 2001, and such connections, either direct or indirect, should be explored.
   - **Social history:** The patient's places of residence and employment should be ascertained. The health status of close contacts should also be explored.
3. **Isolation**
   - Based on the information so far and the differential diagnosis, there is no indication for isolation above the level of standard precautions.
4. **Decontamination**
   - The patient's clothing should be placed in an isolation bag because cutaneous anthrax remains a possibility. Further decontamination procedures are unnecessary.
5. **Diagnostic Specimens**
   - Cultures of the skin lesion and a nasal swab culture should be obtained for processing by the public health department.
6. **Notification**
   - The local health department should be notified because of the suspicion of possible anthrax. Local law enforcement authorities should be notified either by the hospital or by public health authorities, preferably the latter.

   Hospital infection control staff should be alerted.

SCENARIO: PART II

The patient reports low-grade fever at home, although she is currently afebrile. She denies respiratory symptoms and reports that the lesion is painless. She has no lymphadenopathy.

She was born and raised in New York City and denies any travel outside the New York area in the past 3 months.

She works in the mail room at a large office building.

QUESTIONS: PART II

1. How does this information affect your differential diagnosis?
2. What additional questions would you ask regarding her place of employment?
3. Should anyone else be notified at this point?
4. How should she be managed pending final diagnosis?

ANSWERS: PART II

1. **Differential Diagnosis**
   - The history of fever suggests infection rather than basal cell carcinoma and makes spider bite less likely.
   - The absence of a significant travel history reduces the likelihood of fungal or mycobacterial infection and eliminates leishmaniasis.
   - The absence of pain reduces the likelihood of herpes simplex infection and supports the diagnosis of anthrax.
   - The leading diagnosis is cutaneous anthrax.
2. **Additional Information**
   - Important details about the patient's place of employment:
     - What are her duties?
     - How long has she worked in her present position?
     - Does she sort mail?
     - Does she open mail?
     - Does she recall handling any suspicious packages?
     - Does she know of any coworkers with similar skin lesions?
3. **Additional Notifications**
   - The postal service and her employer should be notified that cutaneous anthrax is suspected (this task should be assumed by public health authorities or police unless you are instructed otherwise).
   - Therapy for cutaneous anthrax should be initiated immediately with ciprofloxacin or doxycycline.

SCENARIO: PART III

The patient indicates that she has worked at her present job for the past 5 years.

She sorts, but does not routinely open mail.

She indicates that many types of packages arrive in the mail and she is not sure if any recent packages could be considered suspicious. She does not recall any direct exposure to powders on delivered mail.

She knows of no one else at her job with similar skin lesions. She indicates, however, that her immediate supervisor called in sick yesterday because of a "bad cold."

QUESTIONS: PART III

1. What conclusions do you draw from her description of her job and workplace?
2. What concerns are raised by the information she reports?
3. Should anyone else be notified at this point?

ANSWERS: PART III

1. Her occupation carries a high risk of exposure to anthrax carried through the mail.
2. Respiratory complaints in a coworker should raise suspicion of inhalational anthrax and a common source of infection.
   Many other individuals at her workplace may have been exposed.
3. The health department should be notified of the details of her workplace and of the existence of the sick coworker.

SCENARIO: PART IV

A 50-year-old male has just arrived by ambulance, intubated, hypotensive, and febrile to 105°F.

A reporter telephones the front desk of the emergency department seeking to confirm a rumor that there is a suspected case of anthrax at your hospital. The reporter is referred to the triage nurse who indicates that "we might have a bioterrorism victim."

It is determined that the new patient works in the same office building as the initial patient with suspected cutaneous anthrax.

You are informed that 25 other employees of the initial patient's company are in the waiting room requesting to be tested for anthrax and to undergo decontamination.

QUESTIONS: PART IV

1. Should the intubated patient be treated empirically for inhalational anthrax?
2. What radiographic findings would support the diagnosis?
3. Should he be placed in isolation?
4. Should he undergo decontamination?

5. How should the diagnosis be confirmed?
6. Was the reporter's inquiry handled properly?
7. What information should be given to the press and public at this point?
8. How should the employees seeking testing and decontamination be evaluated?
9. If asymptomatic, do they require treatment for anthrax?
10. Should they undergo decontamination?

ANSWERS: PART IV

1. Culture confirmation is required to confirm the diagnosis. After blood cultures are obtained, the intubated patient should immediately be treated for inhalational anthrax as well as other causes of septicemia.
2. Roentgenographic findings of hilar fullness and/or pleural effusions would be consistent with a diagnosis of inhalational anthrax.
3. Standard precautions are adequate.
4. He does not require decontamination, but his clothing should be bagged and handled as biohazardous waste.
5. The reporter should have been referred to public health authorities.
6. Speculation should be avoided. Further press inquiries should be processed in the same manner until public health and hospital public affairs staffs have communicated and reached a consensus on the nature of the information to be released to the public.
7. The other employees should be rapidly assessed for symptoms of cutaneous or inhalational anthrax.
   Nasal swab cultures should be obtained, stored, transported, and processed under the guidance of the public health authorities.
8. Advice to asymptomatic workers pending the results of nasal cultures and further investigation of the incident should be coordinated by public health authorities.
9. Some may be advised to initiate preventive therapy for anthrax prior to the availability of culture results for anthrax depending on the nature of their potential exposure.

SCENARIO: PART V

Inquiries from the press, both print and broadcast, flood the telephone lines in the emergency department and the general hospital switchboard.

Journalists arrive and begin to interview physicians and nurses leaving the hospital.

In an on-camera interview, one emergency department physician indicates that the hospital is rapidly becoming overwhelmed with victims of anthrax and that he fears for his own safety and that of the other staff members.

LESSONS OF THE EXERCISE

Many decisions can and must be made prior to culture confirmation of anthrax.

Travel and occupational history may represent the most useful information in assessing the likelihood of a biological attack.

Rumors and addressing the needs of the worried well will pose a substantial challenge to hospitals in the event of an attack. Hospitals should develop a pre-event strategy of responding to inquiries by the press and public.

Chapter references: 2, 3, 7, 9, 10, 11, and Appendix A.

Tabletop Exercise: Ricin

Suggested participants:

Director of Emergency Department
Emergency Department; Critical Care Physicians
Emergency Department Nurses
Director of Pharmacy
Chief Operating Officer
Safety Supervisor
Housekeeping Supervisor

SCENARIO

The Centers for Disease Control and Prevention (CDC) announces that a powder, which on preliminary testing has been tentatively identified as ricin, has been found at a postal facility near Washington, D.C.

Final identification of the powder is expected within 24 hours; no cases of ricin poisoning have been identified.

QUESTIONS

1. What additional information would be helpful at this point in hospital planning?
2. What is ricin?
3. How might it be weaponized?

ANSWERS

1. To assess the risk of local cases of ricin poisoning appearing, several facts would be helpful:
   - How long has it been since the first potential exposure to employees at the postal facility?
   - Does mail in your locality pass through that facility frequently?
   - What did the powder look like? Smell like?
   - Has the particle size been determined?
2. Ricin is an extract of castor beans.
   - It is a natural by-product of the processing of castor beans into castor oil. For this reason, it is readily available.

- It can be disseminated as a powder or mist or could be dissolved in water.
- Depending on the route of transmission, as little as 500 μg can be lethal, making ricin one of the most poisonous compounds known.

3. Theoretically, ricin could be effectively weaponized for aerosol distribution. It could also be used to contaminate food or water.
   - Inhalational ricin poisoning has never been documented in humans, although poisoning by the intestinal route (both accidental and intentional) has occurred in a small number of cases.
   - It is thought that effective aerosolization of ricin powder would be difficult, requiring a very small (5 microns or less) particle size.

QUESTIONS

1. What symptoms would be expected to result from inhalational or gastrointestinal exposure to ricin?
2. What other entities could mimic ricin intoxication by these two routes?

ANSWERS

1. **The Symptoms of Inhalational Ricin Poisoning**
   - Several hours after significant exposure to inhaled ricin, the following symptoms would be anticipated:
     - Respiratory distress
     - Fever
     - Cough
     - Chest tightness
     - Cyanosis
   - A picture of noncardiogenic pulmonary edema would rapidly emerge
   - Ingestion of significant quantities of ricin would result in:
     - Vomiting, diarrhea (bloody at times).
     - Mental status changes.
     - Shock.
     - Exposure of the skin or eyes would cause redness and irritation.
     - Depending on the route and significance of exposure, death typically occurs within 36 to 72 hours. If death has not occurred within 5 days, complete recovery is the rule.
2. **Differential diagnosis of gastrointestinal ricin poisoning**
   - Enteric bacterial pathogens
   - Poisoning due to arsenic, mushrooms, caustic substances, etc.
   - Differential diagnosis of inhalational ricin:
     - Toxic shock syndrome
     - Influenza
     - Anthrax

- Pneumonic plague
- Exposure to various chemical toxins (nitrogen oxides, phosphene, etc.)

QUESTIONS

1. How can the diagnosis of ricin intoxication be confirmed?
2. What forms of therapy would potentially be effective?
3. What equipment needs would the hospital likely confront?

ANSWERS

1. **Diagnosis and Therapy of Ricin Poisoning**
    - There is no diagnostic test.
    - There is no known antidote.
    - Ricin is not dialyzable.
2. **Potential Means of Therapy**
    - Decontamination to avoid repeated exposure might be appropriate.
    - Therapy would be supportive.
    - In gastrointestinal poisoning, gastric lavage and/or activated charcoal might be beneficial.
3. **Equipment Concerns**
    - Unlike other biological attack scenarios, a ricin attack would require ample decontamination facilities because, as a powder, the compound is stable and can persist on clothing and environmental surfaces, posing an ongoing risk of poisoning.
    - High-level personal protective equipment would be needed to protect first responders and certain health care workers. However, little data is available on the need for or effectiveness of personal protective equipment.

QUESTIONS

1. How should issues of patient decontamination and staff protection be approached?

ANSWERS

1. **Decontamination**
    - There are no data on the need for or effectiveness of decontamination of victims. Nonetheless, the following measures have been recommended:
        - Field decontamination should be conducted if feasible.

- Gross decontamination: removing clothing and jewelry and showering with warm water and soap.
- Skin decontamination is not required for gastrointestinal poisoning victims.
- Environmental surfaces (e.g., ambulance equipment) should be cleaned with soap and water.
- Victim's clothing should be double-bagged.
- Staff involved in decontamination of victims should wear a chemical-resistant suit with gloves, surgical mask, and face shield or goggles, and should shower afterward.
- Staff caring for victims should follow standard precautions (gown, gloves) as well as use mask and face shield to reduce the risk of inoculation onto mucosal surfaces.

Staffing Needs

- The availability of hospital personnel in the following categories should be determined:
  - Emergency room staff, including those trained in decontamination procedures
  - Intensivists
  - Housekeeping
  - Safety and security
  - Public affairs

LESSONS OF THE EXERCISE

Ricin intoxication may reflect exposure through the respiratory or gastrointestinal tract.

Little is known regarding management of exposed individuals.

There is no known effective therapy; supportive care would be of critical concern.

Because of the rapid onset of the symptoms of ricin poisoning, the finding of weaponized ricin would necessitate hospital preparations to be put into place before it is known if there are any victims.

Tabletop Exercise: Hemorrhagic Fever

Suggested participants:

Director of Emergency Department
Emergency Department; Critical Care Physicians
Emergency Department Nurses
Microbiology Laboratory Supervisor
Infection Control; Infectious Disease Clinician
Chief Operating Officer
Legal, Risk Management Staff
Medical Records Supervisor
Housekeeping Supervisor
Public Affairs Staff

SCENARIO: PART I

A 42-year-old male presents with a 5-day history of fever and worsening muscle aches, sore throat, cough, and eye irritation. In triage, he is found to have a fever of 104°F and a heart rate of 120. On examination, he is found to have a diffuse maculopapular rash and gingival bleeding.

QUESTIONS: PART I

1. Which of the Category A agents would be most likely to present in this fashion?
2. What other disorders should be considered?
3. Does the patient require isolation?
4. Does the patient require decontamination?

ANSWERS: PART I

1. Because the patient has a generalized rash, smallpox and hemorrhagic fever viruses would represent the most likely of the Category A agents based on the very limited information so far. In view of the gingival bleeding, a generalized bleeding diathesis should be considered. If present, this would favor a hemorrhagic fever virus such as Ebola or Marburg.

2. Of course, many more likely possibilities would have to be considered in this and any patient presenting with fever and rash. Among the most dangerous would be meningococcemia or other overwhelming bacterial sepsis syndromes; and toxic-shock syndrome or rickettsial infection, such as Rocky Mountain Spotted Fever, any of which could be accompanied by a bleeding diathesis. Other possibilities would include secondary syphilis, primary HIV infection, enteroviral infection, measles, and hypersensitivity reactions.
3. The patient should be placed in respiratory isolation with airborne precautions because of the possibility of meningococcal infection. This procedure would also be appropriate for Ebola or Marburg virus infections as well as smallpox.
4. Decontamination is unnecessary, although clothing and other materials in contact with the patient should be handled as biohazardous if smallpox is suspected. Based on the information given so far, smallpox would be unlikely unless other cases have already been reported, because the described rash is atypical for smallpox.

SCENARIO: PART II

The patient is placed in respiratory isolation. Routine blood tests reveal anemia, leucopenia, and thrombocytopenia.

QUESTIONS: PART II

1. How do the laboratory abnormalities affect your opinion of the diagnosis?
2. What questions should be asked of the patient?
3. Should public health authorities be notified?
4. Should anyone else be notified?
5. What diagnostic studies should now be ordered?
6. What therapy, if any, should be initiated?

ANSWERS: PART II

1. Thrombocytopenia supports the diagnosis of a bleeding diathesis. Meningococcemia, other bacterial sepsis syndromes and toxic shock syndrome, and other entities remain possible. The diagnosis of viral hemorrhagic fever is supported but not established.
2. The patient should be questioned about contact with other individuals with fever and rash.
   Travel, occupational, and sexual histories should be taken in detail.
3. Notification of public health authorities is appropriate because of concern regarding meningococcemia. Although the syndrome is not specific enough to draw firm conclusions as to the diagnosis, the health department

may have been notified of similar cases from other hospitals or require information through syndromic surveillance on all cases of fever and rash.

4. Hospital infection control officers should be notified.
5. Routine cultures (blood, urine) should be obtained and lumbar puncture considered. Hospital laboratories would not have the capability of processing specimens for hemorrhagic fever viruses.

   Serum samples can be obtained for storage for future processing for antibodies to these and other possible agents. Public health officials may request specimens for viral culture.
6. Therapy for bacterial sepsis, including meningococcemia, should be initiated and therapy for rickettsial infection considered.

SCENARIO: PART III

You have notified the department of health and your hospital's infection control officer, and you have begun therapy with broad-spectrum antibiotics.

The patient denies contact with anyone with a similar illness.

He has not traveled outside the country in the past 5 years and denies travel to rural or wooded areas in the past 6 months.

He works as a legislative assistant for your district's congressman.

He is heterosexual and denies sexual contact within the past few months.

QUESTIONS: PART III

1. Does his lack of known exposure to others with similar illnesses alter the differential diagnosis?
2. How does his travel, sexual, and occupational history help?

ANSWERS: PART III

1. The absence of a known exposure to anyone with similar complaints does not alter the differential diagnosis.
2. The absence of travel to rural or wooded areas makes tickborne infections such as Rocky Mountain Spotted Fever unlikely. The absence of foreign travel, particularly travel to areas endemic for hemorrhagic fever viruses, means that such infections, if diagnosed, would likely represent an intentional release of these agents.

   As an employee of a member of Congress, he may be at increased risk of becoming an early victim in a biological attack.

SCENARIO: PART IV

You are notified by the health department that 5 suspected cases of viral hemorrhagic fever have been reported from area hospitals within the past 12 hours and that health department investigators are coming to your hospital to interview the patient.

A telephone call comes to the emergency room front desk. An individual identifying himself as a congressman asks if a member of his staff is being seen in the emergency department.

Two police detectives arrive and ask to question the patient and to review his medical record.

A television news reporter and cameraman arrive in the waiting area. They indicate that they were informed by the office of your congressman that a member of his staff may have been the victim of a bioterrorist attack.

QUESTIONS: PART IV

1. How should the inquiry from the congressman be addressed?
2. Are the police detectives entitled to interview the patient or to review the medical record?
3. What information can be given to the reporter? What procedure should be followed in answering their questions?
4. Should anyone else be contacted?
5. Who should serve as the hospital's spokesperson?

ANSWERS: PART IV

Information regarding a patient's diagnosis is generally privileged. Release of information under most circumstances requires the written, informed consent of the patient. Health department clinicians are normally permitted to interview patients and their contacts. Legal advice, from hospital counsel or risk management staff, should be sought if uncertainty exists regarding the release of information to anyone without the permission of the patient.

The hospital's public relations or senior administrative staff should coordinate the release of any information in conjunction with public health officials. Individual physicians, nurses, and other employees should avoid speculation regarding the likelihood of bioterrorism without guidance from these individuals.

LESSONS OF THIS EXERCISE

Viral hemorrhagic fevers resemble many far more common infections.

Specific diagnosis is impossible without the assistance of public health laboratories.

Occupational and travel history may be helpful in determining the likelihood that a patient is the victim of a biological attack.

Releasing medical information may raise complex legal questions requiring the advice and guidance of the hospital's legal counsel.

Chapter references: 3, 9, 10, and 11.

Tabletop Exercise: Botulism

Suggested participants:

Director of Emergency Department
Emergency Department; Neurology; Critical Care Physicians
Emergency Department Nurses
Microbiology Laboratory Supervisor
Infection Control; Infectious Disease Clinician
Director of Pharmacy
Chief Operating Officer
Safety Supervisor

SCENARIO: PART I

A 23-year-old female presents to your emergency department with a 12-hour history of double vision, hoarseness, and difficulty speaking. She denies any prior significant illnesses. She has no fever and her neurological examination is notable for photophobia, ptosis, bilateral opthalmoplegia, and slight weakness of both arms.

QUESTIONS: PART I

1. Of the Category A agents, which would be most likely to present in this fashion?
2. Based on the information given so far, what is the differential diagnosis?
3. What other information would you wish to obtain from the patient?
4. Should the patient be placed in isolation?
5. Should the patient undergo decontamination?

ANSWERS: PART I

1. Of the Category A agents, only botulism is suggested by the presenting complaints, which implicate paralysis of multiple cranial nerves and symmetrical paralysis of the arms.
2. Other than botulism, the differential diagnosis based on the information given includes Guillain–Barre syndrome, tick paralysis, shellfish toxin poisoning, myasthenia gravis, and a variety of other primary neurological conditions.

3. Because naturally occurring botulism typically results from the ingestion of home-canned foods or from a wound infection with *Clostridium botulinum*, the patient should be questioned about such potential exposures.

4/5. Neither isolation nor decontamination are appropriate.

SCENARIO: PART II

The patient denies ingestion of home-canned foods, or any recent injuries, or exposure to ticks or shellfish within the past several weeks. She mentions that her 34-year-old husband has had transient diplopia for the past several hours but went to work rather than coming with her to the emergency department.

QUESTIONS: PART II

1. How does this additional history help?
2. What diagnostic tests are appropriate?
3. Should therapy be instituted?
4. Who, if anyone, should be notified?

ANSWERS: PART II

1. The similar, though milder, symptoms experienced by her husband suggest a common exposure to a toxin or infectious agent rather than an underlying primary neurological disorder.

   As no common exposure to home-canned foods is suggested, the possibilities of contamination of commercially preserved products and of a biological attack with botulinum toxin must be considered.
2. A tensilon test may be appropriate to fully exclude myasthenia gravis. Electromyographic studies may aid in the diagnosis of botulism.

   Confirmation of the diagnosis requires isolation of the organism from stool or identification of the toxin in serum or stool.
3. Antitoxin to botulinum toxin is effective if given shortly after or, preferably, prior to the onset of symptoms of botulism and must be obtained from the CDC. In view of these logistical issues, the patient should be observed closely for extension of the paralysis with the expectation that mechanical ventilation may be necessary.
4. Because the diagnosis of botulism is strongly suggested by the apparent clustering of cases, the health department should be notified.

SCENARIO: PART III

You are notified by the health department that four other hospitals have reported suspected cases of botulism and nine other cases of unexplained paralysis are under evaluation.

QUESTIONS: PART III

1. What is your level of suspicion that a biological attack is underway?
2. What resource needs should your hospital address?
3. What surge capacity issues should you anticipate?

ANSWERS: PART III

1. The scenario as described strongly suggests a widespread outbreak of botulinum toxin. It is, as yet, unclear if this represents an intentional release of toxin into the atmosphere or the food supply, or naturally occurring exposure through contaminated, commercially processed food.
2. In either case, additional patients with paralysis should be anticipated until the scope of the outbreak or attack is characterized. Because botulinum toxin causes paralysis and supportive care represents the only effective approach to management, the number of ventilators and critical-care beds available in your hospital is of primary importance.
3. These needs would have to be addressed as areas where surge capacity must be developed rapidly, either through cooperative arrangements between hospitals or the deployment of additional ventilators and monitoring equipment, or both. Because there is no risk of person-to-person transmission of botulism, isolation capacity and personal protective equipment would be relatively unimportant issues, and stabilized patients could potentially be safely transferred to other facilities.

   As in other attack scenarios, the emergency department should anticipate the arrival of "worried well" patients after information about the outbreak is made public.

   Decisions regarding the distribution and administration of antitoxin must be made by health department officials in collaboration with the CDC.

LESSONS OF THE EXERCISE

Confirming the diagnosis of botulism and distinguishing between an intentional release of botulinum toxin and naturally occurring botulism may be impossible in the early stages of an attack.

Therapy of botulism is supportive and requires ventilatory support in some cases.

Issues of contagion, isolation, and decontamination are irrelevant, and the focus of planning and response must be on surge capacity to accommodate large numbers of patients with respiratory paralysis.

Chapter references: 9, 10, 11, and Appendix A.

Section V

Appendices

Appendix A: Drug and Vaccine Compendium

INTRODUCTION

This chapter summarizes therapy and prevention of the Category A agents of biological attack. The material is presented in two ways: by biological agent and by antibiotic and/or vaccine. Although novel therapies and vaccines are under investigation for a number of the agents, we limit the discussion here to strategies that have been established and included in consensus recommendations. This is not intended as an exhaustive discussion of the therapeutic agents mentioned but rather as a concise presentation designed for easy reference. The pharmaceuticals reviewed are typically present in the pharmacy of any hospital. Vaccines discussed are available only through public health authorities.

The reader is referred to Chapter 10 for discussions of containment and additional information regarding treatment.

DRUGS OF CHOICE AND PREFERRED THERAPEUTIC STRATEGIES

ANTHRAX (INHALATIONAL/GASTROINTESTINAL)[1]

Postexposure Prophylaxis

On the basis of animal data, ciprofloxacin, doxycycline, and procaine penicillin G have all been approved by the U.S. Food and Drug Administration for the prevention of inhalational anthrax among exposed individuals.[2,3]

Recommended regimens: Ciprofloxacin 500 mg by mouth twice daily for 60 days (adults); ciprofloxacin 30 mg/kg by mouth twice daily for 60 days (pediatrics).

Therapy

Recommended regimens:

- Ciprofloxacin 400 mg intravenously every 12 hours (adults); 10–15 mg/kg intravenously every 24 hours (pediatrics), *or*
- Levofloxacin 500 mg intravenously every 12 hours (adults), *or*
- Doxycycline 100 mg intravenously every 12 hours (adults); 2.5 mg/kg (pediatrics), *plus*

- Rifampin 600 mg by mouth daily (adults); 10–20 mg/kg (pediatrics), *or*
- Clindamycin 900 mg intravenously every 8 hours (adults); 5–10 mg/kg every 12 hours (pediatrics), *or*
- Vancomycin 1 g intravenously every 12 hours (adults), *or*
- Imipenem 500 mg intravenously every 6 hours (adults), *or*
- Ampicillin 500 mg intravenously every 6 hours (adults), *or*
- Clarithromycin 500 mg by mouth every 12 hours (adults)

Anthrax (Cutaneous)

See postexposure prophylaxis and treatment guidelines in the preceding text.

All patients receiving postexposure prophylaxis should be offered the acellular anthrax vaccine (see the following text).

Smallpox

Postexposure Prophylaxis

Immediate vaccination is recommended for all potential contacts of a proven or suspected case of smallpox. If more than 7 days have elapsed since exposure, vaccinia immune globulin is also recommended by some authorities.[4]

Therapy

There is no therapy proven to be effective after the onset of symptoms. Cidofovir has shown activity against related viruses in an animal model.[5]

Tularemia[6]

Postexposure Prophylaxis

Doxycycline (100 mg by mouth twice daily) or ciprofloxacin (500 mg by mouth twice daily) for 14 days may provide protection.[4]

Therapy

- **First choice:**
  - Streptomycin (15 mg/kg twice daily) or gentamicin (5 mg/kg intramuscularly or intravenously once daily) (both are adult doses) for 10–14 days
    Streptomycin is in very limited supply in the U.S.
- **Alternatives:**
  - Tetracyclines or chloroamphenicol for 14 days
    Higher failure and relapse rates than aminoglycosides
  - Ciprofloxacin for 10 days
    Limited human data

Plague[7]

Postexposure Prophylaxis

Little data exist regarding the effectiveness of postexposure antimicrobial prophylaxis. The following regimens have been suggested based on published data.[8]

Doxycycline (100 mg by mouth twice daily) (adult dose) for 7 days, *or*

Ciprofloxacin (500 mg by mouth every 12 hours) (adults); 7.5–15 mg/kg intravenously every 12 hours (pediatrics)

Therapy

Therapy must be initiated within the first 24 hours of the onset of symptoms and continued for a minimum of 7 days.

- **First choice:**
  - Streptomycin (1 g intramuscularly every 12 hours) (adults); 15 mg/kg every 12 hours (pediatrics), *or*
  - Gentamicin (5 mg/kg intramuscularly or intravenously daily) (adults) *Streptomycin is in very limited supply in the U.S.*

Plague Meningitis

- *Add:*
  - Chloramphenicol 1 g intravenously every 6 hours (adults); 75–100 mg/kg every 6 hours (pediatrics)
- **Alternatives (*limited data*):**
  - Doxycycline 100 mg intravenously every 12 hours (adults)
  - Ciprofloxacin 400 mg intravenously every 12 hours (adults); 7.5–15 mg/kg intravenously every 12 hours (pediatrics)

Botulism

Postexposure Prophylaxis

Antitoxin must be administered prior to the onset of symptoms for maximum effectiveness. The currently licensed antitoxin is administered as follows:

10-ml vial diluted 1:10 in 0.9% saline by slow intravenous infusion.[9]

Therapy

Antitoxin should be administered as stated in the preceding text as soon as possible after the onset of symptoms. Supportive therapy, including ventilatory support in some patients, is the mainstay.

Viral Hemorrhagic Fevers

Postexposure Prophylaxis

Little information is available regarding postexposure prophylaxis of viral hemorrhagic fevers. Ribavirin, administered orally, may be effective in preventing Lassa fever.[4]

Therapy

Lassa Fever: Ribavirin 30 mg/kg intravenous loading dose followed by 15 mg/kg intravenously every 6 hours for 4 days followed by 7.5 mg/kg every 8 hours for 6 days.[8]

Commonly Recommended Antibiotics for the Treatment of Agents of Bioterrorism

In this section we briefly present information regarding forms of drugs described above as well as major potential side effects and conditions under which dosage adjustments should be made.[10] For specific recommendations regarding dosing regimens for the Category A agents of bioterrorism please see the preceding section.

Amoxicillin

Routes of administration: oral, chewable tablets, oral suspension
Notable side effects: hypersensitivity reactions, rash
Dose adjustment in renal insufficiency: yes if glomerular filtration rate (GFR) is less than 50 ml/min
Safety in pregnancy: probably safe; no known toxicity

Amoxicillin/Clavulanate

Route of administration: oral
Notable side effects: hypersensitivity reactions, nausea, and vomiting
Dose adjustment in renal insufficiency: yes if GFR is less than 50 ml/min
Safety in pregnancy: probably safe; no known toxicity

Chloramphenicol

Routes of administration: oral, intravenous
Notable side effects: blood dyscrasias, GI disturbance
Dose adjustment in renal insufficiency: no
Safety in pregnancy: not established; gray syndrome in newborn. Should be used only if no safe alternative available.

Ciprofloxacin/Levofloxacin/Ofloxacin

Routes of administration: oral, intravenous
Notable side effects: nausea, vomiting, and CNS effects
Dose adjustment in renal insufficiency: yes for GFR less than 50 ml/min

Safety in pregnancy: not established; associated with arthropathy in animal studies. Should be used only if no safe alternative available.

Doxycycline

Routes of administration: oral, intravenous
Notable side effects: GI disturbance, bone lesions and staining, and deformity of the teeth in children under 8 years of age and in the newborn when given to the mother during pregnancy after the 4th month
Dose adjustment in renal insufficiency: no
Safety in pregnancy: contraindicated

Erythromycin

Routes of administration: oral, intravenous
Notable side effects: GI disturbance
Dose adjustment in renal insufficiency: no
Safety in pregnancy: considered safe

Gentamicin

Routes of administration: intravenous, intramuscular
Common side effects: vestibular damage, renal failure, and rash
Dose adjustment in renal insufficiency: yes
Safety in pregnancy: not established; possible eighth nerve toxicity in fetus. Should be used only if no safer alternative is available.

Penicillin G

Routes of administration: oral, intravenous
Notable side effects: hypersensitivity reactions
Dose adjustment in renal insufficiency: only in severe renal insufficiency
Safety in pregnancy: probably safe; no known toxicities

Rifampin

Routes of administration: oral, intravenous
Notable side effects: Hepatitis, hypersensitivity reactions, orange discoloration of urine and tears, and accelerated metabolism of many other drugs including methadone, hypoglycemic agents, and corticosteroids
Dose adjustment in renal insufficiency: no
Safety in pregnancy: probably safe; teratogenicity reported in animal studies

Ribavirin

Route of administration: intravenous
Notable side effects: nausea, abdominal cramps, anemia, and headache
Dose adjustment in renal insufficiency: use of drug not recommended
Safety in pregnancy: contraindicated

Streptomycin

Route of administration: intramuscular
Notable side effects: eighth nerve damage, renal insufficiency, fever, and rash
Dose adjustment in renal insufficiency: yes
Safety in pregnancy: Possible eighth nerve toxicity in fetus. Should be used only if no safer alternative available.

Trimethoprim-Sulfamethoxazole

Routes of administration: oral, intravenous
Notable side effects: hypersensitivity reactions, nausea and vomiting, photosensitization, neutropenia, and hepatitis
Dose adjustment in renal insufficiency: yes
Safety in pregnancy: Contraindicated at term. Earlier in pregnancy should be used only if no safer alternative is available

Vancomycin

Routes of administration: oral, intravenous
Notable side effects: diffuse erythematous rash ("red man syndrome"), thrombophlebitis, and fever
Dose adjustment in renal insufficiency: yes
Safety in pregnancy: Not established; possible eighth nerve and renal toxicity in fetus. Should be used only if no safer alternative is available.

VACCINES

Effective vaccines are currently available for only two of Category A infections: smallpox and anthrax. Both of these vaccines are currently in use in the military and are available for civilian use only under the guidance of public health authorities. Vaccines for other Category A agents of bioterrorism are currently in the investigational stage. A large-scale program to provide smallpox vaccination to selected health care workers and first responders was initiated in 2003 (see expanded discussion that follows). Anthrax vaccination has not been employed in this fashion for civilians, although approximately 1700 individuals exposed during the 2001 anthrax attacks received the vaccine in conjunction with preventive antibiotic therapy under an investigational protocol through the CDC.[11]

Anthrax Vaccine

The current anthrax vaccine available in the U.S. is a cell-free preparation of an avirulent strain of the organism. It is currently not available for civilian use and its use and distribution in the event of a biological attack would be controlled by federal and local public health authorities. The effectiveness of postexposure vaccination has not been evaluated.

Side Effects

Erythema and tenderness at the injection site, fever, malaise, myalgia, and headache are accepted side effects. A variety of more unusual side effects, including bronchiolitis obliterans with organizing pneumonia (BOOP) and arthritis have been ascribed to the anthrax vaccine.[12]

Clinical Uses (Acellular Vaccine)

Preexposure

At the time of this writing no strategy for preexposure vaccination of civilians against anthrax has been implemented, although it has been mandated for military personnel.

Postexposure

Vaccine, if available, should be administered as follows: 0.5 ml subcutaneously as soon after exposure as possible, and again at 2 and 4 weeks and 6, 12, and 18 months. Annual booster doses are required to maintain protective immunity. Vaccine should be given in conjunction with a 60-day course of antibiotics as outlined in the preceding text.

Tularemia Vaccine

An investigational vaccine is available from the CDC. It is not recommended for postexposure use.[4]

Plague Vaccine

Plague vaccine previously in use is not currently available in the U.S. and was not protective against inhalational infection.[4] A newer vaccine is under development.

Smallpox Vaccine

Please see the expanded discussion of smallpox vaccination in Appendix B.

REFERENCES

1. Inglesby, T.V. et al., Anthrax as a biological weapon 2002: updated recommendations for management, *JAMA*, 287, 2236, 2002.
2. Food and Drug Administration, Prescription drug products; doxycycline and penicillin G procaine administration for inhalational anthrax (post-exposure), *Fed Regist*, 66–55679–82, 2001.
3. Friedlander, A.M. et al., Postexposure prophylaxis against inhalation anthrax, *J Infect Dis*, 167, 1239, 1993.
4. The Medical Letter, Drugs and vaccines against biological weapons, *Med Lett*, 43(W1115A), 87–89, 2001.
5. Bray, M. et al., Cidofovir protects mice against lethal aerosol or intranasal cowpox virus challenge, *J Infect Dis*, 181, 10, 2000.
6. Dennis, D.T. et al., Tularemia as a biological weapon: medical and public health management, *JAMA*, 285, 2763, 2001.
7. Inglesby, T.V. et al., Plague as a biological weapon: medical and public health management, *JAMA*, 283, 2281, 2000.

8. Weinstein, R.S. and Alibek, K., *Biological and Chemical Terrorism: A Guide for Healthcare Providers and First Responders*, Thieme, New York, 2003.
9. Arnon, S.S. et al. Botulinum toxin as a biological weapon: medical and public health management, *JAMA*, 285, 1059, 2001.
10. The Medical Letter, *Handbook of Antimicrobial Therapy*, 16th edition, The Medical Letter, New Rochelle, New York, 2002.
11. Tierney, B.C. et al., Serious adverse events among participants in the Centers for Disease Control and Prevention's Anthrax Vaccine and Antimicrobial Availability Program for persons at risk for bioterrorism-related inhalational anthrax, *Clin Infect Dis*, 37, 905, 2003.
12. Sever, J.L. et al., Safety of anthrax vaccine: a review by the Anthrax Vaccine Expert Committee (AVEC) of adverse events reported to the Vaccine Adverse Event Reporting System (VAERS*), Pharmacoepidemiol Drug Saf*, 11,189, 2002.

Appendix B: Smallpox Vaccination

RECENT HISTORY OF SMALLPOX VACCINATION IN THE U.S.

Routine smallpox vaccination ended in the U.S. in 1972, 23 years after the last U.S. case of the disease, although the U.S. military continued to vaccinate recruits until 1990. In 1980, after an intensive campaign of surveillance and vaccination led by the United Nations' World Health Organization, the disease was declared eradicated worldwide. It was an achievement universally hailed as one of the greatest triumphs of the century. The only remaining smallpox virus consisted of specimens held by the U.S. and the Soviet Union.

Then, in the 1990s, it was revealed that the Soviet Union had been running a vast bioweapons research and manufacturing enterprise that had produced hundreds of tons of pathogen, including smallpox, for potential use as weapons. Ken Alibek, a former leader in Soviet germ warfare effort who defected to the U.S. in 1992, wrote in his frightening memoir, *Biohazard*, that he had authorized work on combining smallpox genetically with another pathogen, such as Venezuelan equine encephalitis virus or Ebola virus, to make it a more dangerous weapon. The upshot of this work was not known.[1]

With the breakup of the Soviet Union, concerns rose that such research in biological weapons would be disseminated to terrorist groups or rogue nations. After the September 11, 2001, terrorist attacks, the U.S. began bolstering its antiterrorist activities. At the same time, the U.S. was preparing for war with Iraq, amid apparently unfounded fears that Iraq had stockpiles of biological weapons, including smallpox, which it might use if the U.S. invaded.[2–5]

In that context, President George W. Bush announced on December 13, 2002, that the U.S. would quickly inoculate 500,000 military personnel, and about 450,000 civilian doctors, nurses, and emergency workers. If smallpox were unleashed on the nation, the civilians would serve as emergency teams, inoculating others and treating infected people. The plan included a second stage, in which vaccine would be offered to as many as 10 million health care workers, police, firefighters, paramedics, and other emergency workers, and, finally, a third stage in which it would be available to civilians who wanted it. Bush himself was vaccinated on December 21.[6,7]

The military vaccination program was largely complete by the summer of 2003, but the civilian plan ran into obstacles.[8] Federal officials had hoped to complete the first stage of the civilian program within 30 days. But many health care workers thought that the risks of a bioterrorist release of smallpox were not great enough to warrant taking the risks of vaccination. On the basis of data from 1968, when vaccination in the U.S. was routine, the risks were estimated at 1 or 2 deaths and up to about 50 life-threatening reactions per million people vaccinated, with up to 1,000 lesser but serious adverse reactions per million.[9,10] Some hospitals declined to participate in the program. Many health care workers objected that a system of compensation for possible injuries was not in place. One commonly expressed concern was that recently vaccinated health care workers might accidentally infect household contacts, patients, or other hospital employees with vaccinia virus, the virus used in the vaccine. Some local health officials said the program was too costly. And, with the war underway, Iraq had shown no ability or intent to wage a smallpox attack.[11]

The program stalled. As of April 30, 2004, only 39,512 civilian health care workers had been inoculated, less than 10% of the number once contemplated. A state-by-state breakdown showed figures ranging from 17 in Nevada to 4,632 in Texas. In New York and the District of Columbia, scenes of the September 11 terror and the anthrax attacks, the figures were 816 and 105, respectively.[12]

SMALLPOX VACCINES

The smallpox vaccine is a live-virus preparation of vaccinia virus. It does not contain variola, the smallpox virus.

Dryvax

The vaccine used in the 2003 campaign and in the 1970s global eradication campaign was Dryvax, made by Wyeth Laboratories, Inc. The U.S. had 15.4 million doses of Dryvax in 2002, when a federally sponsored study showed the vaccine could be diluted 1:5 without loss of potency, in effect giving the U.S. a stockpile of 75 million doses.[13] As of May 2004, Dryvax was the only smallpox vaccine licensed for use in the U.S.

During the 2003 vaccination campaign, health care providers were required to give potential recipients a package of vaccine information materials, including a consent form, developed by the Centers for Disease Control and Prevention (CDC). Copies of these materials, as well as a wealth of information about many aspects of smallpox, are available on the CDC smallpox website at www.bt.cdc.gov/agent/smallpox/index.asp. In addition, the package insert for Dryvax is available at www.fda.gov/cber/label/smalwye070303LB.pdf.

Other Vaccines

Federal health officials have been evaluating U.S. stockpiles of other vaccines:

- Some 200 million doses of Acambis' ACAM1000 and ACAM2000, produced for the U.S. under contract since 2000. They were derived from the same vaccinia strain as Dryvax, the New York City Board of Health (NYCBH) strain, but were grown in cell culture, a more modern technique, rather than on the skin of calves, as Dryvax was.

- Some 70 to 90 million long-frozen doses of Aventis Pasteur's vaccine, which the company donated to the U.S. in 2002. The Aventis Pasteur vaccine, like Dryvax, used the NYCBH strain cultured in calves' skin.[14,15]

In addition, the National Institute of Allergy and Infectious Diseases (NIAID) has been testing a possible alternative vaccine, called modified vaccinia Ankara (MVA), in hopes it might be safe for individuals at high risk of complications from existing vaccines.[14,15]

Administering the Vaccine

Smallpox vaccine is administered by scarification, not injection. A special bifurcated needle is dipped into the vial of vaccine, picking up a tiny drop of liquid between its prongs. Holding the needle perpendicular to the recipient's upper arm, the health care worker jabs the needle in quickly, making 2 to 3 punctures for a first vaccination and 15 for a revaccination, all within a 5-mm area. The punctures should produce a trace of blood within 15 to 30 seconds. The needle is discarded after each use; it should never be dipped back into the vaccine. To avoid transmitting virus to other people or other parts of the body, the site should be covered loosely with gauze and, for health care workers, a semipermeable membrane. It should be kept covered until it is fully healed and the scab has dropped off. Until then, to guard against accidental transmission, dressings should be considered contaminated and carefully disposed of, and hands should be washed after contact with dressings.[16]

REACTIONS TO THE VACCINE

Normal Reactions

Normally a papule appears in 3 to 4 days, and develops into a vesicle with surrounding erythema by the 5th to the 6th day. This becomes a pustule, which crusts over and forms a brown scab. After 2.5 to 3 weeks, the scab detaches. At this point, the site can be left uncovered.[16]

Vaccinated people usually have soreness and redness at the site and often have malaise, local lymphadenopathy, chills, nausea, fatigue, fever, and headache about 8 to 10 days after vaccination.[16]

The vaccination site should be checked 6 to 8 days after vaccination. If it did not "take" — that is, if the reaction is equivocal or lacking — vaccination can be repeated on the other arm and, if possible, using vaccine from a different vial or lot.[17]

COMPLICATIONS

Accidental transmission of the vaccinia virus to other parts of the body or to other people has been the most common complication of vaccination historically. Such inadvertent transmission may occur if recently vaccinated people rub or scratch their inoculation site and then touch other parts of their body or other people. The vaccinia virus can also be transmitted through contact with contaminated clothes or dressings. Accidental transmission can cause lesions on any part of the body, similar to the reaction at the primary vaccination site and usually no more harmful than that. But the lesions can proliferate on eczemous skin or in the eyes, and inadvertent transmission to another person can be dangerous if that person is immunocompromised or otherwise not a safe candidate for vaccination. (Counterindications for vaccination are listed in the Section "Persons at higher risk of complications.")

Historically Established Complications

Before the 2003 vaccination campaign, the following complications were seen as the major risks of vaccination.[18,19] The first three listed here, while extremely rare, were held responsible for most vaccination-related deaths.

- Progressive vaccinia (vaccinia necrosum): This condition, which can occur in people with impaired immunity, involves progressive necrosis from the inoculation site followed by viremia, virus in the bloodstream. Vaccinia immune globulin (VIG) is indicated in suspected cases.
- Postvaccinial encephalitis: It can appear 10 to 14 days after vaccination, with fever, headache, and somnolence. VIG is not thought to be effective treatment. No predisposing factor has been identified, although the incidence was slightly higher in babies vaccinated before age 1.
- Eczema vaccinatum: Extensive vaccinia lesions can occur in persons who have active or inactive atopic dermatitis (eczema). Hospitalization and treatment with VIG are required.
- Generalized vaccinia: This condition, with vesicles and pustules appearing on normal skin distant from the vaccination site, is usually mild and self-limited but can be serious in immune-compromised people. More severe cases may be treated with VIG.
- Autoinoculation: Localized sites of vaccinia infection may appear anywhere on the body as a result of accidental autoinoculation. This is usually self-limited, but VIG should be considered for more extensive lesions.
- Vaccinia keratitis: Direct autoinoculation into the eye can cause lesions on the cornea that, left untreated, can produce scarring that permanently impairs vision. VIG is contraindicted in this condition. Topical antiviral medications are used. The CDC recommends consulting an experienced ophthalmologist about this rare condition.
- Erythema multiforme major/Stevens–Johnson syndrome: This is a hypersensitivity reaction to vaccine components and is usually self-limited.
- Fetal vaccinia: Infection of a fetus, caused by vaccination during pregnancy, is a very rare complication that can cause stillbirth.
- Bacterial superinfection: Bacteria, especially staphylococcus, may infect the vaccination site. This may require systemic antibiotic therapy.

Historic Rates of Complications

In a 1968, 10-state survey, postvaccination events included:

- Inadvertent inoculation (529.2 per million primary vaccinations)
- Generalized vaccinia (241.5 per million primary vaccinations)
- Eczema vaccinatum (38.5 per million vaccinations)
- Progressive vaccinia (1.5 per million primary vaccinations)
- Postvaccinial encephalitis (12.3 per million primary vaccinations).

Death occurred in about one per million primary vaccinations, usually as a result of progressive vaccinia, postvaccinial encephalitis, or severe eczema vaccinatum.[9,10]

A review of the literature about the U.S. experience during 1963–1968 found that postvaccinial encephalitis and vaccinia necrosum occurred in at least 3 and 1 per million primary vaccinations, respectively. Death occurred in 29% of those with postvaccinial encephalitis and 15% of those with vaccinia necrosum. No vaccinees died from eczema vaccinatum, but 2.3% of nonvaccinated contacts with eczema vaccinatum died. People who had been vaccinated before had a sharply reduced risk of postvaccinial encephalitis, generalized vaccinia, and eczema vaccinatum, and a slightly reduced risk of accidental infection and vaccinia necrosum.[20]

Recent Experience with Complications

The 2003 vaccinations of U.S. military personnel and U.S. civilian health workers saw fewer of the traditional side effects, such as postvaccinial encephalitis and progressive vaccinia, than were feared. This may in part reflect careful screening of the vaccinees for contraindications and the demographics of the population being vaccinated. As expected, adverse events were especially rare in people who had been vaccinated previously. Both programs, however, saw a small but unexpected number of suspected or probable cases of myopericardiopathy (see Figure B.1, Figure B.2, Figure B.3, and Figure B.4).

Myopericarditis

Myopericarditis — inflammation of the heart and/or membranes around the heart — can range in severity from mild to life-threatening. In the military program, myopericarditis occurred at a rate of about 1 per 12,000 vaccinees. In persons getting vaccinated for the first time, the rate was about 1 per 8500; no cases occurred in previously vaccinated personnel.[21,22,23] Among civilian health workers, the rate was about 1 per 1800.[24]

Myopericarditis had been reported earlier as a rare occurance after vaccination by researchers in Australia and Europe. But it was not identified as a problem in reviews of the U.S. vaccination experience in the 1960s. While a causal link has not been fully proven, the 2003 data is consistent with a causal link, according to the CDC.[25] Potential vaccinees should be warned of this possible complication and should seek medical attention if they have chest pain or shortness of breath after vaccination.

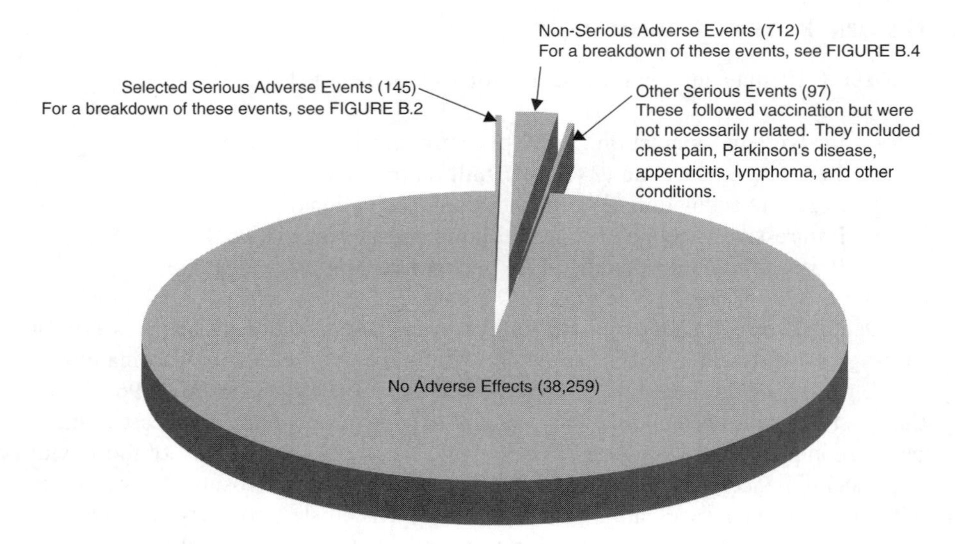

Figure B.1 Civilian smallpox vaccination, 2003.[28]

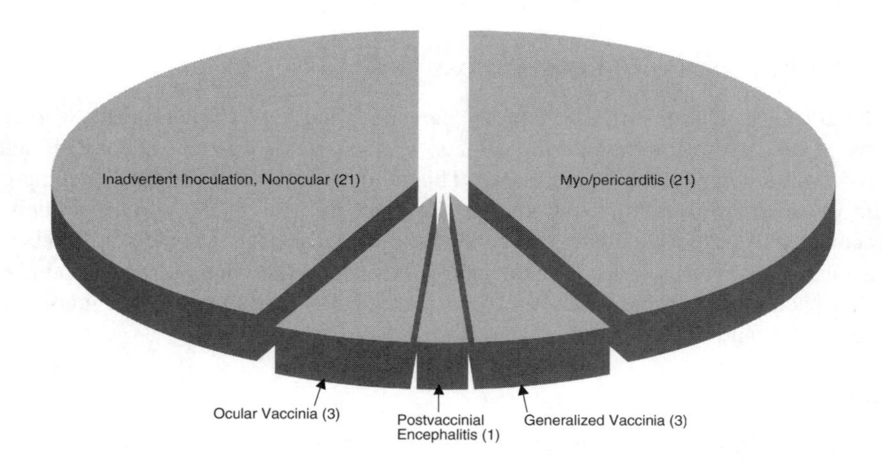

Figure B.2 Selected adverse reactions in civilian smallpox vaccination program, 2003.[28]

According to Cassimatis and colleagues, besides treatment with nonsteroidal antiinflammatory agents, temporary limits on exertion, and conventional heart failure treatment as necessary, immune suppressant therapy with steroids may be beneficial in myopericarditis related to smallpox vaccination, as opposed to other types of myopericarditis (Figure B.2).[23]

Other Cardiac Events

In March 2003, based on these unexpected cardiac side effects, the CDC recommended excluding from vaccination anyone who had been diagnosed as having a heart condition or who had three or more known major cardiac risk factors.

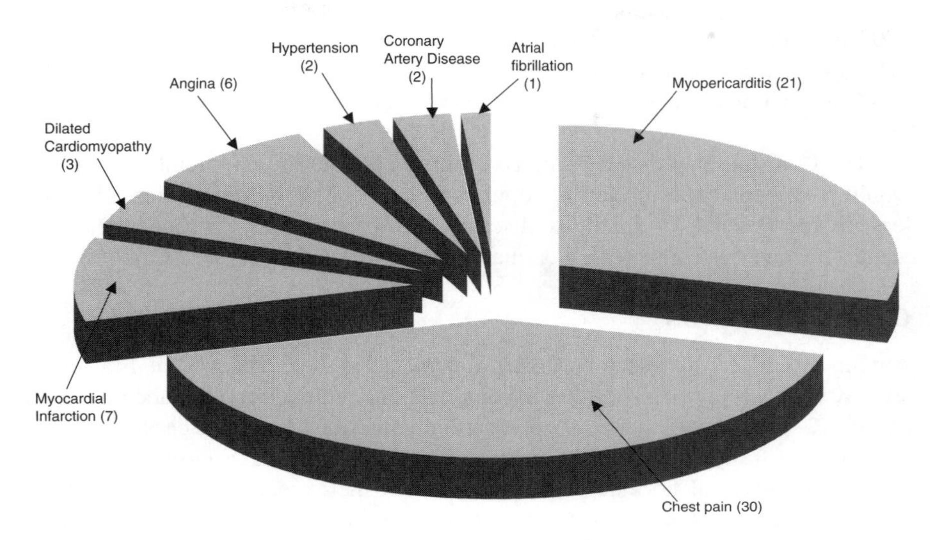

Figure B.3 Adverse cardiac reactions in civilian smallpox vaccination, 2003.[28a]

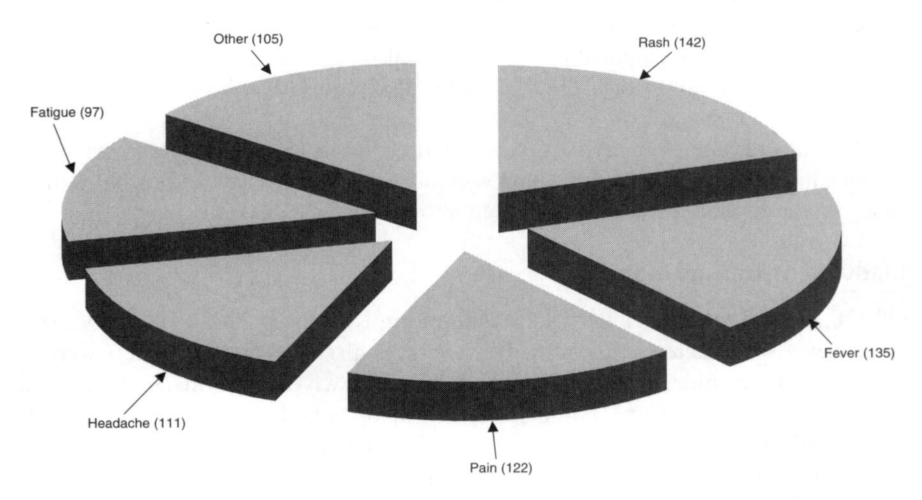

Figure B.4 Nonserious adverse events in civilian smallpox vaccination program, 2003.[28]

The agency was reacting in part to the first of three ischemic cardiac deaths in vaccinees, two in civilians and one in a military member. All were in their 50s, with multiple cardiac risk factors.[26] Autopsy findings did not link these deaths to myopericarditis. Also recognized in vaccines were other nonfatal ischemic events. In an effort to look for a link between the vaccination and the ischemic deaths, Frieden and colleagues conducted a retrospective analysis of New York City death records following a mass smallpox vaccination in 1947. To contain an outbreak then, health officials had vaccinated approximately six million people — 80% of the city's population — during a 4-week period, using the same vaccinia strain used in the

2003 inoculation programs. The study showed no statistically significant increase in risk of all-cause deaths, atherosclerotic deaths, or myopericarditis deaths after the 1947 vaccinations, suggesting that the 2003 cardiac deaths were unrelated to vaccination.[27]

The CDC has said that the cardiac events were consistent in number with what would have been expected in the population independent of vaccination. Nonetheless, in the absence of smallpox disease, it has maintained its recommendation against vaccinating those with a cardiac history or risk factors.[25]

Other Complications

Among 39,213 civilian health workers vaccinated in 2003, there were 145 serious adverse events reported. The cardiac complications in this group included myopericarditis (21 cases), chest pain (30), myocardial infarction (7), dilated cardiomyopathy (3), angina (6), hypertension (2), coronary artery disease (2, including one death), and new onset atrial fibrillation (1). Instances of the expected serious side effects included inadvertent nonocular inoculation (20), generalized vaccinia (3), ocular vaccinia (3), and one case of postvaccinial encephalitis. There were no cases of progressive vaccinia, eczema vaccinatum, or erythema multiforme.[28,28a]

Other serious events were temporally related to vaccination but not necessarily causally related. They ranged from Parkinson's disease and lymphoma to appendicitis to seizure. The vaccinated health workers also reported 712 nonserious adverse events, most commonly rash (142), fever (135), pain (122), headache (111), and fatigue (97).

No transmission from civilians was reported, but in 16 cases (14 nonocular, two ocular), military vaccinees transmitted vaccinia to civilians. The CDC includes those cases in the civilian adverse events cited above.

Inadvertent Transmission

Of 578,286 military personnel vaccinated during December 2002 to January 2004, there were 30 suspected cases of inadvertent transmission. The transmitters were all male primary vaccinees; the recipients included 12 wives, 8 intimate contacts (all adult females), 6 male and 2 female friends, and 2 children. Of the 30 cases, 18 were confirmed, including 2 cases of tertiary transmission. In one, vaccinia was transmitted to a service member's wife and their breastfed infant; in the other, it was serially transmitted among male sports partners.[29]

Despite the fears expressed by many health care workers who declined to participate in the program, no cases of transmission from health care workers, either civilian or military, were reported.

The data indicates that the risk of transmission of vaccinia is extremely small if the vaccine site is carefully dressed. In a study of 148 civilian vaccine recipients reported by Talbot and colleagues, in which site checks and dressing were conducted every 3 to 5 days, no instances of autoinoculation were documented.[30] Although vaccinia virus was detected at the vaccination site in all subjects, it was found on only 0.65% of the outer layer of dressings and only 0.22% of all contralateral hand cultures. Each dressing in this study consisted of both a waterproof gauze-impregnated transparent bandage and a second outer waterproof semi-permeable bandage. In most cases dressings were not changed by the subject themselves, but by trained personnel. These data provide reassurance that meticulous dressing and site care can virtually eliminate the risk both of autoinoculation and, by extrapolation, transmission to household contacts, patients, and coworkers

Persons at Higher Risk of Complications

According to the CDC, people in the following groups should not get smallpox vaccination unless they have been exposed to smallpox or are at high risk of exposure.[25] In other words, they should not be vaccinated "pre-event." If a smallpox release actually occurred, the risk equation would be dramatically altered and the CDC recommendations almost certainly would be modified.

- Persons who have ever been diagnosed with eczema or atopic dermatitis, even if the condition is not currently active, or whose household contacts have a history of eczema or atopic dermatitis.
- Persons with other acute, chronic, or exfoliative skin conditions, or whose contacts have such conditions.
- Persons with Darier disease (Keratosis follicularis), a genetic skin disease that usually is noticed in childhood.
- Persons who have altered immune states (such as HIV/AIDS, organ or stem cell transplant, generalized malignancy, leukemia, lymphoma, or agammaglobulinemia) or who have a household contact with such a condition. Before vaccination, HIV testing is recommended for persons who have any history of a risk factor for HIV and are not sure of their status.
- Persons with severe cases of some autoimmune diseases (e.g., systemic lupus erythematosus).
- Persons being treated with immune-suppressing agents (such as radiation, antimetabolites, alkylating agents, high-dose chemotherapy agents, or organ transplant medications) or persons who have household contacts undergoing such treatment.
- Pregnant or breast-feeding women or pregnant women's household contacts.
- Children younger than 1 year.
- Persons who have a serious allergy to any component of the vaccine.
- Persons with moderate or severe acute illness, including inflammatory eye diseases, which can make inadvertent inoculation more likely due to rubbing of the eye.
- Persons with known cardiac disease such as previous myocardial infarction, angina, congestive heart failure, cardiomyopathy, stroke, or transient ischemic attack.
- Persons with three or more known cardiac risk factors, including hypertension, diabetes, hypercholesterolemia, smoking, or having an immediate family member who had a heart condition before age 50.

EFFICACY OF THE VACCINE

The first dose of the vaccine induces protection in 95% or more of recipients.[31] It offers high-level protection from smallpox for 3 to 5 years, with decreasing immunity after that. If a person has been vaccinated more than once, immunity lasts longer. Studies have show antibodies present many years after vaccination, but the level of protection this affords is not clear.[32]

It should be noted, nonetheless, that 90% of volunteers vaccinated 25 to 75 years earlier maintained substantial humoral or cellular immunity (or both) against vaccinia. In a study by Hammarlund and colleagues, antiviral antibody responses remained stable 1 to 75 years after vaccination, while antiviral T-cell responses declined, with a half-life of 8 to 15 years.[33]

In a study of a European smallpox outbreak, the death rate in people who had been vaccinated 20 years or more before was 11%, compared to 41% in unvaccinated people.[32]

Postexposure Efficacy

In people who have not been previously vaccinated, vaccination has an estimated median effectiveness of 93%, 90%, and 80% if administered at 0 to 6 hours, 6 to 24 hours, and 1 to 3 days after exposure. In those who become ill, its effectiveness in modifying the disease is estimated as 80%, 80%, and 75%, respectively. Effectiveness is greater for those vaccinated previously.[34]

Certain problems with postexposure vaccination must be noted:

- The rate of protection is somewhat lower.
- If widespread exposure is expected, it may be difficult to quickly vaccinate all those who need protection.
- People may not immediately know they have been exposed, making it difficult for them to get vaccinated within a few days of exposure.
- In some cases, vaccination does not "take" and must be repeated. Since the lack of an immune reaction does not become apparent until several days have passed, revaccination probably would be delayed beyond the period of vaccine efficacy.

LIABILITY AND COMPENSATION

Section 304 of the Homeland Security Act establishes that liability claims for injury or death stemming from smallpox vaccination or other smallpox countermeasures can be brought only against the U.S., not against doctors, hospitals, drug manufacturers, or other individuals or entities that administer the countermeasures. This provision covers smallpox vaccines, Vaccinia Immune Globulin (VIG), and cidofivir and its derivatives. This provision took effect from January 24, 2003; its 1-year term was extended to January 24, 2005, and could be extended again. If, however, the U.S. paid a claim because of gross negligence or misconduct on the part of a medical professional, the government could then recover the money from the provider.[35,36]

In addition, the Smallpox Emergency Personnel Protection Act of 2003 (SEPPA), enacted during the 2003 vaccination campaign, established a no-fault program to provide benefits to health and emergency workers injured by administering smallpox countermeasures, and to individuals injured by accidental vaccinia inoculation through contact. The program's payments would be secondary to any other coverage available to the individual.[37]

REFERENCES

1. Alibek, K. with Handelman, S., *Biohazard*, Random House, New York, 1999, chap. 19.
2. Bumiller, E., In Blunt Words, Bush Threatens Hussein Again, *New York Times*, A1, November 21, 2002.
3. Miller, G. and Drogin, B., Iraq Arms Inspector Resigns, Casts Doubt on Prewar Data, *Los Angeles Times*, A1, January 24, 2004.
4. Pincus, W. and Milbank, D., Kay Cites Evidence of Iraq Disarming; Actions Taken in '90s, Ex-Inspector Says, *Washington Post*, A1, January 28, 2004.
5. Kay, D., Testimony to Senate Armed Services Committee hearing on Iraqi weapons of mass destruction and related programs, FDCH Political Transcripts, Jan. 28, 2004.
6. Connolly, C. and Milbank, D., U.S. Revives Smallpox Shot; Bush Says He Will Receive Vaccine with Military, Emergency Workers, *Washington Post*, A1, December 14, 2002.
7. Allen, M., Bush Receives Smallpox Vaccination, *Washington Post*, A11, December 22, 2002.
8. Connolly, C., U.S. Smallpox Vaccine Program Lags; Workers Decline Immunizations, *Washington Post*, A3, April 13, 2003.
9. Lane, J.M. et al., Complications of Smallpox Vaccination, 1968: results of statewide surveys, *J Infect Dis*, 122, 303, 1970.
10. CDC, Smallpox Response Plan and Guidelines, executive summary, 2000.
11. Davenport, C., Smallpox Strategies Shifting; Inoculations Fall Far Short of Goals in Nation, Region, *Washington Post*, A1, May 12, 2003.
12. CDC, Smallpox Vaccination Program Status by State, chart, accessed May 19, 2004, at www.cdc.gov/od/oc/media/spvaccin.htm.
13. Frey, S.E. et al., Clinical responses to undiluted and diluted smallpox vaccine, *NEJM*, 346, 1265, 2002.
14. FDA Center for Biologics Evaluation and Research, Smallpox Vaccines Questions and Answers, fact sheet, accessed May 22, 2004, at www.fda/gov/cber/vaccine/smallpox.htm.
15. NIAID, Summary of NIAID Accomplishments in Biodefense Research, fact sheet, 2003, accessed May 22, 2004, at www2.niaid.nih.gov/newsroom/biodresaccomp.htm.
16. CDC, Smallpox Vaccination Method, fact sheet — information for clinicians, accessed at www.bt.cdc.gov/agent/smallpox/vaccination/administration.asp.
17. Dryvax package insert, accessed at www.fda.gov/cber/label/smalwye070303LB.pdf.
18. CDC, Adverse Reactions following Smallpox Vaccinations, fact sheet — information for clinicians, accessed May 19, 2004, at www.bt.cdc.gov/agent/smallpox/vaccination/reactions-vacc-clinic.asp.
19. Mandell, G.L., Bennett, J.E., and Dolin, R., *Mandell, Douglas, and Bennett's Principles and Practice of Infectious Diseases*, 5th edition, Churchill Livingstone, Philadelphia, 2000, p. 1554.

20. Aragon, T.J. et al., Risks of serious complications and death from smallpox vaccination: a systematic review of the United States experience, 1963–1968, *BMC Public Health*, 3, 26, 2003.
21. Halsell et al., Myopericarditis following smallpox vaccination among vaccinia naïve US military personnel, *JAMA*, 289, 3283, 2003.
22. Grabenstein, J.D. and Winkenerder, W. Jr., US military smallpox vaccination program experience, *JAMA*, 289, 3278, 2003.
23. Cassimatis, D.C. et al., Smallpox vaccination and myopericarditis: a clinical review, *J Am Coll Cardiol*, 43, 1503, 2004.
24. CDC, National Immunization Program, Update, Adverse events following civilian smallpox vaccination — United States, 2003, *MMWR*, 53, 106, 2004.
25. CDC, Questions and Answers: Smallpox Vaccination Program Implementation: Adverse Events and Vaccine Safety, accessed May 22, 2004, at www.bt.cdc.gov/agent/smallpox/vaccination.
26. CDC, Update: adverse effects following smallpox vaccination — United States, *MMWR*, 52, 492, 2003.
27. Frieden, T. et al., Cardiac deaths after a mass smallpox vaccination campaign — New York City, 1947, *MMWR*, 52, 933, 2003.
28. CDC, National Immunization Program, Update: adverse events following civilian smallpox vaccination — United States, 2003, *MMWR*, 53, 106, 2004.
28a. CDC, National Immunization Program, Update: Cardiac and other adverse events following civilian smallpox vaccination — United States, 2003, *MMWR*, 52, 639, 2003.
29. Barkdoll, T.W. et al., Secondary and tertiary transfer of vaccinia virus among U.S. military personnel — United States and worldwide, 2002–2004, *MMWR*, 53, 103, 2004.
30. Talbot, T.R. et al., Risk of vaccinia transfer to the hands of vaccinated persons after smallpox immunization, *Clin Infect Dis*, 38, 536, 2004.
31. Mandell, G.L., Bennett, J.E., and Dolin, R., *Mandell, Douglas, and Bennett's Principles and Practice of Infectious Diseases*, 5th edition, Churchill Livingstone, Philadelphia, 2000, p. 3221.
32. CDC, Questions and Answers: Smallpox Vaccination Program Implementation, Smallpox Vaccine: Smallpox Vaccine Characteristics, accessed May 19, 2004, at www.bt.cdc.gov/agent/smallpox/vaccination/.
33. Hammarlund, E. et al., Duration of antiviral immunity after smallpox vaccination, *Nat Med*, 9, 1131, 2003.
34. Massoudi, M.S., Barker, L., and Schwartz, B., Effectiveness of postexposure vaccination for the prevention of smallpox: results of a delphi analysis, *J Infect Dis*, 188, 973, 2003.
35. CDC, Smallpox Vaccination: Legal and Liability Issues, fact sheet, accessed May 19, 2004, at www.bt.cdc.gov/agent/smallpox/vaccination.
36. HHS, Amendment to Extend January 24, 2003, HHS Declaration Regarding Administration of Smallpox Countermeasures, accessed May 19, 2004.
37. CDC, Benefits and Compensation for Smallpox Vaccine Injuries, fact sheet, accessed May 19, 2004, at www.bt.cdc.gov/agent/smallpox/vaccination/legal.asp.

Appendix C: The Lessons of National Readiness Exercises

INTRODUCTION

Since 2000, many tabletop and role-playing exercises have been held around the country to prepare responses to terrorist attacks. Described in this chapter are three major exercises that illuminated many of the problems hospitals and public health agencies might face in a bioterrorist emergency. TOPOFF 1 and 2 are part of a congressionally mandated series of terrorism-response exercises to be run every other year. Their name refers to "top officials," who are supposed to be involved in the exercises. TOPOFF 3 has been announced for April 2005, with scenarios in Connecticut and New Jersey and additional activities in the U.K.[1]

TOPOFF 1

As part of efforts to upgrade U.S. preparedness, in the late 1990s Congress directed the Justice Department to conduct a domestic preparedness exercise "with the participation of all key personnel who would participate in the consequent management of [an actual chemical, biological, or cyber] terrorist event."[2]

The first such exercise, a $3 million drill, was held in May 2000. It involved simulated attacks with a chemical weapon — mustard gas released in a bombing at a 5K run in Portsmouth, NH — and a biological weapon, aerosolized plague bacteria covertly released in a performing arts theater in Denver, CO.[3,4] (At the same time, a separate radiological exercise, NCR-2000, was held in the Washington, D.C., area.[4,5])

TOPOFF 1, which occurred in real time, involved real activity: CDC staffers went to Denver, some mock patients staged unrest at a pharmaceutical distribution point, and local officials consulted with the real U.S. Attorney General by phone. Certain elements were notional. Only three of Denver's acute care hospitals participated, for instance, and one dropped out early. News reports for participants were provided by a Virtual News Network (VNN) created for the occasion.

THE TOPOFF 1 SCENARIO

The bioterrorism scenario played out as follows, according to Inglesby, Grossman, and O'Toole's account, based on interviews with 11 people involved in the exercise:[4]

Day 1: Saturday, May 20 — The Colorado Department of Health and Environment learned that, starting the previous day, Denver area hospitals had been seeing excess patients with fever and cough. The Centers for Disease Control and Prevention (CDC) in Atlanta was notified, and it sent 31 staff members. A suspected terrorist was found dead in a motel room. *Yersinia pestis*, the plague bacteria, was confirmed in the laboratory, a public health emergency was declared, and the governor restricted travel in the Denver metropolitan area. People with symptoms or contact with cases were told to seek treatment; other people were ordered to stay in their homes. Interviews with patients pointed to a release at the Denver Performing Arts Center on May 17. By the end of the day, there were 783 cases of pneumonic plague, with 123 deaths.

Day 2: Sunday, May 21 — With hospitals already running out of antibiotics, the CDC brought in a push pack from its National Pharmaceutical Stockpile (now called the National Strategic Stockpile), but there were not enough staff to distribute prophylaxis efficiently, and violence broke out at a distribution center. By the end of the day, several hospitals were overloaded with patients. Other states reported cases and competed for CDC staff and pharmaceuticals. Plague was seen in London and Tokyo. The number of cases rose to 1871, with 389 deaths.

Day 3: Monday, May 22 — Hospitals had insufficient staff, antibiotics, ventilators, and beds. Denver residents were advised to wear face masks. The CDC advised closing Colorado's borders, but state officials worried about getting food and supplies. By the end of the day, more than 3000 cases had been reported, with 950 deaths.[6]

Day 4: Tuesday, May 23 — With plague in at least 11 states[4] and spreading,[7] TOPOFF ended. Statistics conflicted, but the toll may have reached more than 4000 cases and more than 2000 deaths.

Key Problems Identified

Accounts of the exercise identified the following problems:

- Lack of surge capacity in handling patients and dispensing antibiotic prophylaxis: With an incubation period of only 2 to 3 days, the infection spread fast enough to quickly overwhelm available resources, according to a report by officials of the Colorado Department of Health and Environment. "The hospitals had too many patients and worried-well persons and too few healthcare workers and empty rooms to permit isolation of pneumonic plague patients. Case reporting was delayed, and there were too few trained public health workers to conduct interviews and locate contacts in a timely manner."[6] As a result, 2 million people — all of metropolitan Denver — were ordered quarantined in their homes.
- Difficulties in decision making, coordination, and communication: Participants did not agree which agency was the highest authority in the exercise.[4] Each agency maintained its own command center, with no central command center.[5] Debate and decision making took place through conference calls involving as many as 50 to 100 people, a procedure

widely seen as inefficient and unwieldy.[4,5] Some decisions were made, then reversed.[4]

- Lack of speed and clear direction on disease containment: There was disagreement about who should receive antibiotic prophylaxis. The governor's committee eventually decided to offer it to first-line workers and their families, in part to win the workers' support.[5] There was also strong disagreement on whether to bar all movement into or out of the state. Even after the exercise had ended, participants disagreed on whether the governor's committee had actually decided to close the borders; according to Inglesby and colleagues, they had not officially made the decision. Some participants felt that not enough emphasis was placed on containing the epidemic, in part because hospitals' energetic pleas for help directed attention toward needs for treatment and care.[4,5] By Day 3, according to Hoffman, "it became clear that unless controlling the spread of the disease and triage and treatment of ill persons in hospitals receive equal effort, the demand for health-care services will not diminish. This was the single most important lesson we learned by participating in the exercise."[5]

Although many problems surfaced in the exercise, its design may have eased others. The exact nature and date of the exercise were secret, but the probable data and possible pathogens were suggested, and the Colorado Department of Public Health and Environment began preparing 8 weeks in advance. Employees were recruited for disaster response teams, and a command center was established with communications and computer equipment installed.[5]

In addition, the exercise included "injects" of information that allowed early identification of the outbreak's terrorist origins, the time and place of the pathogen's release, and the rate of secondary spread. According to some experts, most health departments are unlikely to have information resources equal to those assumed in the episode.[4]

DARK WINTER

Dark Winter, a tabletop exercise conducted from June 22 to 23, 2001, was designed to examine how senior level policy makers would handle a covert smallpox attack. Its 12 players were all current or past public officials playing members of the National Security Council (NSC). They were led by Sam Nunn, cochairman of the Nuclear Threat Initiative and a former senator from Georgia, who played the role of the president. Frank Keating, then the governor of Oklahoma, played himself. The players were observed by 50 persons involved in biological preparedness and 5 journalists, who also participated in a mock press conference.[8] The exercise was produced by the Center for Strategic and International Studies (CSIS), Johns Hopkins Center for Civilian Biodefense Strategies, and the Analytic Services (ANSER) Institute for Homeland Security.

The following account of the scenario is based on three sources: the final script for the exercise,[9] testimony to a congressional subcommittee by Dr. John Hamre, president and chief executive officer, Center for Strategic International Studies,[10] and a paper by members of the Johns Hopkins Center for Civilian Biodefense Studies.[8]

The Dark Winter Scenario

The exercise presumed three simultaneous releases of smallpox in shopping malls in Oklahoma City, Philadelphia, and Atlanta on December 1, 2002, that initially infected 3000 people with smallpox.

First NSC meeting: The scenario began on December 9, 2002, when the fictional NSC members were told that about two dozen smallpox cases had been confirmed by the CDC in Oklahoma, with suspected cases in Georgia and Pennsylvania as well. They learned that the U.S. had 12 million doses of vaccine available out of a stockpile of 15.4 million doses. After debate about vaccine issues, the national leaders decided to implement ring vaccination to conserve vaccine, while reserving some for the Department of Defense. In this plan, vaccine would be given only to patient contacts, health care workers, and public safety personnel in the three states. The leaders also decided to try to initiate accelerated vaccine production.

Second NSC meeting: The next NSC meeting played out in the scenario occurred on December 15, 6 days into the epidemic. By then 15 states had reported a total of 2000 smallpox cases; isolated cases had also been seen in Canada, Mexico, and the U.K. Investigation pointed to three shopping malls, in Oklahoma, Georgia, and Pennsylvania, as the initial sites of release. Little vaccine was left; there were food shortages, public unrest, and violence. The medical care system was overwhelmed, schools were closed nationwide, and some states limited travel and public gatherings. An emergency program to produce more vaccine was underway, but first deliveries were not expected for 5 weeks. After debate, the leaders decided not to federalize the National Guard. They also voted to accept 4 million vaccine doses offered by Russia, if tests proved it safe.

Third NSC meeting: By December 22, almost 2 weeks into the epidemic, 25 states had reported 16,000 cases, with 1,000 deaths. Of the cases, 14,000 were reported in the previous 48 hours, a surge that probably represented secondary cases but could have reflected a second or continuing release. Ten other countries reported cases, all believed caused by travelers from the U.S. Canada and Mexico had closed their borders. Demands for vaccine had sparked riots and looting.

The epidemic was now in its second generation, which was expected to total 30,000 cases, including 10,000 deaths. For the third generation, worst-case projections were for 300,000 cases, with 100,000 deaths. Emergency vaccine production of 12 million doses a month was supposed to become available by the fourth generation. Unless a large-scale vaccination campaign or other disease containment efforts were successful, fourth-generation cases are projected to total 3 million, with 1 million deaths.[10]

The leaders learned that three U.S. newspapers had received anonymous letters, accompanied by a genetic fingerprint matching the smallpox strain in the outbreak. The letters demanded the removal of all U.S. troops from Saudi Arabia within a week, or more biological attacks would follow. On that chilling note, the scenario ended.

Key Problems Identified

Participants in the exercise said that one of the most difficult aspects of their decision making was the lack of information on which to base judgments about containing the spread of the disease.[11,12] If participants had known with reasonable certainty that the cases were initially confined to certain geographic areas, they could have isolated them, Nunn said in congressional testimony. "But there was no clarity. We kept asking, 'Do we know that it hasn't already spread all over?' And the answer was, 'It could have spread everywhere,' because we didn't know for 10 or 12 days that it had even happened and those people that were in those shopping centers had dispersed in all directions."[11]

The lack of knowledge was of particular concern to Nunn when the NSC began contemplating "impinging on the civil liberties," by using the National Guard to forcibly impose in-home quarantines. "You know that your vaccine's going to give out and you know the only other strategy is isolation," Nunn said, "but you don't know who to isolate and that's the horror of the situation."[11]

Dark Winter's developers said what it showed was that the U.S. was not prepared to meet a biological attack, lacking adequate vaccine and antibiotic stockpiles; adequate means of distribution; strategies and plans for response; information systems and coherent protocols for decision making; and a vigorous public health infrastructure.[10,13]

Since Dark Winter, the nation has made progress in these areas. The greatest advance, in terms of the specific Dark Winter scenario, was the acquisition, by September 2003, of 155 million additional doses of smallpox vaccine. In 2003, about 500,000 members of the military and about 39,000 civilian health care workers were vaccinated as part of antiterrorism preparations.

TOPOFF 2

TOPOFF 2, a 5-day, $16 million exercise held in May 2003, was the largest, most elaborate readiness exercise to date. It was designed as an "open" exercise; a series of seminars were held before the exercise to help educate participants in readiness and response issues and to help build relationships among them. It was the first exercise run by the recently created Department of Homeland Security and the first time that public agencies had to respond, if only fictionally, to a "threat condition" of red, or severe, under the Homeland Security Advisory System.

Responders knew in advance that the scenario would feature terrorists releasing pneumonic plague in Chicago and setting off a "dirty bomb" in Seattle, with release of radioactive material. Officials said they decided to run a bioterrorist scenario again because TOPOFF 1 had revealed how fragile the public health system is and how difficult the issues raised by bioterrorism could be, compared to the issues that might be seen in a chemical attack.[14] In both cities, officials said they had prepared over a period of months. In Chicago, preparations included equipping and training several specialized public health and tactical teams. Despite all the preparation, the scenario was said to have included some surprises.[14]

The design drew some criticism from those who said it was too tightly scripted to be useful — for instance, hospitals got to specify in advance how many patients they would see — and cost too much.[15,16] However, officials of the Department of Homeland Security said that the process was chosen to strengthen preparedness, not simply to test it. They and others who participated said the exercise had been very valuable.[1,14,17,18] Some Illinois rescue personnel who participated said they thought the state exercise should have focused on the plague release alone, without adding other disasters. Nevertheless, they said the exercise had left them much better prepared.[18]

The overall exercise involved 8500 people and 25 federal, state, and local agencies, as well as the American Red Cross and the government of Canada. Tom Ridge, the secretary of the U.S. Department of Homeland Security, played himself.

The TOPOFF 2 Scenario

The scenario, as described in news reports at the time and testimony later,[15,19–21] began with a fictional terrorist group releasing aerosolized plague on a Saturday at Union Station, O'Hare Airport, and the United Center sports stadium in Chicago. Hospitals "saw" their first patients on paper — descriptions of cases, symptoms, and histories were faxed to emergency departments. The fax patients included some who had other conditions. On Tuesday, the hospitals began seeing their first role-playing patients in the flesh. On Thursday, with patients still showing up and treatment centers set up around the city to provide antibiotics, the scenario saw fictional complications: a building collapsed, trapping people in the rubble; a chemical plant suffered a release; and a medical helicopter crashed into a plane at Midway Airport, leaving more than 100 dead and some critically injured.

Sixty-four hospitals in Illinois participated in the exercise. After public health workers had worked 48 hours straight, the federal government brought in an additional 150 public health nurses and 25 doctors.[21] By the end of the exercise on Friday, 5000 people had been infected, almost 1100 had died, and the plague had spread around the world.[16]

Meanwhile, in Seattle, a dirty bomb had exploded on Monday near a coffee roasting plant, injuring 150 people and trapping some in the rubble. About 200 firefighters and 60 police officers participated. Simultaneously, at a university about 40 miles south of Seattle, a fictional car bomb exploded.

Once again, VNN reported on the crisis. Former CNN reporter Frank Sesno anchored its broadcasts, which were seen only by participants in the exercises.

Key Problems Identified

The Department of Homeland Security's 200-page assessment of the operation was classified. Its 14-page public summary deemed TOPOFF 2 "an innovative, useful, and successful exercise" and "a tremendous learning experience."[22]

The principal problems cited in the public report — problems with communications, coordination, scarcity of resources, and allocation of prophylaxis — were similar to those seen in TOPOFF 1.

"The outward communications, plus the internal communications of how we work, interagency and intergovernmental, are probably the number-one thing that we need to address," Michael Brown, undersecretary for emergency preparedness and response in the Department of Homeland Security, was quoted as saying when the TOPOFF 2 public assessment was released.[23,24]

One of the main problems occurred in Seattle, where federal agencies differed over how far the radioactive plume from the dirty bomb would extend. As a result, the mayor was unsure which residents should be instructed to stay indoors, with windows shut. The question took about an hour to resolve. There was also confusion about the value of plume models and other predictive data, as opposed to real data from the site.[17,21,22]

The report identified several problems in the bioterrorist response, including:

- Hospitals lacked adequate emergency communications systems and relied heavily on regular telephone and fax lines, which were overwhelmed by volume. In one location, three HAM radio operators were used to maintain communications.
- Data transmission was slow and involved error-prone manual copying and collecting. Hospital personnel were taxed by having to compile and transmit huge amounts of information tracking the status of beds, specialized spaces, and medical equipment. "Blast fax" transmission, designed to transmit information to large numbers of recipients in a short span of time, took up to 2 hours.
- Hospitals did not have enough staff or enough isolation and negative-pressure rooms to handle the patients. They activated staff phone trees to recall medical personnel; used conference rooms, lobbies, and Clinical Decision Units (closed units) as isolation wards; and used same-day surgery, radiology, and endoscopy labs, as well as an off-site tent, as negative-pressure rooms.
- The shortages occurred even though, as the report notes, "Topoff 2 did not last long enough to fully explore the impacts of mass casualties on the medical system. Much less than half of the infected population was visible to the medical system at the conclusion of the exercise."
- Officials had problems determining who among first responders and local residents should get prophylaxis from the National Strategic Stockpile. The decisions were complicated by the difficulties inherent in distributing medications across a large metropolitan area and the limited amounts immediately available.
- Different agencies gave conflicting information on who should get prophylaxis, and when they should get it. (They also gave different information on the location of the plague-release sites.) However, the actual distribution of the medication was said to have gone well.[22]

A participating police officer was quoted as saying that disputes over antibiotic distribution strategy were "our greatest and biggest fight" during the drill.[18]

An analysis of the costs of containing the plague, including business losses, ranged from $1.7 billion to $25 billion. The cost was estimated at $1.7 billion to $5.5 billion if containment relied largely on voluntary mass prophylaxis with rapid distribution of antibiotics. The cost went as high as $25 billion if containment relied on shutting businesses and schools, and keeping 80% of the population at home.[25]

References

1. Department of Homeland Security, Department of Homeland Security Announces Exercise Participants, press release, April 5, 2004.
2. U.S. Department of Justice, State and Local Domestic Preparedness Stakeholders Forum, executive summary of the Topoff exercise planning conference, 1999.
3. Wade, B., Drill tests response to terrorism, *American City & County*, 115, 46, August 2000.
4. Inglesby, T.V., Grossman, R., and O'Toole, T., A plague on your city: observations from TOPOFF, *Clin Infect Dis*, 32, 436, 2001.
5. U.S. Department of Justice, Justice Department, Federal Emergency Management Agency to Conduct Domestic Counterterrorism Exercises, April 27, 2000, press release, 2000, accessed Oct. 31, 2003, at www.ojp.usdoj.gov/odp/docs/230ag.htm.
6. Hoffman, R.E. and Norton. J.E., Lessons learned from a full-scale bioterrorism exercise, *Emerg Infect Dis*, 6, 652, 2000.
7. O'Toole, T., Quotes in U.S. Totally Unprepared for Bioterrorism, *UPI*, August 22, 2000.
8. O'Toole, T., Mair, M., and Inglesby, T.V., Shining light on "Dark Winter," *Clin Infect Dis*, 34, 972, 2002.
9. Dark Winter bioterrorism exercise — Andrews Air Force Base, June 22–23, 2001, final script, accessed from www.hopkins-biodefense.org/DARK%20WINTER,pdf.
10. Hamre, J., Transcript of testimony at hearing by House Government Reform Subcommittee on National Security, Veterans Affairs, and International Relations, July 23, 2001, accessed from nexis.com.
11. Nunn, S., Prepared testimony to the House Government Reform Subcommittee on National Security, Veterans Affairs and International Relations, July 23, 2001, accessed from nexis.com.
12. Keating, F., Testimony to the House Government Reform Subcommittee on National Security, Veterans Affairs and International Relations, July 23, 2001, accessed from nexis.com.
13. Johns Hopkins Center for Civilian Biodefense Strategies, Dark Winter — Lessons Learned, slide presentation, accessed from www.Hopkins-biodefense.org/darkwinter-slides/slide 30.html.
14. Ridge, T. et al., Remarks on the Announcement of the Topoff Exercises, Department of Homeland Security press release, May 5, 2003.
15. Turnock, B., Comments on NPR's Talk of the Nation/Science Friday, transcript, May 16, 2003.
16. Meserve, J. and Sesno, F., Comments on *CNN Newsnight*, transcript, May 16, 2003.
17. James, F., Ridge Sits Back to Assess Good, Bad of Drills; Mock Terrorist Exercises End, *Chicago Trib*, 9, May 17, 2003.
18. Fiorill, J., TOPOFF 2 participants recommend narrower drills, better dissemination of results, *Global Security Newswire*, accessed Oct. 31, 2003, at www.nti.org.

19. Cox, C., comments at House Committee on Homeland Security Hearing, transcript, May 22, 2003.
20. Kestenbaum, D. and McCormick, J., comments on NPR's Talk of the Nation/Science Friday, transcript, May 16, 2003.
21. Gillespie, E.M., Early assessments rate Topoff 2 a success — glitches and all, *AP*, May 16, 2003.
22. Department of Homeland Security, Top Officials (TOPOFF) Exercise Series: TOPOFF2 After Action Summary for Public Release, 2003.
23. Fessler P., Lessons Learned from a National Counterterrorism Exercise Conducted, *NPR Weekend Edition* transcript, December 20, 2003.
24. Doyle, J.M., Topoff 2 exercise exposed flaws in communications, DHS reports, *Aviation Week's Homeland Security & Defense*, 2, 3, 2003.
25. Risk Management Solutions, RMS Provides Cost Estimates for Bioterrorism Attack Simulation Conducted by Department of Homeland Security, press release, August 6, 2003.

Index

B

C

D

E

F

G

H

M

N

O

P

Q

R

S

T

U

V

W

Y

Z